The Quiet Time Companion writing team

Julia Cameron
Claire Evans
Alistair Hornal
Mary-Jane Kirkland
Helen Mynors
Susan Penfold
Deborah Reed
David Stone
Steve Walton
Phyllis Wells
Bob Willoughby
Ro Willoughby

General editor
Ro Willoughby

THE QUIET TIME Companion

A Daily Guide through the Bible

General editor: R. Willoughby

INTERVARSITY PRESS
DOWNERS GROVE, ILLINOIS 60515

Introduction

Any book that helps people to study the Bible is worth buying. *The Quiet Time Companion* by IVP makes an excellent contribution in this field. It takes you through the basic message of the Bible in just two years and uses different methods of study to achieve that. This is important not only because variety keeps your interest going, but also it teaches new ways to glean spiritual truth. What I like best is the fact that the studies are structured without cramping your style. There's room for the Holy Spirit to speak and opportunity for you to think.

If you like pre-packaged easy-to-digest 'blessed thoughts' – keep away from these studies. If you want to get into a well-thought-out guide that respects your intelligence – start here!

Ian Coffey

Publisher's note

You are holding in your hand a unique introduction to the whole Bible.

Too often we keep to well-worn paths in our Bible reading and study, as if much or most of the Bible is not for us! *The Quiet Time Companion* is distinctive and unique in combining a vivid introduction to *all* parts of God's Word, in twelve digestible sections, with a variety of tested and proven approaches to using the Bible practically, effectively and devotionally.

There are no limits to God's imagination but the ordinary Christian needs a non-technical resource to help us find our way around the rich storehouse of the Bible. The Bible, God's Word, is of course the main way God has chosen for us to know him as a person in all his glory.

The Quiet Time Companion assumes no specialist knowledge, but avoids spoonfeeding, in the conviction that the Bible is meant to be understood by ordinary people. The team of writers has a wide experience in leading Bible study groups and in Bible teaching.

This book provides you with a compact learning guide that encourages you to encounter in a first hand way the living God and his very practical message for today!

How to use this book

Encountering the living God on a daily basis is the most
life-changing experience possible for any Christian.
Confronted by God's standards and his view on life as we
find them in the Bible, we either turn away from him or
plead, in confidence, for him to change us and make us like
Jesus.

As you use these Bible studies, make it your overall aim to meet
with God and become like him. If you never have had a regular
time with God you might find it helpful to use the guidelines at the
end of the book.

We all need variety; we so easily get into a rut. So you'll find in
this book different approaches to getting to know your Bible.
Basically, there are nine different types of study:

- Fairly detailed study of short consecutive passages in one book
  of the Bible.
- 'Bird's-eye' study, taking long passages to get a broad view of a
  long book.
- Whole book study, concentrating on major themes from a Bible
  book.
- Meditative study, where we dwell on one passage for several
  days, looking at it from different angles and letting its message
  really sink in.
- Word study, looking at key words in the Bible.
- History, getting the general flow of the story.
- Character study, showing how God dealt with an individual.
- Topics, outlining the Bible's teaching on particular aspects of
  the Christian life.
- Problem studies, pointing to what the Bible has to say on
  difficult or controversial issues.

We also need frameworks in which to work and worship, and
each week of studies has been designed to occupy **five daily
sessions** of prayer and study of about **half an hour.** Then there
are suggestions for **further, less structured projects** for the
weekend.

The idea is to use the daily sections through the regular working week, Monday to Friday, and then weekends can be used for something slightly different. Eventually, you will no longer need this kind of guide, developing your own plan and variety of Bible study. The less structured projects aim to encourage you to do this.

We all have patterns that work best for us, but do make sure you *have* a regular pattern. It's a good idea to use the checklist which follows to keep a track on your progress! You can also use it to organize your sequence of study (for example, you may wish to do a series of character studies). To get most out of the series, you will need a notebook in which to record your discoveries. If you like, you could keep your own Bible study diary to which you can return. This will be especially useful if you jot down the reference of the Bible passage as well.

Don't be tempted just to 'do it in your head' – it's a great help to concentration and clear thinking if you actually write down your responses.

Nor is this meant to be just an academic exercise. A true understanding of the Bible affects our lives, so try hard to apply what you discover to your own life and the lives of those around you.

Many suggestions have been given to help you and it is most important to *pray* about what you have learned. Having key Bible verses tucked into the corners of your memory will also help you to retain what you have discovered.

Bible study has torn apart my life and remade it. That is to say that God, through his Word, has done so. In the darkest periods of my life when everything seemed hopeless, I would struggle in the grey dawns of many faraway countries to grasp the basic truths of Scripture passages. I looked for no immediate answers to my problems. Only did I sense intuitively that I was drinking drafts from a fountain that gave life to my soul.

John White, *The Fight*

Part Eleven

Part Twelve

Your Checklist for Your Study of the Bible

Part and *week* numbers are indicated. Check when completed.

Part One

Solomon
The letters of John
Growth and maturity
The Judges
Leadership
Songs at Christmas
Amos

Part One/Week One
Solomon (A character study)

Mention the name 'Solomon' and whom do you think of? The last king who ruled over the united kingdoms of Israel and Judah? Or the fabulously rich and wise king who wrote many of the proverbs in the Bible? Or the man who had woman problems, but who had such a sensitivity to the woman he loved that he could write the exquisitely beautiful love poem, the Song of Songs? Or the king who was responsible for the building of the first temple in Jerusalem? There are indeed many intriguing facets to this man.

This week we shall try to unravel some of these. Solomon is an example for us to follow, but his life is also a warning of how the rot can set in, leading to behaviour which displeases God.

1. Meet Solomon, the king
1 Kings 1

King David was deeply repentant not only over his act of adultery with Bathsheba but also his schemes which were to lead to the death of her husband (see Psalm 51). After this he married her and we read in 2 Samuel 12:24-25 that Bathsheba gave birth to Solomon, or Jedidiah, meaning 'loved by the LORD'.

Solomon however was only one of David's many sons. As David approached the end of his life, the big question remained – who would be king in his place? The eldest son did not become king automatically.

1 *Read 1 Kings 1:1-53, trying to capture its atmosphere of intrigue.*
2 *The desire for personal power will drive some to extraordinary lengths. How would you summarize the efforts of both Adonijah and Solomon's backers? Write down your summary. Is there any evidence that either group was motivated by a desire to do what was pleasing to God or for the good of the kingdom?*
3 *Reflect on what you most desire in life. Marriage? Financial security? Status? Are your motives or the means you might use to achieve such ends always ones that would please God?*
4 *Solomon appears to play a fairly passive role in his accession to the throne. What impressions of him have you gained already? What early signs are there that he is going to be a king of high calibre?*

2. Solomon – with a secure throne
1 Kings 2

1 *Read 1 Kings 2:1-12, making a list of each of the instructions David gave to his son.*
2 *Then read verses 13-46, noticing how many of these commands Solomon obeyed. He was clearly removing any opposition, placing*

15

men loyal to himself in positions of responsibility. In the twentieth century Solomon's ruthlessness seems shocking. But why do you think such violence was necessary? How prepared are you to root out evil in your own life, however painful?

3 Solomon was determined to get his rule off to a good and reliable start. You may have been involved in evangelistic activities or projects which are done in the name of Christ. As was the case with Solomon, how important do you think it should be that members of the team are
a) committed to the project from the start
b) loyal to the leadership
c) are not carrying around with them unconfessed sin from the past?
Do you need to take any action now to establish on a firmer footing any team with which you are involved?

Note: Solomon's leadership was becoming apparent. But he was a king in peacetime and one area where his leadership was seen was in administrative reorganization. Read 1 Kings 4:1-19 to see the extent of his household and organization.

3. Solomon – wealthy and wise
1 Kings 3:1-28; 4:29-34

You may remember the high priority Solomon gave to wisdom – his proverbs are devoted to it.

Memory verse: The fear of the LORD is the beginning of knowledge, but fools despise wisdom and discipline (Proverbs 1:7).

1 Read 1 Kings 4:29-34 to see how great was his wisdom.
2 How Solomon acquired such wisdom is less well known. So turn to 1 Kings 3:1-15. What particularly strikes you about the character of Solomon?

If you have ever been in a position of responsibility, how have you prayed for yourself? – help me to survive? don't let me appear a failure? Is there anything you can learn from Solomon's example?

Pause to pray for those you know in leadership in the light of Solomon's request. James 1:5 could be your prayer.

3 God does not promise to reward his children with wealth. Solomon is not the norm. But what does this incident show about God's character?
4 Solomon's wisdom was put to the test many times. Read 3:16-28 for one example of this. How did this make Solomon more secure as king?

4. Solomon – the master builder
1 Kings 5;7;8;9

David had wanted to build the temple but in 2 Samuel 7:13 God had declared that it would be his son who would perform this task. And what a job it turned out to be!

1 Today we shall be reading parts of the story of the building. As you read the following verses, notice firstly how much attention Solomon paid to detail and the organization that this involved. Secondly, try to identify what it was that motivated Solomon.

1 Kings 5:1-18; 7:13-14, 40-51; 8:1 – 9:9.

2 *Only the best would do for God. How have you offered him the second best on occasions?*

3 *Taking the first part of Solomon's prayer at the dedication of the temple (8:22-32), how does Solomon pray? How does his understanding of God affect the way he prays? Let his example be a challenge to your own prayer life. Take time now to remind yourself of God's greatness and then in humility ask him to forgive and bless you. You may find it helps to write your prayer down on paper.*

5. Solomon – the rot sets in

1 Kings 11

His reign began on such a wave of hope – his father urged him to obey God which would lead to God's blessing. God himself reminded Solomon of his promises. Look up 1 Kings 3:14 and 6:12-13 for two such occasions.

1 *But Solomon failed. Turn to 1 Kings 11:1-8. How would you summarize the cause of Solomon's failure? You may know of Christians whose Christian life was full of promise, yet they slipped away from God. Why was this? Did wrong relationships, or sexual sin, or*

outright disobedience play any part? Pray for them now.

2 *Any one of us could find ourselves similarly disobeying God. How can we guard against it? Pray for yourself in the light of Solomon's example.*

3 *Read 11:9-13. God's judgment and yet his mercy are seen combined in his words to Solomon. When you think of God, how far do you hold in balance these two aspects of God's character?*

4 *To complete the picture, finish reading chapter 11. The reign closes with a whimper. Yet what overall impression do you have of Solomon? What has particularly struck you about him? Write down your thoughts.*

Weekend

Read through the Song of Songs at one sitting, appreciating it for what it is, a love song. If you are married or are contemplating marriage in the near future, pray for your relationship in the light of this. If you are not in that position, pray that your own expectations of love and marriage will come more into line with what we read here rather than with the sullied or slushy views of marriage which we often encounter in our society.

In the New Testament, what is Solomon remembered for? Look up the references to him in a concordance.

The letters of John (A whole book study)

Wrong thinking about God the Father or about the Lord Jesus Christ has existed ever since man began to worship. False teaching which stems from such ideas (or no teaching at all!) always has disastrous consequences in the church. Not only do people not know the truth intellectually but eventually it affects their day-to-day lives.

When this letter was written it is likely that the idea was circulating that, since Jesus is God, he surely never lived a fully human life; it only seems that he did. And as we might imagine, this was not without some very serious results. Speaking out of his own personal experience, John seeks to straighten out a few facts.

1. The letter itself
1 John

The first letter of John is not easy to divide. Themes keep popping up throughout and all are mixed together. It deals, however, with some fundamental issues for a Christian.

Before reading pray that God will help you to gain an overall grasp of the issues that are being dealt with.

1 *Read through the whole letter quickly and look out for its general themes, passing over the finer details. Watching out for recurring*

statements or phrases, noticing the first point in each paragraph and picking up the subheadings which may have been inserted into your version, may help you to do this.
2 *Make a note of what you see as the general themes, and any initial reflections that you have on whether these issues are still around in the church today.*

2. The importance of truth
1 John 2:18-27; 4:1-6

Read 1 John 2:18-27.

1 *Note down what was the basic error that these people were making (see especially verses 22 and 23). What other things might they deny (1:1; 4:15; 5:5, 10; 4:2; 4:9-14)?*

Most heresy focuses on or derives from a distorted understanding of who Jesus is.

Pray that your own knowledge and understanding of him might always be true to the Bible. Do you know of any person or people who have left a church through backsliding or following false teaching? Pray for them, asking God to restore them.

2 *Read 1 John 4:1-6. How would you sum up the kind of discernment that*

John writes about here? Pray for yourself and your church leaders, that you may be discerning, and may be prevented from straying into error.

[The letter] was called forth by the activities of false teachers who had seceded from the church (or churches) to which John is writing, and who were attempting to seduce the faithful (2:18-26). They formed an esoteric group, believing that they had superior knowledge to ordinary Christians (cf. 2:20, 27; 2 John 9) ... and claimed a special knowledge of God and of theology ...

Illustrated Bible Dictionary, 2 (Tyndale)

---

3. Sin and a God of light
1 John 1:5 – 2:17; 2:28 – 3:10

Christians know the joy of sins forgiven – the fact that their sin need never again cut them off from God. But sin does remain a problem in our everyday living.
Read 1:5–2:17.

1 *What evidence do you find for the assertion that sin remains a problem for the Christian?*
2 *What is God's remedy for this state of affairs (1:9–2:2)? How does sin find expression in our lives?*
3 *Jot down specific areas which you need to bring before God now.*

Read 1 John 2:28–3:10.

4 *What do these verses say about continuing to sin?*
5 *How would you use these verses to answer someone who believes that Christians will automatically live sinless lives?*

...John is not denying the possibility of sin in the Christian. But he is not asserting its impossibility either ... John is arguing rather the incongruity than the impossibility of sin in the Christian.

John Stott, *Tyndale New Testament Commentary on the Epistles of John*
(Eerdmans)

Thank God that we can find forgiveness for all our sins.

---

4. God's love and ours
1 John 3:11-24; 4:7-21

'All you need is love ... love is all you need'.

The Beatles

We all have different ideas about what love is. For some it conjures up the idea of a romantic honeymoon. Others think of a mother's love for her children. And still others see it as nothing more than enlightened self-interest. There are probably as many ideas as there are people.

1 *Read 1 John 3:11-24. Try to compose a Christian definition of love.*
2 *Jot down the practical examples given here of love in action. Can you*

add any further possible ways of showing love? Pray that God may give you opportunities to show practical love today.

3 Read 1 John 4:7-21. Take some minutes to meditate upon what showing love meant to God.

4 Look back to the introduction to this study. Are there any ways in which your ideas about love should be corrected?

Memory verse: This is love: not that we loved God, but that he loved us and sent his Son as an atoning sacrifice for our sins (1 John 4:10).

5. Certainty and assurance
1 John 5:1-21; 1:1-4

Who wants to be adrift in an open boat without oars or sail on a sea without shores? For the non-Christian it is hard to be certain about a great many things, such as what happens after death, or the purpose of life. But the Christian is much stronger in his faith for as a child of God, he can experience real assurance and certainty.

1 How, according to chapter 5, can you be sure that you are born of God (verses 1, 10-11, 20)?

2 How do we show that we love God (verse 3)?

3 What is it that puts us on the 'winning side' (verse 4)?

4 Many Christians lack assurance and certainty in their lives. Think how you might use these passages to help such a person to a stronger faith. Pray for any you know who are like this.

5 John wants us to be certain of the things that he is writing about. Read 1:1-4 and then reflect upon 5:13.

Thank God for such certainty. It is worth reading *Doubt* by Os Guinness (Lion, 1983), which deals with some of the questions surrounding uncertainty.

Weekend

1 Return to the themes noted down on the first day. Reread the letter and pray over what God has been saying to you this week.

2 Read 2 John and 3 John as if they were letters you had received this morning. Why do you think they were written? Do you know of any similar situations today?

3 John Stott's Tyndale Commentary on The Epistles of John (IVP) is an excellent guide for a deeper study of the letter.

Part One/Week Three
Growth and maturity (A topic study)

'That's simply amazing – I just can't believe it!' Ever heard anyone say that? Ever said it yourself? The problem for many Christians is that they've an inadequate grasp that, through Jesus, they really have been put right with God. It's such good news and so earth-shattering a reality that most of us, at rock bottom, find it very difficult really to believe. This is a particularly important starting point when we begin to think about Christian growth and maturity.

1. This is where we start
Romans 5:1-11; 6:1-14

These passages will be studied again in Part Four on 'conversion' – looking at them today we can see how 'conversion' is closely related to 'going on with God'.

1 *Jot down why and in what ways (if at all) you find it hard to accept what God has done for you. Then pray that God will make real to you the crucially important lessons contained in this passage. Ask him to show you what* practical *results should follow.*

2 *Christians are people who have been 'justified' before God (5:1). Read Romans 5:1-11 and as you do so, jot down in your notebook a list* of practical benefits that arise from this. How does this tie in with the list you made in answer to question one? **3** Read quickly through Romans 6:1-14. How does Paul follow up his argument in this letter?

Take time to ponder the significance of 6:14: '... sin shall not be your master ...'. As you do, memorize verses 12 to 14.

2. Don't be a dry twig
John 15:1-16; Galatians 5:22-23

Used symbolically the vine was the emblem of prosperity and peace among the ancient Hebrews. More particularly it symbolized the chosen people. They were the vine which God had taken out of Egypt (Psalm 80:8-14; Isaiah 5:1-5) and planted in a particularly choice land. They had been given all the attention necessary for the production of outstanding fruit, but instead yielded only wild grapes ...

Illustrated Bible Dictionary, 3
(Tyndale)

In this passage Jesus takes the Old Testament picture of the people of God as a fruitful vine and uses it to describe the new situation that through him makes Christians the people of God.

1 *See what John 15: 1-16 indicates about the closeness necessary between Jesus and his disciples (e.g. verses 5-7, 10, 14-15).*
2 *What major lessons is Jesus teaching about our growth and maturity (verses 5, 7, 16)? Note these down.*
3 *The initiative is God's but what is the role of obedience (verses 10, 12, 14)?*
4 *What does Jesus say here about the hopelessness of seeking to grow unless we are directly relying on Jesus? What are to be the objectives of our relationship to him (verses 8, 11, 16)?*

Today's passage from John is part of Jesus' farewell message and final prayer. Don Carson provides a riveting basic study of this in *The Farewell Discourse & the Final Prayer of Jesus* (Baker, 1981).

Pray that the closeness and intimacy of your relationship to God through Jesus may stimulate the growth of good fruit in your life and witness. Use Galatians 5:22-23 as a basis for your prayer.

---

3. A new set of clothes
Colossians 3:1-17

'Let go and let God...' – there's a certain amount of truth in such a saying. We saw in our previous study that the initiative for both our salvation and our growth is essentially God's. There is, however, a need for us also to work hard at it, allowing Christian character to develop within us, avoiding things which would grieve the Spirit of God (Ephesians 4: 3).

1 *Glance through Colossians 3: 1-17 and write out as many reasons for motivation in living as a Christian as you can find (e.g. verses 1-4, 12, 17).*

Praise God that there are so many positive reasons for living as God wants us to. Thank him that growth and obedience are not simply a matter of obeying a set of rules but arise from an appreciation of his love and our privileges.

2 *Make two columns in your notebook: one of things to avoid (or take off) (verses 5-11), and the second of things and attitudes to cultivate (or put on) (verses 12-14).*
3 *Do a quick spiritual 'check-up'. Are you characterized principally by the bad practices of verses 5-11 or the positive virtues of verses 12-14? Notice the importance of knowledge of the Word of Christ in all of this (verse 16).*

Pray that God would enable you to grow in practical holiness (verse 12) during the coming week. Think of specific areas in your life where this might be particularly important and pray about this.

---

4. But that's not fair, Lord!
Hebrews 12:1-13; 5:7-10

Nobody likes suffering or pain. C.S. Lewis lost his mother, father and wife through cancer.

> *God whispers to us in our pleasures, speaks in our*

consciences, but shouts in our pains; it is his megaphone to rouse a deaf world.

C.S. Lewis, *The Problem of Pain* (Macmillan).

The same may be said of discipline. Few of us are keen to accept further discipline and as our passage says, 'No discipline appears pleasant at the time, but painful' (verse 11).

The Jewish Christians to whom Hebrews was written were experiencing a time of extraordinary hardship and testing. The writer urges them that this could work out for their growth and maturity.

1 *Read Hebrews 12:1-13. Consider the intensity of the struggle which faced these Christians. What reasons does the writer give for their suffering? What encouragements?*
2 *Then turn to Hebrews 5:7-10. Clearly Jesus' suffering had meaning. What was the purpose of it?*

You may be going through a time of testing or suffering or you may know of others who are. It may seem meaningless. Pray that God will use this time to develop Christian maturity.

---

5. We need each other
Ephesians 4:1-16

> *No man is an* Island, *entire of it self; every man is a piece of the* Continent, *a part of the* main; *if a* clod *be washed away by the* sea, Europe *is the less, as well as if a* promontory *were, as well as if a* manor *of thy*

friends *or of* thine own *were; any man's* death *diminishes* me, *because I am involved in* Mankind; And therefore never send to know for whom the bell *tolls; It tolls for* thee.

From *Meditation XVII*, John Donne (1571?–1631).

Society in the west is predominantly individualistic. This, however, is not how Paul or the early church saw things. He spoke of the church as a whole, as one body (1 Corinthians 12:12, 14; Ephesians 4:4) of which all individual Christians are members.

1 *Why does Paul think unity is so important (verses 1-6)? How do you think a lack of unity could hinder the spiritual growth of Christians?*
2 *What is the purpose of leaders and others serving in the church (verses 11-16)?*
3 *Why is doctrinal truth important for maturity? Look back for help to your notes on last week's studies on John's letters, where truth was seen in action.*

> *It is not enough to use the phrase 'born again' and then behave as though we have been born as orphans in the wilderness. We must recognize that if God has begotten us again, then we have been born into the new family, the new household of God.*

Michael Griffiths, *God's Forgetful Pilgrims* (Eerdmans)

Pray for the leaders of your church that they might know how to help the congregation grow in maturity and unity. Pray also that you might be the means of growth for other people in your fellowship.

Weekend

'Follow me'

1 Paul often encouraged new believers and indeed more mature ones too, to follow the example of God and of Christ (e.g. Ephesians 5:1; Philippians 2:5). Interestingly enough he even encouraged them to follow his own example (Philippians 3:17; 4:9). Why was this so?

2 Hebrews chapter 11 also gives us many examples of 'saints' of the past who pleased God. Read this chapter and look up the references quoted in the previous question.

3 Most of us learn more from watching and imitating other people than we ever do from study. What examples are we choosing to follow? Are they all good ones? In many ways we cannot imitate Christ, such as his work upon the cross. How can we, however, learn from the example of his day to day life? Seek out a copy of Michael Griffiths' excellent The Example of Jesus (IVP, 1985).

4 Over this weekend consider where your major influences are to be found – television, your peers, magazines? Are they good influences? Are they helping you to mature as a Christian? Do you need to make any changes?

The period recorded in Judges – stretching from the end of the exodus (around 1200 BC) to the beginning of a more settled period (around 1050 BC) – is one of the darkest in the history of the Jewish people. Time and again the people fell into depravity, making pacts with their enemies which compromised their worship of God. On each occasion God raised up a 'judge'. We use the term 'judge' in a more limited sense today than is meant in this book. They were more than mere judiciaries, being leaders, warriors, deliverers and people of moral courage. Sadly they were also just as fallible as the rest of us in their service of God.

Nowhere does the Bible commend the mistakes of the 'judges' (and some of them were pretty bad). Neither does it suggest that sinful actions disqualify you from God's use. One of the themes of the book is that God uses people because of their faith and in spite of themselves.

It isn't certain who was the author of this book. Twelve judges are mentioned; six of them – Othniel, Ehud, Deborah, Gideon, Jephthah and Samson – are dealt with at length.

Ancient writers are not as concerned with chronology as we are today. Judges is reckoned to cover the period 1200-1050 BC approximately. Yet if you added together all the dates given in this book, they total 390 years. There are many reasons for this such as an overlap between the lives of the judges. These discrepancies need not cast doubt on the author's accuracy. He simply has a different way from us of looking at time.

For further information you could look at the *Tyndale Old Testament Commentary on Judges and Ruth* by A.E. Cundall and L. Morris (IVP, 1968), pp. 28–34, or the *New Bible Dictionary* (Tyndale, 1982) or the *Illustrated Bible Dictionary* (Tyndale, 1980) – entry under 'Chronology of the Old Testament'.

---

1. Unfinished work
Judges 1:1 – 2:5

The first two studies cover what has been called the introduction to Judges, before coming onto the history of the 'judges' proper. These are a necessary background, though a little difficult to absorb because of the unfamiliar places mentioned.

Note: 1:1 is a general heading for the section, which leads up to Joshua's death (2:8).

Under Joshua, the tribes of Israel entered the promised land, ending their wanderings in the wilderness. Gradually, they drove out the former inhabitants. God willingly gave them the Canaanite land, but he insisted that the Israelites 'break down their altars' (2:2), and keep their worship of him pure.

Note: 'angel of the LORD' (2:1) was an authoritative messenger who spoke in God's name.

1 *Military superiority is not usually enough to stop the march of God's army. Note down the deeper reasons for the Israelites' failure to take the land.*
2 *Notice that the further south the Israelites venture, the more incomplete their conquest becomes. Suggest reasons for this.*
3 *Make a list of the bitter consequences of their compromises.*

Ask God what compromises you tolerate in your daily living. Ask him to give you the strength to both repent and follow him wholeheartedly.

---

2. Past glory, present failure

Judges 2:6 – 3:6

Under Joshua's leadership, the tribes united and were able to drive out much of the Canaanite resistance. Mopping up was left to the individual tribes. But without the strength of definite leadership the people soon turned to paganism and making pacts with those they should have defeated.

1 *A tradition of past godliness wasn't enough to meet the challenge. What importance does the writer attach to passing on God's ways to succeeding generations? What else does he say about serving God wholeheartedly? How might these*
truths *apply to the church today?*
2 *This passage falls into a pattern which we'll see is often used in Judges. Note down the four phases of this cycle from:*
(a) 2:10-13;
(b) 2:14-15;
(c) 2:16, 18;
(d) 2:17, 19.

Being a Christian has been aptly described as a bicycle ride! You've got to keep going forward because if you stop you'll fall off. Ask God to prevent you ever relying on past achievements and to keep going forward.

Note: 2:13 'Baal' and 'Ashtoreth' (Astartes, GNB) are Canaanite fertility/vegetation gods.

---

3. Othniel and Ehud

Judges 3:7-31

Othniel and Ehud are the first of the twelve 'judges' we meet in detail.

Note: v. 15 Left-handedness was considered a defect but it meant the movement of Ehud's hand aroused no suspicion in Eglon.

Compare Othniel and Ehud closely. In each case, make notes on the following:

1 *What was the cause of the Israelites' 'trouble'?*
2 *What could the Israelites have learnt at the time about God's sovereignty?*
3 *What qualities did these judges possess (or were given) which enabled God to use them?*

God sometimes takes the most

unlikely characters and uses them. What encouragement is that to you personally? Also, how does that affect the way that you respond to those whom God is obviously using? Turn to 1 Corinthians 1:26–31 and allow that to direct your prayers.

4. 'Has not the Lord gone ahead of you?'
Judges 4:1 – 5:31

The scene switches from the southern to the northern tribes. No less than six of them will be involved in battle. This was the earliest major threat to Israel since their occupation of Canaanite territory. Again they were their own worst enemies. Deborah was already established as a prophetess, wife and judge and it is because of proven qualities that the people come to her to lead them in a time of peril.

1 *A glorious victory indeed! Go carefully through these chapters and pick out all the evidence of God's hand at this time.*
2 *Make notes on the characters of Deborah and Barak – their qualities and weaknesses. Why shouldn't Barak have displayed hesitancy (4:8)?*
3 *Put into your own words the relationship between God and the nation, described in chapter 5 (e.g. verses 3-4, 10, 31).*

Many of the great characters in the Bible hesitated at the magnitude of the task God called them to (e.g. Moses and Jeremiah). They learned that God never calls without providing the strength necessary to

the task. Pray you'll learn the same lesson.

5. Gideon
Judges 6:1 – 8:21

The victories over Sisera result in forty years of peace. Such a triumph doubtless led to a renewal in Israel's fickle faith. But it wasn't a lasting return to the Lord, and God had to chastise them again by allowing the Midianites to plunder them. These nomads came from south of Edom and probably raided the Israelites' land annually. In response to their cries for help, God raises up Gideon – an unlikely candidate.

1 *It was not that Gideon needed guidance. Rather, he needed to know that God would go with him. God is patient with Gideon. In what ways did God confirm his call? How does this incident reassure you that God will keep his promises to you? Pause to think this over in prayer.*
2 *Put yourself in Gideon's position when told to tear down the altar (6:25). What made this job especially difficult?*
3 *Trace Gideon's growing confidence as a leader throughout the story. Notice how he deals with the opposition from the Ephraimites and the Midianites.*

Nowhere in the Bible is there another example of anything resembling fleece-setting. It seems to me inappropriate for Christians to behave like semi-pagan Gideon.

John White, *The Fight* (IVP).

Weekend

Backsliding – Christians often use the term 'backsliding' to mean that someone has stopped putting God first in his or her life. The Israelites were guilty of this during that period. There are all sorts of reasons why this should be, such as deliberate sin, lack of fellowship, false teaching. Read Psalm 51, the words of David after he had sinned (2 Samuel 11) and come back to God. How did he view the sin which had caused him to be far from God? What was his attitude to God as he turned to him? In the light of this, pray for any you know who once were close to God, but are not so any longer.

Any good book on discipleship should help you to know how to go on with God, or to return to him, such as *Discipleship* by David Watson (Hodder, 1983) or *Knowing God* by J. I. Packer (IVP, 1973). Try to find such a book this weekend, to see what it says about 'backsliding' and how to avoid it.

1. An anticlimax
Judges 8:22 – 9:57

The trust in God and reliance upon him for guidance which Gideon displayed in his younger years seems to have deserted him in peacetime.

Note: The ephod (idol, GNB) that Gideon built is likely to have been based on the one described in Exodus chapter 28. The law forbade such action.

1 *What actions of Gideon in 8:22-35 would have pleased or displeased God? What warning is this to anyone who wishes to please God continually?*

2 *What sort of man was Abimelech? Why did he want to be king (chapter 9)?*

3 *In what ways did God show his disapproval of Abimelech? What reassurance is that to you that the Lord is not blind to injustice and godlessness? Skim through Deuteronomy chapter 32 in which Moses rejoices at God's sense of justice. Are there areas of your life now where you need to be aware of this aspect of God?*

2. Jephthah
Judges 10:6 – 12:7

10:1-5 are concerned with Tolar and Jair, also judges. In verse 6 the familiar formula of Israel's waywardness preludes the record of Jephthah's role as judge. With Philistines threatening them to the west and Ammonites to the east, they look to the despised Jephthah's 'adventurers' for help.

1 *Try to summarize Jephthah's communications with the Ammonites. Numbers 21:26 suggests Moab had a better claim to this land than Sihon, but why isn't that the thrust of Jephthah's argument? What does that suggest about Jephthah's acceptance of the Lord's sovereignty?*

2 *Jephthah's rash act of devotion and zeal goes horribly wrong. Yet, to their credit, he and his daughter treated the vow as sacred. What was wrong with making the vow in the first place? Think back over some of the things you have promised or said these last few days. How wise have you been in God's eyes? Let Jephthah's example act as a stimulus to prayer.*

3 *Jephthah's treatment of the Ephraimites in chapter 12 recalls that of Gideon in 8:3-21. Note down the way in which the two incidents differ. The Israelites were fighting each other. How might this have weakened them?*

3. Samson: birth and marriage
Judges 13:1 – 14:20

Three judges follow Jephthah, but it is to Samson that a major part of the biblical record is devoted. Unlike the other 'judges' we have studied in detail it was made known at his birth that Samson was to be God's special servant. Yet he turned out to be quite a contradictory character!

Philistines had settled in large numbers on the coast, establishing themselves in five cities. You'll remember Shamgar's brief success against them (3:31). The real menace lay in the insidious way they polluted Jewish thinking and in the way their presence was meekly accepted.

1 *Examine Numbers 6:1-21 to see what a Nazirite was. Make a list of the ways in which Samson departed from the norm.*
2 *What do you notice about the faith of Manoah and his wife and their role as parents? Pray for any you know who are, themselves, learning how to bring up their children to trust God.*
3 *Though God could hardly have approved of Samson's proposed marriage (14:1-20), in what ways does God use the occasion to demonstrate his opposition to Philistine domination? What principle of God's character does this illustrate?*

---

4. Samson: revenge and folly
Judges 15:1 – 16:31

Samson is insulted to learn that his intended bride has been married to another. He vows personal vengeance. God uses this grudge to challenge the rule of the Philistines.

Note: 15:4 Probably a pack of jackals or foxes.

1 *How would you describe Samson's behaviour in these verses? What place does the Lord have in his life?*
2 *God allows Samson to reap the consequences of his sin, yet in what ways does God show his faithfulness to Samson? Pause to thank God for his faithfulness.*
3 *How far would you say that his succumbing to sexual temptation caused his downfall? Sexual emotions are very powerful. What warning is this to us not to give a free rein to our sexuality in a wrong situation? If this is an issue for you at the moment, let Samson's example act as a challenge. If you have not already done so, ask the Lord to help you.*

---

5. '…as he saw fit…'
Judges 17:1 – 21:25

This final section of Judges is markedly different from the rest. Instead of concentrating on the heroes themselves we are given two stories by way of an illustration of the poor state of Israel's spiritual life. They are included to demonstrate that, 'In those days Israel had no king; everyone did as he saw fit' (Judges 21:25).

Choose just one of these two records for today's study, returning to the other at the weekend.

1 *17:1 – 18:31. Trace the ways in which the religion of Micah and the Danites falls short of true faith. To what extent should Micah share in the guilt of the Danites?*

Chapters 19-21 describe events which occurred shortly after Joshua's death.

2 *Make a list of all the evils described in this section. In what ways did they contribute to the downfall of the tribe of Benjamin?*
3 *What good came out of all this?*

Backsliding, unfaithfulness and ungodliness seemed to be the order of the day in the time of the 'judges'. May this be a warning to us. Use Psalm 119:9-16 as a prayer that, unlike so often the people at this time, you will grow in the likeness of God.

Weekend

1 *Read again the final verse of Judges. This is the judgment of a writer looking back from the times when Israel did have a king. But would you consider this sufficient explanation for the unspiritual state of the Israelites? Going through your notes on Judges from the last fortnight make a list of those factors that undermined them spiritually and morally. Work out the parallels that exist between this list and the evils that might undermine the individual Christian, present day church and Christian Union. Use these thoughts to pray for yourself and your fellowship.*
2 *Some of the judges such as Jephthah and Samson are not exactly saints. Why do you think that God uses imperfect people for his purposes?* There is an excellent chapter on this issue in John Wenham's The enigma of evil: can we believe in the goodness of God? (Zondervan, 1985), p. 89.

Consider: The Bible is ruthlessly candid about the sins of its saints, and this is often regarded as an argument against the Bible's morality. It is in fact just the opposite; it is an illustration of its moral integrity. The Christian wants desperately to hide his sins, not only for his own comfort of mind, but so that God's name shall not be blasphemed on his account. But God usually rules otherwise. His name needs no defence, and he is not one to hide the truth when man needs to learn a lesson. While the disease is still only partially cured, God does not normally suppress the symptoms. So it is that the very heroes of faith who are commended in the New Testament are clearly delineated in the Old as men with dubious records.

Part One/Week Six
Leadership (An issue study)

Leadership is very much in vogue as something for Christians to think about and discuss – if the current flood of books, magazines and conferences on the subject is anything to go by! During this week, we will be looking at some of the things the Bible has to say on this important topic.

If you are in a position of Christian leadership, pray that God will use this week's studies to deepen your understanding of what it is he has called you to do. But if this doesn't apply to you (or at least, not yet), don't skip on to next week! Pray that God will teach you to understand better, and so support more effectively, those he has provided to lead you ...

In some ways though, we all lead others by the often unconscious influence we have on people through the example of what we say and do. So even if we have no formal position of leadership, the subject is an important one for all of us.

1. A heart in the right place
*1 Samuel 15:10-26; 16:1-13;
1 Chronicles 28:9*

The life story of David, the shepherd boy who became Israel's greatest king, makes thrilling reading. (You can find it in the books of 1 & 2 Samuel and 1 Chronicles.) He showed many great gifts of leadership during his lifetime, but we shall concentrate today on the essence of what made him great in God's eyes.

1 *Initially, David's predecessor Saul had looked promising – just the sort of leader Israel needed (see 1 Samuel 9:1-2). But appearances were deceptive as you can see by reading 1 Samuel 15:10-26. Write down in your own words what led to his being rejected by God.*
2 *Read 1 Samuel 16:1-13. Samuel doesn't seem to have learnt from his experience with Saul. What sort of characteristics was he looking for? What was God more interested in?*
3 *Towards the end of his life David gave some sound advice to his son Solomon. Look at 1 Chronicles 28:9 and note down the key phrases. What is it that God looks for in the heart?*

Memory verse: 'The LORD does not look at the things man looks at. Man looks at the outward appearance, but the LORD looks at the heart' (1 Samuel 16:7b).

As you pray, ask God to show you what he sees in *your* heart. You might like to use David's prayer in Psalm 51: 10. Ask God to give you a new desire and resolve to be wholehearted in acknowledging and serving him. What changes will that mean for your life today?

2. Trust and obey
Exodus 3:1 – 4:17; Numbers 11:10-17

Today we look at Moses, regarded by the Jews as their greatest leader, who led the Israelites out of captivity in Egypt. When God called him to be a leader, Moses himself was in exile.

1 *Read Exodus 3:1-14. Notice the way God says, 'I have come down to rescue them ...' in verse 8 and 'I am sending you ...' in verse 10. What does this tell you about the way God works?*
2 *Read on to Exodus 4:17. List the objections that Moses raises against what God is calling him to do. How does God respond? What does this say to any you know who are reluctant leaders?*
3 *We may not have quite the same need to perform dramatic miracles with our walking sticks but we still need the promise of God's presence and the support of fellow believers. Look at Numbers 11:10-17. What encouragement is this to the leader who is confronted by grumblers?*

The Christian life is an adventure of faith! Pray for the ability to trust and obey God, even when you don't understand exactly what he is up to!

3. The good shepherd
Ezekiel 34:1-10; John 10:1-21

1 *Read Ezekiel 34:1-10. In this sobering passage, God makes clear to the leaders of his people what he expects of them. Write out a list of the things mentioned. How do these apply to the leadership of God's people now?*
2 *Later in the chapter, God promises that he himself will be the shepherd of his people in a way and with an authority which no man can have over others. Read John 10:1-21. What do you notice about the relationship between the shepherd and his sheep?*
3 *Use what you have found as you spend time in praising and thanking God for all he means to you as your 'shepherd'. (You could also look at Psalm 23.) Then pray for the ability to carry out the 'shepherding' responsibilities that he has given you.*

4. As one who serves...
Mark 10:41-45; John 13:1-17

We look today at some of the key teaching on leadership given by Jesus to his followers.

1 *Read Mark 10:41-45. In the preceding verses, we read that James and John asked Jesus for the honour of sharing in his glory. Write down the distinctive differences which you find in this passage.*
2 *Shortly before his arrest, Jesus gave a practical example of what he meant. Read the account in John 13:1-17. What is the particular significance of verse 3? How does that apply to leaders in the church today – on both a local and national level?*
3 *What modern equivalents of washing one another's feet can you think of?*
4 *Peter is initially unwilling to have his feet washed (verses 6, 8). What does his reaction tell us about him?*

Why does Jesus respond in the way he does?

It's especially easy for leaders to fall into the trap of giving constantly but not bothering to receive from God and their fellow Christians. Pray that you will allow others to help you as much as you help them. Pray too that you might have an attitude of humble service, not glorying in your own importance.

think about how they apply to your own situation.

Note: Jesus is described as the 'Chief Shepherd' (verse 4). Look at 1 Corinthians 1 :10-17 and 3:1-9 to see what happens when this is forgotten.

Spend time praying for Christian leaders who are facing persecution in the world today or are under extreme pressure, that they will stand firm in their faith.

5. 'Feed my lambs'
John 21:15-19; 1 Peter 5:1-11

1 *Read John 21:15-19. Peter, the natural leader among the disciples, boasted that he would never desert Jesus. He failed. Despite this failure, Jesus later gave him the opportunity to make amends and recommissioned him. What does feeding and taking care of the sheep involve? What did it cost Peter ultimately? How costly to you is leadership? How much do you resent or accept the cost?*
2 *Read 1 Peter 5:1-11. Peter writes to the leaders of a Christian community facing persecution. As he thinks back to the time when Jesus commissioned him, he naturally thinks of the shepherd picture to illustrate Christian leadership. List the different points he makes and*

Weekend

1 *Pick an example of a leader in the Bible – either one we have looked at this week or another one that interests you – and put together a brief biography. What influences shaped his or her life? How was he or she equipped for service? What secrets of success can you find? Use a concordance to find references to look up, and a Bible dictionary for background information.*
2 *The classic* Spiritual Leadership *by J. Oswald Sanders (Moody, 1962) is well worth reading. You might also like to look at* Excellence in Leadership *by John White (IVP, 1986),* Leadership *by Philip Greenslade (Bethany, 1986) or* The Making of a Leader *by Chua Wee Hian (IVP, 1987).*

Part One/Week Seven
Songs at Christmas (A meditation)

If you are using this week's studies as Christmas approaches, you could skip them and return to them for Christmas week.

Luke, alone of all the gospel writers, included these songs at the beginning of his account of the early days of Jesus' life. And they have been sung by Christians down the centuries. We shall be taking a week to meditate upon them. They are to be appreciated and enjoyed.

Remember that these are songs using poetic devices for effect.

1. Nothing is impossible with God
Luke 1:46-49

The Christmas story is so familiar that we often fail to appreciate what was actually happening.

1 Read Luke 1:26-38, trying to imagine just how Mary must have felt at the angel's stunning pronouncement.

Note: Being Jewish Mary would have had a knowledge of Old Testament history which served as a background to her song.

2 Look up 1 Samuel 2:1-10 to see what influence Hannah's song might have had upon Mary.

3 Take verses 46-49. What do you make of Mary's response and relationship to God in the light of her circumstances? Even though no one would ever be in a position similar to hers, what example of humble acceptance of the will of God is she setting to men and women of all time?

4 Reflect on how this is worked out in your own life. Where do you need to submit humbly to God's plan right now?

> Tell out, my soul, the
>   greatness of the Lord!
> Unnumbered blessings, give
>   my spirit voice;
> Tender to me the promise of
>   his word;
> In God my Saviour shall my
>   heart rejoice.
>
> Timothy Dudley-Smith

2. God has done great things
Luke 1:46-55

Returning to Mary's song, refresh your memory on what was the course of your meditation yesterday. Pray for a quiet meditative spirit.

Mary knew of God's dealings with his people in the past and lived in the expectation of the glorious age to come.

1 *Read the passage several times, identifying which aspects of God's character she was acknowledging.*
2 *From your own knowledge of the Old Testament, what specific examples of God's dealings with his people might Mary be remembering (e.g. verse 51 could be referring to the exodus)?*

Note: But Mary might also be looking to the future, for God is the same throughout all generations.

3 *Take each of his attributes and actions which Mary mentions and ponder what significance each has for your own circumstances.*

> Tell out, my soul, the
> greatness of his might!
> Powers and dominions lay
> their glory by.
> Proud hearts and stubborn
> wills are put to flight,
> The hungry fed, the humble
> lifted high.
>
> Timothy Dudley-Smith

3. Salvation has begun
Luke 1:68-75

The lives of the cousins Jesus and John the Baptist are interwoven. Luke clearly draws out the parallels of their births – an angel announced the birth of each; Jesus was referred to as 'Son of the Most High' (1:32) while John was called 'prophet of the Most High' (1:76). After the birth of each, Luke includes in his account a song in praise to God for his purposes to be worked out in the life of each child.

This particular song sung by Zechariah, John's father, after John's birth, is divided into two – first of all praising God and then a hymn in honour of the birth of John.

1 *Zechariah had good cause to praise God. Read Luke 1:5-25, 57-66 to see what Luke tells us about Zechariah.*
2 *From childhood Zechariah, like any Jew, would have been longing for the time when God would step into history to keep his promise by rescuing his people. Read Luke 1:68-75 several times, trying to capture that deep longing in his heart for God's salvation to become evident. There was no doubt in his mind that God would keep his word.*
3 *Zechariah himself may not have been aware that non-Jews would also be included in this salvation. But he did expect that when the Messiah came, people's behaviour would be affected. Meditate upon how far the coming of Jesus, the Messiah, has enabled you to live out verses 74 and 75, thinking of your behaviour among both Christians and non-Christians.*

4. A new father's joy
Luke 1:68-80

Any new father can identify with Zechariah's joy and hopes for his son. But in Zechariah's case, his hopes were even greater because he saw in John the fulfilment of specific promises of God.

1 *Reread Luke 1:13-17, then turn to verses 68-80. Zechariah took up the prophecy of Isaiah 40:3-5, seeing it fulfilled in his son, John. What sort of* a role in life awaited John (you could glance at Luke 3:1-19)?

2 John had a unique calling which he faithfully obeyed at great cost. Such a calling cannot be repeated. Meditate on how you respond to God's role for you in life, even though it may not be as clear cut as. John's was.

3 If you are a parent you could pray that your child will know and obey God's call, as Zechariah did. Otherwise pray for the Christian parents in your church.

4 What else does Zechariah say about the coming Saviour's role? Reflect on how Jesus did and does fulfil that role. Turn your thoughts into praise.

Note: Verse 78b probably refers both to the shoot from Jesse (Isaiah 11:1) and the star from Jacob (Numbers 24:17) – both Old Testament images which are usually understood as pointing to the Messiah.

5. Salvation at last
Luke 2:25-35

Simeon was another man who was longing for the coming of the Messiah, the consolation of Israel, bringing salvation. We know little about him.

1 What does the passage tell you about his relationship to God? How far is your heart set on a similar closeness to God?

2 Read verses 29-32 again several times. What is the main thrust of his words? In what ways do you rejoice that God's salvation is so far-reaching? Spend time thinking over this. How much concern do you have for vast areas of the world without a proclamation of the good news of salvation?

Weekend

1 All three songs were sung by three very ordinary people who rejoiced that God had stepped into their own personal circumstances, but also that he was involved in the wider world. This weekend, make time to note down all the reasons why you can praise God for his involvement in your own life and the world around.

2 It sometimes helps to understand something if you put it into your own words. Try to rewrite each of these songs and see if that adds to your understanding of them. If you are musically inclined you could try setting them to music.

3 Mary has been over-venerated by Roman Catholics, and neglected, perhaps, by evangelical Christians. Write a brief biography of Mary with the help of references from a good Bible dictionary. Notice some of her larger family, e.g. cousin Elizabeth, and Mary (wife of Cleopas) who seems to have been Mary's sister-in-law. Her son James, Jesus' brother, is likely to have been the author of the New Testament letter (see J.A. Motyer, The Message of James (Bible Speaks Today series, IVP, 1985), pp.17ff.)

Part One/Week Eight
Amos (A detailed study)

A southerner trying to put a northerner in his place! That's just what Amos, as directed by God, was trying to do. He was a shepherd or sheepbreeder sent from Judah to Bethel, on the edge of the kingdom of Israel, around 760-750 BC. He prophesied the just end of Israel and eventually Judah. His pleadings with God delayed but did not prevent judgment falling on an unrepentant people.

1. Too close for comfort!
Amos 1:1 – 3:2

Amos pronounces against the atrocities of the heathen nations before rounding on the Jews. The latter will suffer the fate they have heaped upon their fellows. That they have attempted to stifle and mislead the prophets will not prevent judgment falling, despite God's prolonged patience – 'for three sins... even for four'.

1 *What are the sins of each of the pagan nations (1:1 – 2:3)? And what is to be God's punishment? Even though they did not follow God, why did he judge them? (Romans 1:18-25 will give further help.)*
2 *Then list the sins of Judah and Israel (2:4 – 3:2). What are the equivalent sins of God's people today? How appalled are you by such sin?*

3 *In what ways had God shown his mercy to Israel (2:9-12)? What are God's unmerited gifts to us? Do we fully appreciate them?*

Lord, protect me from the sin of presuming on your goodness and mercy.

2. Be sure your sins will find you out!
Amos 3:3 – 4:5

To be chosen for a team or special task imposes great responsibilities. Only the best must be offered in way of service. Israel had failed to understand this.

1 *Causes and effects – note them down, showing how the illustrations come nearer home. 'Evil' or 'disaster' (3:6) denotes calamity, not moral wrong. Does the Lord ever act without warning? How much is that an important part of God's character to you?*
2 *Both Bethel and Gilgal (4:4) had been important places in Israel's history. Read about them briefly in Genesis 28:10-22 and Joshua 4:19-24. Yet by the time of Amos they had become altars of unholy worship. What does this say about how far Israel had fallen from the closeness to God they once knew? Are there places or events which were milestones for you, yet which have become a snare subsequently? Why*

was this? And what are you now prepared to do about it?

Lord, help me to live a consistently holy life.

3. Prepare to meet thy doom!
Amos 4:6 – 5:27

The ancients clearly believed that God spoke through natural disasters. The judgment pronounced will bring them to Assyria, home of Sakkuth, god of war, whom they have worshipped in place of God – poetic justice?

1 *Read Amos 4:6-13 out loud. Disaster came on Israel, yet how did they respond? What was God's response to be? Think back to national disasters that have occurred recently and public statements made. How did people respond? Did they turn to God anyway?*
2 *Read chapter 5. The 'gate' or 'court' of 5:10, 12, 15 was the place where it should have been possible to receive just judgments by the elders. How had the Israelites committed social injustices? In what ways can a Christian or the wider church condone such injustice today?*
3 *Depressed by Amos' utterances? Meditate on 5:8-9 – the mighty, righteous Lord, and verse 24 – the unbribable judge!*

Praise the Lord for his justice and righteousness which will eventually be brought to bear on all injustice in this life.

4. Pride comes before a fall!
Amos 6:1 – 7:9

'The Assyrian came down like a wolf on the fold' (Byron). The 'shepherds' of Israel were proud, complacent and rich and they failed their 'flocks' miserably. Amos gives up interceding for Israel, probably realizing the futility of expecting repentance.

1 *Write a thumb-nail sketch of the life enjoyed by Israel's leaders. In what ways were they exploiting their privileged position? What was God's response? Pause to pray that your own church leaders will not fall into similar sinful attitudes.*
2 *Israel preened itself on winning skirmishes, but in a real battle what was to be the outcome? Who or what would be responsible for the coming devastation?*
3 *God repents in that he changes his mind in response to Amos' pleading (7:3,6). You might like to compare this situation with that of Abraham and Sodom (Genesis 18:22ff.).*

What is my part to be, Lord, in interceding for those who are so deliberately committing sin?

5. A light at the end of the tunnel?
Amos 7:10 – 9:15

Amos dares to prophesy at 'the temple of the kingdom', Bethel. Amaziah gets his just deserts for trying to stop God's message from reaching home. A total eclipse of the sun occurred in June 763 BC, providing a picture of the end to come – 'I will never again pass by them'!

1 *Note down the characteristics of Amos which emerge here as he talks with the professional priest. What contrasts are there between God's prophet and the representative of the religious establishment?*
2 *It was not just the leaders who were unjust. How were the retailers being dishonest?*
3 *There is no escape from God's judgment for his enemies – it is terrible and final. Read these last verses, aware of this. But then what are the riches that await the faithful, including Amos? (The language of 9:13-15 is agricultural but symbolic.) Surrounded by injustice in our world as well as our nation, what hope does God's judgment give?*

Praise God that there is a light in the darkness, many promises to be faithfully kept into eternity.

Weekend

1 *Read* The Message of Amos *by J.A. Motyer (IVP), which gets to grips with the details of the book.*
2 *Amos is a book of many negatives. Read the book, noting the corresponding positives which could have been there if Israel and Judah had been faithful. What picture emerges of a people worthy of God?*
3 *Following on from the fifth study, choose an area in the world where you know of injustice. (There is no shortage of places to choose.) Read up about it in the newspaper and think over how the message of Amos could be relevant. Is there any way in which you can take action?*

Part Two

The letter of James
Jacob
Lamentations
Living more with less
The birth of the church
Psalms of the king
Messiah
Songs of the Servant

Part Two/Week One
The letter of James (A whole book study)

Action! That's what James calls for.
The evidence points towards his
being the brother of Jesus. This letter
seems like a collection of sermon
notes – each theme capable of
expansion. It states clearly that faith
without resulting actions is *dead*!
Beginning in 721 BC (when they were
transported to Assyria) the Israelites
were scattered across the world. In
addressing it to the scattered 'twelve
tribes' of Israel he refers to all who
are redeemed by God throughout the
ages.

*The Bible is being translated,
commented on, read, studied,
preached and analysed as
never before. But it is
questionable whether it is
being obeyed to a comparable
degree.*
*All this suggests that the
message of James is one that
we all need to hear – and obey.
No profound theologian,
James' genius lies in his
profound moral earnestness;
in his powerfully simple call
for repentance, for action, for a
consistent Christian life-style.
His words need to thrust
through our theological
debates, our personal
preconceptions, our spiritual
malaise and set us back on the
road to a biblical, invigorating,
transforming Christianity.*

Douglas J. Moo, *Tyndale
New Testament Commentary
on James* (Eerdmans)

1. Faith tested
James 1

If I sin, well so what? Are there any
absolutes anyway? Can't everyone
do what is right in their own eyes?

1 *Note down some of the differences
between the doubter and the
steadfast, persevering person (e.g.
verses 4, 6). What produces a firm
faith?*
2 *How can you decide which values
you should use as your standards to
live by (e.g. verses 5, 12, 17)? How
can they be achieved (e.g. verses
21-22)?*
3 *'Actions speak louder than words.'
What makes you think that James
would have agreed?*
4 *Jot down some of the vivid images
James characteristically uses (e.g.
the mirror, verse 23).*
5 *How can you have an active faith
in your own situation? Are you
involved in evangelism? Do you
support a missionary in a practical
way, for instance, writing to him or
her regularly?*

Write out 1:2-4 on a piece of paper or
card and memorize these verses in
spare moments.

right strawy Epistle

Martin Luther (1483-1546)

---

2. Action for the needy
James 2

It's easy to believe – even the demons do. It doesn't cost them anything to demonstrate belief – does it you?

1 *What is the principle illustrated in verses 1-7? How do your attitudes compare in terms of wealth, nationality, position...?*
2 *'Well officer, I was doing only 80 mph' or 'But it was only a little dent'. Guilty or not guilty according to verses 8-13 – and why?*
3 *What does James teach about the relationship of actions to faith? Note down some examples.*

Who is my neighbour and what is his or her need?

> *There is many a good saying in it.*
>
> Martin Luther on the letter of James

---

3. A controlled tongue
James 3

Usually hidden in the mouth, yet a slip of the tongue may end a friendship, start cruel rumours, endanger lives...

1 *Verses 1-12. Note down the illustrations used to picture the*

power of the tongue and its ability to reflect the heart of the owner. What is the main point each is teaching?
2 *Verses 13-18. Consider the nature of earthly and divine wisdom. What kinds of speech arise naturally from these sources?*
3 *What fires does your tongue start? How can you stop lighting them? Think back over this past week to conversations you have had, cross words spoken, speech that has encouraged your hearer. Let these verses act as a challenge to you.*

Meditate on James 3:17.

> *If a sudden jar can cause me to speak an impatient, unloving word, then I know nothing of Calvary love.*
>
> Amy Carmichael (1867-1951)

---

4. I want...
James 4

How can I be something of value for the Lord when I don't even 'value' myself – I'm always struggling within?

1 *War – a strong word! How often are you at war with yourself and thus with others? What are the signs of this inner lack of peace, and social disquiet? Write them down as given by James.*
2 *Verses 7-10. What does the Lord require that he may 'lift you up'? Does humility mean becoming a 'door-mat'? Consider the active nature of Jesus' submission and humility (Philippians 2:5-8). What difference would active humility make in your life right now?*
3 *Verses 13-17. How does the*

quality of your life in God's eyes square with all human life being like a mist?

Pray that your life may count for Christ. Express your dependence upon him as the source of power for a Christ-like humility and an active faith.

> ...full of instruction ... the benefit of which extends to every part of the Christian life.
>
> John Calvin (1509-1564) on the letter of James

5. Test your faith
James 5

Had your faith road tested lately? Is it 'road worthy'?

1 *Is your faith of the quality that neither acknowledges God's rights in all areas of life nor your responsibilities to your fellow human beings? How may you guard against this, even in small things?*
2 *Note down the characteristics of those who are waiting for Christ to return. How would you explain the meaning of patience (verse 7) or*

perseverance, in the light of these qualities?
3 *What are we shown about the power of prayer coming from people of faith? Is your prayer life like this? How can you learn to pray as Elijah did?*

Pray that you may have an active faith towards others, steadfast towards Christ, patiently waiting for the coming again of the Lord.

Weekend

1 *Moffat found 54 commands in 108 verses! Find as many of them as you can and look out for what James teaches about the relationship between faith and action.*
2 *Luther thought that the letter taught salvation by deeds instead of faith – in what ways was he wrong?*
3 *Read* The Message of James *by Alec Motyer (The Bible Speaks Today Series, IVP, 1985). As you read let the Lord speak to you concerning the relationship of your own faith to its day to day practical use.*

For a more detailed study of the text the *Tyndale Commentary on James* by Douglas J. Moo (Eerdmans, 1986) is helpful.

Jacob (A character study)

A quarter of the book of Genesis is taken up by a man of intrigue, romance, deception and godliness who lived probably in the 18th century BC. He was the spoilt child of a weak, selfish father and a doting schemer of a mother. Yet in fulfilment of God's promise to Abraham (Genesis 12) Jacob became father of the Jewish nation.

1. Mama's boy
Genesis 27

The giving of a father's blessing was a symbolic act, meaning that the recipient would receive the double inheritance due to any elder son. Today we discover how Jacob, the younger son, stole the birthright.

1 *List the actions which show the differing attitudes of Isaac and Rebekah towards Jacob.*
2 *In a few words sketch Jacob's character.*
3 *Loyalty towards parents and honesty between parents and children was sadly missing here. With what consequences? Is this an area of difficulty in your own life? Ask God for his wisdom and courage to face up to such difficult relationships.*

Whatever your situation pray that you may be honourable towards your parents, children and Jesus Christ.

2. Love your brother!?
Genesis 25:27-34; 32:3-21, 33

Whilst Jacob's dealings with his elder brother were devious, the outcome was in God's plan (Genesis 25:23). Esau sacrificed his future for an immediate gratification of his material needs – he was hungry! Later in life, because of his own actions, Jacob would go in fear of Esau.

1 *Note down Jacob's actions and Esau's responses; show any distinctions between those before and at the end of Jacob's exile. How do they differ?*
2 *What do we learn from Jacob about the 'art' of manipulation? In what ways could you ever 'use' people?*
3 *What does Genesis 32:9-12 show you about an underlying relationship which Jacob had? How does it influence his daily living?*

Pray that you may always be straightforward in your relationships with others.

3. More than he bargained for!
Genesis 29 – 32

Jacob got a dose of his own medicine

from the man to whom he became a 'slave-heir'. Laban too was a fully qualified deceiver. Does God give retribution in this life? It would seem so.

1 *Putting your notes into three columns, jot down the contrast in treatment given to Rachel and Leah by Jacob, Laban and the Lord. How much pain must have been given to both women!*
2 *How did Laban's actions influence Jacob's character for good or bad? In what ways do we see God's purposes at work?*

Pray that you may be able to accept the hard times as part of God's character-building plan for you. Sometimes, however, hard times may be of our own making, e.g. pride or deliberate sin may cause us and others much suffering. As you consider how the Lord is forming your character, are there things you yourself need to put right?

4. Like father, like son?
Genesis 34; 37:1-4, 25-36; 48:8-22

Jacob chose to repeat Lot's mistake by choosing the rich grazing lands of Shechem instead of staying in the country chosen by Abraham. In going amongst aliens looking for material gain, nothing but trouble resulted.

1 *What were the sins of Jacob's sons? How might their father have prevented trouble in both situations?*
2 *Note down the parallels between Jacob's attitude to Joseph and*

Rebekah's attitude to him. What, if anything, had he learned about the dangers of favouritism? Is this particularly relevant in your life, or as you think about family life in the future?
3 *What was the difference between Isaac's blessing of his sons and Jacob's of his grandsons (Genesis 27 and 48)?*

Pray that you may seek the Lord's will for your choice of place and job, not going after the good situations for the wrong motives.

5. 'I will not let you go, unless...'
Genesis 28:10-17; 32:22-32

Jacob was God's man! But the progress towards this relationship was hard. It really began with a dream and reached a climax in a wrestling match. There followed later the great prophecy to the tribes of Israel – 'Israel' being Jacob's new name (Genesis 32:28).

1 *What promises were made through the dream? What do you think the ladder may have represented?*
2 *Why did God have to disable Jacob in order to give him a blessing? May God have to deal with you in a similar way? What easier pathway is there?*

What does it all mean? It means that Jacob had been struggling against God all his life. The conflict by the Jabbok symbolizes his lifelong struggle. His early life had led down to this point, and the

47

rest of his life would ascend from it. Up to this crisis his life had been a long endeavor to resist God's goodness. As is so often the case, it had been a struggle against a God who was determined to bless and to help him.

John White, *Daring to Draw Near* (IVP).

3 *You may have been a Christian a long time or a few months. Spend time reflecting on how the Lord has dealt with you so far. It may be in a climactic event or more gradually.*

Pray that you may be content to listen to God as was the habit of Abraham, Jacob's grandfather.

Try reading the chapter about Jacob in *Daring to Draw Near* by John White.

Weekend

1 *Read Genesis 25:19 – 50:21 at one sitting, noting down the 'high' points in Jacob's life, for instance, those times when he is particularly close to God. Why do you think that the New Testament speaks of the God of Abraham, Isaac and Jacob?*
2 *What has the study this week taught you about having fair dealings with people? Think about your own relationships within and outside your immediate family. Are there situations which need to be put right with God, and with the people involved, in which only you can be the peacemaker? How will you go about resolving them?*

Lamentations (A whole book study)

Lamentations is a book of five poems written following the destruction of Jerusalem in 587 BC by the Babylonians. It describes the sorrow felt by God's people and also opens up the reason why the city of God has been destroyed by pagan invaders.

Each chapter of the book is a poem in Hebrew. In chapters 1, 2 and 4 the verses each begin with the letters of the Hebrew alphabet in turn. In chapter 3 each group of three verses begins with the letters of the Hebrew alphabet in turn. Chapter 5 has no pattern of this kind to it.

The key question the author of Lamentations (who is anonymous) is facing is 'Where is our God, when his city and his temple have been destroyed?', and the author's answer is to try to help the people of God to see what their God is doing through the events that have taken place.

1. Sorrow for the city
2 Kings 25:8-12; Lamentations 1

This chapter compares the city of Jerusalem to a friendless widow (verse 1), whose situation is described (verses 1-11) and who then speaks for herself (verses 12-22).

1 *Read 2 Kings 25:8-12, which gives a historical account of the fall of the city of Jerusalem. Looking at the whole of Lamentations 1, note down the marks of the widow's sorrow. How does she express her grief over the fall of Jerusalem?*

2 *What reasons are given for the events that have taken place (see especially verses 9, 12-19, 21-22)? Make two lists – first of all, the things which the people did to cause the fall of the city and, secondly, the things which God did to cause the city to fall.*

3 *C.S. Lewis wrote that 'God whispers to us in our pleasures and shouts to us in our pain'. Think of painful or sorrowful events in your life, or in the lives of those you know. Was God speaking in these situations to rebuke sin and show his judgment? Are you conscious of areas of sin in your life that God is speaking about now? Spend time in quiet thought and repentance over these areas.*

You could follow up the idea of how God speaks through suffering by reading chapter 6 of John White's book *Daring to Draw Near* (IVP), which is a study of Hannah.

2. 'The Lord is a warrior'

Lamentations 2

1 This chapter focuses on what God is doing in the destruction of the city. Read verses 1-9 and notice all the things that God does in these verses. What marks of the character of God emerge? Do you usually think about God in this way?

2 Read verses 10-13 and note the effects of all of these events on the people. Look on to verses 14-17. What does the writer pick out here as a primary reason for the fall of the city? What was the particular sin of the prophets (verse 14)? Pray for those who have the responsibility of teaching in your church or Christian group, that they would be fearless in teaching the whole truth of God, however uncomfortable that may be to their hearers.

3 The last three verses of the chapter are a prayer to God. What evidence do they (and the rest of the chapter) give that the disaster of the judgment is beginning to have its intended effects?

---

3. 'A cloud no bigger than a man's hand'

Lamentations 3

1 Verses 1-20 are the writer speaking as a representative of the whole people, describing the suffering God has brought on him. Yet in verse 21, the whole atmosphere of the book changes. Read verses 21-39 and notice the grounds for hope the writer finds in the face of the tragedy. These aspects of God's character certainly complement those you found yesterday in chapter 2. So what do you learn about facing hardship and tough times when God is acting in judgment? Why is it foolish to complain in times of hardship?

2 In verses 40-42, the writer speaks to the people and calls them to repentance for sin, and then, in verses 43-54, lists the results of their sin. Note the various effects of the people's sin in God's eyes. What are the effects of your sin on God and on your relationship with him?

3 Finally, the writer turns to God in prayer (verses 55-66). What is his prayer in these circumstances? Use the themes of this prayer to pray for Christians under pressure, and suffering.

Memory verse: 'Because of the LORD's great love we are not consumed, for his compassions never fail. They are new every morning; great is your faithfulness. I say to myself, "The LORD is my portion; therefore I will wait for him"' (Lamentations 3:22-24).

---

4. Past, present and future

Lamentations 4

1 Read the whole chapter and divide a piece of paper into three columns headed 'Past', 'Present' and 'Future'. Note in each column pictures of the past, of the present and what God is going to do in the future.

2 What a contrast between the past and the present! Looking particularly at verses 12-20, what are the reasons for this contrast, both on God's side and on the people's side? What particular groups does the writer single out as especially responsible in these verses? Spend some time praying for those with responsibility for leadership amongst God's people today, that they may lead wisely and have ears open to hear what God is saying to them.

3 Edom (the people of Israel's age-old enemies) was gloating over the fall of Jerusalem. What do verses 21-22 say will happen to the Edomites in the future and why? Pray for those unbelievers who despise God's people, that God may give them repentance before they face judgment, especially those close to you.

---

5. Our God reigns!
Lamentations 5

1 The first part of this chapter (to verse 14) forms a sustained cry to God for mercy. Notice the different groups who have suffered because of the people's sin. Everyone has been affected in a devastating way. This chapter seems to have been written some time after the fall of Jerusalem (for example, because of the reference to the previous generation as being dead in verse 7).

2 Verses 15-18 turn to mourning for sin and then the focus shifts to God in the final verses of the book (verses 19-22). Looking at this second half of the chapter, what gives the writer hope in the face of disaster?

3 Consider how the effects of God's judgment on his people can be seen in the world today. From the lessons of the book of Lamentations, how would you help a Christian from a land where suffering has been part of life for a very long period? You might like to write an imaginary letter to such a Christian.

Weekend

Read through the whole book again and try to note down one or more of the following:

1 Places where the writer is honest with God about his feelings and suffering. Can you find places in the rest of Scripture where a similar attitude to honesty in prayer comes out? How honest are you with God in prayer? Consider the example of Jeremiah's prayer life in Jeremiah 20:7-18 as a study in honesty.

2 Evidence of the writer identifying himself with the sin and suffering of his people. How far do you identify with the suffering of your church or nation? Read Nehemiah 1 for another example of a pray-er who stood alongside his people, and consider how you can pray for your nation in the light of that chapter and the lessons of Lamentations.

3 The different ways the writer appeals to God. What kinds of prayer are present in the book? Consider whether your prayer life has the variety of styles of prayer in this writer's prayer life.

4 What God does to lead people back to himself and what responsibility people have to respond to God. Note verses emphasizing one and verses emphasizing the other. What do you learn from this of the balance of the sovereignty of God in drawing people to himself and the responsibility of people to repent?

Living more with less (An issue study)

*Wherever riches have
increased, the essence of
religion has decreased in the
same proportion... religion
must necessarily produce both
industry and frugality, and
these cannot but produce
riches. But as riches increase,
so will pride, anger, and love of
the world in all its branches...
Is there no way to prevent this
– this continual decay of pure
religion?*

John Wesley (1703-91)

1. The right attitude to wealth
Luke 12:13-34

By and large Christians in the west
are wealthy. They own most of the
world's goods and property while
others in the world starve and suffer
desperate injustices.

1 *Verses 13-21. What are the main
points of Christ's parable?*
2 *Try to retell the story from a
modern situation.*
3 *Verses 22-34. Make a note of all
the reasons that Jesus gives for not
being anxious about material
possessions. Can you find any
evidence for believing that such
possessions are not in themselves
sinful?*

Pray about your own attitude to
possessions. Be honest with God and
yourself. Ask him if you need to
change your style of life.

2. Paul's contented life
Philippians 4:4-20

It would be putting it mildly to say
that Paul's life contained many ups
and downs! Not only had he known
severe persecution, hard work,
shipwreck, danger and want, but
hunger and thirst as well (2
Corinthians 11:23-29). Yet he had
also known God's provision for him
in all his needs. One of his main
sources of support was the church at
Philippi.

1 *What in the passage reveals Paul's
attitude to material things? Why was
he able to remain free from anxiety
about his material needs?*
2 *What does the passage tell us
about Paul's overall attitude to life?*

Note: Verse 13 is not an assertion
about Paul as a Christian 'Superman',
but is about how he had learned to
be content in all circumstances
(compare it with verse 12).

3 *Are there any people to whom you
feel a sense of gratitude like that of*

Paul's towards the Philippians?

Pray for the above people. Give thanks to God for them. Pray also that you may learn to live the life of real contentment which Paul had learned (verse 11).

4 *Some today believe that Christians can claim material prosperity as a right. Why would the apostle Paul's attitude and experiences make him reject such a view?*

3. What if I'm a rich person?
1 Timothy 6:6-10, 17-19

It is frequently difficult for Christians to find the balance between being a responsible steward of what God has given (*e.g.* 1 Timothy 5:8) and living a really radical discipleship such as the Lord required of the rich young man (*e.g.* Mark 10:21). In this first letter to Timothy Paul suggests ways in which those who are rich might approach their wealth.

1 *Verses 6-10. Make a note of the basic attitudes to wealth that you find in the passage. Does this challenge your own ideas?*
2 *Christian history has many examples of rich people who have used their wealth to forward the kingdom of God on earth – people such as the Countess of Huntingdon in the eighteenth century supported George Whitfield, the evangelist. Do you know any such people today? Pray for them especially that they might maintain their integrity and not use their wealth to control others.*

3 *If you are particularly rich pray also that our Lord might show you any practical ways of using what you have to his glory. If you are a Christian in the rich west you might pray specifically about your responsibilities towards the poorer parts of the world. Ronald Sider's* Rich Christians in an Age of Hunger *(IVP, 1984) is worth buying!*

4. Generosity
2 Corinthians 8 – 9

The famine which hit Christians throughout the Roman empire had been prophesied beforehand (Acts 11:27-30). For this reason Paul and Barnabas had time to organize aid for the Judean churches amongst the Gentile churches (*e.g.* 1 Corinthians 16:1-4).

1 *Read through Paul's account of the collection in today's passage. What can be learnt from the giving of the Christians of Macedonia?*
2 *What indications are there as to their motivation for such generosity?*

Do you know of any similar situations which might evoke a Macedonian-style response from you? What about situations near to home? Or aid to Christians in poverty, or in other difficult situations?

Pray for generosity of spirit. Pray also for Christians who are suffering lack and hardship. Ask God what you can do to help.

> *Generosity towards the poor goes hand in hand with contentment or inner freedom. One can only give to the extent to which one recognises that*

all things belong to God and can be possessed only when they are put in relation to the kingdom of God and his righteousness.

Rene Padilla, *Mission Between the Times* (Paternoster).

5. 'Let justice roll on like a river'

Amos 5

One of the prophets raised up by God to speak about injustice in Israel was Amos. In this chapter Amos pinpoints several of the areas of injustice in public life.

1 *What does today's chapter indicate about God's attitude towards injustice?*
2 *What precise public injustices does the passage highlight?*
3 *Can you think of similar injustices in our society? Does the passage help to indicate what to do about it?*

Try reading John Stott's *Involvement*, 2 vols. (Revell, 1984), which is concerned with social justice. Find out about Evangelicals for Social Action, World Vision, Prison Fellowship or any other organization working towards a

Christian response to injustice in our society.

The God we know in the Bible is a liberating God... a God who intervenes in history in order to break down structures of injustice and who raises up prophets in order to point out the way of justice.

Emilio Castro, *Amidst Revolution* (Belfast, Christian Journals Ltd, 1975).

Weekend

1 *Look up some literature on Christian responsibility in our world and simple lifestyle, e.g. R. Foster,* Freedom of Simplicity *(Harper & Row, 1981). Those interested in the connection between mission and social action might try one of the following: J.R.W. Stott (ed.),* Evangelism and Social Responsibility *(Paternoster, 1982); Rene Padilla,* Mission Between the Times *(Paternoster, 1985); Ronald Sider,* Rich Christians in an Age of Hunger *(IVP, 1984).*
2 *Social action is not an individual thing!! Make a point of discussing with someone else what you have been learning this week and together consider what you can be doing.*
3 *We are often blind to how materialistic we have become, so ask a good friend to comment on your own lifestyle.*

The birth of the church—Acts 1:1—11:18 (A historical study)

Today, about one third of the world's population would claim allegiance to Jesus – that's roughly 1,400,000,000 people – a big increase on the 120 who were present on the day of Pentecost! Church history is the account of how we got from one to the other – and this is the start of it all.

1. How it all began
Acts 1:1 – 2:42

We tend to think of Acts as the book that tells us how the church began, but for its author, Luke, the beginning of Acts is the middle of the story. His gospel, volume 1, tells what Jesus did during his earthly ministry, and this book takes the story of Jesus a stage further, as we see what the Holy Spirit did through the church.

1 *Read 1:1-11. Jesus tells his followers to wait for the Holy Spirit. What does he say will happen when the Spirit comes?*
2 *Find a map, such as the one on page 108, and look up the places in verse 8. As you go through these studies, keep track of where the disciples have got to.*

Notes: The *New Bible Atlas*

(Tyndale) is a useful reference tool. One reason for having twelve apostles was to show the continuity of the church with the twelve tribes of Israel (see Luke 22:30) – but the twelve had a specific job to do.

3 *Read 2:1-42. Imagine you are a journalist reporting these events for a secular newspaper (if you have time you could try writing a complete article – keep it short!). How would you describe the main characters involved? What explanation might you give of these events?*
4 *Peter's explanation is in his speech. Can you pick out the main points he makes?*

> Almighty God,
> who on the day of Pentecost
> sent your Holy Spirit to the
>   disciples
> with the wind from heaven and
>   in tongues of flame,
> filling them with joy and
>   boldness to preach the
>   Gospel:
> send us out in the power of the
>   same Spirit
> to witness to your truth
> and to draw all men to the fire
>   of your love;
> through Jesus Christ our Lord.

2. Jerusalem, 1
Acts 2:43 – 4:31

It seems almost inevitable that when God is at work, sooner or later someone will cause trouble for the church. And in Jerusalem it was sooner rather than later!

1 *When you have read the whole passage, concentrate first on the healing, and then on Peter's sermon. Can you think of two adjectives which describe the reactions of the following people to these events:
a) the lame man
b) the Jerusalem crowds
c) the Jewish authorities?*

Peter's sermon in the temple (3:12-26) is an explanation both of what has just happened, and also of the gospel.
2 *In what ways does he describe Jesus?*
3 *Which events of Jesus' life does he pick out as specially significant?*
4 *The Jewish authorities clearly wanted to stop Peter and John. Why did they find that difficult? (You can probably think of more than one reason.)*

The church's response to difficulties is to pray, and to remember that Jesus faced similar difficulties, but that that did not stop God working things out according to plan. Write your own prayer, asking God for his help as you witness to him, and include in it any difficulties you face in telling others about Jesus.

3. Jerusalem, 2
Acts 4:32 – 6:7

1 *Read right through the passage, and as you do so, make a list of all the activities the church was engaged in. Are there any you want to add from yesterday's study (see especially Acts 2:42-47)?*

It would be easy to react to this picture of the church in Jerusalem by being critical of our own churches. This church is certainly a challenging example to us. But we need to remember that what applied to the first-century church need not necessarily apply to that of the twentieth century. Take time now to pray for your church and its leaders, and especially for your own involvement.

2 *The incident with Ananias and Sapphira is a reminder that even this church wasn't perfect! By putting both incidents together, Luke intends us to contrast their attitudes with those of Barnabas (4:36-37). What differences can you find?*
3 *In 5:17-42 we see the apostles facing more persecution because of their witness to Jesus. What lessons would you draw from this section for someone who was facing active opposition for their Christian faith?*
4 *In yesterday's study you thought about some of the difficulties you face in telling others about Jesus. Do any of these lessons apply to you?*

4. Judaea and Samaria
Acts 6:8 – 8:40

So far all the action has been set in Jerusalem, but the scene is about to change. Read through the passage to get the gist of the story, but skip over Stephen's speech (7:2-53).

1 *As you read, make a list of all the different factors God uses to cause the gospel to be preached in new places.*

Look up Romans 8:28 and write it out on a slip of paper. Put it somewhere where you'll learn it today.

2 *Which incidents from this passage could be used to illustrate this verse?*

The gospel's power clearly extends beyond Jerusalem! But why didn't the Samaritan converts receive the Holy Spirit when they were converted, as the Jews had (see 8:14-17)?

Endless ink has been spilt over this event... Most interpreters look... to the ancient division between the Jews and the Samaritans. Both claimed to worship Yahweh, but as separate nations, with separate temples and priesthoods. Crossing into Samaria was the first critical expansion of the Christian Church. Would it retain its unity in the Spirit, or would it divide along the old national lines?

Luke records that God withheld the Spirit in a surprising way because an unexpected but crucial lesson had to be learned. For the Samaritans it was the

unmistakable discovery that they were part of the one new Church of Christ. For the Jews, on the authority of the eyewitness accounts of Peter and John, Samaritans had come into an identical experience of the Spirit. Jews could no longer claim national superiority, for all were equal in the one new people of God.

Rob Warner, *Rediscovering the Spirit* (Hodder)

If Samaritan converts were hard to imagine, witnessing to an Ethiopian was unthinkable – he was a Gentile! But God made the way clear to Philip, both in his initial guidance and in all the details of the incident.

3 *How many signs of God at work can you find in this passage (8:26-40)?*
4 *Which of the people you are in regular contact with do you least expect to become Christians? Why?*

Pray that God will give you opportunities to tell others about him, and pray too that you'll recognize and make use of them, however unlikely they seem.

---

5. To the ends of the earth
Acts 9:1–11:18

In God's plan the Ethiopian was to be the first of many Gentile converts, but before the Gentile mission could take off, there was a small matter of personnel to be sorted out...

1 *Read through Acts 9:1–31. Make a*

list of all that changed for Saul when he became a Christian.

2 *What would be different in your life now if you weren't a Christian? Is there anything that should be different, but isn't?*

One barrier to Gentiles becoming Christians was that Jews didn't associate with Gentiles (see 10:28), especially not by eating with them (11:3) in case they ate foods considered unclean, like the animals in Peter's vision. But did you really have to become a Jew before you could become a Christian...?

3 *Read through chapter 10, and pick out all the points that emphasize God's guidance to Peter (enough for him to be sure he wasn't mistaken!). Are they the same as the points Peter picks out in 11:1-18?*

In this case the church had to change its customs so that Gentiles could join it. Are there any changes your church or Christian group needs to make to remove barriers to others joining? Is there anything God wants *you* to do about it?

Weekend

The Holy Spirit

In many ways 'The Acts of the Holy Spirit' would be a more appropriate title for this book than 'The Acts of the Apostles' – none of it would have happened without him!

1 *Look back through these chapters and see how many references you can find to the Spirit's activity. What different things does he do here?*
2 *Many Christians find themselves confused by talk of the Spirit. One step to finding out more might be to read a helpful book. You might try the section in* Know the Truth *(pp. 176-208) by Bruce Milne (IVP), or* I believe in the Holy Spirit *by Michael Green (Eerdmans, 1975) or* Filled with the Spirit *by Charles E. Hummel.*
3 *Don't just read what others think – make sure you read what the Bible has to say about the Spirit for yourself. The Holy Spirit inspired Scripture (2 Peter 1:21) – he'll help you understand it, if you ask. You could try the following passsages to start with: John 14:15-31; 16:5-15; Romans 8; 1 Corinthians 12-14; Galatians 5:16-26. Books on the Holy Spirit will give you other ideas – make sure you look at whole passages, not just odd verses. This could be a major project – why not take a whole week over it?*

Psalms of the king (A detailed study)

The monarchy was to play an important part in the life of the nation of Israel, especially during the time of David. His kingship was a pattern which later developed into a fuller understanding of the kingship of Jesus, David's greater Son – Jesus, the Messiah.

A number of the psalms reflect the centrality of the king for Israel, both in daily life and in worship. We shall look at some of these royal songs this week.

1. Long live the king!
Psalm 2

This psalm may have been used at the time of a coronation, or else may have recalled such an occasion as a means of encouragement when times were tough. We can clearly trace a progression through such a coronation ceremony, *e.g.* anointing the king (verse 2); enthroning him (verse 6); proving his right to rule (verse 7); empowering him (verse 9).

Read the psalm twice, trying to picture the occasion.

1 *How might the king have felt, confronted by all these enemies as his reign began? What assurances had he received from the Lord? What does this tell us about how our God encourages his people as they take on new responsibilities for him?*

If you know of anyone in such a position pray for them in the light of this psalm.

2 *The New Testament takes up this psalm several times. In Acts 4:25-26 it is specifically quoted. How has Luke, the writer of Acts, taken this psalm and expanded its meaning to apply to Jesus (Acts 4:27-28)? Look up Hebrews 1:5 for another reference. Spend time thinking over any new things which may have struck you about Jesus.*

2. The wedding of the king
Psalm 45

A royal wedding was both a national and a religious cause for celebration. This psalm would have been used regularly at such an event. It must initially be read as a powerful poem written for a splendid occasion.

The poem is divided into three sections:

■ verses 2-9 addressed to the bridegroom.
■ verses 10-15 addressed to, and then referring to, the bride
■ verses 16–17 addressed again to the bridegroom.

1 *Read the psalm and sum up what*

the writer says in each section.

2 *What is the groom's relationship to God? To be in such a relationship to God demanded that he should hate wickedness. How was this to be demonstrated? Pause to pray for all Christian leaders you know, that they may consciously 'shun evil'.*

Note: Israel's king never claimed to be divine. The king might be addressed as 'God' in verse 6 but it is clear in verse 7 that there is a God greater than the king.

3 *What responsibilities does the bride have to undertake? What does she receive in return? How does this contrast with views, commonly held today, on the marriage relationship?*
4 *The New Testament again takes up this psalm and extends its meaning. Look up Hebrews 1:8-9 to see the application made to Jesus.*

> But what is a royal wedding-song doing in the Bible? First, love and marriage are topics the Bible treats as God's concerns; indeed he invented them (Gn.1-2). The Song of Songs offers a whole series of lyric evocations of this theme ... God declared that marriage, like food, was something good, and something to be accepted with thanksgiving, as a gift (1 Tim. 4:3-5) ... But then a king's marriage will be especially important. Anything to do with the king was of significance for the whole people, because his life so affected theirs. Their happiness, their prosperity, their righteousness, were tied up with his. So, before God, they celebrate his wedding,

pray for God's blessing on him and challenge him to fulfil the royal responsibility that God has given him.

> John Goldingay, *The Message of Psalms 42-51: Songs from a Strange Land* (IVP)

3. The perfect king
Psalm 72

Most kings of Israel could be labelled 'bad kings'! Even the good ones failed in some area. Yet the Bible presents a high ideal of kingship in Israel which, of course, is ultimately only fulfilled in Jesus. This psalm, traditionally written either by or for Solomon, presents such an ideal.

1 *Read through the psalm, then make a note of all the evidence that the king had a God-given commission and could rule only with God's help. Notice particularly his responsibility to care for the oppressed.*
2 *Paul develops the theme that earthly authorities are appointed by God, even though they, like the kings of Israel, fail to live up to what is expected of them. Read Romans 13:1-7 to see what he says about this.*

Pause to pray that the government, local and national, might be sensitive to the needs of the poor, even though it may not acknowledge God.

3 *Only in Jesus, the Messiah, were these claims for the king totally fulfilled and even some of these statements have yet to be realized in the age to come. Read through the psalm again to see in which ways Jesus is the ideal king.*

Take verses 18 and 19, using them to lead you into worship of God.

4. God is king

Psalm 93

The Bible frequently speaks of God as king, with the human king acting as his representative. Although many pictures are used to describe God's kingship (an example is this psalm), we should be careful not to treat these descriptions too literally in case we inadvertently limit God's infinite greatness. For example, of course God does not have a literal throne or robes, though these pictures are necessary for describing his position.

1 As you read this psalm, allow your imagination to dwell on these powerful pictures of God's kingship. Notice the literary device in which a statement is made and is then echoed to emphasize the point.
2 What key facts about the Lord is the writer emphasizing? Write these down on the left hand side of a page. Beside each, note down what importance this fact has for you today, e.g.

God is more powerful than the fiercest of waves.

> Sometimes life seems out of my control – personally and nationally – but God is still in control.

Spend time thinking over what you have written down.
3 The God who is seen here as a distant, powerful king is in contrast to the king of Psalm 72 who comes to mingle among his people. Glance

back at the notes you made on yesterday's study. In your own understanding of God, do you have a balance of both views?

5. Jesus is king

Psalm 110

Jesus and the early church acknowledged that David was the author of this psalm (see Mark 12: 36). Only in this psalm does King David pay homage to his greater Lord, the Messiah. Here, more clearly than in any other psalm, is the coming of the Messiah predicted, particularly as a priest and king. The psalm may have been used when the king was crowned, for verses 1 and 4 contain the words of God Almighty to his Messiah, while verses 2–3 and 5–7 consist of truths generally applicable to a king.

1 To help us understand the words of the Lord in verses 1 and 4, we shall have to refer to the rest of the Bible. Look up the following verses, and note how they serve to explain this psalm: Genesis 14:17-20; Acts 2:34-36; Acts 5:31; 1 Corinthians 15:25-28; Hebrews 1:13; 7:15-28; 10:11-14.
2 David was able to proclaim the Messiah as a king who ruled, and as a priest who provided a sacrifice and acted as a mediator between God and man – facts which became reality in the first century AD, and are still being fulfilled. What does this tell you about how God, by his Spirit, spoke through the writers of the Old Testament?
3 God the Almighty identified in a unique way with the Priest-King, the Messiah, Christ the Lord. In a lesser way he was to identify with the earthly king. God would fight for him,

as this psalm declares. *How willing are you to join in what is, in effect, God's battle, making his name known in a world which scorns him? Are you part of his kingdom in more than name?*

Weekend

Many subjects have been touched upon which could be pursued this weekend. Here are a few suggestions:

1 *Look up how Israel came to have a king by reading Deuteronomy 17:14-20 and 1 Samuel chapters 8 – 10.*
2 *Study and meditate upon other psalms which exalt God as king (e.g. Psalms 95 – 99).*
3 *Study Isaiah chapter 11 to see how*

Isaiah pictured the Messiah as the ideal king who brought about justice. Christians are called upon to be involved in seeking to bring about justice in God's name. Are there ways in which you could be more actively involved in this?

Jesus shall reign where'er the
                 sun
Does his successive journeys
                 run;
His kingdom stretch from
           shore to shore,
Till moons shall wax and wane
           no more.

Hymn-writer Isaac Watts (1674–1748) was inspired by Psalm 72 to write this.

Part Two/Week Seven
Messiah (A word study)

We sing about it; we read it in our Bibles; but what does it actually mean that Jesus is the Christ, the Messiah? 'Christ' is not simply another name which we tack on to the end of Jesus. It is much more than that.

To the Jewish people in biblical times a name was very important. It said something about a person's character. The various names given to the Son of God have special meanings: 'Jesus' in Hebrew means 'Saviour'; 'Immanuel' means 'God with us'. And so also to the first-century Jews and Jewish Christians 'Messiah', or the Greek equivalent, 'Christ', was packed full of meaning and significance.

1. A king like David
Psalm 89:3-4, 20-29; Matthew 22:41-46

The word 'Messiah' is rarely used as an official title in the Old Testament, though many passages speak about the coming Messiah. The Hebrew *māšîaḥ* means 'anointed', as does the Greek New Testament word, *christos*. God anointed certain men in Old Testament days for specific tasks.

1 *Read Psalm 89:20. 1 Samuel 16:1, 13 will shed more light. Why is David described as 'anointed'? Read on in Psalm 89:3-4, 21-29. Note down any other promises made to David in these verses.*

2 *David was regarded as the greatest king in Israel's history. The Jews of Jesus' time expected that the coming Messiah would be from David's line. Read Matthew 22:41-46. Jesus tries to show the Pharisees that the Christ prophesied by David in Psalm 110:1 would be greater than David. How does he prove this?*

Note: 'Son' can mean a descendant as well as an immediate son.

You are the King of glory,
You are the Prince of peace,
You are the Lord of heav'n and
        earth,
You're the Son of
        righteousness;
Angels bow down before You;
Worship and adore
For You have the words of
        eternal life
You are Jesus Christ, the Lord.
Hosanna to the Son of David!
Hosanna to the King of Kings!
Glory in the highest heaven
For Jesus, the Messiah reigns!

Mavis Ford

In response you might like to sing the chorus above. If you do not know the tune then read it through, thanking God for these different characteristics of Jesus the Messiah.

2. A prophet like Moses
Acts 3:18-23; Hebrews 3:1-6

> The history of Israel is not merely the preparation for the coming of Christ. Jesus the Messiah is the fulfilment of all that Israel ever stood for in the purposes of God.
>
> H.L. Ellison,
> *Men Spake from God*
> (Paternoster)

1 *Read Acts 3:18-23. What is the background to these verses?*
2 *Verse 22 is a quotation from Deuteronomy 18:15, 18-19. The Jews were expecting the great prophet to come, as Moses had foretold. What are the features of a prophet? In what ways did Jesus fulfil the characteristics of a prophet? Turn to Hebrews 3:1-6 to see how else Jesus was greater than Moses.*

Note: Christ has still to fulfil some of the Old Testament expectations. Look up the entry on 'prophet' in a good Bible dictionary for more light on this important function.

3 *What are the consequences for rejecting the Messiah? Peter may have been speaking to a Jewish audience, and Moses' words were directed to the people of Israel. What was Peter saying, nevertheless, about anyone who refuses to listen to the words of the Messiah?*
4 *How seriously do you take these words as they affect anyone you know who is deaf to the gospel? Pray for them. (Look at 2 Corinthians 4:3-6 for further clarification.)*

3. Who do you say I am?
Luke 9:18-36

We have already seen in the first study, that one of the expectations of the Messiah was that he would be a king like David. But there were also false expectations of the Messiah. Around this time many thought that he would be a political figure, and were looking for someone to deliver them from the Roman occupation of the day.

1 *Read Luke 9:18-22. Jesus was becoming well known as a religious leader and there was obviously some controversy about his true identity. Why was Peter's response an important one? How had he reached a different conclusion from 'the crowds' (see also Matthew 16:17)?*

Note: Perhaps it was because of false expectations of the Christ that Jesus warns his disciples not to tell anyone who he is.

2 *What other facts about Jesus, the Messiah, does Luke write about in verses 23-36? How might this confirm or run contrary to the disciples' expectations of the Messiah?*
3 *What wrong views do people have of Jesus today? How would you explain the importance of Christ to a non-Christian friend? Pray for such a friend, and your relationship with him or her.*
4 *Jesus uses the name Christ of himself rarely before his resurrection (e.g. Mark 9:38-41). After this, the early church realized the importance of this truth, and*

Paul uses the name of Christ over 400 times in his letters! The disciples themselves even became known as Christians: those belonging to Christ (see Acts 11:26).

4. The suffering Messiah
Isaiah 52:13 – 53:12

Even though there were Old Testament prophecies about the suffering Messiah, yet the disciples could not see this as part of Christ's mission. The fact that they deserted him at his death may have been partly because they felt he had failed. The mistaken idea of a strong political Messiah and deliverer did not really mix with someone about to be strung up on a cross! Yet, as Jews, they would have been very familiar with Isaiah 53.

Notes: Notice how the key term 'servant' is used in this passage. The 'servant' is another name for 'Messiah' (see how Philip identified the two in Acts 8:26-38. Look also at Matthew 8:14-17). 53:2 'tender shoot' or 'young plant' – an image used of the Messiah, see e.g. Isaiah 11:1; Jeremiah 23:5; John 15:2.

1 *In Hebrew, the language of the Old Testament, a future event can be so certain to come about that it is described in the past tense, as if it had already happened. Much of Isaiah 53 is written like this, and yet it is one of the most moving passages in the Bible about Jesus, the future suffering Messiah.*
2 *How were these prophecies fulfilled in Jesus' life and death? If you have cross-references in your*

Bible, these will help you at this point. (Luke 22:37 specifically quotes from this chapter.)
3 *Read verse 5 again slowly and aloud. What does it mean that Jesus suffered and died for you? Take time to meditate on this and to thank him for loving you so much.*

Take Isaiah 53:5 with you on a slip of paper and try to memorize it through the day.

5. Different reactions to the Messiah
John 1:35-41; 4:29; 20:31

Also look up Mark 14:61-64 (*N.B.* Why was Jesus condemned?) and John 7:40-43 (in connection with 2 Samuel 7:12 and Micah 5:2). As you read these verses about Jesus as Messiah, try to answer the following questions:

1 *What is the general context?*
2 *What do people learn or expect of the Christ in this situation?*
3 *How is it significant here that Jesus is the Christ?*

What have *you* learned from them?

Many Jewish people today still do not believe in Jesus Christ as the Messiah. Pray that they will come to realize who he really is.

Weekend

1 *Look up some other Old Testament references to the coming Messiah and consider how Jesus*

fulfilled these:
- *Isaiah 9:1-7 (compare Matthew 4:15-17; Luke 1:32-33, 68-79)*
- *Isaiah 11:1-5*
- *Micah 5:2 (cf. John 7:42)*
- *Zechariah 9:9-10 (compare Matthew 21:5; John 12:15)*

- *Jeremiah 33:14-18*

2 *Further reading: have a look at the article on 'Messiah' in* The Illustrated Bible Dictionary *(Tyndale, 1980) or* The New Bible Dictionary, *2nd ed. (Tyndale, 1982).*

Part Two/Week Eight
Songs of the Servant (A detailed study)

Isaiah was probably the greatest of the Hebrew prophets. He lived in Jerusalem in the 8th century BC and his prophecies spanned the reigns of four kings of Judah, for a period of over forty years. He had a glorious vision of God in the temple (ch. 6) which dramatically convinced him of his own sin and God's forgiveness and indelibly marked the start of his mission.

Some of the most beautiful prophecies are found in chapters 40–66. They predict the fall of Babylon in the 6th century BC and also the perfect Servant of God who would fulfil his purpose and look forward to the time when there would be a new heaven and earth.

Out of sixteen prophets in the Old Testament, four are 'major' prophets (Isaiah, Jeremiah, Ezekiel and Daniel) and the rest are known as 'minor' prophets – referring to their size, not importance! Isaiah deservedly stands at the head of them all and is the most quoted book in the New Testament.

1. Preparing the way
Isaiah 40:1-31; 41:8-16

There are four passages in Isaiah commonly known as the 'Servant Songs' because they are about a man who would be the perfect servant of God: he would bring light and justice to the nations; he would be despised by people and eventually suffer and die a death which would pay for the sins of others. Sounds familiar, doesn't it?

Chapters 40 and 41 are an introduction to the second part of Isaiah's prophecies and also a backdrop to the Servant Songs. Isaiah is seeing a future time when the people of Judah are exiled captives in Babylon. It is a sad time: Jerusalem is in ruins and the people have no king or place to sacrifice. Perhaps they are in despair, asking: Where is their God who is supposed to be so mighty? Is this the end of the nation of Israel?

1 *Isaiah 40:1-31. As you read these verses, imagine yourself to be one of the Judeans in exile. Isaiah's prophecy here is a message of 'comfort'. Write down what comforts you would find in these verses to reassure you about God's character. Pause for reflection – just how much do you think God loves you?*

2 *Isaiah 40:3-5. These verses are quoted in the New Testament in Luke 3:1-6. What can you learn here about the role of John the Baptist in relation to Jesus?*

3 *Read Isaiah 41:8-16. Israel as a nation is called the servant of God. List some other vivid pictures God uses to describe a) himself, b) Israel.*

67

Note: Jacob's name was changed to Israel (Genesis 32:28).

4 *The promise of 41:10 was written to a particular situation. But it is still true of God's relationship with Christians today. Memorize this verse and remind yourself of it in the routine of this day.*

---

2. Song 1
Isaiah 42:1-9

In 41:8-9 the servant theme was applied to Israel as a whole. But in the 'Servant Songs' it revolves around one man in particular, chosen by God.

1 *Notice the specially close relationship that God will have with the Servant. Divide a page into two columns, and on the left-hand side make a list of the things which God commissioned the Servant to do.*
2 *Are there any ways in which you think Jesus actually fulfilled these things in the New Testament? If so, make a parallel list of these in the column on the right.*

Notes: Verses 1-4: Matthew applies these to Jesus, to show his humble refusal of publicity. Look up Matthew 12:15-21. Verse 1: see Luke 3:22; a combination of Isaiah 42:1 and Psalm 2:7 is used at Jesus' baptism. Verse 6: see Luke 2:32.

Think through the implications of this description of Jesus, then thank him for what he was prepared to do.

---

3. Song 2
Isaiah 49:1-13

In this song God is again the speaker, addressing the Servant. But in the first part the Servant himself is speaking.

1 *Read Isaiah 49:1-13. Continue your lists from yesterday. Add to them any more tasks which the Servant is to perform. What similarities are there in the life and work of Christ?*

Notes: Verse 6: see Acts 13:47. Verse 8: see 2 Corinthians 6:2. Verse 10: see Revelation 7:16.

2 *Verses 6-13 are a message of hope, that God will restore his people. Remember that they would be captives to the Babylonians. What part will the Servant play in this?*
3 *Verse 6 speaks of the missionary activity of the Servant. 'Nations' means the Gentiles or people outside Israel, who were therefore usually also outside the salvation given to Israel. Compare this with Acts 1:8. It is not until Pentecost that the message of salvation is taken throughout all the world.*

Pause for reflection. How much do you associate the coming of Jesus with the good news of God going as light to the whole world – in other words, how great is your concern for the growth of the church throughout the world?

Note: Verse 3: the Servant is called 'Israel' here. This does not refer to the nation as a whole. God was not being glorified in them, but in the Servant who deserved the name of Israel.

Pray that, like the Servant in this chapter, God will give you a servant heart and mind to tackle your responsibilities today.

4. Song 3
Isaiah 50:4-11

1 *Add any other similarities between the Servant and Christ to your lists.*

Note: Verse 6: see Luke 22:63.

2 *Isaiah 50:4-6. So far the Servant has been seen as the teacher; what do these verses show of him as the perfect Learner?*

> He listens to God before he speaks with others, and then when he speaks it is as a disciple, repeating and applying the Master's words.
>
> Henri Blocher, *Songs of the Servant* (IVP)

3 *Verses 10-11 paint a very vivid picture of those who trust in God and those who do not. What should be the Servant's proper relationship to God?*

It has often been said that God has given us two ears and one mouth, to be used in that proportion! It is much easier to talk, even with God, than to listen. Pray that God will help you to listen attentively to him today, and to others.

5. Song 4
Isaiah 52:13 – 53:12

You will most probably have noticed by now the striking similarities in the Servant with the character, mission and suffering of Jesus Christ. This is no fanciful conjecture, trying to read back into the Old Testament what wasn't really there.

> Isaiah's description fits the real Jesus so precisely that one could not but interpret the one in terms of the other.
>
> Henri Blocher, *Songs of the Servant* (IVP)

1 *One of the first names applied to Jesus was Servant – see Acts 3:26; 4:27, 30. Compare Peter's sermon in Acts 3:13-15, and his letter 1 Peter 2:20-25, with this fourth song. Write down the comparisons.*

Note: Because the concept of 'Servant' was so firmly rooted in the Old Testament it was probably dropped later as the gospel went out to the Gentiles.

2 *The New Testament has many allusions to the Servant Songs – the writers keep pointing back to the Old Testament to show how Jesus fulfilled all that was expected. Examine this by looking up Matthew 8:17; 12:15-21; Romans 10:16; 15:20-21.*

Note: Jesus would have found the blueprint of his mission in Isaiah. So he quotes it in Luke 22:37.

3 *In football a substitute is sent on to play instead of a man who is unable to play himself. Although he had done no wrong himself, the Servant here is a substitute for sin on behalf of those who would otherwise suffer eternally for the wrong they have done. What more does chapter 53 tell you about what Christ has* done for your sins as your substitute and sacrifice?

4 Turn this most moving passage into a prayer. Make it personal by putting 'I' instead of 'we' or your own name wherever appropriate.

Weekend

1 Isaiah prophesied about the Saviour who was to come. As you read the following passages, how were they fulfilled in Jesus? Isaiah 7:14; 9:1-7; 11:1-5,10; 40:3-5, 9-11.

2 Look up Isaiah in a Bible Dictionary to find out more about this prophet, probably the greatest and most important in the Old Testament. Or you could look up 'Messiah' in a Bible Dictionary to see what is said about the servant Messiah.

Part Three

Job
Moses
The resurrection of Jesus
Death
Haggai, Zechariah and Malachi
Romans 8
The sacraments
The church in Corinth

Part Three/Week One
Job (A bird's-eye study)

Tragedy strikes – the death of a close friend, terminal illness in the family, the loss of a job – and our immediate reaction is 'Why, God?'

This is the problem that confronts Job. However, it goes further than that. Through his doubts and questions, he is searching for something more. He thought God prospered and blessed those who were good. Then came calamity and everything Job believed about God was contradicted. Yet he did not let go of his faith in God – 'Though he slay me, yet will I trust him.'

If, in studying this book, you are simply wanting to know why God allows suffering, you will be disappointed. However, if you go along with Job, through his turmoil and confusion, you may find, like him, that beyond even the worst circumstances of life God is present. He is the great Creator God and he can be known to sinful man.

You may find it helpful, in understanding who is speaking at any one time, to use a Bible that has headings, such as the Good News or New International Version. We shall be reading large sections of the book at a time. You may not have time to read all of what is recommended but do go back at a later date (possibly this weekend) to the parts you have missed out.

1. The Lord gave and the Lord has taken away
Job 1:1 – 14:2

It is of supreme importance in understanding this book to recognize that God, not Satan, was the initiator of the whole drama. When Job was questioning if God cared about him, he did not appreciate that God never lost control of his circumstances.

1 *Read the first three chapters and try to get a picture of the type of man Job was. Make a list of all his qualities we are told about. How would you describe the different roles of God and Satan in the account?*
2 *The next section, chapters 4–14, is a dialogue between three of Job's friends – Eliphaz, Bildad and Zophar – and Job. If you have time, read all these chapters. What are their arguments and how does Job respond? If you cannot manage that, read just Zophar's argument in chapter 11 and Job's answer in chapters 12–14.*

Perhaps you are facing a difficult situation, or have questions in your mind about God's dealings with his people. Come to God in the same honest way that Job did and tell him

73

exactly how you feel. It may help you to write down your thoughts.

2. Look at ancient wisdom
Job 15:1 – 21:34

Chapters 15–21 make up the second dialogue between the three 'comforters' and Job. As you read their words, try to imagine what you would feel if you were in Job's shoes.

1 *What do his friends think is the cause of Job's suffering? See especially 15:1-16; 18:17-21; 20:4-11, 29.*
2 *Read chapter 19. Where does Job see the problem as lying? Even in the midst of his distress, where is there still hope (see 19:25-27)?*

Pray today for anyone you know who is going through a difficult time. Ask God to give you the right response to their needs, even though, like Job, you may not know the cause of their distress.

3. You also must praise him
Job 22:1 – 37:24

In chapters 22–31, Eliphaz, 'the pious mystic', Bildad, 'the traditionalist' and Zophar, 'the dogmatist', hold their final dialogue with Job, with chapter 28 as an interlude on the subject of wisdom.

1 *Read chapters 32–37 where Elihu joins the debate. What contribution does he make to it?*

2 *'[God] has always been praised for what he does; you also must praise him' (36:24, GNB). Take some of the positive statements Elihu makes about God and use them to praise God for who he is.*

4. Spiritual warfare

Job may have thought that he was just a victim of circumstances. But, as the first two chapters describe, he was really engaged in a spiritual battle.

1 *Satan has many ploys to try to defeat God's people. Look over Job's words and see if you can discern evidence of Satan's strategies in areas of:*
a) temptation
b) deception
c) self-accusation
d) destruction and despair.
Especially look at 3:11-19; 6:8-15; 16:6-14; 23:8-17; 30:20-31. When have you been aware recently of such strategies being directed at you? How did you react? How did you call on God to come to the rescue? With what result?
2 *We, like Job, are engaged in a mighty battle and Satan has declared war against God's people. He will not win because Christ has gained the victory on the cross, but don't be surprised if he continues to assault you. Turn to 1 Peter 5:6-11. What advice is given here for a Christian in standing firm in the spiritual battle?*

Pray today and every day for the Lord's protection. Like Job, you can never assume immunity.

5. Out of the storm the Lord spoke

Job 38:1 – 42:17

1 How does God counteract Job's confusion? Do you think he answers Job's questions? Look at Job's responses in chapters 40:3-5 and 42:2-6.

2 In what ways is the final chapter not merely a happy ending? What principles are here to follow? See if you can apply these to your own situation, then use what you have learnt this week in your prayers.

Weekend

1 Why not read a book on 'spiritual warfare'? Here are some suggestions: The Hidden Battle: *David Watson (Shaw)*
The Fight: *John White (IVP)* – especially chapter 5

2 Look up and memorize strategic verses so you will have ammunition to use against the devil. Here are some suggestions from which to choose (from the Appendix of The Hidden Battle):

> 1 John 4:4
> 1 John 3:8
> 1 John 5:4
> James 4:7
> Romans 6:11
> Luke 10:19
> Ephesians 6:11
> Colossians 2:15
> 2 Corinthians 10:4
> Revelation 12:11
> Hebrews 2:14-15
> 1 Peter 5:8-9
> Romans 8:31
> Romans 8:37
> 1 Corinthians 15:57

3 You might wish to read a good book on evil and suffering, such as The Problem of Pain *or* The Screwtape Letters, *both by C. S. Lewis (Macmillan);* The Enigma of Evil *by John Wenham (Zondervan),* or Is God Really Fair? *by Dick Dowsett (Moody).*

4 You could read the chapters of Job there wasn't time for during the week!

Moses (A character study)

Help wanted

Wanted – leader for Israelite nation wishing to travel across desert to promised land. Must be good negotiator, deal with difficult clients, plan escape route ...

Had Moses seen this ad when he was 40 he might have jumped at the chance. Later, when God chose him, he tried every argument to get out of the job. Moses' life is covered by the books of Exodus to Deuteronomy. We can only dip into it, briefly looking at some of the highs and lows, showing that even great men and women of God are only human when they forget the Lord.

1. Born and prepared
Exodus 1:22 – 2:25

Jacob's descendants had been in Egypt for some 370 years and were now slaves. Pharaoh considered them a threat. Since their numbers grew daily, he instructed the midwives to kill the male babies. Indirectly they refused. So, orders were given to the Egyptians to toss the babies into the Nile (1:22).

1 As the adopted son of the Royal House, what kind of upbringing would Moses have had? Consult a Bible dictionary now or at the

weekend. Use your findings to consider how his future leadership may have benefited.
2 In considering his actions in verses 12 and 17, what can you learn of his mother's influence?
3 Does Moses strike you as having leadership qualities? Note down factors for and against his selection for the post.

Look to the past and see how God has used people and situations to shape your character. Pray with thanks for how God has worked.

2. Called and equipped
Exodus 3 and 4

Moses comes to Mount Sinai as a shepherd! What an opportunity for a prince to learn meekness or to become embittered. For all he knew that was a life-time occupation. God, however, was using it as a period of teaching.

1 What did Moses learn about God at the burning bush?
2 List Moses' attempts to wriggle out of God's plan for him, and the Lord's answers. Ever struggled with God in this way? Is it any use?
3 How was Moses enabled to convince the people that he was appointed to be their leader? What

was Aaron's role in all this? What is the importance of providing fellow helpers for those in a position of leadership?

Thank the Lord that the power available to Moses can be yours today. God does not change.

3. Negotiator
Exodus 5; 11; 12:21-28, 50; 13:11-22; 14

Moses' negotiations are interspersed with encouragement and instructions from the Lord. To the last, Pharaoh tries to stop the exodus. Eventually, however, the Red Sea is crossed and the promised land beckons.

1 *What picture do you get in chapter 5 of the relationship between Moses, Pharaoh and the people?*
2 *By chapters 11–13 things have changed. Skim read the verses above. How would you judge Moses' chances now of leading the people?*
3 *From chapter 14 list the features which show the quality of Moses' leadership. What has brought this about?*

Pray that you may use your God-given abilities in his service. If you are not certain what they are, ask the Lord himself, your Christian friends or the leader of your church.

4. Leader
Exodus 31:18 – 32:35; Numbers 11 and 12

Through Exodus to the book of

Numbers we follow the wanderings of Israel – unnecessarily long due to disobedience. Most of the time the Israelites grumble and a harassed Moses turns again and again to his Lord.

1 *What problems does Moses face from the people and his own family? How does he cope? List the events and the Lord's provision.*
2 *What can you learn here of God's concern for you as an individual in the variety of different situations you face every day?*
3 *How has Moses matured since the day when he slew the Egyptian? Write down his qualities.*

Teach me not to be a grumbler, Lord!

5. The man
Numbers 20:1-13; Deuteronomy 31:28 – 34:12

Moses, like you and me, was prone to disobey God by thinking that he could manage on his own. How the mighty fall! Though the punishment was devastating, he motivated his people to the end. He left a legacy of faith both to them and to us (Hebrews 11:23-29).

1 *What did Moses gain in self-knowledge and God-knowledge in taking authority upon himself? What can be learnt here?*
2 *Moses the poet and historian – scan the Deuteronomy passage, noting down the evidences justifying the comment 'Moses ... whom the Lord knew face to face' (Deuteronomy 34:10).*

Pray that through the study of the

Bible, prayer and meditation you also may come to know your Lord 'face to face'.

Weekend

1 *Read the whole story of Moses, especially picking out the development and qualities of his relationship with the Lord. See how* this may influence your daily life with Christ, by application of the same principles.

2 Using a concordance discover the influence and use of Moses' name throughout the Bible. Consult Tyndale's New or Illustrated Bible Dictionary and the Lion Handbook to the Bible for background information.

The resurrection of Jesus (A historical study)

The resurrection of Jesus is the key to the truth of our faith. If it did not happen, and the corpse remains buried somewhere in Jerusalem, then we are wasting our time. This week we will be looking at the historical evidence from the Bible. This evidence comes, of course, from convinced believers: but this need not rule it out of court immediately. Although their Christian outlook has shaped the way they record and interpret events, *something* must have happened for them to have had this outlook in the first place!

Every day this week we will look at a part of the resurrection story as told in each of the four gospels. As we do so, we will notice differences between them, differences which some people take to indicate the unreliability of the witnesses. But before agreeing with this, we should pause to note that such differences need not be contradictory but simply the different emphases and details given by the different authors. This actually gives us *more* confidence in the accuracy of the biblical record because it shows that the gospel writers did not feel the need to toe a particular party line.

Make five parallel columns in your notebook and head them 'Matthew', 'Mark', 'Luke', 'John' and 'Others'. During the week note down the evidence which each contributes.

1. Dead and buried
Matthew 27:45-61;
Mark 15:33-47; Luke 23:44-56;
John 19:28-42

For Jesus to have been raised from the dead, he must first have died. Some have suggested that he merely *appeared* to die but that in reality he only fainted or even that someone else was crucified in his place.

1 *Read through Matthew 27:45-61. What evidence can you find to show that it was Jesus himself who was on the cross and that he really died? Put the points down in your notebook, in the 'Matthew' column.*
2 *Now look at Mark 15:33-47 and Luke 23:44-56. How do they fill out and confirm what you have gained from Matthew's account?*
3 *Read John 19:28-42. What important information does John add about*
a)being an eyewitness
b)prophecy in the Jewish scriptures
c)the fact that Jesus was dead?

Note: 19:34 'a sudden flow of blood and water' is strong evidence for major clotting and separation of the blood which could only occur after death.

Now summarize how you would answer someone who said Jesus

merely swooned. Spend some time quietly worshipping Jesus, 'the Lamb of God, who takes away the sin of the world' (John 1:29).

---

2. The empty tomb
Matthew 27:62-66; 28:1-8, 11-15; Mark 16:1-8; Luke 24:1-12; John 20:1-9

1 *Read Matthew 27:62-66 and 28:11-15. What precautions did the Jewish leaders take? And what is absurd about the explanation in 28:13?*
2 *The discovery of the empty tomb by some of Jesus' women friends is told by each of the gospel writers. Read through Matthew 28:1-8, Mark 16:1-8, Luke 24:1-8 and John 20:1 and note down in the appropriate columns the information given by each.*
3 *Luke and John add the visit of Peter and John to the tomb. Read Luke 24:9-12 and John 20:2-9. What was it that caused them to believe?*

Note: Although we today do not have the *direct* evidence of the empty tomb, we are able to understand the Scriptures which demonstrate that 'Jesus had to rise from the dead' (John 20:9), an advantage which the first disciples did not have at the time.

Praise God for the historical evidence from the Bible which helps you to be sure that the tomb of Jesus is empty.
   What evidence in your own experience convinces you that Jesus is alive and reigning in your life (e.g. your relationship with him, your attitude to death)?

---

3. The risen Jesus, 1
Matthew 28:8-10; Luke 24:13-35; John 20:10-18; 1 Corinthians 15:3-8

It was not just that the tomb was empty; the disciples knew that Jesus was alive because they met him for themselves. Some say it was a case of hallucination or mass hypnosis.

1 *Read Paul's summary in 1 Corinthians 15:3-8. How many groups of people did Jesus appear to?*
2 *The evidence of women was normally inadmissible in Jewish legal tradition (which may be why Paul doesn't mention them in 1 Corinthians 15). How like Jesus to appear first to them!*
   Read John 20:10-18 and then Matthew 28:8-10 (these may have been separate incidents). How did these women react to the risen Jesus?
3 *Later that day, Jesus appeared to two other disciples. Read Luke 24:13-35. How did their reaction to Jesus change in the course of the conversation? What caused this change?*
4 *How would you now respond to the argument that the disciples were suffering hallucinations?*

'Were not our hearts burning within us...?' (Luke 24:32). Thank God for the Scriptures and pray that he will continue to open them and reveal the risen Jesus to you as you study.

---

4. The risen Jesus, 2
Matthew 28:16-20; Luke 24:36-49; John 20:19-31

One of the extraordinary things which points to the truth of the gospels is the candid way in which they describe the way some of the disciples refused to believe at first.

1 *Read Matthew 28:16-20. How did the disciples react? What did Jesus see as the main implication of his resurrection?*
2 *The same note comes in Luke 24:36-49. How did the disciples know that Jesus was not a ghost? Having dealt with that, what did Jesus go on to emphasize? Why?*

Note: If you are interested and have the time, have a look at 1 Corinthians 15:35-57 to see what Paul has to say about the difference between an ordinary 'natural' body and a 'spiritual' body such as Jesus had after his resurrection.

3 *John tells the story of doubting Thomas in some detail. Read John 20:19-31. What do you think prevented Thomas from believing?*
4 *From these passages, can you discover two ways in which it is possible to believe without seeing (John 20:29)? (Clue: see John 20:25 and Luke 24:44-45.)*

Pray for those known to you who, like Thomas, *refuse* to believe, that they might become more aware of the life and love of the risen Lord.

---

5. The after-effects!
Acts 2:22-33; 3:12-16; 17:16-34

The final strand of evidence we shall look at this week is that which points to the significance of the resurrection in the life of the early church.

1 *Read Acts 2:22-33 and 3:12-16, extracts from two of Peter's early sermons. Note down what Peter says about the resurrection of Jesus. How does he use it?*
2 *Read Acts 17:16-34. For Paul too, the resurrection was central, so much so that his mention of 'Jesus and the resurrection' was interpreted by his hearers as 'foreign gods' (verse 18)! Note down what Paul says about the resurrection. How does he use it?*

Is the resurrection of Jesus a key part of the good news of Christianity you present to your friends? Thank God for the evidence we have discovered this week and pray for opportunities to help others who are unsure of this central pillar of our faith.

Weekend

1 *Spend a bit of time going back over your notes in the five columns and summarize what you have discovered about the evidence for the resurrection.*
2 *During this week we have looked at some of the biblical evidence for the resurrection of Jesus. But how would you respond to the person who said , 'OK, it happened, but so what?'? Have a look at the following passages and verses and make a list of all the implications of Jesus' resurrection. Romans 1:4; 6:8-9; 1 Corinthians 15:17; Ephesians 1:18-21; Romans 8:11; Matthew 28:18-20; 2 Corinthians 4:13-14; 1 Thessalonians 4:14.*
3 *A very helpful discussion of the evidence for the resurrection is John Wenham's* Easter Enigma *(Paternoster), in which he reconstructs the events of the first*

Easter weekend. The Day Death Died by Michael Green (IVP) is another good book which presents the evidence and draws out the implications for us today. The whole question of the historical basis of Christian belief is discussed by Sir Norman Anderson in Jesus Christ: the Witness of History (IVP). See also Sir Norman's booklet The Evidence for the Resurrection (IVP). Another booklet to give or lend to interested friends is Exploring Easter (UCCF Booklets) which sets out and comments on some of the relevant Bible passages.

Death (A topic study)

Death is a rather taboo subject in our society. Indeed, most people in Britain have never even seen a dead body – except perhaps on TV! The Bible's stark treatment of subjects like this can make us feel a bit uncomfortable. But for its writers, death was very much a fact of life, something with which they were all too familiar.

But it's not all grim news! On the positive side, it's all about God's decisive intervention to bring about the abolition of sin and evil, together with their consequences of suffering and death, through his son Jesus Christ. In order to understand the wonder of God's rescue operation more fully, we need to consider what we have been saved from. As we look this week at the dark background against which the wonderful picture of salvation is painted, pray that God will help you to see more clearly and grow in your appreciation of his gift of eternal life.

Make a point throughout this week of praying for anyone known to you who at the moment is confronted by 'death' in whatever shape or form.

1. In the valley
Psalm 88:1-18;
Ecclesiastes 9:2-10

1 *Read Psalm 88:1-18. Make a list of the particular things about death that the author of this psalm mentions, looking especially at verses 4-5 and 10-12. Are these the things that you would naturally think of? What does your list show you about the psalmist?*
2 *This has been described as the saddest of all the psalms, written by someone undergoing particularly severe suffering. But it does contain flashes of faith and hope. What are they?*
3 *The 'Preacher' in Ecclesiastes reflects a common view of death in Old Testament times. Read Ecclesiastes 9:2-10 and add to your list of death's characteristics. Since death is, as far as we can see, the end, what does the Preacher advise?*

'Be very careful, then, how you live – not as unwise but as wise, making the most of every opportunity, because the days are evil' (Ephesians 5:15-16; *cf.* Ecclesiastes 9:10). As you pray over the events – known and unknown – of the coming day, ask God to help you to use it to serve him to the full.

2. Death comes to life
Genesis 2:15-17; 3:1-24;
John 17:3

How was it that death intruded into a world which had been made by God and which was 'very good' (see

Genesis 1:31)? Or has it always been a part of God's creation?

1 *Read Genesis 2:15-17. Write down how God sets clear boundaries for what Adam may and may not do. What would happen when men and women disobeyed God?*

2 *Adam and Eve were tempted to doubt God and went on to disobey him. Read Genesis 3:1-24 and note down all the things that went wrong as a result.*

3 *By 'death' we usually mean the absence of physical life. Yet the physical existence of Adam and Eve continued for quite some time (see Genesis 5:5!). Look back at your list of the consequences of their sin. How would you explain the deeper meaning of death in the Bible?*

4 *Jesus summed up what eternal life was all about on the night before his death. Look at John 17:3. How does this help you to understand the essence of what death is all about?*

Is there anything which is spoiling your relationship with God and preventing you from walking closely with him? Confess it to him now and ask for his forgiveness and the strength to live as he wants you to.

Memory verse: 'For the wages of sin is death, but the gift of God is eternal life in Christ Jesus our Lord' (Romans 6:23).

---

3. Back from the dead!

John 11:1-53

Jesus had become well known for his healing miracles and his ability to prevent physical death from occurring. Not until this point in his gospel does John show how the power of Jesus reaches even beyond death to bring Lazarus back to life.

1 *Read John 11:1-16. Why did Jesus delay before going to Bethany to heal Lazarus?*

2 *Read on to verse 37. How did Jesus respond to the death of Lazarus and the suffering it brought to his friends? What other reactions were there? What differing views of death lay behind these reactions?*

3 *Read on to verse 45. What was the effect on the bystanders of the raising of Lazarus? What could they have come to understand about 'death'?*

Note: Lazarus' raised body was a physical body, unlike Jesus' resurrected 'spiritual' body.

4 *Others reacted differently. Read on to verse 53. Why did the Jewish leaders refuse to change their attitude to Jesus – in spite of the evidence of Lazarus' resurrection? What does this tell you about the effectiveness of evidence in convincing someone of the truth of Christianity?*

'If they do not listen to Moses and the Prophets, they will not be convinced even if someone rises from the dead.'

(Luke 16:31)

We are given enough light for those who only desire to see and enough obscurity for those who have a contrary disposition.

Blaise Pascal (1623–1662)

Pray for those known to you who refuse to consider the evidence of the resurrection or who have no hope of life with Jesus after death.

4. The last enemy defeated!

2 Timothy 1:8-12; Hebrews 2:9, 14-15; 1 Corinthians 15:13-26; John 14:1-3

1 In 2 Timothy 1:8-12, Paul says that part of God's purpose in history is to save us from death (in the sense of being eternally separated from God) through the gospel. Read through the passage. Why is it important to grasp the extent of Jesus' victory?
2 Write down in your own words how Jesus has 'destroyed death' (2 Timothy 1:10). Now check with Hebrews 2:9. What does this verse say that Jesus has done for us? Now look on to Hebrews 2:14-15. What good news does the Bible have for those who are afraid of death?
3 Look at 1 Corinthians 15:13-26. How can we be sure that Jesus really has drawn the sting of death?
4 Turn to John 14:1-3. Spend some time meditating on these verses and thanking God that death is a defeated enemy. Praise him that Jesus has pulled out death's teeth so that it can no longer bite! Pray for those known to you who are trapped by the fear of dying.

Memory verse: The reason the Son of God appeared was to destroy the devil's work (1 John 3:8).

5. Dying we live

Romans 8:1-17; Colossians 2:13-15; 2:20 – 3:14

We look today at some passages which use the picture of 'putting to death' to describe the way in which Christians should abandon their old sinful ways and imitate Christ's way of life instead.

1 Start by thinking of the characteristics of 'death', e.g. cold, decay, no response. Then, what comes to mind when you think of 'life'?
2 Turn to Romans 8:1-17. Make a list of the contrasts Paul makes between living under the control of the sinful nature and living under the control of the Spirit.
3 What 'misdeeds of the body' (verse 13) can you think of which you need to put to death? How does Paul suggest you go about it (also in verse 13)?
4 Look at Colossians 2:13-15, a further reminder of what God has done about the problem of sin and death. Now read on from verse 20 to 3:14. Paul is saying that, as Christians, we are identified with Christ. When he died, we died. When he rose again, we rose with him. How does Paul say that this pattern of dying and living is to be reflected in our lives now?

'Count yourselves dead to sin but alive to God in Christ Jesus' (Romans 6:11). Pray for an increasing ability to resist temptation and live the new life God wants you to enjoy.

Memory verse: I have been crucified with Christ and I no longer live, but Christ lives in me. The life I live in the body, I live by faith in the Son of God, who loved me and gave himself for me (Galatians 2:20).

Weekend

1 *Pick out all the references to 'death' in Romans 5 and 6. How do they fit in with what you have discovered this week?*

2 *Many modern biographies describe Christ's transforming effect on death. Begin to read one this weekend – like* Sandy: a heart for God *by Leighton Ford (IVP, 1985),* A Severe Mercy *by Sheldon Vanauken (Harper & Row, 1980) or* Fear No Evil *by David Watson (Shaw, 1985).*

Haggai, Zechariah and Malachi
(A historical study)

After the seventy years of exile prophesied by Jeremiah (Jeremiah 29:10), some of the people of Israel returned from Babylon in 537 BC and began to rebuild Jerusalem, starting with the temple. The book of Ezra tells the story. But the job wasn't finished – until Haggai and Zechariah started prophesying in 520 BC, which got things moving. The temple was eventually finished in 516 BC. The books record their prophecies, which encourage the Jews to persevere by promising that God's intervention will once again bring prosperity to the defeated and demoralized nation.

This will inevitably be a brief look at some of the major themes of these books. If you'd like to study them in more detail, Joyce Baldwin's *Tyndale Old Testament Commentary on Haggai, Zechariah, Malachi* (IVP, 1972) would be a good guide.

1. Get on, and build
Haggai

Haggai addressed his message to Joshua, the high priest and Zerubbabel, governor and heir to the now defunct throne of Israel. They were the key leaders – the religious and civil authorities – though their power was severely limited, as Israel did not exist as an independent political unit.

Haggai continues to call God's people to zealous service. Half-hearted allegiance is no allegiance. To think that any time will do to become serious about His cause is to fail Him completely. He is waiting to bless, but He cannot do so while His people are apathetic and self-centred. Moreover, in this mood they experience only shortfall, whereas He wants to shower them with good things.

Joyce Baldwin, *TOTC Haggai, Zechariah, Malachi* (IVP).

Read Haggai's first sermon in chapter 1. It was delivered in August, 520 BC, the time of harvest.

1 *There were obviously good excuses for not building (1:2) – the time was wrong, life was tough (see verses 6, 9, 10). How does Haggai answer these excuses?*
2 *Then read the second sermon in Haggai 2:1-9. This one was proclaimed in October, 520 BC, a month after the work was restarted. Progress must have seemed slow, and there was no chance of building anything as fine as Solomon's temple. What do you think is the most important thing the Lord promises here?*
3 *The next sermons (2:10-23) come two months later. The point of the*

debate about ritual is that Israel herself is defiled, and no offering can change that (2:14). God's promise of blessing is in effect an acceptance (and so forgiveness) of the nation, despite their defiled state. In what ways does God promise to bless the nation here?

4 This God is our God. What characteristics of God have struck you today? Let them form the basis of your prayers today.

2. Visions to encourage God's people
Zechariah 1:1-17; 3; 4; 6:9-15

Zechariah started prophesying in the same year as Haggai, but in a different style. We shall read extracts from his visions, which show in pictorial form what God is doing for Israel.

1 Read 1:1-17, an introduction to the book, and the first vision. Visions aren't always easy to understand! What message do you think the Lord intended to give his people through this vision (verses 7-13) and the oracle that accompanies it (verses 14-17)?

2 Read chapters 3; 4; 6:9-15, which relate to Joshua and Zerubbabel. From these chapters, make a list of what God promises to do for these men.

Memory verse: 'Not by might nor by power, but by my Spirit', says the Lord Almighty (Zechariah 4:6).

3 What do you think this verse

would have meant to the Jews of Zechariah's day?

Use this verse to pray for the things you will do during the coming day.

3. Should we fast?
Zechariah 7 and 8

The fast was held throughout the seventy years in exile to remember the destruction of the temple. These chapters start with the question of whether it should continue now that the Jews are back in their own land, and work on a new temple is well under way.

1 The original question is about a religious custom, the fast. What does Zechariah say are the real issues? What does God most want the people to do?

2 Think of the 'religious customs' you observe (e.g. Bible study, church on Sunday). How do they fit in with the issues Zechariah raises?

3 What lessons does Zechariah draw from the past history of Israel (e.g. 7:11-14)?

4 From chapter 8, make a list of all that the Lord promises to do for his people in the future.

5 What effects are the Lord's promises supposed to have on the people? What did they have to do?

6 How often have you wanted God's blessing without being prepared to play your part in obeying him?

4. Future prosperity
Zechariah 9 – 11

The oracles of chapters 11-14 are in

a different style from the rest of the book, and probably belong to a later period. They look into Israel's future – a glorious future, guaranteed by the Lord – and what must happen to bring that future state about.

1 *9:1–11:13 describes the defeat of Israel's enemies and the future prosperity of the nation. What features of this future state does Zechariah draw attention to here?*

One of the reasons for Israel's current problems was her leadership (see 10:2-3). In 11:4-17 the prophet is told to act the part of a good shepherd (11:7-14) and then a foolish one (11:15-17). Some of the details of this passage are obscure, but it should be possible to pick out the main features.

2 *Why does the good shepherd give up his responsibility for the flock?*
3 *What were the results for the flock?*

Let these truths inspire you to pray for the national leadership of the church.

4 *There are several references to these chapters in the gospels. 9:9 is quoted in the account of Jesus' entry into Jerusalem on Palm Sunday (Matthew 21:5). 11:12-13 is referred to in the account of Judas betraying Jesus (Matthew 26:14-15, 47-50). And Jesus refers to himself as the Good Shepherd (John 10:11-18). If you have time, look at this passage, and see how many parallels you can find between Zechariah's description of the good shepherd, and Jesus' description of himself.*

5. The day
Zechariah 12 – 14

There are many references to 'that day' in these chapters. They pick up some of the same themes as chapters 9–11, but seem to point to the Lord's final intervention in world affairs – to defeat Jerusalem's enemies, but also to put things right within God's chosen people. They end with a glorious vision of the whole world worshipping the Lord as King.

1 *Read through these chapters, and list:*
a) References to the defeat of Israel's enemies;
b) The judgment and suffering which will fall on Jerusalem herself.

Note: It's not at all clear who Zechariah thought was the 'one they have pierced' (12:10), but in John's gospel it is quoted as referring to Jesus himself (John 19:27).

2 *In 12:10 – 13:1, what are the results of this man's death?*
3 *What parallels can you think of between his death and Jesus' death?*
4 *The end of the book (14:16-21) describes a future Utopia when the Lord will be acknowledged as King over all, and even everyday life will be sacred to him (14:20). How far does your life match up to this picture now?*

Weekend

This is a chance to read through the book of Malachi! It comes from a later date than Haggai and Zechariah – the temple is finished, and it is obvious that religious duties are being observed, but as yet there is no sign of the Lord's dramatic intervention.

Malachi's prophecy is particularly relevant to the many waiting periods in human history and in the lives of individuals. He enables us to see the strains and temptations of such times, the imperceptible abrasion of faith that ends in cynicism because it has lost touch with the living God. Even more important he shows the way back to a genuine, enduring faith in the God who does not change (Mal.3:6), *who invites men to return to Him* (3:7), *and never forgets those who respond* (3:16).

Joyce Baldwin, *TOTC Haggai, Zechariah, Malachi* (IVP)

1 *What picture does Malachi give of religious life in his day?*
2 *List the specific charges the Lord brings against his people.*
3 *What promises are there for those who repent and serve the Lord whole-heartedly?*

Memorize Malachi 4:2.

Part Three/Week Six
Romans 8 (A meditation)

A dictionary definition of meditation is 'to consider thoughtfully, deeply, reflect upon; to resolve in the mind'.

You will already have found that these studies are not intended to do all the work for you! 'Meditation' may sound an easier option than a 'word study', but it isn't. It involves our minds in deep thought and reflection. So stay awake!

1. A letter to read
Romans 8

Contrary to what the little girl may have said, an epistle is not the wife of an apostle! It is a letter. We can often get bogged down in one or two verses, isolating them from the rest of the writing and forgetting that a letter is not usually read that way. To make the best sense of it we need to read it through in its entirety. Like a jigsaw, the details fall into place more easily if we have a glimpse of the whole picture first.

But if time does not permit, at least read all of chapter 8 today, before we look at verses in more detail during the week.

1 *Read Romans 8. Then read it again in another translation, which will help you to see the chapter through a different set of eyes.*
2 *As you read, note down any word, phrase or thought which particularly strikes you. This may be something which is often repeated, meaning*

that Paul thought it was important (e.g. 'Spirit' is mentioned about 19 times in this chapter!). Alternatively, it may be something you had not realized before or a question to ask an older Christian later.
3 *Now turn your notes into prayer, perhaps like this:*

> *Lord, show me more about your Holy Spirit. May he help me today to say and do the things that will please you ...*

2. No condemnation
Romans 8:1-4

> No condemnation now I dread;
> Jesus, and all in Him is mine!
> Alive in Him, my living Head,
> And clothed in righteousness
>   divine,
> Bold I approach the eternal
>   throne,
> And claim the crown, through
>   Christ my own.
>
> *And can it be, that I should gain*, a hymn by Charles Wesley (1707–1788).

1 *No condemnation! Freedom! To a guilty man these are marvellous words. But what was the condemnation for? What do these verses teach about the freedom of those in Christ Jesus? Write down in your own words what God has done to set you free, and from what.*

91

2 *Verse 4 talks about 'the righteous requirements (demands, GNB) of the law'. What are these? You may like to look up Romans 13: 9–10 or Exodus 20:1-17. Is it possible to keep these requirements absolutely and all the time?*
3 *Spend a few minutes looking back over the past day. In what ways did you fall short of God's 'righteous requirements'? Mention these by name, ask God's forgiveness and thank him that there is no condemnation because Christ has been punished instead of you.*

---

3. Under new management
Romans 8:5-12

The believer is delivered from the condemnation or penalty of his sin, but not yet from its presence. Chapter 7 shows how the Christian still has a struggle with sin, but chapter 8 encourages us to live as those who are forgiven and now under the management of the Holy Spirit.

Note: Some have interpreted Romans chapter 7 differently, as Paul speaking of his conversion. There is an excellent look at the chapter in J.I. Packer's *Keep in Step with the Spirit* (Revell, 1984), p. 263.

1 *Make a list of the differences in verses 5-8 between those who live according to the flesh or sinful nature and those who live according to the Spirit. Where do you fit in?*
2 *'Flesh' (RSV) (human nature, GNB) in the New Testament may often refer to the fleshy part of the body, or a person's physical existence,*

without implying any moral judgment. But here Paul is using it to mean the dark side of a person with its lusts and desires. You may like to look up Galatians 5:19-21 and 5:22-23 to see the difference between the 'works of the flesh' and the 'fruit of the Spirit'.
3 *What motive is there from verses 9-12 for living by the Spirit rather than by the flesh?*
4 *Take a few minutes to reflect on these verses. What areas of your life need to be brought to God today, to be placed under his control?*

---

4. Adopted sons
Romans 8:12-17

The following testimony is from a girl who had been involved in transcendental meditation before she became a Christian. Notice the difference:

We used to descend down into ourselves, firmly and consistently pushing away all distracting thoughts. Our goal was to arrive at a state of nothingness, which we called peace. I would settle down into a void of blackness, a darkness which could be felt.

What a difference biblical meditation has brought to my life. Here God's Word is the focus instead of self; satisfaction instead of emptiness; insight instead of darkness. Here was revelation from God instead of another mystical experience. I found power in God's Word to heal me and cleanse my mind, feed and satisfy my soul, and strengthen my spirit. ... I learned to hear God's voice.

Campbell McAlpine, *Alone with God* (Bethany).

1 *Read Romans 8:12-17. Some people say that every living person is a child of God. How would you answer them from this passage?*
2 *What differences are there in being 'sons' rather than 'slaves'?*
3 *A good father is interested in the smallest details of his children's lives, even things which escape the notice of others. Spend time in meditating on what it means to have God as your heavenly Father.*

Note: 'Abba' means 'father' in Aramaic, the language which Jesus would have spoken.

4 *Think of three people you know who are not yet children of God. Pray that God will use you to bring them into his family.*

5. Help for when we're weak
Romans 8:18-27

1 *As well as today's passage, you may like to look up Genesis 3:17-19; 5:29 and Revelation 22:3. If you were a doctor, what diagnosis would you give about our world today from these verses? What hope is there?*
2 *Verses 18-25 show the rest of the created world sharing in our suffering. How central should the theme of suffering be in your view of life? How can Christian hope take the reality of suffering seriously?*

Prayer is the soul's sincere desire,
Unuttered or expressed;
The motion of a hidden fire
That trembles in the breast.

Prayer is the burden of a sigh,
The falling of a tear,
The upward glancing of an eye,
When none but God is near.

O Thou by Whom we come to God,
The Life, the Truth, the Way;
The path of prayer Thyself hast trod;
Lord, teach us how to pray!

From a hymn by James Montgomery (1771–1854)

3 *Read verses 26-27. 'We do not know how to pray as we ought.' Paul could well have taken the words out of our mouths! We often imagine that great Christians such as Paul could not possibly have the same problems in prayer as we do. But how reassuring that Paul was a learner too. Pray that God will make you a learner in prayer, and that his Holy Spirit will help you.*

Norman Anderson builds his varied and moving life story, *An Adopted Son* (IVP, 1985) around the theme of verses 22 to 24 (and also the similar passage in Hebrews 2:10-11).

Weekend

1 *Read Romans 8:28-39. This is a wonderful passage of encouragement for the believer. How many promises can you find in these verses? God's promises are very personal, so try going through these, substituting the pronoun 'I' wherever you can; claiming these things for* yourself. Example: verse 31, 'If God is for me, who is against me?'

2 Every Christian should know Romans 8:28 by heart! Meditate on it ... rephrase it in your own words ... chew it over ... repeat it often throughout today and thank God that he has a purpose for your life.

3 Why not find a commentary on Romans and look up 8:28-39? The Tyndale New Testament Commentary on Romans by F.F. Bruce (Eerdmans, 1985) would be a good one to start with.

94

The sacraments (An issue study)

Much Christian disagreement centres around two things which Christ commanded us to do (baptism and the Lord's Supper). These are usually called sacraments. So what is the meaning of these two ordinances and what is the meaning of baptism or the taking of bread and wine? Are they optional extras to the Christian life or central to its practice and nature?

We shall look at baptism in days 1 to 3, and the Lord's Supper in days 4 and 5.

1. Beginnings – baptism in the Acts of the Apostles
Acts 2:37-47; 8:12-24, 35-39; 10:44-48; 19:1-7

1 *Prepare a table with four columns, headed as follows:*
WHO? – *note here the people who were baptized.*
WHY? – *note here what led to their baptism: how did they hear about baptism at all?*
WHEN? – *note here the timing of their baptism relative to their conversion.*
WHAT? – *note here the results which followed from the baptism(s) in the passage.*

2 *Using the material in the table, what would you say makes a baptism a Christian baptism? (See especially 2:37-47; 10:44-48; 19:1-7.)*

3 *What do you notice about how the earliest Christians practised baptism? (Notice in passing, how little is said about the mode (immersion, pouring, sprinkling, etc.) of baptism!) How would this change your church's practice of baptism if applied today?*

4 *Have you been baptized? If so, how does your experience of baptism link in with these examples in Acts? Is there anyone there whose experience is similar to yours? Don't worry if there isn't. The events in the Acts of the Apostles are describing what happened, not laying down examples which must be followed by everyone. If you haven't been baptized, talk to an older Christian friend, or your minister or pastor, about the subject.*

5 *If you have time, continue your study by reading Acts 9:17-19 (with 22:12-16) and Acts 16:13-15, 29-33; 18:8.*

Thank God that he has provided baptism as an act whereby Christians can declare that they have already entered into a new relationship with him.

2. Dead and alive

Romans 5:20 – 6:14

This is the only passage in the New Testament which discusses baptism at any length and it has been very important to Christians thinking about the meaning of baptism. We are going to look at what it has to teach us about the implications of baptism for the Christian life.

1 *Read Romans 5:20–6:1. These verses explain the problem Paul is tackling in the remainder of our section. Summarize briefly the objection Paul is dealing with.*

2 *Paul begins his answer in 6:2 and then develops it in terms of the meaning of baptism in 6:3-10, rather than the way many of us might develop it in terms of the meaning of conversion.*
Note down from 6:3-10 what Paul says about:
a)baptism and the death of Christ
b)baptism and the resurrection of Christ.

3 *In 6:11-14 Paul then spells out the implications of baptism in the Christian life. What difference should our identification with Christ in our baptism make to daily Christian living in the battle against sin and temptation?*

What are the areas of your life where you give in to sin most? How determined are you to live a new life, united with the risen Christ, because you have been baptized into his death? Pray that God will give you strength to live out the implications of your baptism.

3. Baptized into the church

Matthew 28:19;
1 Corinthians 1:15-17; 12:13;
15:29; Galatians 3:26-29;
Ephesians 4:5;
Colossians 2:11-12;
Hebrews 6:2; 1 Peter 3:21-22

1 *Consider each of the passages in its context. Write down what is the main topic under discussion in the verses that surround the reference to baptism.*

1 Corinthians 1:15-17 – see 1:12
1 Corinthians 12:13 – see 12:12, 14-20
Galatians 3:26-29 – see 3:28
Ephesians 4:5 – see 4:3
Matthew 28:19 – see 28:18-20
Colossians 2:11-12 – see 2:6-10, 16-19
1 Peter 3:21-22 – see 3:13-17, 4:12-19

2 *From these passages note down the outcome of baptism for:*
a) Christian unity
b) Christian lifestyle
c) Christian assurance.
Notice how many different areas of Christian doctrine and lifestyle are linked with baptism! How has your baptism affected the way you think and live? How hard are you working to break down divisions in your church?

Pray that your own church will demonstrate your common baptism into Christ. Also pray that this will be seen in your unity, your distinctive lifestyle and your assurance of God's acceptance.

4. The Lord's Supper – what it means

Matthew 26:26-29;
Luke 22:14-20;
1 Corinthians 10:16-17; 11:17-26

The Lord's Supper (or communion service) began in the context of a Passover Supper, which was the annual celebration by the Jews of God bringing them out of slavery in Egypt (see Exodus 12). Now Jesus was giving his followers another meal to celebrate his bringing his people out of slavery to sin.

1 *Read 1 Corinthians 11:17-22. The situation in Corinth was one of disorder and disharmony amongst believers meeting for the Lord's Supper (vv. 17-18). We shall look at the causes of this in the next study.*
2 *Paul goes on to give positive teaching about the meaning of this meal (vv. 23-26). What does he say about Jesus' intention in instituting this meal? Look at one of the accounts of the Last Supper in the gospels, in Matthew 26:26-29. How does this demonstrate Jesus' intention?*
3 *Read again Matthew 26:26-29 and then Luke 22:14-20. What does Jesus say that the bread symbolizes? And the wine? Compare this with 1 Corinthians 11:26. Write down, in your own words, what the central focus of the Lord's Supper should be from these passages.*
4 *Read 1 Corinthians 10:16-17 and 11:26. The Lord's Supper is not only a 'look back' to what Christ did for us on the cross, but has present and future dimensions as well. How does Paul spell those out here?*

5 *Consider the way that your church celebrates the Lord's Supper. How do the ideas in the passage we have read come out in the celebration? If you use a set service, get hold of a copy and read it through, looking for those ideas. If you do not, think about the pattern of your communion services and their different elements.*

5. The Lord's Supper – what to do

Matthew 5:23-24;
1 Corinthians 11:18-34; 13:4-7

1 *Read 1 Corinthians 11:18-34. What problems related to the Lord's Supper existed in the church in Corinth? What was the cause of these problems?*
2 *What preparation does Paul recommend before eating the bread and drinking the wine? How do you do this before you go to a communion service?*

A suggestion for preparation
Read 1 Corinthians 13:4-7, and then read it again, putting your own name in place of 'love' throughout. Think in each phrase where your life falls short of God's standard of love and confess these failures to God. Then spend time praising God for the cross (which is the focus of the Lord's Supper) through which our sins are forgiven.

3 *How does Paul say the problems of 1 Corinthians 11:18-22 should be tackled? What practical steps does he recommend? What importance do you attach to relationships with other Christians in the context of the* communion service? Matthew 5:23-24 may help here. What principle emerges about the worship that God desires? Think about your relationships with other Christians in your church or Christian group. Is there anyone with whom you need to make peace before you next come to the Lord's Supper with them?

Weekend

1 Read either Donald Bridge and David Phypers, The Water that Divides *(IVP, 1977)* – a book by an Anglican and a Baptist about baptism, which considers both sides of the debate over who should be baptized – or Donald Bridge and David Phypers, The Meal that Unites? *(Shaw, 1983)* – the same team of authors considering the varying views on the Lord's Supper.

2 Go with a Christian friend of another denomination to a baptism service or communion service in his or her church. Get your friend to explain why things are done as they are in their denomination. See how the biblical emphases you have found about the two services come out in this different setting to your own church.

3 If you didn't have time to look up all the references in days one and three, you could do so now, adding to your chart and notes.

The church in Corinth, 1 (A bird's-eye study)

Ancient Corinth and Julius Caesar's new city (46 BC) has given history the term 'Corinthian' – synonymous with 'loose living' – a term derived from the materially prosperous but morally corrupt sea port. It was around AD 50 that Paul arrived and preached the gospel, with the result that an infant church was born.

But the members of this church had many problems, partly due to its birthplace. So after Paul's departure they wrote, quizzing him regarding aspects of faith and indicating a less than healthy outlook.

1. The church's background
Acts 18:1-17; 1 Corinthians 1:4-9

Greeks, Latins, Syrians, Asiatics, Egyptians and Jews bought and sold, laboured and revelled, quarreled and hob-nobbed in the city and its ports, as nowhere else in Greece.

T.C. Edwards

1 What atmosphere is conjured up by the above quotation? Read Acts 18:1-17. How far is life in the synagogue any different?
2 Yet Paul could say, 'I always thank God for you.' Read 1 Corinthians 1:4-9. List the evidence of God's work in the church.
3 *Just how strong is a gospel which can withstand the evil opposition in the city of Corinth? What is the source of this strength?*

Write down the names of those known to you who strongly resist the gospel. Ask the Lord for the willingness and power to witness to them.

2. The church's disagreements
1 Corinthians 3:1-9; 6:1-11

No law but his own desires.

von Dobschutz

Read 1 Corinthians 3:1-9 and 6:1-11.

1 *A quarrelsome church – in what areas does this quarrelsome spirit show itself?*
2 *From these verses, how do God and man work together in seeing people come to faith? Make a note of this for your own benefit. Do you ever lose sight of your partnership with God in this?*
3 *How should grievances amongst Christians in Corinth be settled? How was the past catching up on the church?*

3. The church and marriage
1 Corinthians 5 and 7

Sexual laxity was rife in Corinth. Read chapter 5 to see how this was influencing the church and how the Christians were failing to take a firm stand.

1 *Read 1 Corinthians 7:1-11. In what ways does Paul see marriage as necessary in the presence of such immorality? What responsibilities accompany marriage? Write down your answers.*
2 *Read the rest of the chapter. What positive things does Paul say about being married and about being single? Put into your own words what advice Paul is giving in general to this church about contentment.*
3 *You may be distressed by your marital status, whatever it is. Write a letter to God, pinpointing exactly what is troubling you. Then reflect on the relevance of Paul's words to you.*

Do you know of marriages where only one partner is a Christian? Spend time praying for them in the light of this chapter.

Note: Paul himself had probably been married since any orthodox rabbi would have been married around the age of eighteen. His wife may have died or have left him.

4. The church's scruples
1 Corinthians 8; 10:12-33

From the vantage point of the twentieth century it's easy to exclaim in horror at the thought of eating meat offered to idols, but 'it was all part and parcel of the formal etiquette in society' (Moffat).

Read 1 Corinthians 8 and 10:12-33.

1 *What are Paul's arguments against eating meat offered to idols? What do these arguments suggest about Christian 'liberty' or 'freedom' in any age?*
2 *What modern equivalents are 'part and parcel' of society, e.g. the use of alcohol? What guidance are we given by Paul?*
3 *1 Corinthians 10:12-13 teach an important lesson. Put them into your own words, then learn them to enable you to stand strong in your faith from day to day.*

What 'freedoms' do you need to restrict for the love of a fellow Christian?

5. The church and worship
1 Corinthians 12; 14

The church at Corinth obviously had many questions about the role and contribution of individual members. This led on to questions about how worship should be conducted.

1 *Read 1 Corinthians 12. Divide a page of your notebook into two columns. On one side write down what Paul says these Christians have in common. On the other side, note down the differences. (The differences column may be longer than the other one. But this doesn't* mean that the things held in common are outweighed by the differences.)

2 Try to put into your own words this important fact of emphasizing unity but allowing differences to exist for the common good. Why is this an essential requirement for worship in the church?

3 Read 1 Corinthians 14. What does Paul say about right and wrong motives for wanting to exercise spiritual gifts? Are you eager to exercise a spiritual gift in your church? If not, why not? Reflect on your motives.

4 Summarize Paul's teaching about the importance of orderliness in worship from 14:26-39.

Much has been written about this matter. You could look up *The Message of 1 Corinthians*, by David Prior, in IVP's The Bible Speaks Today series.

Weekend

1 Questions about the Lord's Supper were raised by the church; Paul discusses them in chapter 11. Since this chapter was looked at in the series on the sacraments we shall not be studying it here, but you might like to look back at your notes to enable you to get a complete picture of this church.

2 'When Christ comes to live in a man's heart, his face is often seen at the windows' (Samuel Rutherford). Meditate on 1 Corinthians 13 with the aim that the love of Christ may be seen at your 'windows'.

1. The church and hope
1 Corinthians 15:1-28, 51-58

'The Archimedian point on which all else turns' (Künneth). To the mind of the Greeks, resurrection was untenable. Hades was the place where the soul had a shadowy existence. To the Christian, resurrection is a sure hope, though the mechanics may remain a mystery.

1 *What is the significance of Christ's resurrection? How were the Corinthians failing to appreciate it? How does Jesus' resurrection relate to his death?*
2 *The Christian hope – list the areas which it encompasses. What is its superiority over Hades?*
3 *Several weeks ago we looked at the topic of death. Meditate on how that aspect of hope enables you to confront death with courage. Pray for any known to you who are having to come to terms with death right now.*

2. The church's acceptance of Paul
1 Corinthians 9; 2 Corinthians 11

In several of Paul's letters his right to speak out, indeed his right to be an apostle, is under attack, *e.g.* Galatians 1:11-12. The church at Corinth was no exception in being critical of him. Read 1 Corinthians 9.

1 *What criticisms had been levelled at Paul? How did he defend himself? What motivated him to preach? At what personal cost to himself?*
2 *Read 2 Corinthians 11. False teachers had infiltrated the church at Corinth. What does Paul say about these false apostles? How does he compare himself with them?*
3 *Are you aware of any false teaching in the church today? From what Paul says about the church at Corinth, how might you discern whether or not people are speaking the truth?*

Pray that the leaders of your own church will be able to discern right from wrong, and that as a church you may accept the truth when it is preached.

3. The church and evangelism
2 Corinthians 5:9-15; 6:1-13

Paul uses a defence of himself and his ministry to stir the Corinthians to evangelism and to righteous living.

1 *Read 2 Corinthians 5:9-21. What*

differences lie between pleasing God and pleasing self and others? What do the verses suggest had been happening in the church?

2 An ambassador was sent to bring terms of peace in war. In what practical ways can the Christian be an ambassador in bringing peace and reconciliation?

3 From 6:1-13 note down the qualities of those who belong to God which cause them to be recommended. The Corinthians were too blind to see this in Paul.

Spend time reflecting on how willing you are to be an ambassador for Christ whatever the cost. For example, in what ways have you been inconvenienced (humanly speaking) because you have witnessed for Christ?

4. The church and giving
2 Corinthians 8 and 9

'There is an amazing divide between the givers and the non-givers' (Baughen). The Corinthians were definitely in the latter group. In the first letter (16:2-4) they had been reminded about giving – and they still hadn't got the gift together, some twelve months later. Glance back at these verses, then read 2 Corinthians 8 and 9.

1 Note down the indicators suggesting that the Corinthians didn't part easily with their money. What would be their reward if this didn't change?

2 What are the benefits to and signs of a cheerful giver (9:7)? Think back over the last month – how generous

and caring have you been (not just in financial terms either)?

3 From what you have learnt about Paul's involvement at Corinth, would you say that stewardship involves more than just money? Why?

Ask the Lord continually to teach you the lessons of good stewardship.

---

5. Paul's love for the church
2 Corinthians

It has been said that Paul's first letter to the church at Corinth says more about the church, but his second letter more about Paul himself. As you have read both letters you will have been struck by his deep affection for these Christians. In this study we shall be looking at the second letter only.

Note: He had already made two visits to Corinth when he wrote this letter, anticipating a third visit. His second visit had caused him great pain.

1 If you have time read through the whole of the second letter, noting down the various ways (plus references) in which Paul expressed his care for this church. Look especially at 1:23 – 2:4; 7:2-15; 12:11–13:11.

2 Is this the quality of care and discipline that you expect in your church? How prepared are you to give and receive such care?

Pray for yourself and your church leaders from this point of view.

Weekend

1 2 Corinthians, A Spiritual Health Warning to the Church *by Baughen (Marshalls) is a very readable but challenging book which puts this letter into the present church situation.*
2 *What has your study over the past two weeks taught you about the* importance of understanding the basics of faith and its practical outworking as you rub shoulders with the world, whether rough and ready as in the docksides of Corinth or sophisticated as amongst the Greek intellectuals? Use this weekend for a spiritual check-up, noting down the areas which you need to work on in the coming months.

Part Four

Travels with Paul
Conversion
The book of Numbers
Law
The book of Joshua
Authority
Paul's letter to the Colossians

Part Four/Week One
Travels with Paul (A historical study)

This week we are going to follow Paul around on his travels, focusing particularly on his strategy in bringing the gospel to the various situations he encountered.

1. Early days – Lystra, Iconium and Derbe
Acts 14:1-23; 16:1-5

1 Find these three towns on the map. Lystra and Derbe lay along the Via Sebaste, an important road through Asia Minor (modern Turkey). All three were Romanized to some degree and Derbe was an important frontier city in the Roman Empire. A religious hotch potch existed in all three cities: in Iconium there was the worship of a mother goddess, led by eunuch priests, as well as worship of the Roman gods and a Jewish synagogue (cf. 14:1); in Lystra the local Lycaonians had a legend of a visit from the gods, Zeus and Hermes. These were hardly very promising places to which to take the gospel.
2 Read the accounts of the initial evangelism of the three towns in Acts 14:1-21a. Given the presence of so many religions, what are the key elements of the gospel which Paul speaks about in each place? What provided him with the opening to speak? What does he say about God

in each place? How does this confirm or contradict the views of God held by the locals?
3 What is the key area of Christian truth which needs to be proclaimed where you live or work? Perhaps it is that Jesus is the only way to God, or that forgiveness is available to all. Yet what ideas about God do people already have? How right or wrong are these ideas? Pray for wisdom and courage in sharing those truths with those around you.
4 Read the accounts of Paul's later connections with these places in Acts 14:21b-23 and 16:1-5. What example is set for following up those who have recently come to faith in Christ? How would you help a friend who has recently become a Christian?

A useful book to help a new Christian to grow is *Grow Your Christian Life* (IVP). Buy two copies: read one and give the other to a new Christian you know!

2. Prison and praise! – Philippi
Acts 16:6-40

Philippi (modern Filibedjik) was a Roman colony named after Philip of Macedon. Thus citizens of Philippi were Roman citizens and had all the

107

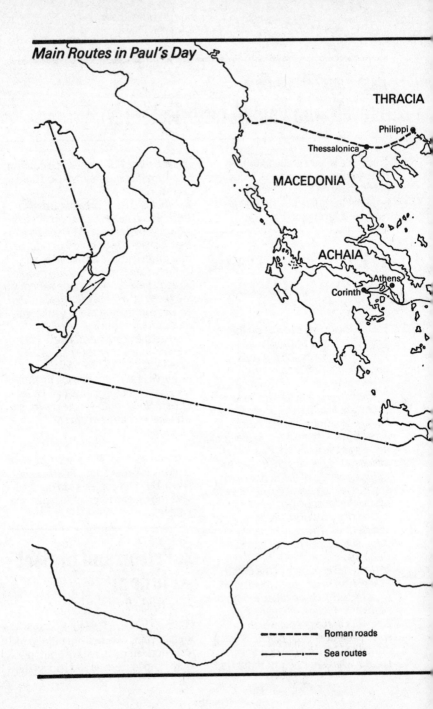

Main Routes in Paul's Day

THRACIA

Philippi

Thessalonica

MACEDONIA

ACHAIA

Athens

Corinth

- - - - - - Roman roads
———·——— Sea routes

BITHYNIA
AND
PONTUS

GALATIA

Troas

Caesarea

ASIA

CAPPADOCIA

Hierapolis
Colossai
Antioch
Iconium
Lystra
Ephesus
Laodiceia
Derbe
Tarsus
Antioch

CYPRUS

Mediterranean Sea

Caesarea
Philippi

Caesarea

Samaria

Joppa

Samaria

Jerusalem

Judea

rights linked to that citizenship – anything not sanctioned by Rome was out (see Acts 16:21)! Look it up on the map. Philippi was 10 miles inland from its port, Neapolis, which lay at the Eastern end of the Egnetian Way, a very important Roman road for travel from Italy to Greece.

Like other Roman cities, there was a climate of melting religious boundaries: 'All religions lead to God (or the gods)' was the slogan of the day. There was Roman worship of their gods, the emperor and there was Thracian religion, worshipping Bendis and Myndrytus. There was, however, no synagogue, which is why Paul and the others went outside the city to find a place of prayer (Acts 16:13).

1 *Read Acts 16:6-12. Why did Paul go to Philippi? Notice how he tried to go to other places, but received negative guidance from the Lord about them.*
2 *Read Acts 16:13-15. What was Paul's initial approach to evangelizing Philippi? Why do you think he did things this way? (Compare his approach to Iconium in yesterday's study.) What is the correspondingly most open ground you know? How could you go about gaining an opening for the gospel there?*
3 *Read Acts 16:16-24. What appeared to be an opening for the gospel rapidly looked the opposite as the missionaries were imprisoned and flogged. How would you have felt in Paul and Silas' shoes? Can you think of situations where an apparent opening for the gospel has gone sour? What did you do in response? Pray now for those around you who oppose the gospel.*

Note: Acts 16:25-34. Look at Paul and Silas' reaction! On the earthquake, the jailer would know that he would have to take the punishment due to any prisoners who escaped (verse 27). God turned the situation round so that an apparently closed door to the gospel reopened.

4 *Read Acts 16:35-40. Paul exercized his rights as a citizen. Why do you think he waited until this point to do that? What effect do you think that would have on the believers left in Philippi after Paul left? Are there situations where you should waive your 'rights' for the sake of the gospel? Are there other situations where exercizing your legal rights could open doors for the gospel or help those who are believers?*

3. The gospel in a pagan society – Athens
Acts 17:16-34

Athens was an ancient university town. Within the Roman Empire it was a free city because of its reputation. Much of its art and sculpture was linked to temples and images of pagan gods. The Areopagus exercised jurisdiction over visitors in the areas of religion and moral teaching and this is why Paul was summoned to address the Court (Acts 17:19). Look up Athens on the map.

Two main schools of philosophy existed in Athens. The Stoics were rationalists, who believed that the individual is self-sufficient, not needing God's help in human life. This produced spiritual pride. They thought of God (if there was one at all) as being identified with the universe. The Epicureans treated pleasure as the chief end of life, although not in a modern pleasure-seeking way. They wanted a tranquil life without fear, especially fear of death. They regarded the gods as having no interest in their affairs.

1 *What does Paul do to show that he understands the world views of those he speaks with? At what points does he agree with their views and at what points does he challenge them?*
2 *Trace Paul's teaching about God in his speech to the Areopagus (vv. 22-31). What statements does Paul make about God, both negatively (what he is not) and positively (what he is)? Write out two lists of the positives and negatives. How might this list of truths about God, both positive and negative, help you to explain the gospel to others?*

Pray that your non-Christian friends will have a true grasp of who God is. Pray too that you will have opportunities to share the truth about God with them.

4. Things take time – Corinth
Acts 18:1-18

Corinth was another Roman city. Its strategic position made it an important trading centre and a very cosmopolitan place, leading to large groups of ethnic minorities. The cult of Aphrodite practised cult prostitution and Corinth as a city was a byword in the ancient world for its loose morals. Nevertheless, there was a Jewish minority there

too. Look up the city on the map. You could also refer back to your studies on Corinth (Part Three, Weeks Eight and Nine).

1 *Read verses 1-8. Paul was not, at this stage of his travels, a full-time missionary, but had to support himself through tent-making (verses 2-3). Nevertheless, he looked for and found opportunities to explain the gospel. What approach did he adopt in Corinth initially? Why did he later change his tactics, both in terms of time (verse 5: cf. 2 Corinthians 11:8f.; Philippians 4:15) and his target audience (verse 6)?*
2 *Read verses 9-11. God knew Paul felt under pressure in Corinth. How did Paul receive encouragement? In what ways has God encouraged you when you have been under pressure from sharing the gospel in difficult situations? What can you learn from Paul's further activity about the needs of a young church in a difficult situation (especially verses 11ff.)?*
3 *Read verses 12-18. How does God continue to protect Paul and the young church in Corinth when further attack comes?*
4 *Imagine you are writing a letter to a Christian under pressure and attack because of his/her witness to the gospel. What are the three most important things you would say to encourage him/her to keep on keeping on?*

5. A regional centre – Ephesus
Acts 19:1-41

There was enormous religious variety in Ephesus. The worship of Diana or Artemis took place in a temple, which was the largest building of the Greek world. Emperor worship was also promoted. Yet the Jewish colony was substantial in size and enjoyed a privileged position amongst the Romans, with freedom to worship and observe the Sabbath.

1 *Read verses 1-10. What was Paul's initial strategy in evangelizing the area of Ephesus? Why and how did that change? Paul did not leave Ephesus, and yet notice verse 10! How did that happen? Notice, like Corinth, how Paul spends a long time in one place (verse 10). Why do you think he did this in Ephesus?*

Note: Ephesus was a large city (300,000+ in New Testament times), and had been under Roman control since 133 BC. It was a seaport at the mouth of the River Cayster and a great commercial centre. It had excellent road links with the rest of Asia Minor (see map), and especially with the valley of the River Lycus.

2 *Read verses 11-22. As usual , the gospel attracted opposition. Here, it was openly from the powers of darkness (verses 13-15). What lessons emerged from this episode about the relationship of Christianity to spiritism and the occult? Pray for any you know involved in such practices today.*
3 *Read verses 23-41. Why did the attack on the gospel come this time?*

Notice the mixture of religious and financial opposition Paul encountered here. What modern parallels are there to this kind of attack on Christian faith? Notice again how God defends the gospel through pagans (verses 33-41)!

Pray for confidence in the Lord of the gospel to present it in all its fullness today, especially where the religious and social climate works against the truth of the gospel.

Weekend

1 *Most of the places you have been reading about have a non-existent, or only very tiny, Christian community today. Get hold of P.J. Johnstone's* Operation World *(STL) and read up on Greece and Turkey. Get in touch with one of the groups working in one of those countries today and pray for the work they are doing in a difficult climate. You could also look for newspaper cuttings about Greece and Turkey and go to a travel agent's to find pictures and information on both these countries.*
2 *Write down all the areas of opposition to the gospel in our society that you can think of. Then think of ways in which God is at work, through individuals and structures, to bring about change in a Godward direction on all levels – individual and corporate.*

Part Four/Week Two
Conversion (An issue study)

People become Christians in a variety of ways. Some, from Christian backgrounds, are able to build on a wealth of knowledge gained from their upbringing. They may be unable to point to a particular date of conversion. A few have a life-changing revelation, such as Saul. For others it is a slow process of discovery over many months.

Some people talk about their conversion as though nothing else has ever happened in their spiritual life since. We should not live always on past spiritual experiences. It is important though that we understand what happened when we turned to God (however and whenever that occurred.) There is much muddled thinking about conversion today. Our studies will try to clarify what the Bible teaches.

---

1. Dead ...
Romans 1:18-32;
Ephesians 2:1-10

What were you like before you turned to God? If you can still remember life without Christ, try briefly to recall some of your attitudes and expectations of life.

1 *Read Romans 1:18-32, which graphically describes a society where godlessness prevails. What particularly strikes you about this bleak description?*
2 *Your own life may not have been*

as seemingly desperate as that but, according to Paul in Ephesians 2:1-3, what was your position in relation to God? How did that affect the way you lived your life?
3 *'To be saved' – these are indeed the right words to describe God's deliverance. From Ephesians 2:4-10 note down all the things God has done for us, and then the reasons why he has done them.*

Use these verses to thank God for what he has saved you from. Pray too that you may realize just how desperate is the plight of those without God, which should provoke you to urgent prayer for them.

---

2. ... set free from sin
Romans 5:6-8; 6:15-23

From God's perspective, how is it possible for you to turn to him?

1 *Read Romans 5:6-8 and then put these verses in your own words. What does it mean to you personally that 'Christ died for the ungodly'? Let the enormity of his actions sink in, causing you to praise him.*
2 *It is not enough to understand the facts. A personal response is also called for. Read Romans 6:15-23. What action does Paul urge upon his readers? With what results?*
3 *We live in a world where freedom is a commodity much talked about. Yet true freedom can be found only*

through Christ. In what ways do you know a freedom that would be totally foreign to an unbeliever?

> "Lord Jesus, I believe you. I accept you. Please come into my life. I commit it to you." With these few words that morning, while the briny sea churned, came a sureness of mind that matched the depth of feeling in my heart. There came something more: strength and serenity, a wonderful new assurance about life, a fresh perception of myself and the world around me. In the process I felt old fears, tensions and animosities draining away. I was coming alive to things I had never seen before; as if God was filling the barren void I'd known for so many months, filling it to its brim with a whole new kind of awareness.

> Charles Colson, *Born Again* (Revell).

3. The conversion of two men
Acts 8:26 – 9:19

God had his way of dealing with Chuck Colson. But as we said at the beginning, there is no set way of becoming a Christian. Satan can rob us of our certainty by causing us to compare unfavourably our own experience of God with that of others. To show the variety of experiences, we shall look today at the conversions of Saul and of the Ethiopian eunuch – which like our own, were unique.

1 *Draw two columns in your notebook. In one column note down all the features of the eunuch's conversion and in the other, the features of Saul's. Pay particular attention to the similarities and differences (e.g. the eunuch appears to have been longing to understand, unlike Saul; yet both were religious).*
2 *What part did other believers have to play in their conversion? At what cost? How willing are you to be used by God in this way? How expectant are you? Pause to pray about this.*
3 *What was the connection between the conversion of these two men and their baptism? What does that suggest is part of the purpose of their baptism?*

Churches vary in the view they take on baptism. If you have not been baptized, make a point of talking about it with a leader of your own church, and refer back to your earlier studies in this book (Part Three, Week Seven).

4. It's real and lasting
1 Peter 1:3-12; Ephesians 1:3-14

So many choruses we sing rejoice in the closeness to God that we can feel. What happens though if God seems far away, or if we distrust our feelings, or when doubts assail us? Where do we stand then?

1 *Read 1 Peter 1:3-12. According to Peter, what thoughts could cause us to be unsure of where we stand with God (e.g. verses 6, 8)?*
2 *How does Peter encourage these believers to be certain of their faith? Make a list from these verses of all that God has done and is doing for us.*

3 Turn to Ephesians 1: 3–14 and add to the list you have just made. What has God done for us? What especially does Paul see as the purpose of the Holy Spirit in this work of salvation?

4 Too often we see conversion as being important now without thinking about the long-term effects. How do both Peter and Paul explain that the effects of conversion are lasting? How important is this to you?

Pray a prayer of thanksgiving based upon your list of all God has done and is doing for us.

---

5. From now on...
2 Corinthians 5:11 – 6:2

However God brought it about, conversion is the beginning of our Christian life. Our future hope is a source of inspiration. In the meantime, we have God's presence, his gifts and his commission to tell others about our hope in God.

1 Read 2 Corinthians 5:11 – 6:2. How does Paul see conversion as a genuine turning point in the life of a believer?

2 Put in your own words what Christ has done that is worth telling others about.

3 What does God intend to do through us? In what practical ways can we respond? What motivated Paul? Are you similarly motivated?

Try writing a letter to God thanking him for reconciling you to himself and all that that involved. In what specific ways are you willing to act as his ambassador on this earth? Are you holding back in some areas? Pray about what you should be doing; and write down some specific things.

Weekend

1 Look back over your notes of this week to see what is the balance between God's part in conversion and the response of the potential believer.

2 Are our lives transformed because we meet an interesting philosophy, or view of life, or because we have an encounter with Jesus? Think through examples of how some people reacted to him, for better or worse. Luke 5:17-26; 7:36-50; 9:18-26; 18:18-30; 19:1-10.

3 Being a mouthpiece of God's goodness is a natural consequence of conversion. You could learn more about this by reading Out of the Saltshaker by Rebecca Manley Pippert (IVP, 1979) or How to Give Away Your Faith by Paul Little (IVP, 1966).

The book of Numbers, 1 (A bird's-eye study)

'Guide me, O Thou great
  Jehovah,
Pilgrim through this barren
  land;...'

    From a hymn by William
        Williams (1716-1791)

It's sung everywhere, from church, to the football terraces and pubs. And it's usually thought of as describing the Christian's pilgrimage through this difficult world to our 'promised land' in heaven. But it's based on Israel's desert wanderings en route

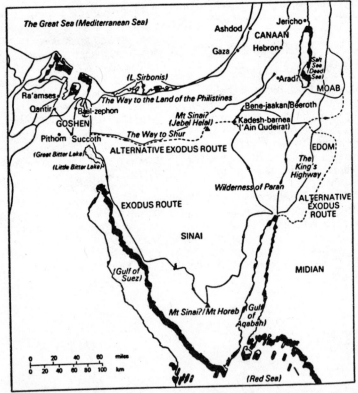

Possible route of the Exodus. From Illustrated Bible Dictionary *(Tyndale, 1980), p. 491.*

from Egypt to the promised land of Canaan. But what really happened? Why did it take forty years for such a relatively short journey? And what lessons are there for us?

Numbers is the English translation of the Greek title of the book Arithmoi, *a title no doubt given to it because of the census returns found in chapters 1 – 4 and 26. The fifth word of the book,* b^emidbar *'in the wilderness', constitutes its Hebrew title. This more aptly describes its contents, for it is wholly concerned with the forty years the tribes of Israel spent wandering in the wilderness between Mount Sinai and the plains of Moab.*

Gordon J. Wenham, *The Tyndale Old Testament Commentary on Numbers* (IVP)

1. 'Getting going'
Numbers 9:15 – 10:36

The people of Israel left Egypt as a disorganized rabble, with Moses at their head, and made their way to Mount Sinai. It was there that things changed, for a covenant was made between God and the people. That is, God gave them his laws and promised to be faithful in his care of them, and required their loving obedience. The tabernacle (the Tent of the Lord's presence) was built, Aaron and his sons were appointed as priests, and regular sacrifices instituted. The people were counted and sorted into tribes, with their marching order for the journey decided (Numbers 1 – 4). They were ready to set off!

Note: Paul comments on this covenant and its relationship with the law and the earlier covenant of Abraham in Galatians 3:16-29.

1 *Try to put yourself in the place of one of the people on that journey – what might you have thought of these events? Perhaps you might try writing an imaginary diary entry for the first day.*

Note: 9:15 'cloud' – see Exodus 13:21. 10:11 date reckoned from when they left Egypt; 10:33 the Ark or Covenant Box contained the stones with the Ten Commandments on them. It was kept in the most holy place in the tabernacle.

2 *The Israelites received clear guidance when they should move. How do you know what God wants you to do? How easy is it to know?*

Let the fire and cloudy pillar Lead me all my journey through...

William Williams

3 *The cloud wasn't just a signpost – it was the symbol of God's presence, the greatest blessing possible (see Numbers 6:24-26). How do you experience God's presence? Are you consciously enjoying it now? Pray for a sense of God's presence with you throughout today.*

Need help with guidance? – try reading John White's *The Fight* (IVP, 1977); or Paul E. Little's booklet *Affirming the Will of God* (IVP).

2. The problems begin
Numbers 11 and 12

Chapter 10 ended on a high note as the people set off on their journey – but the first signs of hardship as they moved on into a desert region led to discontent.

1 *Read the passage, and then try to describe the state of morale of the Israelites.*
2 *Do you think their various complaints were justified?*
3 *Make a list of all that God does in answer to Moses' prayer (11:10-15).*
4 *In chapter 11 the grumbles were directed against God. How would you describe Moses' attitude to personal criticism in chapter 12?*

Note: 12:1 Miriam and Aaron: Moses' sister and brother.

Grumbling and criticism can characterize many Christian groups and churches. Are you guilty of it? If so, stop and ask God's forgiveness.

5 *What lessons and encouragements can you find here for those who are the targets of criticism?*

---

3. Turning point
Numbers 13 and 14

The Israelites have now reached the southern borders of Canaan, and their spies are sent out to explore it by crossing from south to north (about 250 miles each way). This land – a good land – has been promised to them ever since God first called Moses to be their leader (Exodus 3:8). Indeed the promise goes back to God's covenant with Abraham (Genesis 15:18-21).

1 *What differences are there between the reports of Joshua and Caleb on the land (14:7-10) and the report from the rest of the spies (13:27-29, 32-33)? Why might the reports have been so different? When faced with a difficult situation are you more like Joshua and Caleb or the others?*
2 *What is Moses' chief concern in his prayer for the people (14:13-19)?*

The Lord answers Moses' prayer (14:20) and does not strike them down as he had threatened (14:12), but their sin still has serious results – results the people have to accept, as it is now too late to fulfil the Lord's original command (14:39-45).

3 *In what ways does God's judgment on the people (14:20-38) seem appropriate to their sin?*
4 *When Paul talks of these events in the desert, he says they were written down as warnings for us (1 Corinthians 10:11). What warnings can you find here for your own Christian life?*

---

4. Yet more problems
Numbers 16 and 17

Some people never learn! God had given the tribe of Levi a special role, looking after the tabernacle and other holy objects. Within that tribe Aaron's family were appointed priests, to offer the sacrifices for the people. Korah and his followers questioned the exclusive right of

Aaron's family to be priests (16:3, 8-11), and Dathan and Abiram (from a different tribe, Reuben) were just generally fed-up with where Moses was leading them (16:12-14).

1 *Jot down the ways in which God shows his approval of Moses' and Aaron's special positions of leadership.*
2 *What issues are really at stake?*

Note: The passage ends with the people's realization of God's holiness (17:12-13). It is followed by a repetition of the roles of the priests and the Levites (18:1-7), who do the work of the sanctuary on the people's behalf as a protection against the awesome effects of God's holiness.

> *Within the veil I now would*
> > *come,*
> *Into the Holy Place to look*
> > *upon thy face.*
> *I see such beauty there, no*
> > *other can compare,*
> *I worship thee my Lord within*
> > *the veil.*

> (Copyright Genesis Music, P.O. Box 26, Auburn 2144, Australia.)

3 *Does God's holiness arouse the same feelings of awe in you? Jesus has made a way into God's presence for all God's people (see Hebrews 10:19-22). In what ways could we take that privilege for granted?*

---

5. Rock bottom

Numbers 20

1 *In the light of what you have read*

so far this week, why were the Israelites wrong to grumble?
2 *In verses 9-11, how did Moses exceed God's instructions (verse 8)?*
3 *Why do you think that this dishonoured God (verse 12)?*

Note: The people made a detour round Edom – presumably they were unwilling to fight because Edom was Israel's 'brother'.

4 *Moses did not totally disobey God, but he failed to carry out his instructions properly. How careful are you about your obedience to God? Are you ever tempted to think it doesn't matter?*

Weekend

1 *The book of Deuteronomy is a sermon preached by Moses to the Israelites as they are about to enter the promised land. In it he recalls their history after leaving Mount Horeb (another name for Sinai) and reminds them of how they should live as the people of God. If you read Deuteronomy 1:1–2:8 you will review what you read in Numbers this week – and of course, you can read on, to see what happens next!*
2 *Obeying God has been a common theme this week. Think over the last few months. What examples have you experienced of God asking you to obey his Word, perhaps a change in attitude, or in doing something for him that you found difficult? Did you obey or disobey him? With what results? Can you do something now to rectify any mistakes made?*

The book of Numbers, 2 (A bird's-eye study)

The whole book of Numbers looks forward to the occupation of the land of Canaan. Chapters 1–10 describe the preparations for the journey from Sinai to Canaan, 11–12 the journey itself, 13–14 the abortive attempt at conquest. The rest of the book describes the subsequent period of wanderings and their period of waiting in Transjordan prior to their entry. Canaan is the ever-present goal of the people, that is never quite reached in Numbers.

Gordon J. Wenham, *Tyndale Old Testament Commentary on Numbers* (IVP).

1. The tide turns
Numbers 21;
Deuteronomy 2:26 – 3:11

The time for victory has now come! The complete destruction recorded here (verses 2-3) may seem brutal, but it was a means of destroying idolatry. The people and goods of the idolatrous nations were given to the Lord and completely destroyed, rather than being kept by Israel, with the risk of God's people compromising with idols (more on this in study 4).

1 *Numbers 21:1-9. Why is the bronze snake (verse 9) not simply another idol, an object of popular worship and superstition? This snake is seen, centuries later, in the New Testament as a 'picture' of Christ on the cross (see John 3:14-15). What parallels can you think of between the problem and cure talked about here, and Jesus being lifted up on the cross?*
2 *Numbers 21:10-35. Israel now moved on, travelling round the south and east of the promised land until they were confronted with Sihon, a powerful king, who had conquered other nations (verses 27-29). The story of the victories over Sihon and Og is retold in Deuteronomy 2:26 – 3:11. Read these verses, for they are an easier account to follow!*
3 *What was the secret of Israel's success on this occasion (see verse 34, and Deuteronomy 2:30-36)?*

These victories over Sihon and Og were recalled as especially significant to Israel (see Psalms 135:11; 136:19-20). What special events do you recall, when God has acted on your behalf? Praise him for them, as Israel praised God for these victories!

2. To curse, or not
Numbers 22 – 24

At one level, this is an amusing story.

Balak, king of Moab, hires Balaam, a prophet from Mesopotamia (22:5), to put a curse on Israel for him. But things don't go quite according to plan...

1 *When you have read the whole story, concentrate on Balaam's oracles about Israel (23:7-10, 18-24; 24:3-9, 15-19). List the promises to Israel in these oracles.*
2 *God's original promise to Abraham contained three elements: land (Genesis 12:1; 13:15), descendants (Genesis 12:2; 13:16) and a special covenant relationship with himself (Genesis 12:3; 17:7). In what ways are these promises restated here?*
3 *Israel faced more opposition before she occupied the promised land. How might these oracles have been an encouragement to the people?*
4 *Balaam carried out God's will – but you wouldn't regard him as a hero! No Israelite prophet would have prophesied in order to get money (see also 2 Peter 2:15; Revelation 2:14). Look at Matthew 7:21-23. What is the difference between service and obedience?*

3. Nearly there
Numbers 26 and 27:12-23; Deuteronomy 31:1-8

Numbers 26 starts with another census – in preparation for the battles ahead (26:2) and the division of the promised land (26:52).

1 *Read quickly through chapter 26. As you do, list the people who are said to have rebelled against God.*

Numbers has been full of people who

disobeyed God – but that didn't stop God keeping his promises. Can you think of times when God has been faithful to you, even though you haven't trusted him? Stop and praise him for them now!

2 *The other question to be settled was that of leadership, as Moses was forbidden to enter the promised land. Read Numbers 27:12-23; Deuteronomy 31:1-8 with this question in mind.*

Note: Numbers 27:21 'Urim and Thummin' – high priest used these to consult God (Exodus 28:30).

3 *From study 3 of last week, what sort of a man would you say was Joshua? How had he already shown signs of leadership and courage?*
4 *Joshua is told to be 'strong and courageous'. Jot down all the things you can find in these passages which might encourage him. How would these help a Christian today entering a new situation where leadership was called for?*

4. Defeat and vengeance
Numbers 25 and 31

1 *Chapter 25. What was the nature of Israel's sin?*
2 *What feature of this account shows how seriously the Lord took Israel's sin?*
3 *Read chapter 31 and notice how the command in 25:16-18 is fulfilled by the events recorded.*

Note: The severe treatment given to the Midianites seems harsh to us, but is typical of warfare in the ancient

Near East, and was then the normal practice which the Lord demanded of Israel (see Numbers 21:1-3; Deuteronomy 7:1-5). It was a means of destroying idolatry and the grossly immoral and even brutal practices that went with it. It also emphasized the horror of idolatry. For further reading, see *The Enigma of Evil* by J.W. Wenham (Zondervan, 1985), chapter 8.

4 *Idolatry is a desperately serious sin, and it happens whenever something else becomes more important than the Lord (e.g. material possessions – see Colossians 3:5; Matthew 6:24). How does what you read here change your estimate of the seriousness of idolatry (or worldliness) to God?*

If you want to take this further, John White's *The Golden Cow: Materialism in the Twentieth Century* (IVP, 1980) tackles the problem.

5. To go, or not...?
Numbers 32

Israel had defeated Sihon and Og (Numbers 21:21-35), but their lands lay east of the Jordan – outside the boundaries of the land promised to Abraham and his descendants. Yet it was here that some of the people of Israel proposed to settle.

1 *Verses 6-15. Moses likens their request to Israel's rebellion in Numbers chapters 13 and 14. What*

similarities are there between the two incidents?
2 *And what differences?*
3 *How far do you think Moses' anger at their request was justified?*

Note: 1 Chronicles 5 shows what happened to the Gadites, Reubenites and the half-tribe of Manasseh.

4 *Some commentators think that Reuben and Gad's refusal to settle in Israel meant they missed God's best for them, because they were attracted by immediate material prosperity. Do you agree? Is that a temptation you face in other ways (see e.g. Luke 18:18-25)?*

Weekend

1 *After a recap in 33:1-49, the rest of the book of Numbers deals with plans for settling in Canaan. Read through these chapters. What sort of society do they anticipate?*
2 *The one major event before the crossing of the Jordan was the death of Moses, and the commissioning of Joshua as his successor. You can read about these in Deuteronomy chapters 31–34, and Joshua chapter 1.*
3 *The wilderness wanderings – told with painful realism – are part of the story of faith, outlined vividly by the writer of Hebrews chapter 11. Read this chapter and look back over your notes of the last two weeks with this theme of faith in mind. How does your own 'story' fit in with this momentous story of faith? Let the encouragement of Hebrews 12:1-2 sink into you.*

Part Four/Week Five
Law (A word study)

The word 'law' has a bad press with Christians – perhaps because it tends to be associated with legalism, and we know that both Jesus and Paul condemned legalism. But is 'law' a bad thing? Or is it applicable only in Old Testament times, and no longer relevant today? Read on and find out....

The word 'law' is used in several different ways throughout the Bible – even having different meanings in one passage. Look out for this throughout the week. If you have time to do some preliminary research, read the article on 'law' in a Bible dictionary, or the article 'The Commandments' in the *Lion Encyclopaedia of the Bible* (1978), pp.132-133.

1. Given for God's people
Deuteronomy 4:44 – 6:25

At the heart of this passage is the idea of the covenant (5:2), the special relationship between God and his people. It is a bit like a treaty between a powerful king and a weaker state. In the ancient Near East such treaties would contain
■ a history of the relationships between the two states;
■ promises by the powerful king to protect the weaker state;
■ a list of conditions to be fulfilled by the weaker state;

■ the penalties for breaking the treaty.

Israel has already experienced God's protection (5:6), and so stands in a special relationship with God. This passage tells how that relationship can continue.

1 *As you read the passage, make three lists:*
(a)what God has already done for Israel; (b)what he promises to do in the future; (c)what the people of Israel are to do.
2 *The people are told to pass on these laws to their children (6:7). Imagine yourself in their place; from these chapters, how would you explain to a child why he or she should obey God?*
3 *Why do you obey God? How similar are your reasons to those you have found from this passage? Are there any differences?*

Notes: 4:44-49 – see Numbers 21:21-35. 5:2 Horeb was another name for Sinai.

2. Precious to God's people
Joshua 1:1-9; Psalm 19:7-14

To the Jews, the Law or Torah consisted of the first five books of the Old Testament. Thus it was more than just a set of rules – it also contained some of the history of

God's dealings with his people Israel.

1 *Read Joshua 1:1-9. How would you describe the importance of the law to Joshua?*

Now go on to read Psalm 19:7-14. Use verse 14 as a prayer, before going on to read the verses again (several times) slowly and meditatively. Think about the passage for yourself, before going on to these questions.

2 *Make a list of all that the psalmist says the law means to him. Try to explain each point in your own words.*
3 *How does that match up with your appreciation of God's law?*

In verses 12-13 the psalmist is concerned that God's law should affect the way he lived his life. How far is that your concern? Use these verses to pray for yourself.
    Psalm 119 — the longest psalm — is an extended meditation on the law of God. Read some, or all, of it to see how much the law meant to the psalmist.

---

3. The law's limitations
Romans 7:7–8:4

The law is one of the major themes in Paul's letter to the Romans. Some Jewish people thought that keeping the law was the most important thing God asked of you. They thought that it put you in a right relationship with God – whereas, in fact, keeping God's law expressed a loyalty to his covenant (Exodus 20:6). The children of Israel had been chosen as God's covenant people – they did not

earn that right by keeping the law (Deuteronomy 7:7-9).
    Some Christians mistakenly thought that all of Christ's followers, whether or not they were Jews, should keep the Jewish law, as well as believing in Jesus. Paul says quite clearly that this isn't correct – because righteousness (a right standing before God) cannot come through law-keeping, as no one manages to keep the law perfectly (Galatians 2:16; 3:10). Instead, righteousness comes through faith in Jesus, and those who have faith are beyond the condemnation of the law. But that leads inevitably to the question, 'Does that mean that the law is a bad thing?'

1 *Read the passage carefully, and then try to decide whether the following statements are true or false. Give reasons, and say which verses are relevant.*
A. The law doesn't give the right instructions.
B. Knowing what's right is easy; doing it is more difficult.
C. The law makes you sin more, not less.
D. The problem is not the law, but me.
2 *Do any parts of the passage ring bells with your own experience – perhaps verse 19?*

We all know how hard it can be to do what's right. But Paul's message is that God has solved our problem (see 8:1-4) – and that should encourage thanksgiving as you turn to God in prayer now!

---

4. Jesus and the law
Matthew 5:17-48

Paul's teaching on the law has led some Christians to think that the law applied only to the Jews in Old Testament times, and is no longer valid. But what did Jesus think about the law?

1 *From verses 17-20, how would you answer those who think the law has no relevance today?*

The Pharisees were noted for their meticulous observance of the law, but in their efforts to apply it to the society of their day, they ran the danger of distorting its original meaning. In our passage, the clearest example of that is in verse 43 – the Old Testament does not contain a command to hate your enemies!

2 *How might the Pharisees have reacted to Jesus' teaching in verses 21-48?*
3 *What principle do you think Jesus is teaching by his interpretation of these commandments?*
4 *Many people see Jesus' teaching here as an example of the new covenant promised by Jeremiah (see Jeremiah 31:31-34) – not external rules, but a radical obedience from the heart, in all situations. Do you allow God's commands to affect you in this way, or do you merely observe the external conventions in Christian living?*

5. The law and the Christian
Romans 6:15-23; 13:8-14

The New Testament is clear on two points – first: that you can't be put right with God (made righteous) by keeping the law; and second: that

Jesus didn't abolish the law, but fulfilled it, both by keeping it himself, and by being the one to whom the law looked forward.

> *The climax was his death on the cross in which the whole ceremonial system of the Old Testament, both priesthood and sacrifice, found its perfect fulfilment. Then the ceremonies ceased. Yet, as Calvin rightly comments, 'It was only the use of them that was abolished, for their meaning was more fully confirmed.'*
>
> John R.W. Stott,
> *The Message of the Sermon on the Mount* (IVP)

Thus for the Christian, law-keeping does not involve observance of all its rituals – but that does not mean the law has no relevance for Christian living.

1 *Romans 6:15-23. You can imagine the question – if we don't have to keep the law to be right with God – if it all depends on grace – why not sin and enjoy it? God would forgive us anyway.*
2 *What does Paul say in this passage are the results of sin?*
3 *Why then should Christians live holy lives?*
4 *Romans 13:8-14. What further reasons can you find here for holiness?*

Note: In verse 9, Paul is not saying that love is an excuse for breaking the commandments; rather he is pointing to a wider interpretation of them, as Jesus did in Matthew 5.

Christians have much to learn from

from the Old Testament law. For further reading, see *An Eye for an Eye* by Christopher Wright (IVP, 1983) – on the relevance of Old Testament ethics today.

Weekend

1 *Look back over your notes. Try to sum up what you have learnt about 'law' from each study in turn in one or two sentences. Can you write one definition of 'law' from this – or does the word have different connotations in different parts of the Bible?*

2 *If you didn't read Psalm 119 in study 2, find time to read some of it this weekend.*

3 *Read through Paul's letter to the Romans, looking out for all the references to law. Each time you find it, try to see in what sense the word is being used – it usually refers to the Old Testament law, but it can mean other things (e.g. Romans 7:21). As you go, make a list of all that you learn about the word.*

The book of Joshua, 1 (A detailed study)

Moses was dead. It was Moses who had led the people out of Egypt and through the wilderness, but he was not permitted to take them into the promised land of Canaan. Joshua was to undertake that task.

He had served a lengthy apprenticeship. He had figured frequently in the wilderness (see Exodus 24, 32 and 33) and along with Caleb, was the only surviving adult of this period because these two had recommended advancing into the promised land when many had rebelled (see Numbers 14–30). Though God had promised them the land of Canaan, the Israelites still had to fight to enter into that promise.

For us, this book contains graphic lessons about spiritual warfare and claiming the promises God has prepared (compare Hebrews 4 and 12:8-11).

1. 'Be strong...'
Joshua 1 and 2

God is not limited to one person or strategy. The Israelites must learn that although Moses is dead, God will still continue to lead them, but through Joshua. Joshua's earliest tasks are to prepare the people to enter into the promised land (Joshua 1–5:12).

1 *What commands must Joshua obey? And what reassurances does he have for the assignment ahead? Pause to pray for any you know facing a daunting task.*
2 *Imagine yourself in Rahab's position and note down all the different pressures she would have experienced. What were the hallmarks of her character (see Hebrews 11:31)?*
3 *What effect did her faith have on the spies and Joshua?*

Memory verse: 'Do not let this Book of the Law depart from your mouth; meditate on it day and night, so that you may be careful to do everything written in it. Then you will be prosperous and successful' (Joshua 1:8).

How careful are you to allow God's Word a central place in the way you order your life? Then pray that, like Joshua, your life may be based on God's Word.

Note: Joshua 1:12-18 These tribes choose to settle on the east bank, but cross the Jordan to aid in the conquest of the west.

2. The crossing of the Jordan
Joshua 3 and 4

The river was swollen in flood and the promised land stood on the other side of it. The people were neither dismayed, nor did they try to bridge it by their own ingenuity. Instead, God gave Joshua the answer.

1 *List the three actions the Israelites had to perform before they could cross the Jordan (Joshua 3:5,6,13). In each case what was the significance?*
2 *Two piles of stones were built. One was where the priests stood on the east bank, the other was at the base camp on the west. Write down the reasons why these memorials were constructed.*
3 *In what ways was the crossing of the river so significant in establishing Joshua as Moses' successor (read Exodus 14:21)?*

Some events in our lives stand out as 'piles of stones' – testimonies of God's faithfulness and a promise of his future love. What 'piles of stones' are there in your life? Thank God for the events which demonstrate his care for you.

Notes: 3:4 The ark of the covenant which contained the tablets of law. 3:16 This happened again in 1927!

3. A holy war
Joshua 5 and 6

Soon after the construction of the stone memorials, God gave another type of memorial, that of the circumcision and the Passover. Circumcision was a sign of the covenant which God made with Abraham (see Genesis 17:1-14). During the time in the wilderness this had not been observed. The Passover recalled the flight from Egypt (see Exodus 12:1-27). Militarily, it was folly to wound your entire army and then celebrate the Passover, but God's wisdom is not the wisdom of the world.

1 *What was the significance of these two acts on the very eve of battle?*
2 *Put into your own words the importance of Joshua's action in 5:13-15.*

The manna stopped (see Exodus 16). There was no way back into the wilderness. The time of preparation was over and the enormous city of Jericho lay at their entrance to the promised land. By gaining it their tactic would be to cut a wedge into the land and then spread out. Take a look at the map opposite.

3 *What qualities did the Israelites demonstrate during the fall of Jericho? In what ways are they worth imitating? How aware are you that Christians are involved in a spiritual battle? How do you fight in this battle? Use 2 Corinthians 10:3-4 and Ephesians 6:10-18 to see how this applies to you.*

Pray that you will know God's power in the battle and be willing to be on the attack.

4. Sin and defeat
Joshua 7 and 8

Even in the midst of their triumph at Jericho, Achan succumbs to temptation and the people to pride. God requires obedience and the disobedience of even one person affects everyone.

Israel in the time of Joshua

1 *Make a list of the reasons why the Israelites failed to conquer Ai. What remedial action was necessary before Ai could be won?*

Can you recall an incident when the sin of an individual has had a bad effect on a larger group? This can sometimes be the cause of a lack of growth in a church. Pray for your own church in the light of this.

2 *Why is it so important to deal with sins as they occur in your life (Isaiah 59:2; 53:5)?*
3 *Note down the principles for success which emerge from this incident. How did the response of the Israelites to the victory at Ai differ from their response at Jericho (Joshua 8:30-35)?*

Pray that you will learn to keep short accounts with God, being quick to confess your wrongdoings. Is there any need for confession in your life right now?

Notes: 7:14 The guilty party was discovered by sacred lot, the exact procedure of which is unknown. 8:33 The mountains form a natural amphitheatre.

---

5. The southern campaign
Joshua 9 and 10

God promised the Israelites in Deuteronomy 7:1-6 that he would drive out the nations before them. Even though they knew this the Israelites were prepared to make a treaty with Gibeon. Consult the map whilst you read these chapters.

1 *How were the Israelites deceived by the Gibeonites? What errors did the Israelites make?*
2 *Having discovered the deception, what two decisions did the leaders make (9:20-21)?*
3 *Though the oath was made without God's consent, he expected the Israelites to keep it. Read 2 Samuel 21:1-6 to see what happened when the oath was later broken.*
4 *There are no stereotypes as to how God acts. Write down the ways in which the defeat of the five kings differs from both the fall of Jericho and the taking of Ai.*

In what ways are you tempted to compromise? – e.g. the way you spend your time; the thoughts which fill your mind in an idle moment. Pray that God will protect you from making compromises, when he is willing to make you victorious.

Note: Jasher is a lost book of poetry about Jewish heroes.

Weekend

1 *Read chapter 11. Use a map to trace the course of the wars against the Northern kings. What was the basis of Joshua's success?*
2 *The expelled peoples of Canaan were treated very harshly by the Israelites. Use these references to work out whether this treatment was justifiable. Genesis 15:16; Exodus 9:12; Deuteronomy 9:4-5.*

What parallels can be drawn with the Christian life (Matthew 18:8-9)? *Knowing God* by J.I. Packer contains a useful chapter, 'Goodness and Severity', on this topic.

The book of Joshua, 2 (A detailed study)

Chapter 12 summarizes the entire campaign for the promised land, which lasted about seven years. The land was conquered in the sense that the major strongholds were taken, but much of it still had to be secured. God promised in Joshua 13:6 that he would drive out the remaining resistance and decreed that on the basis of this they should divide up the land between the tribes. But a new problem lay before them. They simply did not grasp what was theirs. Sometimes the opposition was too strong (Joshua 15:63), but mainly they couldn't be bothered and chose to extract tribute instead (Joshua 17:13). They opted for an uneasy peace and the pursuit of affluence instead of God's blessing. In our first study we see that Caleb stands in marked contrast to this attitude.

1. Possess your possessions
Joshua 14:6-15; 15:13-19; 16

1 *Using Joshua 14:6-15 and 15:13-19 together with Numbers 13:17-33, compile a character study on Caleb. Make a list of his strengths.*

Caleb's faithful example still speaks to us. If we have believed in Christ for the forgiveness of our sins then the crucial battle has been won, just

as the campaigns of the Israelites claimed the strongholds of the promised land. But what of the mopping up operation?

2 *Are there areas of your life where Christ is not fully in possession? Are you living as someone who belongs totally to the living God? Look up Galatians 5:22-25 and turn that into a personal prayer for yourself.*

Using your answer to question 1, pray that God will give you the sort of faithfulness which Caleb displayed.

2. Sharing out
Joshua 17–19

Chapters 16 and 17 record the inheritance allotted to Joseph's sons, but they proved to be easily deterred in the matter of clearing the Canaanites from the land.

1 *Read Genesis 48:11-20. Then read Joshua 17 and with the help of a map work out how this prophecy was fulfilled in the allotment of the land.*
2 *At Joshua 17:3 we read that a dispute arose involving Zelophehad's daughters. Look at Numbers 27:1-11 to see how decisions were made in this matter. What decisions are you facing now*

*or in the near future? Have you
'brought your case before the Lord'?*

At the beginning of chapter 18 the
Israelites move permanently from
Gilgal to Shiloh. Here the land
allocation of the seven remaining
tribes is made as described in
chapters 18 and 19.

3 *What are the attitudes of the
Israelites displayed in Joshua 18:1-10
which Joshua seeks to correct? Are
you ever slow to act on God's
command?*

3. Cities
Joshua 20 – 21

The Levites, who were the priestly
tribe, were to be given cities rather
than a share of the land. There were
to be 48 in all of which six were to be
cities of refuge.

1 *Find out why the Levites were not
given a division of the land using
these references. Joshua 13:14, 33;
Numbers 3:1-13; 18:21-24; 35:1-3.
Think of some reasons why it would
be useful for the religious leaders to
be dispersed amongst the tribes.
This could be a case of being a 'light
in the world' (Matthew 5:14-16). Is
that something you strive to be?*
2 *Fill in some of the details about
the cities of refuge by reading
Numbers 35:6-34 and Deuteronomy
19:1-14. Would fleeing to a city of
refuge be of any help to a murderer?
Who would be helped in such a
place?*

Meditate on Joshua 21:44-45. Can
you say the same about your life?

4. A misunderstanding resolved
Joshua 22

The map called 'The land shared out'
shows that three tribes settled on the
east side of the Jordan. After helping
to conquer the western side they
returned home. Fearing that they
would be forgotten they built a
second altar, but their symbol of
solidarity is misinterpreted by the
western tribes and a dispute arises.

1 *List the reasons given for building
a second altar.*
2 *Why did the western tribes object
to it? Was their anger justifiable? See
Numbers 25:1-9.*
3 *Happily, diplomacy prevents
bloodshed. What can you find that is
commendable on both sides in the
way this internal trouble is settled?*
4 *Disputes sometimes arise in
churches. What lessons can you
draw from here as to how to deal
with them?*

The Israelites on the west bank acted
with *holiness* (by being prepared to
stand up for God) and *love* in
attempting correction and
reconciliation, instead of just
marching off to civil war. Pray that
you will be able to apply these twin
qualities in everyday situations, *e.g.*
in coping with those with whom you
disagree.

5. Will you serve the Lord?
Joshua 23 – 24

A lengthy time of stability follows the

The land divided

0 10 20
Scale of Miles

PHOENICIANS

Asher

Naphtali

Zebulun

BASHAN

Issachar

Manasseh

Manasseh

Ephraim

Gad

Dan

Benjamin

AMMON

PHILISTINES

Judah

Reuben

Simeon

MOAB

EDOM

133

division of the land. Joshua has reached the end of his long life and has no single successor to follow him. Instead he summons all the leaders and charges them with remaining faithful to God, who has already proved his faithfulness to the people.

1 *What reasons does Joshua give the people for continuing to trust God for their future well-being?*
2 *Write down the conditions necessary for the people to continue to receive God's blessing.*
3 *What choices does Joshua say the people must make?*

Throughout this book the people have at various times had to choose between following God and taking an easy way out. We too have to make these choices. Can you recall any such choices you have made in the past year? Pray that God will give you the strength to make wise choices, echoing Joshua's words: 'But as for me and my household, we will serve the LORD' (24:15).

Notes: 24:9-10 See Numbers 22. 24:12 A dramatic way of describing how God threw Israel's enemies into a panic.

Weekend

1 *Use your notes on the last fortnight to compile a character study on Joshua. What do you think he would have been like to meet?*
2 *Joshua 22:5 is a model for living. Write out this verse, breaking it up into individual sections. Take time over each section and write down ways in which it affects your life now and could do so in the future.*

Part Four/Week Eight
Authority (An issue study)

The question of authority exercises the minds of many people today. We are often unsure as to the source of ultimate authority, whom we should obey, and the degree to which we should be obedient. What is more, society is unclear where to turn for authoritative guidance on the major issues of life. The final authority on all questions of ultimate value must be God himself. And God's will is expressed in the Bible and supremely in the Lord Jesus Christ himself to whom the Bible bears witness (John 5:39). For that reason, our first two studies are concerned with the Bible and Christ; then we shall go on to the derived authority of the state, the church and the home.

1. The final authority: Scripture
Psalm 119:1-16

The whole of Psalm 119 describes the attitude of a devout Old Testament believer towards the Scriptures. He delights to speak about them and to see how he can apply them practically to his life.

1 *Throughout the passage the psalmist tells us how he approaches God's Word. Read through these verses and then write down the possible ways and attitudes of mind with which one can approach the Scriptures.*

Note: Almost every line in the psalm contains a synonym for Scripture, such as 'law' (verse 1), 'testimonies' (verse 2), 'ways' (verse 3), 'precepts' (verse 4).

2 *Make a note of all the benefits for the reader who tries to put God's Word into practice obediently.*

Ask the Lord to give you the same delight in his Word as the psalmist experienced. We have an advantage over the psalmist for we have the whole of the Bible as our guide. Pray also that you might be obedient to what God tells you in the Word.

If you have difficulty accepting the authority of Scripture, try reading *The Authority of Scripture* (IVP) or *God's Book for God's People* by John Stott (IVP, 1982) for some approaches to solutions.

2. The authority of Jesus
Matthew 7:24-29; Ephesians 1:15-23

One of the things which is noticeable in a reading of the gospels is the sheer authority and grip of Jesus, shown in his power over demons (Mark 1:22,27) and his powerful and authoritative teaching. He himself assumed this authority as of right and expected to be obeyed.

1 *Matthew 7:24-29. Consider the consequences of obedience and disobedience. Do you see the outcome quite so dramatically as is stated here? What degree of authority do you give to the teaching of Jesus in practical ways in your day-to-day life?*

Note: The Sermon on the Mount contains much of Jesus' most memorable teaching. Today's passage from Matthew is the concluding part.

2 *Read Ephesians 1:15-23. Write down the specific things Paul wants his readers to know about the Lord Jesus Christ – in particular his complete and total authority now over every competing power or authority throughout the universe.*
3 *Use Paul's words to help you pray that God might reveal to you parts of your life where deep down Christ does not have authority, e.g. in your home, your studies, or a relationship. Pray also for any friends who may have similar issues facing them.*

3. 'Give to Caesar...'
Romans 13:1-7; 1 Peter 2:13-17; 1 Timothy 2:1-4

All Christians are citizens of two kingdoms: one is the kingdom of God and the other is the secular state to which we belong. Both Paul and Peter urge obedience to the state, though sometimes loyalty to it may conflict with our loyalty to God (Revelation 13).

1 *In today's passages, what reasons are given for obedience to the state?*
2 *Do you find any practical*
difficulties or unwillingness on your part to comply with the exhortation of Romans 13:7? Do you find it hard to give respect or honour to those in authority?*
3 *How would you use these verses to answer someone who says, 'You only worry about the law if there is a chance of getting caught.'*

Pray that your attitude to those in authority might be such as God wants it to be. Read 1 Timothy 2:1-4 and use it as a basis for prayer for your own country and its authorities.

4. 'Obey your leaders'
1 Peter 5:1-7; Hebrews 13:7, 17

Some of us see our church leaders as austere, authoritarian figures. Today, however, probably more of us are unsure as to the exact amount of authority that leaders and ministers within the church should be allowed to exercise, and where their authority begins and ends.

1 *Read through 1 Peter 5:1-7 and then Hebrews 13:7, 17, trying to put yourself firstly in the position of a church leader and then of a church member.*
2 *Try to work out what Peter and the writer of Hebrews have to say particularly to your own church.*
3 *What sort of attitude does God expect from leaders? And what sort of attitude does he expect from church members or members of the Christian Union?*

Memory verse: 'Instead, whoever wants to become great among you must be your servant, and whoever wants to be first must be slave of all. For even the Son of Man did not come to be served, but to serve, and to give his life as a ransom for many' (Mark 10:43b-45).

Pray for your immediate church leaders that God might enable them to exercise their authority wisely and with integrity. Pray also for a right attitude towards them on your part.

> Leaders are meant to be facilitators not despots. Their role is essential. But they must use their authority in the way Jesus did. And they must never forget that while (like all of us) they have a line to heaven, unlike Jesus they are open to the wiles of the devil. Such leaders are needed to guide God's people along the disciplined road of freedom.
>
> John White and Ken Blue, *Healing the Wounded* (IVP)

For further reading, see Jerram Barrs, *Shepherds and Sheep* (IVP, 1983).

---

5. 'Dear Mom and Dad...'

Ephesians 5:21 – 6:4; 1 Peter 3:1-7

> It is well known, of course, that marriages are falling apart all around us... There are numerous reasons for the present instability in marriages, but undoubtedly one source of the problem concerns the lack of care with which many marriages are put together.

> Gary R. Collins, *Christian Counselling* (Word)

Family relationships need real care. In today's passage from Ephesians read how Paul urges his readers to examine their attitudes to each other!

1 *Note down what responsibilities and attitudes he commands for different members of the family.*
2 *Take stock of your own family situation. Think about how issues of authority and responsibility are handled by you. Reassess the present situation in terms of Paul's words. How much are you allowing Scripture to mould your thinking, and how much is conditioned by the way everyone else thinks and acts?*
3 *1 Peter 3:1-7. What kind of attitudes is Peter expecting from husbands and wives?*
4 *Make a note of any parts of your family life where you need to take responsible authority. Are there areas which call for a greater degree of submission or obedience?*

Pray for wisdom to deal with any delicate action which your study today may have indicated.
  Chua Wee Hian's '*Dear Mum and Dad...*' (IVP UK) is helpful reading.

Weekend

1 *The book of Deuteronomy represents the words of Moses to the people of Israel before they crossed the river Jordan to enter the Promised Land. In it he gives authoritative teaching from God on how they are to live in obedience and submission to God's will. Read through Deuteronomy chapters 5–8 and reflect on how God's blessing* was conditional upon Israel's submission to God's authority. See how this theme is powerfully emphasized also in chapters 28–30. Do you see evidence of God's 'cursing' or judgment in your own society?

2 Look through a newspaper and remind yourself of all the ways in which authority is being undermined in our world. Use this reminder as a spur to pray for a rediscovery of God's authority and his laid-down means for the exercise of authority.

3 Read through Revelation chapters 1–3 and ascertain why some of the churches were under God's judgment and others commended. How far do you think their failures and successes is an issue of authority?

Healing the Wounded by John White and Ken Blue (IVP, 1985) deals with the whole question of church discipline.

Part Four/Week Nine
Paul's letter to the Colossians (A whole book study)

Most people would agree that the church at Colossae had one or two problems. In Colossae the church seems to have been exposed to a form of teaching called Gnosticism which combined elements of Judaism and other more exotic religions. What was actually being taught can only be deduced from what Paul advises the Colossians, especially in chapter two.

Epaphras, and not Paul, had been the founder of the church at Colossae (Colossians 1:7) but Paul still felt a real pastoral burden for them. As well as giving them a lot of concrete practical advice, he provides them (and us) with one of the most breathtaking visions of Christ in the whole of the Bible. Doctrine and application go beautifully together. It may be that he wrote to them at the same time as he wrote to the Ephesians, during his imprisonment in Caesarea or Rome. This may account for some of the similarities in the two letters. It is helpful and interesting to keep looking at Ephesians whilst reading Colossians.

...doctrine and practice are so intimately related and connected that they must never be divided; Paul cannot deal even with the most practical matters except in the light of doctrine ... Our conduct must always arise from and be dictated by and controlled by our doctrine.

D.M. Lloyd-Jones, *Darkness and Light* (Baker)

For further information on the background to Colossians you might like to consult *The Illustrated Bible Dictionary Vol 1* pp.304f.

1. Praying for strangers
Colossians 1:1-14

Although he knew Ephesus and had been in the area for a long period of time (Acts 19:10), Paul did not apparently know the Colossian Christians personally. So when he comes to his usual opening prayer, he has to pray in a much more general way than is his custom. For this reason Colossians 1:3-14 might be helpful as a 'pattern prayer' for when *we* pray for those we may not know very well – missionaries, for example.

1 *Make a list of all the points of thanksgiving with which Paul begins his prayer.*
2 *Paul prays for specific spiritual qualities to be evident in the lives of the believers. What are they?*
3 *Rather than praying now for*

139

yourself, think of two people –
Christian leaders, missionaries or
believers from another country –
whom you do not know personally.
Make use of what you have learnt
from today's study to pray
meaningfully for them. Paul himself
requested the prayers of the
Colossians so that his own ministry
might be fruitful (4:2-4).

4 You might find it helpful to look at
similar prayers of Paul found in
Ephesians 1:1-23 and 3:14-21. Can
you use these passages in praying for
other people?

2. First place in all things
Colossians 1:11-23

Thanksgiving and prayer lead
naturally to worship. Paul soon finds
himself reflecting upon the glories of
Jesus Christ. This passage is one of
the most beautiful hymns to Christ to
be found anywhere.

1 Begin by reading the passage
through twice and marvelling at the
great things God has done for us in
Christ. Consider his great and
awesome majesty.

2 The passage is something of a
compendium of truth about the
Person of Christ. What does the
passage tell us about
(a)his relationship to God the Father
(b)his relationship to creation
(c)his relationship to the church?

3 Following on from that, what
precisely has Jesus done for us (see
especially verses 12-14 and 20-22)?

4 How does all of this affect our
daily lives (verses 22-23)?

5 The most appropriate response to
this passage is worship. There is so
much material here which can be
used for personal worship. Try to
make some of the truths part of your
thinking as you go about your work
today.

> Reconciliation is a term we
> use quite commonly and in
> much the same way as people
> used it in Bible days. It means
> 'restore to friendship', 'make
> up after a quarrel'... In the New
> Testament redemption is
> deliverance on payment of a
> price and when men's
> salvation is concerned that
> price is the death of the Son of
> God.
>
> L. Morris, The Atonement (IVP)

3. Paul's pastoral concern
Colossians 1:24 – 2:19

Christianity is all about liberty:
freedom from sin, freedom to do
right. We are free to follow Christ
and experience true liberty in the
Father's service. The problem is that
we love to add external
requirements to our discipleship.
Paul was concerned for the
Colossians since it seems that they
were being influenced by teachers
who held to an early form of what
later came to be called Gnosticism.
For more information look up
'Gnosticism' in a good Bible
dictionary.

1 Look at verses 1:24–2:7. Let what
Paul writes act as a stimulus in
praying for any young Christians you
might know. Spend a moment or two
in prayer for them.

2 *Read through 1:24–2:19. A good part of Christian growth is to be experienced through appreciating what we already have. What is this, according to Paul (see especially 2:3,6,9-15)?*

3 *In 2:16-19 Paul warns the Colossian Christians against aspects of false teaching which they were facing. What kind of similar problems and deceptions do Christians face today? How does what Paul writes help us to combat them?*

the very practical lessons of today's reading.

4 *Ephesians 4:1–6:20 gives a very similar list though it is much longer. Read it through if you have time, or save it for the weekend. Are there any further lessons God has impressed upon you from your rapid reading?*

A good book upon the subject of personal holiness is *Overcoming Anger* (IVP, 1987). You might find it useful in tackling some of the issues in this study.

4. A new suit of clothes
Colossians 2:20 – 3:17

Paul now seeks to build upon what he has said before. Christians are people who have been to their own funerals (2:12,20; 3:3); they have also been raised from the dead (2:12; 3:1). His main teaching now could be summed up as 'Be what you are'.

1 *What would Paul say was the essential motivation behind Christian discipleship (see especially 3:1-4)?*

2 *He speaks of discipleship as if it were a matter of changing our clothing. In your notebook make a detailed list on one side of a page of the various habits that Paul commands the Colossians to 'take off'. On the other side list those desirable virtues we are encouraged to 'put on'.*

3 *How much does 3:14-17 characterize your daily walk with Christ? What do you need to do to make it a reality? Spend some time in meditation and prayer concerning*

5. Living with other people
Colossians 3:18–4:18

In Colossians Paul gives equal amounts of teaching on our relationship to God and our relationship to each other. It is often in the way we treat other people that our discipleship is really tested. In this last section Paul gives us a lot of insights into how we ought to act within our families, for example, but he also reveals his own feelings about others.

1 *Read 3:18–4:1. Although Paul is writing to a different society with different expectations of the family, what external principles does he lay down? In the light of this, do you need to examine your own family relationships more closely?*

2 *What other advice do you notice concerning relationships with other people?*

3 *As can be seen from any of Paul's letters, prayer is a most important factor in living as a Christian. What* can you learn from Paul's prayer request (4:2-4) and from the example of Epaphras (4:12-13)?

4 Read 4:7-17. In what ways does Paul express his care for others?

Weekend

1 Reread the whole of Colossians at one sitting. Try to treat it as a practical letter written to real people in a real situation. Get an overall grasp of what Paul is wanting to say and allow the Holy Spirit to bring back to your mind any particularly important lessons.

2 Read through Ephesians. In what ways is it different to Colossians?

3 Colossians 1:15-20 is an excellent passage to memorize.

4 If you want to delve deeper into Colossians, a good commentary would be N.T. Wright, Colossians and Philemon (Eerdmans, 1987).

Part Five

The Sermon on the Mount
Repentance and forgiveness
The first book of Samuel
2 Samuel 7
Paul's letter to the Philippians
Deuteronomy 7
Hope and fear
Some women in the Old Testament
The role of women

Part Five/Week One
The Sermon on the Mount (A detailed study)

Matthew chapters 5–7 are among the most well-known and well-loved chapters in the New Testament. They are often called 'The Sermon on the Mount', since Jesus preached them on a hill by the Sea of Galilee, perhaps near the start of his public ministry.

These are not merely the sayings of a great moral teacher, although they set out the highest ethical ideals. But they do give the characteristics which show those who belong to the kingdom of God, and those who do not. Christians are to be radically different in allegiance, priorities, thought life, spirituality and behaviour. In short, we are to take after our heavenly Father. High ideals indeed, and impossible without the perfect life of the King of the kingdom living in and through us!

1. Attitudes of Christian character
Matthew 5:1-14

'Beatitudes' is the title normally given to these verses beginning with 'blessed' or 'happy' (Latin, *beatus*). Another way of looking at them is as the Be-attitudes; the attitudes of being a Christian, or the behaviour suited to members of the kingdom.

1 *Verses 1-9. Go through the*
beatitudes one at a time. What do they mean? How should each attitude show itself in a believer's life?

Notes: Verse 3 'Poor' here does not mean having no possessions. It refers to spiritual poverty; needing the riches of God's help in our lives. Verse 4 'Those who mourn' are not the bereaved, but those mourning over sin and evil. Verse 5 Meekness does not equal weakness, but humility. Verse 7 The merciful, having experienced God's mercy, show it to others and receive yet more from God. Verse 9 Peacemakers are those who have first known peace with God.

2 *In which parts of your life are you aware of failure? If God is speaking to you through these verses about a wrong attitude spend a few minutes asking his forgiveness and his help in putting it right.*
3 *Verses 13-16. How are Christians to be salt and light in a tasteless and darkened society? What difference should and can we make?*

Ask God to make you effective in his service today.

2. Attitudes to piety
Matthew 6:1-18

145

1 *Verses 1-18. What warnings does Jesus give about piety, the appearance of being religious? Write down in your own words what you think is the general principle which he is trying to teach here.*

Note: Before the well-known Lord's prayer, Jesus tells the disciples, 'This is how you should pray'. In a similar passage in Luke 11:2 he says, 'When you pray, say ...'. So the prayer seems to be used both as it stands and also as a pattern for other prayers.

2 *Notice that the Lord's prayer begins with God and who he is – a good place to start in our prayers. What other patterns for prayer can you find here?*
3 *Read the Lord's prayer out loud, slowly and prayerfully.*

3. Attitudes to possessions
Matthew 6:19-34

1 *Verses 19-24. Is it right for a Christian to have possessions or wealth? What does Jesus mean by 'do not store up for yourselves treasures on earth'? How can you store up treasure in heaven?*
2 *Verses 25-34. What does worrying suggest about our attitude to God? How does Jesus show that God, as our caring Father, will provide all our needs? What condition is attached to these promises?*

Origen, one of the early church fathers, comments:

Ask for the great things and the little things will be added to you, and ask for the

heavenly things, and the earthly things will be given you as well.

3 *How many of us disobey verse 34! Is there anything causing you anxiety? Entrust it to God today, and let him do the caring for you.*

Memory verse: But seek first his kingdom and his righteousness, and all these things will be given to you as well (Matthew 6:33).

(When you memorize verses, always learn the reference as well.)

4. Attitudes to others
Matthew 7:1-12

In Charles Kingsley's *The Water Babies* the names of two characters, Mrs Doasyouwouldbedoneby and Mrs Bedonebyasyoudid, make an appropriate comment on these verses! Attitudes come before actions, and how we see and think of others affects the way we treat people.

1 *Verses 1-5. Notice that in verse 5 we are told that it is still important to take out our brother's 'speck'. 'Judge not' does not mean that we are to ignore the wrong in people as if it did not exist. But what does it say about our motives and the way we are to go about judging?*
2 *Is there anyone that you are wrongly judging or find it difficult to get on with? Why? How can you put verses 1 and 5 into practice?*
3 *Verse 6. No Jewish pagan would invite a person to a religious feast, or throw away consecrated sacrificial meat to scavenging dogs. It would be a useless waste. Can you think of a*

modern application of this for you today?

4 *Verses 7-12. Back to prayer again! How does Jesus encourage us here to be persistent in prayer?*

Note: The verbs in verse 7 really mean 'keep on asking... keep on seeking... keep on knocking'.

5 *How do you know that God hears your prayers? Will he give you anything you ask for? What are the 'good things' or 'gifts' in verse 11? Compare this with Luke 11:13.*

---

5. Attitudes to discipleship
Matthew 7:13-25

... if you and I want to be people who are whole-heartedly dedicated to God, who want to serve the Lord with all we have... then it must be in the power and under the leadership of the Holy Spirit of God. We need to be abandoned to Him, so that He can fill us and use us for His glory.

Michael Griffiths,
Take My Life (IVP)

1 *Verses 13-14. The Christian life is never promised to be a rose garden! Why do you think so many people opt for the wide gate rather than God's way?*
2 *Verses 15-20. Jesus seems to be teaching that it is possible to tell the difference between Christians and enemies of Christ. How? What constitutes 'good fruit' and 'bad fruit'? How can you cultivate good fruit in your life (see John 15:1-8)?*

3 *Verses 21-23. Being a part of the kingdom of heaven is not a matter of repeating a few religious words. Where did those in verse 22 go wrong? How can you 'do' the will of the Father (verse 21)?*

Use these words as a prayer:

> *Take my life, and let it be*
> *Consecrated, Lord, to Thee;*
> *Take my moments and my*
> *   days,*
> *Let them flow in ceaseless*
> *   praise.*
>
> *Take my will, and make it*
> *   Thine;*
> *It shall be no longer mine;*
> *Take my heart, it is Thine own;*
> *It shall be Thy royal throne.*

Frances Ridley Havergal
(1836-1879)

Frances Ridley Havergal's own inspiring example of discipleship is recounted in *Great Christians You Should Know* by Warren Wiersbe (IVP, 1986).

Weekend

1 *Read Luke's summary of the sermon in Luke 6:20-49; 11:1-13. This is slightly different from Matthew's. It may be that Luke selected other parts of the many things which Jesus said at that time, or that he was writing about a different occasion and set of sayings.*
2 *Look up the Sermon on the Mount in a commentary, e.g. John Stott, The Message of the Sermon on the Mount (The Bible Speaks Today series, IVP, 1978); D.M. Lloyd-Jones, Studies in the Sermon on the Mount (Eerdmans, 1971); R.T. France, The Tyndale New Testament Commentary on Matthew (Eerdmans, 1986).*

Part Five/Week Two
Repentance and forgiveness (A topic study)

'"Repent" belongs to the age of the soap-box preachers.'

'I'll never forgive him.'

'I could never forgive myself.'

This week we shall investigate the flaws in the statements above and explore in detail the following quotation:

> *The call for repentance on the part of man is a call for him to return to his creaturely dependence on God ... not just as a feeling sorry, or changing one's mind, but as a turning round, a complete alteration of the basic motivation and direction of one's life ...*

> *IBD, 'Repentance'*

1. Sin matters to God
Genesis 6:5-7; Isaiah 30 – 31

God longs that every man and woman should know and love him. He longs to forgive if only we will let him, by repenting of our sin. Yet he hates evil.

1 *Read Genesis 6:5-7 for one example of how intensely God hates evil. Have you ever thought what an insult it is to God that wickedness seems to prevail in our world? In a limited sense, do you grieve with*

God that this is the case?
2 *Accounts of God's anger are often tempered by evidence of his mercy. Isaiah's prophecy in chapters 30 and 31 is one such example. As you read these two chapters, write down (with verse references) all the sins of Judah and the characteristics of God's wrath and judgment on them. Similarly, note down all the evidence of his mercy and love.*

Isaiah had warned Judah not to attempt to enter an alliance with Egypt. This was not part of God's plan (Isaiah 20). Such a move meant that Judah was not trusting God for protection.

Notes: 30:7 Rahab = dragon. 30:33 Topheth = place of the departed.

3 *Despite Judah's sin and the judgment they deserved, God still offered them hope. In love he called them to repent. He still does that today. How would you explain this to someone genuinely interested in finding out about Christianity?*
4 *Take Isaiah 30:15 phrase by phrase, thanking God for its truth and being aware of the seriousness of its implications.*

2. Repenting together
Nehemiah 9:1-38; 10:28-29

We saw yesterday that God was

calling a people to return to him. Repentance is not just an individual act. Another occasion of this 'repenting together' is recorded in Nehemiah 8 and 9. You may remember that the people of Israel had returned from Babylon to rebuild the city walls of Jerusalem. When this work was completed there was a time of celebration, followed by a period of deep repentance.

1 *Read Nehemiah 9:1-38; 10:28-29. Write down the signs for which the people were seeking God's forgiveness. Were they personally responsible for all of them? Summarize what this says about corporate repentance.*

This is an area of the Bible's teaching which is often ignored today. Does it have any particular relevance to your own set of circumstances?

2 *Note down all that the people understood about God's mercy in forgiveness.*
3 *Being forgiven changes all sorts of things. What change of heart resulted from this act of repentance?*

Has a reluctance to change ever prevented you from fully knowing God's forgiveness?

3. Repenting alone
Psalms 6, 32, 38

The psalms often put into words what we ourselves want to tell God. When it comes to words of repentance, there is no shortage of psalms to help us. Seven in particular are known as the 'penitential psalms'. We shall look at three of these today, all traditionally

written by David. You could look at the others at the weekend.

Read Psalms 6, 32 and 38, out loud if possible, and try to answer the following three questions for each psalm (where applicable):

1 *David knows he needs to be forgiven. What effect does this knowledge of sin have upon his life?*
2 *Why does he believe God can and will forgive?*
3 *What are the results of knowing this forgiveness?*

Your own experiences may be very different from David's, but in the light of his understanding of God and his mercy, ask yourself these three questions:

■ Have I ever failed to realize the seriousness of sin? Am I even proud of my sin?
■ Is anything beyond God's forgiveness?
■ Have I failed to let God's forgiveness affect my daily life?

4. A heart of repentance
Luke 18:9-14; 15:11-24

Jesus taught the importance of turning from sin and receiving forgiveness which affected relationships with God and others too. Today we shall look at what he said about the attitude of those coming to God and needing forgiveness.

1 *Read Luke 18:9-14. In your own words write down the attitudes of these two men. How might an attitude of self-justification prevent*

you from knowing God's merciful forgiveness?

2 Turn to Luke 15:11-24. Read these verses through twice, putting yourself firstly in the shoes of the son and then of the father. What do you discover about the attitudes of each?

3 Then ask yourself these questions:
■ *Do I believe that on my own merits I don't deserve to be called a child of God and need forgiveness?*
■ *Am I committed to turning from unChristlike habits and lifestyle to get right with God?*
■ *Do I rejoice that while I was still far away, God came and accepted me?*

5. As we also forgive...

Matthew 18:21-35; Luke 23:32-34

'Forgive us our sins as we also forgive everyone who sins against us.'

Luke 11:4

If we know we have been forgiven then we shall be aware of how much we need to forgive others.

1 *Turn to Matthew 18:21-35. What attitude lay behind Peter's question of verse 21? Have you ever shared his expectation?*
2 *How would you summarize Jesus' parable in a few sentences? Can you think of a modern equivalent which relates to your own experience? e.g. have you felt bitter after being treated unjustly, yet you refuse to forgive someone else who has slightly wronged you? Let the words of verse 35 speak to you – then, if*

possible, put things right, today.
3 *Jesus himself was willing to forgive, despite being wronged. Read Luke 23:32-34. Pray that your attitude may become more and more like that of Jesus.*

> Forgive me Lord, for thy dear
> Son,
> The ill that I this day have
> done,
> That with the world, myself
> and thee
> I, ere I sleep, at peace may be.

From 'Praise God from whom all blessings flow'

At the end of each day, do you make a point of wiping the slate clean in your relationships with God, yourself and others? Think about it and act!

Note: The 'unforgivable sin' of Matthew 12:31-32 is never defined. Rather than being a specific sinful act, it is more likely to be 'the continuing blasphemy against the Spirit of God by one who consistently rejects God's gracious call' (*IBD*, p.522).

Weekend

1 *Read through the other four 'penitential psalms' – 51, 102, 130 and 143. What do these add to your thinking this week about repentance and forgiveness?*
2 *The apostle Paul majored on the subject of repentance only indirectly. Look up in a concordance all the references in the epistles (not just those written by Paul) to repentance and forgiveness.*
3 *On Sunday reflect on how important a place repentance is given in your church service. Should it have a more prominent place?*

The first book of Samuel, 1 (A historical study)

All the neighbouring tribes around Israel had kings. 'Give us a king to lead us,' the people cried to the prophet Samuel.

'You don't need a king,' replied Samuel. 'God leads you. A king will mistreat you. God never will.'

'Give us a king,' they cried again. 'We aren't a real nation without a king.'

The Lord heard them and told Samuel he would give them what they wanted.

1 Samuel tells the story of the origins of the Israelite monarchy and of their first two kings, Saul and David. The task of being God's mouthpiece through this transitional period falls to the prophet Samuel. Samuel gives his name to two books in the Bible, though he is not the author. He is the last of the judges and the herald of a new era.

Over the next two weeks, as we look at the characters of Samuel, Saul and David, you will be discovering three men who knew God and played important roles in the history of God's people. At times they set a marvellous example to follow. But at other times their lives are a warning of dangers any one of us could fall into. Pray that you will learn from both the good and the bad.

1. Samuel – 'given over to the Lord'
1 Samuel 1:1 – 4:1

The story of Samuel begins before he is born. For many years Hannah prays for a child and her perseverance is finally rewarded. In her gratitude to God Hannah gives Samuel to Eli the priest to be a minister at the tabernacle, the centre of Israel's worship. Samuel is brought up at a time when Israel's spirituality is at a low ebb and there is no prophet who regularly makes known God's Word.

1 *Make a list of the things which Hannah knew about God's character. In what ways did knowing God influence her life? Her faithfulness had a profound effect on the life of God's people. Reflect on how faithful you are prepared to be, however insignificant you may think you are in God's purposes.*

2 *Write down all the ways in which Eli and his sons offended God.*

Note: Read Leviticus 3:3-5 to see how the sacrifice should have been carried out.

3 *Describe Samuel's response to his calling by God.*

Pray that, like Samuel, you will be

compelled to speak out about what God is doing in your life.

You could read more about Hannah's prayer in *Daring to Draw Near* by John White (IVP).

2. The ark of the covenant
1 Samuel 4:2 – 7:17

The ark was the symbol of God's presence with his people. But they tried to use the ark as a lucky charm by taking it into battle against the Philistines. Disaster struck – they lost the battle and the ark with it.

1 *In what ways did the Israelites misuse the ark both in battle and at Beth Shemesh (6:19)?*
2 *Make a list of the occasions on which God shows his power and displeasure amongst the Philistines. How are the Philistines convinced that their afflictions are God's doing (6:7-13)?*
3 *Chapter 7. It took the nation a long time to recover from its foolishness but after twenty years there was a turning back to God. Describe how the Israelites demonstrated the genuineness of their repentance. In what ways is the second battle different from the first?*

The Lord is a holy God who cannot be used for our own ends. Pray that you will learn to take God on his own terms.

3. 'We want a king'
1 Samuel 8:1–10:8

Eli's sons could not be trusted to succeed him and Samuel discovers that the same could be said of his own family. This provides the elders of Israel with fuel in their clamouring for a king. It is not enough that God himself leads them through his prophets – they want to be like other nations.

1 *Wanting a king was not in itself wrong. (Provision had been made for one, see Deuteronomy 17:14-20.) Make a list of all the pointers to the wrong attitude to God which the Israelites showed.*
2 *Write down the ways in which having a king was going to be bad for Israel. Given this, why did God accede to their demands anyway?*
3 *Describe how God intervened in Saul's life to make his will known.*

Are you holding onto ideas which are not necessarily God's best for you? Pray that you will not accept second best in your spiritual life.

4. King Saul
1 Samuel 10:9 – 12:25

Samuel had privately identified Saul as king. Public recognition is yet to come. Though the people were rejecting God by wanting a king, he would not leave them to make such an important choice by themselves.

1 *When God calls he also equips. Describe how Saul is prepared for his new role.*
2 *Not everyone is convinced at first that Saul is the right man. What qualities does Saul's relief of Jabesh city show which confirm him as God's man?*
3 *Write down the warnings which Samuel gives about Saul's kingship.*

What must the people do to ensure God's favour?

Note: The historical survey in 12:9-11 refers to events recorded in Judges chapters 4–16.

Meditate on 12:24: 'Be sure to fear the LORD and serve him faithfully with all your heart; consider what great things he has done for you.'

---

5. Saul disobeys
1 Samuel 13 – 15

Saul's rallying of the people over the fate of Jabesh is an auspicious beginning to his reign. But soon Saul shows he is self-willed and not always so prepared to respond to God's leading. Under God's direction he musters an army but when it begins to disintegrate Saul's nerve cracks and he fails to wait the appointed period for Samuel.

1 Analyse what was wrong about Saul's stated desire to seek the Lord's favour (chapter 13).

2 Contrast the personalities of Saul and his son Jonathan. What made Jonathan so courageous? On the other hand, what made Saul such a flawed leader?
3 Write down what you can learn from Saul about outward religious observances masking an inner disobedience. Can you think of modern examples of this?

In what ways might you have 'sacrificed' when you should have obeyed (15:22)?

Weekend

1 Through the course of this week's studies the figure of Samuel has stood behind events. Reread the passages and compile a character study of the prophet. In what ways does he show true obedience to God?
2 Do you think he was ever tempted to disobey, such as when he discovered that his sons were not to succeed him? Did he ever give Saul a chance?
3 What sort of a person would he have been to meet?

Part Five/Week Four
The first book of Samuel, 2 (A historical study)

Saul was just the sort of man the people had in mind when they asked for a king. We shall see that when Saul disobeyed and God rejected his kingship, he became governed by his unpredictable and unstable temperament.

In this time of need God chose a new man. He was not a natural choice by the standards of the world, but by God's standards he was a man after his own heart. This does not mean that David does not sin. We shall see that he probably does follow God's guidance imperfectly and make compromises out of fear. Still, David proves to be a man motivated more by his desire to see God glorified than anything else.

1. Appearances can be misleading
1 Samuel 16 and 17

Samuel grieves long and hard over Saul's failure. Yet he is still responsive to God's command to seek out a new king. As with Saul, Samuel anoints David privately before he is publicly identified as God's choice.

1 List the reasons why Samuel was surprised by the choice of David.
2 Describe David's reasoning as he heard Goliath's taunts. How did he

use his past experiences of God to understand the present situation?
3 The Lord has left Saul to his own devices. What evidence can you find that his temperament is getting the better of him?

David's ability to confront Goliath shows how proving God's presence in daily life can be a preparation for major events. Pray that you will see God's hand in all your ordinary tasks and learn faithfulness through them.

2. Friendship and envy
1 Samuel 18 – 20

As David grew into manhood he made a lasting friendship with Jonathan and an enduring enemy of Saul. Saul could see that God had chosen David over him. In a fit of pique he tries to spear David. Then Saul's black mood takes a more subtle twist and he tries to get rid of David by setting a bride price which places him in extreme danger.

1 Describe how Jonathan and Michal demonstrated their love toward David. What risks did they take for him? How good a friend are you (1 Corinthians 13:4-7; 1 John 3:16-20)?
2 Make a list of all the attempts made by Saul on David's life. How

were these attempts foiled?

3 *Given that David so obviously had other friends at court, what made Saul treat him as an enemy? How has Saul changed from the early days of his reign?*

Jealousy – that green-eyed monster! Pray that you will allow God to control your emotions in circumstances where you are tempted to jealousy.

---

3. David the fugitive
1 Samuel 21–24

David is on the run. He flees Saul's court for Nob (the main shrine of the period) where he receives help from the priests. Saul is bent on a murderous course and in his fury massacres the priests for helping David.

1 *What evidence is there that David's journeys were based more on fear than guidance? Use the sketch map to help trace his route.*
2 *Make a list of David's reasons for not harming Saul when he gets the opportunity.*
3 *Saul weeps when he hears how David spared him. Does his relief lead to repentance? What does repentance involve? Mark 7:6-7 may help. Write down your answer.*

Pray that you will discern the difference between an outward keeping of rules and an inward love of God.

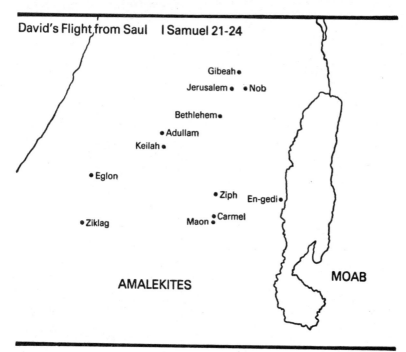

David's Flight from Saul   I Samuel 21-24

Gibeah•
Jerusalem • • Nob
Bethlehem•
• Adullam
Keilah •
• Eglon
• Ziph   En-gedi•
Maon • •Carmel
• Ziklag

AMALEKITES

MOAB

155

4. No short cuts to the throne
1 Samuel 25:1–28:2

Samuel dies without seeing David ascend to the throne. Neither Samuel nor David doubt that David will be crowned and he therefore resists two opportunities to speed things up.

1 *David had done Nabal a favour in the past, so he tries to ask Nabal for a favour in return. In the midst of great wealth what things does Nabal lack?*
2 *Describe what motivates David. What principles does he uphold in his dealings with Saul and Nabal?*
3 *In 27:1 David slips into a black mood and temporarily allows his circumstances to get the better of him. Does this mood lead David to compromise with Achish?*

Pray that you will learn the lesson of not taking things into your own hands, and wait for God's action.

---

5. The King is dead – Long live the King!
1 Samuel 28:3 – 31:13

Saul sinks so low as to consult a medium, something expressly forbidden in Leviticus 19:31. It is one of his final actions before his death at his own hands. By contrast, David extricates himself from his exile with the Amalekites. He demonstrates that the Lord is his shepherd in bad times and his champion in victory.

1 *God turned away from Saul. Reflecting back over his life, how could Saul have avoided the ignominy of spiritualism and suicide?*
2 *David is in the awkward position of being numbered amongst the Philistines. Describe how God gets him out of this difficulty.*
3 *Make a list of the new aspects to David's character you see in his pursuit of the raiding party.*

Pray that you learn to take comfort from the Lord in times of difficulty.

Weekend

1 *The story of David's reign is continued in 2 Samuel and in 1 Chronicles 11–29. Read through one or other of these accounts.*
2 *In what ways did his experiences of friendship, rejection and flight help prepare David for the kingship (see 1 Samuel 16–31)?*

Part Five/Week Five
2 Samuel 7 (A meditation)

In biblical meditation we allow ourselves to absorb what God is saying to us, particularly applying it by personal reflection to our own lives. We take time to think and pray, consciously quietening our minds and using our imaginations as well.

As we look at 2 Samuel 7, it is vital to bear in mind how different David's situation was to our own. None of us (probably) is a king. We live almost 3,000 years later in history, in the nuclear age. But God has not changed and neither has mankind. Try to discover what is eternally relevant to us in this chapter.

1. The Temple of the Lord
2 Samuel 7:1-17

David's motives were good. He wanted to do something for God in gratitude for God's leading and presence with him.

1 *What particular reasons do you have to thank God? The psalms are full of such reasons for gratitude (e.g. Psalm 23). Why not write such a psalm today which includes the particular reasons you have for thanking God? (You may want to leave this till the weekend.)*
2 *What was God's promise to David? Was it better or worse than David wanted? (Notice the different use of 'house' in verses 5 and 13 to that in verse 11.) Turn to 1 Corinthians*

3:16-17. According to Paul, what is God's temple now? Look as well at 1 Corinthians 6:19-20 and see how Paul modifies the picture.

Do you have any ambitions or dreams with respect to the building of these 'temples'? Turn these desires to prayer as David did. Ask God exactly what *he* wants *you* to do.

2. The Covenant, 1
2 Samuel 7:1-29

> *The Davidic covenant became necessary with the development of a new historical situation. The Israelite king was now the mediator between the Lord and his people. A covenant with this king became a necessity.*
>
> *IBD* 1, p.329

1 *As we saw yesterday, God often has much better plans for us than we could ever imagine. Read again 2 Samuel 7:1-17. Then continue to verse 29.*
2 *Make a note of the exact promises that God gave to David. Notice David's response in verses 27-29. Are there any promises of God which you need to pray to receive yourself?*
3 *You may not be able to think of many of God's promises to you, so turn to Paul's account of Christian blessings in Ephesians 1:3-14. Reflect*

on these promises. How far are these blessings only abstract truths and how far have you made them part of your very life?

4 The promises of God are all related to his word. It is the Hebrew for 'word' (dabar) which underlies 'promise', 'word' and 'spoken' in verses 21, 25 and 28 of 2 Samuel 7. Thank God that his word can be completely trusted and especially thank God for the promises and blessings found in his written word.

Read the article on 'Covenant' in the *Illustrated Bible Dictionary* 1, pp. 326-331, or in another good Bible Dictionary.

---

3. The Covenant, 2 – the love of God
2 Samuel 7:1-29

Ideas about love change from generation to generation and from culture to culture. In the Old Testament, God reveals himself much through the idea of 'covenant love' (Hebrew *ḥeseḏ*). Our nearest equivalent today is to be found in the marriage service, where love is seen in the context of a covenant/contract. Briefly note down what commitment in love is called for in a marriage.

1 *Read 2 Samuel 7:8-17. What characterizes God's ḥeseḏ – his covenant love towards David and his family (see especially verse 15)?*
2 *Consider how this love was shown throughout David's life and how he had been called. See how verses 18b and 19 compare with Psalm 78:70-72.*
3 *Turn now to 1 Corinthians 11:23-26 and meditate upon the giving of*

the new covenant. How much did it cost Jesus to forge this covenant with us?

Pray now to him in gratitude. Then read through David's response in verses 18-29.

4 *Think how you would explain God's love in similar terms of covenant-commitment to a non-Christian.*

---

4. The Covenant, 3
2 Samuel 7:1-17

Like our ideas of God's love, our ideas of fatherhood ought not to be limited to human ideas but formed by God's revelation of himself. The fatherhood of God is something taken for granted by many Christians today. Perhaps we don't appreciate what an extraordinary thought it is.

1 *Read God's promises to David and his descendants in verses 11b-16. Consider what a unique promise is being made at this point.*
2 *Jesus addressed his father as 'Abba' and encouraged his disciples to do likewise. Turn to Romans 8:15-17. How did we become sons of God? You could compare this with Galatians 4:6-7.*

Note: The Hebrew word for 'father' in verse 14 is *Ab*.

3 *All models of a human father are imperfect to a greater or lesser extent. So what does it actually mean to you to know God as father? Note down the various ways in which this affects day-to-day life.*

Use the Lord's Prayer as a means of

concentrating on God as your father. You will find it in Matthew 6:9-13, including the footnote for verse 13 in recent translations.

4 *To continue this theme, Floyd McClung's* The Father Heart of God *(Harvest House) and Tom Smail's* The Forgotten Father *(Hodder) are worth reading.*

5. Worship
2 Samuel 7:18-29

The only possible response to such promises of blessing was for David to bow down in worship.

1 *Read these verses and then make a note of the main reasons that David has for worship. It is not just empty rhetoric.*
2 *Notice his sense of unworthiness before God. Does your appreciation of God ever lead you to feel unworthy? Read Psalm 8 to see man in God's perspective. How far does confession of sin form part of your response to God?*
3 *What is the focus of David's prayer? Examine your own prayer life to make sure the focus is on God and not yourself.*

Make up your own prayer in response to what God has done in your life.

Weekend

1 *Write the psalm suggested in Study 1.*
2 *Find out about David's life from a good Bible Dictionary, or read Tom Houston's* King David *(Marc Europe, 1987).*
3 *Arising from Study 2, read the article on 'Covenant' in the IBD, pp. 326-331, or another good Bible Dictionary. Also, William Dyrness's* Themes in Old Testament Theology *(IVP) is worth reading all the way through, although there is a section on Covenant.*
4 *It is not a good idea to base your ideas of God on a hymnbook or chorus book, but find such a book this weekend and look through it. Note how much the hymns about God's love and God as a father are based on God's character as you have been meditating upon it this week.*
5 *For further ideas for how to meditate on God, try J.I. Packer's excellent* Knowing God *(IVP).*

Part Five/Week Six
Paul's letter to the Philippians
(A whole book study)

Paul writes to the church at Philippi with a special, tender regard. After all, he had been involved with its foundation. You can read about this in Acts 16:11-40. Paul was in prison at the time of writing yet this doesn't prevent the letter from being characterized by the overwhelming joy he knows through Christ's Spirit. There do not seem to be any big problems which Paul wishes to deal with, unlike in some of the other epistles, though there are one or two warning notes. Rather, he is writing for personal reasons, such as thanking them for their support and explaining Epaphroditus's return.

4 *Make a list of Paul's attitudes to life and death. What does this tell you about his priorities? How do your priorities compare with Paul's?*

> 'You meant this thing for evil, but the LORD wove it for good.'
>
> Joseph

Reexamine verses 3-11 and your answer to question 1. Pray for your own church today using this prayer as your example.

Note: ' saints' – a general word for Christians emphasizing how they are set apart for serving God.

1. 'Prayer with joy'
Philippians 1:1-26

Paul includes Timothy in his opening greetings as they were together when the church was founded. He begins with prayer for the church, full of love, hope, thankfulness and joy.

1 *Write down the requests which Paul makes to God for the people. What is the basis of his confidence in the future of these Christians?*
2 *In what ways can Christians be prepared for the 'day of Christ' (Christ's return)?*
3 *What are Paul's reasons for rejoicing, despite his circumstances?*

2. 'Complete my joy'
Philippians 1:27–2:18

Divisiveness is creeping into an otherwise thriving church (see Philippians 4:2). There may also be a suggestion that the church is going through a time of suffering (1:29-30). Paul tells them they must dispense with their pride and learn to think as one because of the example of Christ's humility.

1 *Make a list of the qualities which Christ displayed. How should his example affect our actions? What does it mean to 'work out your salvation'?*

160

2 *The Bible talks about salvation as a progression of becoming a Christian and then becoming more Christlike. What positive steps can we take to make sure that our lives are 'worthy of the gospel of Christ' (1:27)?*
3 *Write down the reasons Paul gives why Christians should be united. What power is available to us to achieve this?*

Pray for the preservation of unity in your own church. If there are any specific problems known to you, pray that these may be settled quickly. What action can you take to bring about greater unity, relying on the power available? (Be as specific as possible.)

The basic fact of all faith and fellowship is to own that Christ is Lord.

Notes: 2:6 'Form' – the nature of God, not just the appearance. 2:7 Christ became man but he did not lose any of his deity in so doing. 2:12 'Salvation' – God's rescue of man from sin and death through the death of Christ which paid the penalty for sin.

3. 'Rejoice in the Lord'
Philippians 2:19 – 3:11

After telling of the imminent return to Philippi of two old friends, Paul continues his advice on living the Christian life, using himself as an illustration. It's possible that Paul had heard of a group known as 'Judaizers' operating in Philippi. Paul is angry with this group because they argue that faith in Christ should be supplemented with Jewish observances such as circumcision.

1 *Even from this brief glimpse of Timothy and Epaphroditus you can see something of their characters. Using your answer to yesterday's question 2, write down which qualities and virtues these two men possessed.*
2 *What reasons did Paul have for 'confidence in the flesh'? Can you think of modern-day equivalents which people rely on instead of God? e.g. what gives you status among your friends and colleagues – qualifications? gifts? achievements? upbringing? good looks? relationship to Jesus?*

No-one can gain credit with God through their own achievements. The best of human behaviour means nothing when compared with the offer of life in Christ. Compare your own life to Paul's. Spend a longer time than usual in prayer and reflection today to see if you count everything as 'loss for the sake of Christ'.

> *He is no fool who gives what he cannot keep.*
>
> Jim Elliot

Note: 3:2 'dogs' – possibly the Judaizers.

4. 'My joy and crown'
Philippians 3:12 – 4:1

Becoming a Christian is one thing. Living, growing and standing as one is another. In our own strength it is impossible but God gradually renews us from within.

1 *Write down the factors which make you want to grow as a Christian. Then, from these verses make a list of those things which motivate Christians. What are our interests and expectations?*

2 *By contrast, what should be forgotten?*

3 *What sort of people are described in 3:19? In what ways are Christians different from them?*

How could these priorities affect your day-to-day behaviour? Take time to consider this seriously.

Helen Roseveare, a missionary doctor who survived a massacre of missionaries in the Belgian Congo, was greatly moved by 3:10-14. Read how she lived out these verses in her autobiography *Give me this mountain* (IVP UK). She wrote,

> Above all, I have learned a little of the tremendous privilege of walking with Him, of being identified with Him. Christ not only bore my sin; He was made sin for me. He identified Himself utterly with us sinners that He might redeem us. Now if He should seek a body, a vessel in whom to live, that He might identify Himself with the deepest needs and hungers of Congolese hearts, was I willing to be this vessel? More than willing! I entered into the great privilege of bearing about the One who had paid the supreme cost.

5. 'Again I will say, rejoice!'

Philippians 4:2-23

Rejoice! Rejoice! – amazing words from a man who has suffered persecution, torture, rejection and imprisonment! Most people would be bitter but Paul positively sparkles with joy. Today's study tells us his secret. He empties himself of his worries and allows God to fill him with his own strength. Paul doesn't dwell on the problems – he thinks of the opportunities.

1 *Read Philippians 4:2-23. What difference does it make to know God in your*
a)relationships with others
b)attitudes to plenty and poverty?
2 *In 4:4 Paul exclaims 'Rejoice'. Using 4:5-7, write out in your own words why Paul is able to be joyful.*
3 *Using one's mind plays a significant role in the Christian life. Write down all those things Paul tells us to think about. Why do you think it's so important to use your mind? What can God do for our thought life?*

Memory verse: Do not be anxious about anything, but in everything, by prayer and petition, with thanksgiving, present your requests to God. And the peace of God, which transcends all understanding, will guard your hearts and your minds in Christ Jesus (Philippians 4:6-7).

After learning these verses, put them into practice by thanking God, telling him about your anxieties and requests and then leaving them in his hands.

162

Weekend

1 *Philippians 2:6-11 are well-known verses. It is worth memorizing them or setting them to music. Do this and at the same time analyse them in depth using a commentary.*
2 *What is joy? Is it different from happiness? What is the source of joy? How do we become joyful? Begin to answer these questions using your notes from this week. Read through Philippians again and underline every mention of joy or rejoicing. You could look up 'joy' in a Bible Dictionary.*

3 *No man is an island.*
John Donne

May they be brought to complete unity to let the world know that you sent me.
Jesus Christ

What is life if you have not life together?

T.S. Eliot

Find out more about unity and fellowship by reading Bruce Milne's We Belong Together *(IVP).*

Part Five/Week Seven
Deuteronomy 7 (A meditation)

This is part of a speech Moses makes to the people of Israel before they enter the promised land of Canaan. He looks back and reminds them of the God they worship – the one who has led them throughout their wilderness journey and always kept his promises.

In this chapter he reminds them that God has saved and blessed his chosen people because he loves them; their response is to be one of love and obedience.

They lived many centuries ago. But their God is our God. His commitment to his church today is similar to the commitment he made to them. The principles underlying this speech apply to us in the twentieth century.

1. The Lord your God is God

1 *Read right through the chapter a few times. Try to put yourself in the shoes of the people of Israel. They have been wandering in the wilderness for forty years. At last the promised land is becoming a reality. Despite many hardships and times of rebellion, God has been faithful to them. Pick out three of God's promises to his people. Why would these promises have meant so much to them?*
2 *Take time to meditate and pray over each one – that is, identify the*

aspect of God's character that underlies each promise, then relate it to your life. Allow God's Spirit to open your heart to his love in your own situation.

2. Holy to the Lord
Deuteronomy 7:1-6

God took great pains to keep his people separate from the nations around them.

1 *Read right through the chapter again, if possible in another version of the Bible. Then refer especially to verses 1-6. How were the people of Israel to relate to these other nations? And why was this so?*
2 *What do these instructions indicate about human nature and God himself?*
3 *What action should you be taking to ensure that your life is pure and holy? For example, in what ways do your non-Christian friends or family distract you from serving God wholeheartedly? What idols are there in your life?*

Radical action may be called for!

3. His treasured possession
Deuteronomy 7:6-11

1 *Read verses 6-8 through several times and let them sink into your* very being. Revel in God's choice and his love for his people. Have there been occasions recently when you have tried to earn God's affection? Why is that such a misguided thing to do?

2 Look at the words in verses 9-10 which describe God. Think carefully about each one and then consider how these truths about God speak into your own circumstances. For example, God is utterly committed to keeping his side of a covenant, by loving his people whatever happens. How much do you actually believe that and behave in the light of it?

Pray for any you know who lack the certainty of God's unfailing love for them.

4. Blessings of obedience
Deuteronomy 7:11-15

1 What confidence should these promises have given the people of Israel? What conditions were there to the fulfilment of the promises? Write down all the examples you can think of where God's promise of blessing is conditional upon obedience to him, e.g. think back to Solomon (1 Kings 3:14).

2 Such a state of Utopia has never been realized on this earth, despite claims that are made over a short time. Disease has not been totally defeated (Deuteronomy 7:15); sin still exists. How far do you hold a balance between living triumphantly yet experiencing suffering, either for Christ (see 1 Peter 4:12-19) or just because we still live in a fallen world?

Pray for any you know who are suffering in some way, either because they are Christians, or as a result of sin, or for no apparent reason. Rejoice, too, with those who are experiencing God's blessing at this time.

5. Do not be afraid
Deuteronomy 7:16-26

1 Write down what specific fears you are harbouring in your heart.

2 The people of Israel were told not to be afraid. What were the grounds for this courage? Were they promised instant release from fear? And how conditional was this?

3 From these verses, consider what could be the keys to dealing with fear in your own life. For example, have you any past experience of God dealing with an adversary? Is any action called for on your part?

Spend time asking God to deal with any fears you have. They may be deep-rooted so you may want to find someone to talk with. Pray for courage to face up to the reality of your fears.

Weekend

1 In order to win the world for the Lord we need to be involved with people. How does God's command to his people in this chapter to be separate from their enemies relate to Jesus' commands to be salt and light in the world (Matthew 5:13-16)?

2 'The Lord hates idolatry' (verse 25). Do you think idol worship is a problem today? Refer back to the second study of this week. Can you think of any modern-day examples? Do you think worship of these gods would be 'fatal' (verse 16) today? What can we, as Christians, do about this killer?

3 Learn Deuteronomy 7:6-9 off by heart. Then you can meditate upon these verses even when you do not have a Bible to hand.

4 If you are able, write a poem that includes some of this chapter's themes.

5 To get deeper into the Book of Deuteronomy, The Tyndale Old Testament Commentary by J.A. Thompson (IVP) is excellent.

Part Five/Week Eight
Hope and fear (A word study)

Our century has probably witnessed more fear, anxiety and sheer hopelessness than any other – through the bomb, over-population, poverty, famine, new diseases. All these things, and more, lead people to the brink of despair and over it. Along with this goes a failure to grasp the real hope which God offers us in the Bible. But Paul lists hope as one of the things which will remain for ever (1 Corinthians 13:13). This week we shall see why.

1. 'Whom shall I fear?'
Psalm 27

From flying in an aeroplane to failing our driving test or an exam, many things make us afraid. There is nothing new or unusual about this – it's all part of being a human being and the Bible has plenty to say about it.

1 *Read Psalm 27. Make a note of what appears to be frightening the psalmist (verses 2-3). Write down the sort of things which cause you to fear.*
2 *Analyse the psalmist's remedy for this fear (verses 4-6). How far does any of this apply to you?*
3 *What do verses 7-12 indicate about the place and importance of prayer in dealing with fear? Where does your trust lie in overcoming these problems?*

Look up Philippians 4:6-7 (your memory verse in Part Five, Week Six) and ask for God's peace in each of the situations you noted earlier.

2. The beginning of wisdom
Psalm 111

> Oh how I fear thee, living God,
> With deepest tenderest fears,
> And worship thee with
> trembling hope
> And penitential tears.
>
> 'My God, how wonderful thou
> art'

The Bible urges us to fear just one thing – or rather person – God himself. This 'fear of the Lord' is regarded as the beginning of wisdom (Psalm 111:10; Job 28:28). But what does it mean?

1 *Read Psalm 111. On one side of your sheet of paper note down all the great and mighty things about God (see especially verses 2-4). On the other side list all the ways God acts with mercy towards mankind (especially verses 5-9).*
2 *How is it that the two sides come together? How far have your fears been magnified because you have failed to remember God's greatness?*

> [Hope] transforms man's anxiety about himself and his

167

*world, leaving him with only
this one fear, which is a
trembling adoration of the
transcendent Holy Lord.*

In A. Richardson (ed.), *A
Theological Word Book of the
Bible* (Macmillan)

Read Philippians 2:12-13. Use some
of the verses of Psalm 111 to worship
God, giving thanks that he has seen
fit to draw you to himself.

3. Hope for Christians
*Exodus 19:16-24;
Hebrews 12:18-29*

Hope for the Israelites in Egypt
consisted basically in escape from
slavery and entering the promised
land. The awesome God of the
exodus met with them at Sinai. For
an account of this encounter, read
Exodus 19:16-24.

1 *How was Israel's hope for her
future bound up with the fear of the
Lord in the present, as shown in
yesterday's study?*
2 *Turn now to Hebrews 12:18-29.
The writer clearly has the Exodus
passage in mind. In what ways does
New Testament hope differ from that
of the people of God in the Old
Testament?*
3 *What role does Jesus Christ have
to play in this (see especially verse
24)? Has God changed or have
circumstances changed? How?*

Some Christians fail to grasp the
basics of Christian hope. Maybe deep
down some of your friends are hopeless. Pray for wisdom in how to help
them through what you are learning

from this week's studies.

Try reading *The Message of
Hebrews* by R. Brown (IVP), which
will help you to trace how Jesus has
brought a new and living hope in the
new covenant.

4. A living hope
1 Peter 1:3-21

We live in a society that is
characterized by hopelessness.
People frequently lack meaning for
their lives, direction, security,
assurance and any feeling of being
wanted or valued (*cf.* 1 Peter 1:18).

1 *Read 1 Peter 1:3-12. On what
specific facts or events is Christian
hope based? In what ways do these
facts make a difference to the
hopelessness of life at the end of the
twentieth century? What sort of
results do you expect from such
hope?*
2 *Write down your hopes for the
future. How far are they similar to
those in this passage?*
3 *Read 1 Peter 1:13-21. What kind of
behaviour should Christian hope
produce? What indications are there
that God cares for you?*

*New Testament hope is a
patient, disciplined, confident
waiting for an expectation of
the Lord as Our Saviour.*

NIDNTT 2, p. 243

Memory verse: Therefore, prepare
your minds for action; be self-
controlled; set your hope fully on the
grace to be given you when Jesus
Christ is revealed (1 Peter 1:13).

5. Hope while we wait

Romans 8:18-39

Paul twice describes the Holy Spirit as an *arrabon*, which is translated variously as 'deposit' (*NIV*), 'guarantee' (*RSV*), 'pledge' (*NEB, JBP*), 'first instalment' (Living). It is as though God's gift of his Holy Spirit is a down-payment – promise of even greater things to come in the future. In Romans 8:23 he speaks of the Spirit as 'firstfruits'. So once again we find that Christian hope is not just 'pie in the sky when you die'. It is based on facts from the past (see yesterday's study) and on our present experience of the Spirit.

1 *Read carefully through Romans 8:18-39. Make a list of all the tangible things that Christians can hope for in the future.*
2 *How is this future hope related to the present with all its groaning, suffering and problems?*
3 *This passage naturally leads to praise, worship and thanksgiving. Turn the words of 8:28-39 into a prayer of your own. Write it down, expanding it to fit your own situation.*

The truth that the Messiah reveals is contrary to the lies,

the propaganda, the idolatrous, the untrustworthy in the world. His truth is the truth that holds the freedom and this is what we are called to proclaim... It is not true that our dreams for liberation of humankind, of justice, of human dignity, of peace are not meant for this earth and for this history... This is true: The hour comes and it is now that the true worshippers shall worship the Farther in spirit and in truth... Jesus Christ is the life of the world.

Alan Boesak,
WCC Assembly in Toronto

Weekend

1 *With this weekend's newspapers, make a note of all the circumstances mentioned where hope is lacking and Christian hope might be applied. How would you apply this week's lessons to a world in such need? What practical steps can you or your church take to make such hope available to these situations?*
2 *Read through the Easter story as recorded in one of the Gospels. As you do so, ask yourself what part hope played in those events.*

Part Five/Week Nine
Some women in the Old Testament (A character study)

1. Miriam
Exodus 2:1-10; 15:19-21;
Numbers 12:1-15

1 *We first read about Miriam in Exodus 2:1-10. Read through this passage. Her role was central to God's plan for the people of Israel. What would have happened to Moses if she had not intervened?*
2 *In Hebrew tradition (see Micah 6:4) Aaron and Miriam helped their brother Moses as he led the people of Israel from Egypt to the promised land of Canaan. Read Exodus 15:19-21. What was Miriam's role on this occasion?*
3 *Read Numbers 12:1-15. What sin did Miriam and Aaron commit? What was the difference between them and their brother Moses?*

'If anyone thinks he is something when he is nothing, he deceives himself' (Galatians 6:3). Look up this verse. To prevent any jealousy you may feel towards those who have different gifts, spend some time thanking God for the particular abilities he has given you.

Miriam was a woman in a leadership position but this did not protect her from the temptation to sin. Think of any Christian women you know who exercise a leadership role in your church, at work, or in society at large. Pray specifically for

them in the light of Miriam's experience.

2. Hannah
1 Samuel 1:1-28; 2:1-10, 18-21

How do you react when things go wrong, or you are faced with disappointment?

1 *Read 1 Samuel 1:1-18. Infertility is not a new problem. Make a list of the descriptions in the passage of how Hannah reacted to her continuing disappointment. The pain of childlessness is particularly acute. Yet what can you learn from Hannah's example about facing up to disappointment of a more general kind? Then pray for sensitivity in caring for any you know who long for a child.*
2 *Read 1 Samuel 1:19-28 and 2:18-21. It must have cost Hannah a lot to part with her young son. But the Lord compensated her. What principle of the way God works does this story illustrate?*

Jesus said: 'And everyone who has left houses or brother or sisters or father or mother or children or fields for my sake will receive a hundred times as much and will inherit eternal life' (Matthew 19:29).

Use Hannah's joyful prayer in 1 Samuel 2:1-10 as a basis for your own prayer today.

3. Abigail

1 Samuel 25:1-44

1 *We look today at the beautiful story of Abigail. Read 1 Samuel 25:1-44. Imagine that you have been asked to write her a reference and list all that you can find out about her from the passage.*

Note: In the culture of the time, Nabal's refusal to offer the hospitality requested would have been regarded as a great personal insult to David.

2 *Note down what David and Abigail say about God and his involvement in the situation. What does this tell you about the way God works in the world?*

Are there situations at the moment where you want to step in and see justice done? How do you decide when is the right time to act or to wait? How can David and Abigail's actions be your guide?

'Blessed are the peacemakers, for they will be called sons of God' (Matthew 5:9).

Praise God for the peace-making death of Jesus and pray for the strength to be an ambassador of his peace today.

Pray particularly for peace in an area of the world where many are seeking their own revenge at any cost, which will almost inevitably result in bloodshed.

Make a point of reading today's newspaper for up-to-date information.

4. Jezebel

1 Kings 16:31-33; 18:4,18,19; 19:1-2; 21:1-26;

Revelation 2:20-23

Jezebel, the daughter of the king of Tyre and Sidon, was married to Ahab in order to secure an alliance between Israel and her northern neighbour. She survived her husband and continued as queen mother through the reigns of Ahaziah and Jehoram. As prophesied by Elijah in 1 Kings 21:23, she met a violent death shortly after Jehu came to power (2 Kings 9:30-37).

1 *Read 1 Kings 16:31-33; 18:4,18-19 and 19:1-2. Jezebel's marriage to Ahab may have been politically astute, but what were its other consequences?*

Note: For the 'sins of Jeroboam' see 1 Kings 14:9. 'Baal' and 'Asherah' were foreign deities worshipped by Jezebel.

2 *An incident which shows Jezebel at her worst is recorded in 1 Kings 21:1-26. Read through the passage. How does the writer describe her influence on Ahab (verse 25)?*
3 *By New Testament times Jezebel's name had become a byword for idolatry and immorality. Read Revelation 2:20-23, part of the letter from Jesus Christ to his church in Thyatira. What does he promise to those who urge others to do evil?*

'Let us consider how we may spur one another on towards love and good deeds' (Hebrews 10:24). Make a list of three people whom you influence in any way. Then reflect upon whether you are a good or bad influence. Follow this up with a prayer that your influence on others would be for good rather than evil. What else can you do to ensure that it is?

5. Esther
Esther 2:1-18; 3:1-6; 4:9-16

The book of Esther is the exciting story of what happened after Queen Vashti refused to obey her royal husband's summons to appear at a feast. Her successor, Esther, was in the right place at the right time to prevent the wholesale slaughter of the Jewish people. God is never mentioned – a fact which has led some to doubt whether this book should be in the Bible at all. But the hallmarks of his activity are unmistakable, especially in the character and life of his servant Esther.

1 *Read Esther 2:1-18. List the ways in which God was at work in Esther's life.*
2 *Read Esther 3:1-6. Why did Mordecai refuse to bow down to Haman? What was the result?*
3 *After learning that Haman had gained Xerxes' permission to kill all the Jews in the kingdom, Mordecai passed on a message begging Esther to plead their cause with the king.*

Read Esther 4:9-16. How did Esther respond? How did she demonstrate her dependence on God?

Pray for those (including yourself?) who are tempted to keep quiet about their faith in case it gets them into trouble. As we are thinking this week about women, pray for Christian women you know who live or work in hostile environments, that they may have the courage to speak out for God. Thank God for the example of those like Esther and Mordecai.

Weekend

1 *Yesterday we began to look at the story of Esther. During this weekend set aside some time to read through the whole book. As you go through, note down all the different circumstances and 'coincidences' which show that God was at work.*
2 *We have concentrated this week on some of the lesser-known women in the Old Testament. But the women of the New Testament can teach us a thing or two as well! Use a concordance and/or Bible dictionary to find out all you can about one or more of the following: Anna, Martha, Mary Magdalene, Sapphira, Dorcas, Rhoda, Lydia, Priscilla, Euodia and Syntyche. With each character you choose, ask why they have been included. What good example do they set for us to follow? Or what bad example should we avoid?*

The role of women (An issue study)

This study is not only for women! Roughly half of the world's population is made up of women and, since Adam and Eve, men and women have been working out their relationships with each other. The subject affects *all* of us whether it is in the church, in marriage or in employment. How do we define the role of a woman? Should we simply accept whatever are today's cultural norms? As Christians we want to find out what our *God-given* roles are. So the Bible is the place we turn to.

These passages are aimed to get us looking and searching and learning. They can only be a launching pad. But before digging yourself deeper into any feminist/ non-feminist/don't care presuppositions, ask God to speak through these Scriptures about this important topic.

1. Back to the beginning
Genesis 1:27-28; 2:18-25; 3:14-21

Not only are man and woman together created in the image of God, they are also given joint responsibilities over the rest of creation. Together they are told to have dominion over everything else, and to

exercise stewardship. Sexual differences are built into the man-woman relationship: they are made 'male and female', and are given the job of producing children. However, nothing in the first chapter of Genesis would support any hierarchical view of man and woman. Whatever applies to one applies equally to the other.

Elaine Storkey, *What's Right with Feminism* (Eerdmans)

1 *Read Genesis 1:27-28. It is obvious that this blessing and mandate were given to both man and woman. What do you think the commands to 'subdue' the earth and to 'rule over' other living things mean in practical terms? How does our society today reflect this commission to both men and women?*
2 *Read Genesis 2:18-25. Adam was asleep when Eve was created; it was God who created her, as a helper for him. 'Helper' in no way implies inferiority. Even God himself is sometimes called 'the helper of Israel'!*

Loneliness is one of the great problems facing people today. What does this passage have to say about this, and man's basic need to live in community?

3 *Read Genesis 3:14-21. Things went wrong! With the coming of sin in the fall the relationship between Adam and Eve was changed from the ideal it was meant to be. There would be problems now for men and women. From these verses, can you describe some of these problems? Can or should they be overcome when people become Christians?*

Spend time thinking over how these issues actually affect your attitudes and behaviour.

2. Women in the early church

Luke 8:1-3; Colossians 4:15; Philippians 4:2-3; Romans 16:1-13

1 *Take a piece of paper and list on it any things you think are predominantly or exclusively men's or women's roles today. These may stem from cultural to biological, sociological or biblical reasons. State why you think these are so.*

Keep the list with you this week and check it against the Scriptures you read to see if they shed any light on what you have written.

2 *Read each of the following passages: Luke 8:1-3; Colossians 4:15; Philippians 4:2-3; Romans 16:1-13. As you do so, note down the variety of different roles which women played in the New Testament church.*

Note: Romans 16:1 The NIV reads 'Phoebe, a servant of the church'. This may also read 'deaconess'.

3 *From these passages, what sort of attitude does there seem to have been in the New Testament church towards women?*

Pray today for the contribution that women make in your church.

3. Neither male nor female

Galatians 3:26-28; Acts 2:17-18

A Jewish prayer, recommended for daily use by men, says, 'Blessed (be God) that hath not made me a woman'! In New Testament times Christian attitudes were very different from the Jewish background where women took no part in public life; in worship there was segregation and women were not allowed to participate in learning. A woman was thought of in relation to her husband, father or brothers, not in her own right; neither was she allowed the right to bear witness.

So Jesus' attitude to women was revolutionary, *e.g.* the woman at the well (John 4) or accepting women as witnesses to his resurrection.

1 *Read Galatians 3:26-28. What sort of barriers are broken down through Christ? Obviously it does not mean that there are no longer any differences at all between men and women. What does verse 28 mean?*
2 *Read Acts 2:17-18. The beginning of the church at Pentecost specifically included women's participation. Find out some of the roles of women from the following passages: Acts 1:14; 8:3; 12:12; 16:1,14-15; 18:18, 26; 21:8-9.*

Pray that God will break down any barriers or prejudices you may have to the opposite sex.

4. Women teachers
1 Timothy 2:8-15

The next two studies will look at pasages traditionally thought of as ruling out any public or teaching role for women. These are among some of the most hotly debated parts of Scripture!

We all have preconceived ideas on this subject, but pray that God will give you fresh understanding today to distinguish between Christian tradition or natural bias and biblical truth.

1 *Read 1 Timothy 2:8-10. The world so often wants to squeeze women (and men these days!) into its fashion mould. From verses 9-10 what principles can you find to help us to be different as Christians?*
2 *Read 1 Timothy 2:11-15. Summarize in your own words Paul's teaching in these verses.*

Note: Verse 11 – This was revolutionary for Paul's day. Women were not supposed to learn at all!

The phrase 'to teach or have authority over' in verse 12 has often been thought to mean a total prohibition on women's teaching. (But see Titus 2:3-5 and Priscilla in Acts 18:26.) It is more likely that this unusual word 'have authority over' meant to teach in the sort of way which was wrongly usurping authority or was proud and domineering.

The force of 1 Timothy 2:12 is to warn against the temptation to take part in ministry from fallen, sinful motives.

Howard Marshall, *The Role of Women* (IVP UK)

3 *Now look up 1 Corinthians 14:33-36. How does this work out in your own church, e.g. women leading a group discussion, preaching or participating in public worship?*
4 *If you still feel there is a total prohibition on women teaching men, where do you draw the line? (Many of the studies in this book are written by women. Is this teaching men?!)*

You may appreciate talking this over with other Christians. Can you take the initiative to raise the subject?

5. Headship
Ephesians 5;
1 Corinthians 11:3-16.

Any discussion of the role of women must inevitably involve the role of men!

What is 'headship'? Is it ultimate authority? The only time men are to exercise authority over their wives is in the sexual sense (1 Corinthians 11) where the woman also has authority over her husband's body. Wives are not even asked to *obey* their husbands, but to submit – a more voluntary act set in the context of mutual submission.

For headship means men loving their wives as Christ loved the Church, that is with sacrificial, self-denying love. The example of Christ's relationship with the Church is of that of a servant: he came not to be ministered to, but to minister. *The essence of headship is therefore servanthood. For the word 'head' is used in this sense of source and has little to do with authority.*

Elaine Storkey, *What's Right with Feminism* (Eerdmans)

1 *Read Ephesians 5:21-33. What are the responsibilities of a wife here? How should a husband show his 'headship'?*
2 *Read 1 Corinthians 11:3-16. What point is Paul making about the roles of men and women here?*

Note: NIV translates verse 3 as 'the head of the woman is man'. 'Man' here could also mean 'husband'.

The Corinthian church was obviously having problems in defining women's roles. This is no new discussion! In talking about head covering Paul is probably not saying that women should be veiled for worship, but that their hair should not be cut off to make them look like a man or left loose like a prostitute of the day.

Weekend

1 *Write down the names of all the men and women you know for whom this is a very painful issue. Then pray very specifically for them over this weekend.*
2 *An excellent book to read on this subject is* Women, Authority and the Bible, *ed. Alvera Mickelsen (IVP, 1986).*
3 *What role did women play in the Old Testament? You could look again at the story of Deborah, the prophetess and judge, in Judges 4:4-10. Or read Proverbs 31, which gives an example of a fulfilled woman with many functions and roles in life. Look again at these verses in the light of this week's studies.*

Part Six

Hezekiah
Parables of the kingdom
Issues of life and death
The first letter of Peter
Isaiah 55
The book of Ezekiel
The Revelation of John 21–22

Part Six/Week One
Hezekiah (A character study)

The events of 701 BC were the making of Hezekiah! Physically and spiritually a descendant of David, he was born of an evil father, Ahaz, with whom he was co-regent of Judah (the Southern Kingdom) from 729-716BC. Ahaz had made Judah a vassal of Assyria, exhausting the treasury with the payment of tribute. As Hezekiah begins his reign the Assyrian threat strengthens and eventually Sennacherib, the king of Assyria, writes in his campaign history, 'Hezekiah the Judean like a caged bird within the city of Jerusalem his capital I shut up'.

to rectify this?
3 *In what did Hezekiah find his joy as people began to move towards godliness?*

> *And you may be quite surprised that his very first move in defence preparations... was to call his people back to God.*

> John Hercus, *More pages from God's case-book* (IVP)

When life goes sour do I give top priority to getting my relationship with Christ back on the right lines?

1. Reformer
2 Kings 18:1-12; 2 Chronicles 29

The security of Judah was precarious, to say the least. Yet Hezekiah's cleansing of the nation's worship places and practices showed godly devotion and political good sense. For it both attempted to win freedom from Assyria but angered the Assyrians.

1 *Read 2 Kings 18:1-12 and 2 Chronicles 29. Note down the characteristics of Hezekiah which showed his descent from David to be more than just physical.*
2 *What did Hezekiah take to be signs that the Lord was displeased with Judah? What steps did he take*

2. Strategist
2 Chronicles 32:1-8,30; 2 Kings 18:13-16; 20:20

Hezekiah realized that Sennacherib, having invaded Judah, would make for the capital, Jerusalem. A siege was likely and he wasn't to be caught out. One of the great engineering feats of the ancient world, visible today, brought all-important water into Jerusalem. However, a shameful event also occurred.

1 *It seems that Hezekiah had reasonable time to prepare his defence because the excavation of the conduit through some 600 yards of solid rock was done with hand tools! Read 2 Chronicles 32:1-5, 30* and write a thumb-nail sketch of a prepared Jerusalem.

2 Read 2 Chronicles 32:6-8. How does the king use his spiritual insight to lead his people?

3 Read 2 Kings 18:13-16. How does this episode suggest Hezekiah was feeling?

Can I justify acting independently from God when he actually stands at hand to help? When he seems slow to answer prayer for guidance, do I make a rushed decision? When I am in need of practical assistance, do I try to raise it with little reference to God?

3. Politician
2 Kings 18:13 – 19:4

A king negotiate with a mere envoy? Not likely! Rabshakeh must have been 'speechless' but Hezekiah had shown great political skill in playing Sennacherib at his own game.

1 First read the passage. What were the characteristics of Rabshakeh's performance? How does Satan use similar methods in undermining the Christian's faith?

2 Imagine that you are Hezekiah listening to Eliakim. Note down your feelings as each stab of the envoy's message strikes home.

3 Hezekiah was willing to send to Isaiah for help. What does that tell us about the king's character?

> A man in a slit trench is quite unashamed as he prays, 'God, get me out of this.'
>
> John Hercus

4. Intercessor
2 Chronicles 30; Isaiah 37:1–38:22

No long public prayers are recorded as having been offered by Hezekiah. Yet, at the time of reformation, during the siege and following illness we see that he must have been often in conversation with God.

1 Read 2 Chronicles 30. In the light of that, what does Hezekiah's prayer in verses 18-19 show us that he understood about heart knowledge of God and outward observance of religion?

2 Read Isaiah 37. Summarize the temple prayer and the answer from the Lord through Isaiah. What is the great confidence Hezekiah has? Is it yours?

3 Finally read Isaiah 38. Assyria temporarily crushed, God now has to deal with Hezekiah's health. Read his words of thanksgiving and suggest why he was so unwilling to die.

Lord, help me to accept your ordering of my life, for your ways are best.

5. Penitent
2 Chronicles 32:24-33; Isaiah 39

These passages cover the same period, each assuming familiarity with the other. Hezekiah was prepared to join an unholy alliance with Babylon against Assyria – Judah would pay in Jehoiachin's time. Hezekiah's thoughts should be read with the idea that Manasseh *could* have followed in his ways – but he didn't.

1 *Read both the passages listed above. With God's blessings also came a test – which Hezekiah failed! What can we learn from his response?*

2 *Why was he foolish in displaying his treasures to Babylon? The Babylonians used flattery to get what they wanted. Does the devil still use this ploy today?*

3 *Why was Hezekiah honoured at his death? Had he served Judah well?*

Lord, remind me that my actions may have consequences for the eternity of others.

Weekend

1 *Try to find a copy of* More Pages from God's Case-book *by John Hercus. It gives a lively picture of Hezekiah and is well worth the effort of locating. Older Christians are a likely source!*

2 *Write a character study of Hezekiah, 'Yahweh is my strength', as seen through the eyes of Isaiah. In what ways would you want to follow or avoid his example?*

Parables of the kingdom (A bird's-eye study)

One of the special features of Matthew's gospel is his 'parables of the kingdom'. Although such parables are scattered throughout Matthew, chapters 13 and 23 are little collections. They lie close to the heart of Jesus' message (see Matthew 4:17) and illustrate beautifully various aspects of his teaching about the kingdom. The Parable of the Sower is perhaps one of the most famous, particularly because Jesus gives an explanation of its meaning and also reasons why he uses parables in his teaching.

In the gospels, the kingdom of God (or kingdom of heaven as Matthew calls it) was something that was partially experienced in the ministry of Jesus. But Jesus also talks of it as something that belongs to the future, at his second coming.

1. What on earth is going on?
Matthew 13:1-23

This parable might be better described as the 'Parable of the Soils' because its main point is the reaction of the soils rather than the activity of the sower.

1 *Read through the parable in verses 3-9. Imagine the impact of such a vivid story on the minds of* *the crowds in first-century agricultural Palestine.*
2 *Now move on to the explanation given to the disciples in verses 18-23. Note down the four types of response made to Jesus' message. Do you know of similar situations in the world today? What about your own country? Or your circle of friends? Try to identify the nature of their response to the message of the kingdom, then pray for them on the basis of this insight.*
3 *Read carefully verses 10-17. How would you express the reason Jesus gives for speaking in parables? At the end of the week, look back to your answer to see how it has helped you to understand the parables of the kingdom.*

> *... the passage describes an existing division ... and explains why speaking in parables is appropriate in that situation. It does not discuss how one becomes a disciple ... what it does make clear is that natural insight is not enough: spiritual enlightenment is given (verse 11). But how and to whom it is given is not the theme of these verses.*
>
> R.T. France, *Matthew* (Eerdmans)

2. How the kingdom grows
Matthew 13:24-43

Most of us have complained at the 'state of the world', whether rightly or wrongly. Yet in reality we are unlikely to find perfection in the world, in our churches or in ourselves.

1 *Read the Parable of the Weeds (verses 24-30) and the explanation (verses 36-43). Why, according to this parable, is the world such an imperfect place? What would this parable suggest is the right attitude towards evil of those who live among the weeds of the Evil One? How does this affect your life as a son of the kingdom?*
2 *The terrible fate of those mentioned in verses 42-43 should lead us to urgent and compassionate prayer on their behalf. Pray now by name for any 'weeds' for whom you are concerned.*
3 *Read now the parables in verses 31-33. We say 'tall oaks from little acorns grow'. What do these tell us about how the kingdom grows and is growing?*

Note: Verse 31 The mustard tree can grow from a small seed to a tree as tall as 10 ft.

In our success-orientated society where 'big is beautiful', do you need to revise any of your thinking about the growth of God's kingdom?

3. First and last
Matthew 20:1-16

This parable of the kingdom needs to be read as Jesus' answer to the disciples (Matthew 19:25-26). With that in mind, read the conversation between Jesus and the Rich Young Man in chapter 19:16-30. Notice how this passage ends with a saying similar to that in 20:16. Then read Matthew 20:1-16.

1 *What precise attributes of God does this parable illustrate (see especially verse 16)? Deep down, do you find it difficult to understand why God is like this (cf. verses 10-12)?*

Pray for God to change any wrong attitudes you may have similar to the original workers (such as resentment).

2 *Justice in God's kingdom is often at odds with the standards of contemporary society. How do you think the parable relates to Jesus' own time, especially with respect to the Jewish people? Note down any similar situations you know of today to which the parable might apply.*
3 *The parable reveals the owner's attitude towards outcasts, the unemployed and the unwanted. You may not be an employer yourself, but are there any lessons here for you from his example?*

God has been totally just in his treatment of you. Use the following words in prayer to express your own gratitude to him.

Amazing grace, how sweet the
sound
That saved a wretch like me.
I once was lost but now am
found,
Was blind but now I see.

John Newton

4. An unwelcome visitor: a good host?

Matthew 21:33 – 22:14

The final parables we shall be looking at have been described as 'parables of crisis'. Whereas up to now we have seen how the kingdom of God grows and develops, the emphasis now shifts to an examination of our responsibility in responding correctly to God's call.

1 *Read the Parable of the Tenants (21:33-46). Why do you think the chief priests and Pharisees were so angry (verses 45-46)? What exactly was Jesus teaching about them (verses 41, 43)?*

To reject and kill the owner's son was a serious offence. See how this applies to people's attitude to Jesus (verses 42-44). Pray for any known to you who are rejecting Jesus.

2 *Now read the Parable of the Wedding Banquet (22:1-14). What do you think the religious leaders of 21:45-46 would make of this parable? (Notice that in chapter 23 Jesus actually rebukes the religious leaders.)*
3 *What kept these people from attending the banquet (verse 5)? Note down the sort of things that prevent people today responding to*

God's invitation. What indications do you find that, though God's invitation comes free, it is still costly (verses 11-14; cf. 21:43-44)?

5. Making hay while the sun shines

Matthew 25:1-30

Some of Jesus' teaching about the Second Coming is given in parables (e.g. he uses 'like' and a parable in verses 1, 14 when elsewhere he does not speak in parables on the same subject – see 25:31-46).

1 *Read the Parable of the Ten Virgins (25:1-13). Write down the facts taught about the coming of the kingdom in this parable.*
2 *Now read the Parable of the Talents (25:14-30). What additional information about the kingdom does this parable give? Write down your comments. What should the followers of Jesus be doing whilst they wait for his coming? What does it tell you about the value of our individual abilities and talents? In what ways are you determined to use your own gifts in the time that is left to you before Jesus comes and the kingdom is fully established?*

> ... the sums of money entrusted to the slaves are more likely to represent, not natural endowments given to men in general but the specific privileges and opportunities of the Kingdom of Heaven.
>
> R.T. France, *Matthew*
> (Eerdmans)

Read 2 Peter 3:3-9. Then pray for a greater expectancy of the Lord's coming, both in yourself and in your friends and church.

Weekend

1 Look back over the parables we have studied this week. Take each one and try to recast the story in a modern idiom. First decide what are the main points of the parable and then try not to lose any of them in your retelling of it for a modern audience.

2 Read through the other parables of the kingdom in Matthew (e.g. the Treasure, the Pearl and the Dragnet 13:44-50; the Sheep and the Unmerciful Servant 18:10-35). What do they add to your understanding of Jesus' teaching about the kingdom?

3 Try to explain in your own words why Jesus spoke in parables, looking back over this week's studies.

Part Six/Week Three
Issues of life and death (An issue study)

Deciding what is right and wrong can be very difficult, especially where ultimate issues such as death are involved. But, as Christians, we have a guide-book to help us through the maze of ethical dilemmas. It is through the Bible that God has revealed certain principles which indicate how he views these issues. So we'll be looking at some of the relevant passages in our studies this week. But before we begin, there are a few things we should bear in mind...

For one thing, the modern world is, in many respects, rather different from that of the Bible writers. Human nature is much the same but just about everything else has changed and many of the particular dilemmas we face today were unknown in Bible times. This means that we need to look for general *principles* for action rather than specific *rules* to apply on every occasion.

The Bible does not always give an unambiguously clear line for us to follow and this sometimes results in equally sincere Christians disagreeing with each other on how the Bible's teaching is to be applied today. Our purpose this week will therefore be to look primarily at some of the things the *Bible* itself has to say. We will not exhaust the biblical material on each subject. If you would like to follow through the more controversial implications of

the issues mentioned, see the books recommended for further reading.

---

1. How much are you worth?
Genesis 1:26-28; 4:1-16; 9:1-7

Today we look at three passages which show what Genesis, the 'book of beginnings', has to say about how much God values human life.

1 *Read the account of man's creation in Genesis 1:26-28. What distinguishes man from the rest of creation?*
2 *Genesis 4:1-16 is the account of the first murder in the Bible. Note that the death penalty as such is not carried out at this stage. But what was Cain's punishment (verses 12-14)?*
3 *The distorting effect of sin in the world is recognized in the covenant made by God with Noah after the flood. Read Genesis 9:1-7. What makes human life so valuable?*

Note: The phrase 'in the image of God' (Genesis 1:26,27; 9:6) should probably be translated '*as* the image of God'. In other words, the human being, as a whole person, was created to be the physical image and visible representative on earth of the transcendent and invisible God. See the article on 'Image' in the *New Bible Dictionary* (IVP, p.683ff.) or *In the Beginning* by H. Blocher (IVP, p.79ff.) for further details.

As you consider the privilege of being a man or a woman created in God's image, ask God for the ability to think of yourself and fellow human beings in the light of this truth. How should that help you to love and accept yourself – and others as well?

2. Life before birth
Psalm 139; Jeremiah 1:4-5

Abortion is a complex issue. The Bible refers only to *accidental* abortion (Exodus 21:22), not the deliberate ending of foetal life we face in modern society. The key question is that of the status of unborn children. Are they to be given the same rights as full human persons? Are they of lesser value, so that they may be terminated for what would otherwise be unjustifiable reasons? Or is there a mid-point at which a foetus becomes a human person at some stage after conception?

1 *Some light on this question comes in Psalm 139, a beautiful and poetic account of how the Psalmist understands his relationship with God. As you read through the Psalm, make a note of all the verbs used to describe what God does.*
2 *Look at verses 13-16. What do they tell you about the beginnings of personal life? Does this shed any light on how God views deliberate abortion?*
3 *A number of the prophets were conscious that God's call came before they were born. Read*

Jeremiah 1:4-5. Note down the verbs used to describe what God did before Jeremiah's birth. What does this tell you about the way God treats the unborn?

The biblical evidence clearly does not answer all the questions people raise about the status of the foetus, but does indicate that God's relationship with us begins well before birth. This implies that the unborn child should be regarded as a human person and not as a disposable 'blob of jelly'.

Pray for those who are trapped in the dilemma of abortion, either facing the possibility of an unwanted birth or suffering the deep and lasting consequences of an abortion in the past. Is there anything *you* can do to show practical love and support? You might like to write to Christian Action Council, 422 C St., N.E. Washington, DC 20002 for some suggestions.

3. Capital punishment
Exodus 21:12-17; Leviticus 20:7-10; John 8:2-11

The Old Testament law prescribes the death penalty for a number of offences, including murder, adultery, rape, perjury, sorcery and idolatry. Capital punishment reflects the high standards of holiness which God insisted on among his chosen people. Although the crimes outlawed remain offences, there are now arguably more appropriate ways of administering justice.

1 *Read Exodus 21:12-17 and*

Leviticus 20:7-10, two passages which contain several examples of offences which merited the death penalty. Why do you think there is such an emphasis on how people treat their parents? Then turn to Deuteronomy 19:1-21. How would you describe the provision for those who had killed unintentionally? Overall, what motives lay behind capital punishment?

2 Something of Jesus' attitude towards punishment was shown on one occasion when he was invited to condemn a woman caught in the act of adultery. Read John 8:2-11. What implications does this have for the Christian view of punishment in general?

3 Some of the people who argue the case for capital punishment do so from a standpoint of 'righteous indignation', desiring vengeance. What do these verses say to them? Others, arguing against capital punishment (but not all!), do so from a position of belief that putting an offender to death will achieve nothing. What do these verses say to them?

Pray today for all those who are in prison, for whatever crime, especially for those whose experience has led them to see more clearly their need of God.

4. Violence and warfare
Matthew 5:38-42; Romans 13:1-7

Violent wars were a common feature of the life of Israel during Old Testament times as they established and held on to the territory given them by God. In such warfare it was not unknown for whole communities to be slaughtered. It is, however, clear that this was not wanton destruction but in order to preserve the nation and prevent its people from sliding into idolatry and pagan practices (e.g. Deuteronomy 7:1-6). Furthermore, it was not so much a case of men fighting on God's behalf but God fighting for himself! (See e.g. 2 Samuel 5:24.)

1 All Christians are agreed that wanton destruction is wrong. Read Amos 1:2-15 capturing God's abhorrence of the way Israel's neighbours had acted towards the (apparently) innocent. Can you recall pictures of war-torn countries seen recently on television or in the newspaper? How far do you share God's abhorrence of war?

2 What else does the Bible have to say about violence and warfare? Is there a case for God still using war to preserve his purposes? Is there a case for pacifism? Read Matthew 5:38-42 and Romans 12:17-21. What personal attitude is being urged towards one's enemies?

3 Thinking of these passages, how far does that principle also apply on a wider, national scale? Are there occasions when there is a just cause which demands an active and even armed response? Or is such force never justified? There is no easy answer, but these questions must be responsibly faced.

4 Read Romans 13:1-7. Write down what are the responsibilities the Christian has to the governing authorities. How far could that responsibility go in the event of war?

Because we are liable to realise our own interests at the

expense of other people, coercive government is essential. It sets limits to the harm we can do.

Richard Harries

Whether or not our conscience can accept a distinction between limited and unlimited nuclear weapons, we should be able to agree that the latter should be renounced and abolished as soon as possible.

John Stott, *Involvement*
(Revell)

5. What about the poor?
Deuteronomy 24:14-22; Isaiah 58:1-12; 1 John 3:16-20

We cannot leave 'issues of life and death' without looking at what the Bible has to say about our responsibility to those who are poor and oppressed. There are countless references to them in the Bible. We can only select three passages.

1 *Read Deuteronomy 24:14-22. List the reasons given why the poor are to be cared for.*

2 *The prophets stress that exploiting the poor is incompatible with genuine worship. Read Isaiah 58:1-7. What effects of oppression does Isaiah give here? Read on to verse 12. What are the results of generous giving?*

Memory verse: Religion that God our Father accepts as pure and faultless is this: to look after orphans and widows in their distress and to keep oneself from being polluted by the world (James 1:27).

3 *Read 1 John 3:16-20. Think and pray about what you can do practically to help those in need.*

Weekend

1 *One suggestion for further reading this week.*
Involvement *(2 vols.): John Stott (Revell)*
2 *Spend time praying for those who have to make hard decisions in some of the areas of life and death which we have been looking at this week. If you don't do so already, make a point of beginning to pray for your own senators and congressmen, in particular, and for other national leaders and legislators in general.*

The first letter of Peter (A whole book study)

Remember Peter? He was the blustery, impetuous fisherman who was witness to so much of the life of Jesus; he protested his love for his Lord, yet was unable to own allegiance to him when it came to the crunch.

And do you remember Jesus' words to Peter? 'Feed my sheep' and 'on this rock I will build my church'.

In this letter we see Peter fulfilling Jesus' commission to be a church leader. He is probably writing from Rome to Christians scattered over what is now the greater part of Northern Turkey. It is likely that he is writing on the eve of the outbreak of persecution of Christians in the Roman Empire. This letter could have served to prepare the readers for such a time.

As it stands, it is full of relevant teaching for us in the twentieth century. We shall be drawing out themes from the letter. But make sure that you don't just look at isolated verses. Try to get a grasp of the letter as a whole.

1. Peter

The apostle Peter had come a long way from the days when he was a fisherman on the Lake of Galilee. Some say that such an ill-educated man could not have written this letter in Greek. But Jewish boys were taught in the synagogue and his home town, Bethsaida, was on a commercial trade route. And he was writing with the help of Silas anyway (5:12). He certainly was writing from his deep personal knowledge of Jesus.

1 Read through the whole letter of 1 Peter. As you do so, note names Peter gives to Jesus: see 1:19; 2:4-8,21,25; 5:4.
2 Take each of these names and use them to thank God for Jesus. For example, as the perfect lamb (1:19), Jesus makes it possible (without the sacrifice needing to be repeated) for us to get right with God. What does that mean to you?

2. Suffering

The world is full of suffering. This is more acute for some than for others. Christians are not exempt. Indeed, being a Christian can be the cause of suffering. This was true for Peter's readers as well!

1 The words 'keep', 'kept' or 'shielded' occur several times in 1:4-5. Read 1 Peter 1:3-9. How would the idea of God's purpose and protection help the Christian who is isolated or under pressure?
2 Read 1 Peter 3:8-17 and 4:12-19. Write down the many points he is making about suffering.

When have you suffered for your faith, experienced unjust accusations and the like? Can you think of others suffering right now? Pray for yourself and them with Peter's points in mind.

3 The purpose of suffering is a difficult problem. What indications does Peter give why a Christian suffers? See 1:6-7; 4:1-2; 5:9-10.
4 Pray for Christians around the world who are being persecuted for their faith. You may wish to pray for Christians in an Islamic country like Iran, where churches may be small and illegal, and violent death a possibility.

3. Holy living

'Be holy, because I am holy' (1:16). Peter was quoting from Leviticus. The people of God were to be pure, untouched by the filthy practices of the tribes around them. To be holy and pure means to live life God's way. But what does that mean?

1 Trace the process by which we are set free to be holy (1:13-23).
2 What will be the characteristics of this new life of holiness? See 1:2,22; 2:1,11,12; 3:10-12; 4:2; 5:5-7.
3 How does this affect others? 2:12,15; 3:1-2,15-16; 4:4.

Think through your programme today. Are there any activities which you need consciously to bring to God for him to make them holy?
    Pray then that the holiness of your life will challenge others to think about Christ – and look out for God to act through you.

4. Relationships

Peter has stressed that Christians are individually part of one nation (2:9). We can't live in isolation. We *have* to live in relationship with others – both Christian and secular. How does God affect our relationships?

1 How were these Christians to respond to every authority? Why was this important (2:13-18)?
2 Put the principle in 2:16 into your own words. How should this affect relationships in the work place and in the home?
3 How was Peter transforming the commonly held view of his day about the inferiority of women (see 3:1-7)? What lasting principles about husband and wife relationships is he stating here?
4 In the light of all these relationships, what should our response as Christians be to disrespectful comments about our boss, principal, prime minister, husband/wife?

Pray for those in authority today.

5. Church

Relationships within the church are included in this letter. Before you begin, ask yourself how conscious are you of working at and taking care of relationships with people in your church? Too careful or lazy?

1 What are the characteristics of a good church leader? See 5:1-4. Pray for your leaders now in their responsibilities.
2 Read 5:5 slowly. Are respect and humility the characteristics you

would expect to see in a church? Do your attitudes affect this in your church? Be practical.

3 Put 4:7-11 in your own words, then underline any statements that you feel are lacking in your church life.

Spend time praying that the Lord will enable your church to reflect these characteristics – and again, be specific.

Weekend

1 Read through 2 Peter. Look out for the three main themes:
- Christians are called to be holy.
- False teaching must be rejected.
- The day of the Lord is coming.

You could then read through the book of Jude to see the parallels.
2 Compare 1 Peter 2:21-22 with Isaiah 53.

Part Six/Week Five
Isaiah 55 (A meditation)

This chapter is the climax of a part of the Book of Isaiah which runs from chapter 40 to chapter 55. Set against the background of exile of the people of Israel in Babylon, Isaiah introduces the Suffering Servant to speak of the hardships to be endured by the exiled Jews. Isaiah also speaks in these chapters of the breathtaking majesty and sovereignty of God. (The studies in the Book of Ezekiel next week will be set against the same background of a people in exile.)

1. Refugees!
2 Chronicles 36:1-21

In order to enter fully into the experience of the Jews which Isaiah is addressing, it would be good to get a thorough grasp of what had happened to them. It is for this reason that we must start by turning to 2 Chronicles 36:1-21.

1 *Read the passage through. Try to picture what it must have been like to live through such political instability. Are there any situations described in the news today which resemble Judah at that time?*
2 *Use your imagination to enter into the feelings of distress of the Jewish people. How would you feel about yourself? What about the rest of the nation? Would your belief in a good*

God be shaken? Can you believe in a good God amidst so much evil? How could he let such a thing happen to you?
3 *Try to describe your feelings in writing. Perhaps you could write a letter to a distant cousin. This cousin is a young Christian. You want to be honest but not to shake their faith. What are you going to say?*
4 *Focus again upon a similar contemporary situation. Use the insights gained from your meditation to pray with sensitivity for the Christians and non-Christians involved.*

2. Invitation!
Isaiah 55:1-7

> *Over and over again, when God communicated with those he loved, it was he who took the initiative, by preceding the person and providing him with an awareness of his presence or speaking in clear unmistakable ways.*
>
> Joyce Huggett,
> *Listening to God* (IVP)

Read Isaiah 55:1-7. Try to capture the scene which is being presented to you. It is very graphic and full of real-life action. Cast your mind back to the last time you were in an open-air market. Remember the traders, the hawkers? Maybe some of them are unknown to you. But if it was your local market there may have been others you trust because of long acquaintance.

Read the first five verses and imagine God in the market place speaking the words. He really wants you to receive what he has to offer. The tone is urgent.

1 *How would you describe what God is offering? How far does it tie in with your priorities in life?*
2 *Write down the words of command to be found in verses 1-7, or underline them in your Bible. What is the appropriate response to God's loving initiative?*
3 *Put yourself once again in the position of the exiles in Babylon. How do you think they would respond to the message of these verses?*
4 *Thank God for the way in which he takes the initiative in your life and in the lives of other people.*

---

3. Majesty!
Isaiah 55:6-11

How often we suspect that our lives are out of control! It hardly takes anything to throw us off balance. Of course, we sometimes face major crises and God can appear very far from us. And that was the case for the Jews who are addressed in Isaiah 55. We have already tried to enter into some of their desperation.

Read slowly through the whole of Isaiah 55. Then focus in on verses 6-11.

1 *What do you think it means to seek God (verse 6)? How do you*

personally seek him? Is this something you do only when you have a specific need? What does verse 6 suggest to you about God's availability? Verse 7 indicates that seeking God will entail his making some demands of you. Do you need forgiveness or pardon perhaps for being too casual in your attitude to God?
2 *Have you recently felt like saying, 'Lord, I just don't understand what you're doing'? Perhaps you were being treated unjustly. Perhaps you feel very confused about something; maybe it's your faith. Do verses 8 and 9 help?*
3 *Verses 10 and 11 reassure us about the reliability of God's Word and promises. Thank God now for all the promises of his Word that you can call to mind. Thank him also that no matter what happens he is in sovereign control of your life.*

---

4. Authority!
Isaiah 55:8-11

Truth liberates. It not only reveals a standard but will set you free to keep it. This is what makes Scripture different from other ethical systems, which are powerless to help the struggler.

John White, *The Fight* (IVP)

There is a natural human tendency to think that we know what is best for us. Some of us never grow out of our childhood desire to play with fire. This independence is at the heart of our sin: independence from God. Often we will listen to almost anyone rather than the person who is telling us the truth. And God always tells us the truth.

1 *The world is full of voices, impressions, opinions and other truth claims. Write down on a piece of paper all the various major influences there have been upon you in the past. They have made you what you are. Are they influential now as far as you are aware? Who and what are the major influences upon you nowadays?*
2 *Read Isaiah 55:8-11. God's wisdom is superior to all others, but how much are you allowing God's Word really to bear fruit in your life? Are there clear commands with respect to relationships which you need to obey? What about your language, perhaps the way you speak about people? The issues will be different for each one of us.*
3 *Imagine the springlike freshness described in verse 10. Ask God that his Word might have that sort of effect in your own life.*

---

5. Wholeness!

2 Chronicles 36:22-23; Isaiah 55:12-13

Our chapter, indeed this whole section of the Book of Isaiah, finishes on a triumphant note of promise. Read once again the whole of Isaiah 55, looking with especial care at verses 12 and 13.

All the desires for security and well-being of the Jewish people are summed up here. Here is the antidote to the despair and dejection of their experience of exile. To what extent do joy and peace characterize your own daily life?

1 *Read 2 Chronicles 36:22-23 to get the necessary historical background. Try to enter imaginatively into the experience of the Jews returning to Jerusalem.*
2 *Is there anything in your own past Christian experience which causes you to rejoice in a similar way – perhaps your conversion, or a particularly memorable time of prayer, or maybe an occasion when you have been especially conscious of God's presence? Spend a few moments in recollection, thanking God for his goodness.*

> Peace is more than the absence of anxiety. It is a positive quality arising from inner harmony. A peace which is destroyed by external threats is no peace. God's peace ... defies uncertainty and danger.
>
> John White, *The Fight* (IVP)

3 *Turn to John 14:27 and Philippians 4:6-7. Use these promises to pray that God's wholeness and peace might characterize your life.*

Weekend

1 *Use this weekend to recap on the lessons of the week. Perhaps you would like to read through the chapters which lead up to Isaiah 55 (i.e. from chapter 40) and see how the climax builds up.*
2 *You could try memorizing this chapter. It would be time well spent!*
3 *Perhaps this meditative study has served to awaken a desire to get to know God better on a devotional level. If so, then you might find the*

following book helpful: Joyce Huggett, The Joy of Listening to God *(IVP, 1986.)*

The Book of Ezekiel, 1 (A whole book study)

In 597 BC Nebuchadnezzar captured Jerusalem and deported its king and leading citizens to Babylon (see 2 Kings 24:10-17). It is likely that the young man Ezekiel, a member of an influential priestly family, was taken into exile with them.While in Babylon he received his commission as a prophet from God himself. His message was simple. Awful though the exile itself had been, worse was to follow: the city of Jerusalem and the Temple of the Lord would be destroyed – a prediction which came true in 587 BC. Ezekiel's job was to warn of this impending catastrophe and affirm that it was part of God's plan of judgment on his people's rebellion. This is what most of chapters 1–24 are about, which we shall be looking at this week. Chapters 25-32 form an interlude in which judgment is given against seven nations surrounding Israel, while the remainder of the book focuses on the aftermath of the fall of Jerusalem and the promise of restoration.

1. God above all
Ezekiel 1:1-28

1 *Read verses 1-3. People at this time tended to think that the influence of a god was confined to his own country. In what way is the God of Israel different?*

Note: Verse 1 'the Kebar river': possibly an irrigation channel from the Euphrates to the south-east of Babylon.

2 *As you read through the rest of chapter 1, try to visualize something of what Ezekiel saw in this vision of God's glory. It begins with a spectacular storm (verse 4) and goes on to describe the four living creatures (verses 5-14), the four wheels (verses 15-21), a sparkling platform (verses 22-25) and finally a vision of God himself seated on his throne (verses 26-28). If you can, make a sketch of what Ezekiel describes.*

3 *As we shall see over the next two weeks, a deep awareness of the holiness and majesty of God runs through the whole book. What immediate effect did the vision have on Ezekiel (verse 28)? Do you have a similar sense of God's holiness and majesty? Pray for an increasing grasp of the reality of who God is in your own life.*

All prophecy begins with the character of the God who inspires it.

John B. Taylor, *Ezekiel*, Tyndale Old Testament Commentary (IVP, 1969)

2. Watch out!
Ezekiel 2:1 – 3:19

1 Read through this account of Ezekiel's call. Note down the words God uses to describe his people.
2 What is Ezekiel's reaction (3:15)? How do you react to the sin and evil in the world caused by people's rebellion against God?
3 3:16-19 make clear the prophet's responsibility to declare God's message. What things can you find in this passage that might deter Ezekiel from doing this?
4 Christians have a responsibility to make known God's message of salvation in the world today. Read through 2 Corinthians 5:11-21. In the light of that, pray for the strength to declare God's message in your own family and among your friends and colleagues.

3. No delay
Ezekiel 12:1-28;
2 Kings 24:18 – 25:7

1 Read Ezekiel 12:1-7. This is one of many symbolic actions which Ezekiel is told to carry out as a visual demonstration of the message to follow. Read the message itself in verses 8-20. What is the purpose of God's judgment?
2 It seems that Ezekiel's audience had previous experience of false prophets whose prophecies were not fulfilled. Read verses 21-28. What guarantee is Ezekiel able to give (verse 25)? Now read the account of the fulfilment of this prophecy in 2 Kings 24:18–25:7.
3 How important is it to you that what God says will come true? Have there been times when you have

tried to evade the severity of his truth or the greatness of what he has made known? Is there anything in your life which needs to be put right in the light of this?

> The Lord is not slow in keeping his promise, as some understand slowness. He is patient with you, not wanting anyone to perish, but everyone to come to repentance.
>
> 2 Peter 3:9

4. A look back
Ezekiel 16:1-63

1 Chapters 4–24 spell out to the exiles the inevitable fate of Israel in vivid and often shocking detail. But why is this going to happen? Read verses 1-52, which are an allegory of the history of God's dealings with his people and their response. Refer to the notes below as you do so. What was the Israelites' main sin?

Notes: Verse 8 describes a symbolic act denoting commitment to marriage (cf. Ruth 3:9). Verses 26-29: Ezekiel is referring to alliances with foreign powers that betrayed a lack of trust in God. Verses 46-52: The nation is compared unfavourably with Samaria (representing the Northern Kingdom, destroyed in 722 BC) and Sodom (a byword for immorality: see Genesis 19).
2 Read verses 53-63. What do these verses say about why God decides to punish his people? What hope is there for the future?
3 This is a disturbing chapter, but one which sets out the seriousness of sin as God sees it. Pray that God will give you the ability to be as

disturbed by the awfulness of sin as you are by the graphic details in passages like this one.

---

5. Sour grapes
Ezekiel 18:1-32

1 Read verses 1-4. What was the complaint of Ezekiel's fellow-exiles? How does God answer them?
2 Ezekiel goes on to give the examples of three generations in one family. Read verses 5-20 and list the sins that are mentioned. Which have a direct parallel with modern society? How do the others apply to us now?
3 The individual's personal accountability before God is a much

stronger stress in the Book of Ezekiel than earlier in Israel's history. Read verses 21-32. Looking over the whole chapter, what is the answer to the accusation that God is punishing people for the sins of previous generations?

Weekend

1 We have only been able to look at a few key passages in this first section of Ezekiel during the week. Over the weekend, read as much as you can of chapters 4–24. In particular, ask what is shown about God? How does this add to what we have already found out this week?
2 Try John Taylor's Tyndale Old Testament Commentary on Ezekiel (IVP) for further reading.

Part Six/Week Seven
The Book of Ezekiel, 2 (A whole book study)

1. Judgment on the nations
Ezekiel 25:1-17

Before the account of Jerusalem's eventual destruction in chapter 33, chapters 25-32 come as a series of prophecies denouncing seven surrounding nations who had taken advantage of God's displeasure with his people to further their own ends.

1 List the offences for which each nation in chapter 25 is condemned. What form does the punishment take?
2 What reason is given for such harsh judgments?

Many people find difficulty with the idea that God punishes people. How do you think Ezekiel would respond? Why? Turn to Hebrews 10:26-31, an awful and awe-inspiring passage. Ask God to help you understand this part of his character (as far as that is possible).

2. Jerusalem destroyed
Ezekiel 24:15-27; 33:21-33

1 Read 24:15-27 and 33:21-22. The shock of the news of Jerusalem's destruction will be so great that even the normal customs of mourning will go unobserved. Look at 24:24. Why does God tell Ezekiel not to mourn the sudden death of his wife?
2 Read 24:27. Apart from his prophetic utterances, Ezekiel had maintained a ritual silence throughout this period of his ministry (see 3:26-27). Why is he not allowed to speak freely?
3 Read 33:23-29, a message for those left in the land of Israel. What wrong assumption are they making? Look on to verses 30-33. What mistake are Ezekiel's fellow-exiles in danger of making?

It's easy for us to develop a taste for certain speakers and authors who say only what we want them to say. How far is that a trap you could fall into? Pray against that happening, and pray too for speakers who may be tempted to preach only the message which their audience wants to hear and yet is not necessarily the truth. 2 Timothy 4:2-5 could direct your praying.

3. God's honour
Ezekiel 36:1-36

1 After judging and punishing his people, God now promises to restore them. But what reasons does he give for doing so? Notice again Ezekiel's entirely God-centred perspective.

Write down all the actions that God will take in this work of restoration. Reflect on how far you expect God to act and how far you really see him as inactive.

2 Look at verses 25-27. What resources will God's people now have to enable them to keep his laws? What reason does God give in verse 32 for doing this?

Thank God for this aspect of the Holy Spirit's ministry. Pray that he will help you to live so that God's reputation is honoured rather than disgraced.

4. Dry bones
Ezekiel 37:1-14

1 Ezekiel's hearers have been in exile for ten years and Jerusalem has been destroyed. The promise of restoration must have seemed rather hollow. But that wasn't the end of the story! What had they forgotten?
2 Look at verses 7 and 10. What is it that actually makes the difference to the dry bones? How is Ezekiel involved? How is God involved?
3 Think about a situation known to you which seems hopeless. Spend time praying about it in the light of this passage.

5. The glory of the Lord
Ezekiel 10:18-19; 11:22-23; 43:1-11

1 Chapters 40–48 form the climax of Ezekiel's prophecy, describing a vision of God returning in glory to a new temple in a rebuilt city. Compare 10:18-19 and 11:22-23 with 43:1-5.
2 Read 43:6-12 several times. What characteristics of God is this passage teaching? In what ways is this relevant to your life and behaviour, e.g. in terms of your worship, the manner in which you speak God's name, being aware of God's anger?

As we draw to the end of our two weeks in the company of Ezekiel, think back over what you have learnt about God and his dealings with his people. Praise him for new insights and pray for the ability to live in the light of them.

Weekend

1 Ezekiel's vision of a restored city in which God dwells with his people for ever finds its full expression in the book of Revelation. Look through Ezekiel 47:1-12 and compare it with Revelation 21 and 22. (We shall be looking at these chapters next week.) What difference does looking at Ezekiel from a New Testament perspective make?
2 To go deeper into this fascinating book, why not get hold of John B. Taylor's Tyndale Commentary, Ezekiel (IVP)? Or you could look up a good Bible dictionary to help you to find out more about Ezekiel as a person, following up the Bible references that it gives.

The Revelation of John 21–22 (A detailed study)

Welcome to the last two chapters of the Bible. And what glorious chapters they are! To break into John's vision at this point may be inappropriate, but you have to start somewhere and these two chapters are often put together. If you capture something of the majesty of the book of Revelation in this week's studies, your whetted appetite may drive you to study the whole book. *The Message of Revelation* by Michael Wilcock in the Bible Speaks Today Series would be a valuable tool.

> *Pictures, potent images of Christian truth to use as we use the sacraments – that is what we are given in Revelation ... It is the images which stick. John's pages are studded with them ... that our imagination, as well as our mind, should grasp the key concepts of the faith. So till the bridegroom returns – till the city descends from the sky and the day of the wedding-feast dawns – we do this, in remembrance of him.*

> Michael Wilcock

The sixty-sixth book of the Bible draws on images and truths which recur throughout the Bible. To help you appreciate this and to bring this book of studies to a close, each day we will suggest a theme, relevant to the study, which you can trace through the Bible. You could use a concordance or rely on your memory alone. It is worth noticing the connection between this book and the fourth gospel, strong evidence that they have the same author, probably the apostle John himself.

---

1. God's new heaven
Revelation 21:1-8

1 *Start by reading Revelation 1:1-3, to remind yourself of who first received this revelation. Why was it given? What was the effect on those who then received it? Pray that you will fully respond to these truths presented so graphically.*

Note: Revelation 21:1-8 records the seventh vision which John saw. We are told of the previous six in Revelation 19:11–20:15. This seventh vision is in fact a prelude to the final scene of the book.

2 *Make a list of what John saw of the new world. Contrast this with the features of the old world that he saw. As you do so, try to capture the wonder of the new heaven and earth.*

Notes: 'the sea' verse 1 stands for all that was evil. 'The city' (verse 2) stands for the church.

3 *What evidence is there of God's commitment to his church?*
4 *In the last few days, what if anything has caused you to despair of life in the 'first heaven and earth'? What hope does this vision of John give you?*

Pray for those known to you who are particularly downcast by the evidence of the fallen world around us. Pray too for those in the world who are oppressed in any way.

Theme for the day 'Newness' Try John 3; Romans 6:4; 2 Corinthians 5:17.

2. God's holy city
Revelation 21:9-27

Of this city the reborn are citizens, and to it all pilgrims of faith tend. The city is also described as the Lamb's bride; it is in another respect his church for which he died, the pattern and goal of all human society. In the last analysis this chief of scriptural cities is men, not walls: just men made perfect, the city of the living God.

The Illustrated Bible Dictionary (Tyndale)

Michael Wilcock writes: 'The most fruitful question we can ask concerns the vision's object. What is it about the city that John is meant to notice in particular, and why?' (see page 207). How would you answer that question from these verses?

Notes: verse 9 relates to 15:1. 4:4 the 24 elders represent the 12 tribes of Israel and the 12 apostles – the foundation stones of Israel and then the church.

1 *Read verses 9-21. In what ways would you describe this holy city? How far could this description apply to the church today, for God is already preparing his bride?*

Use this to pray for your own church, leaders and members.

2 *Read verses 22-27. In what ways is the city so perfect that it sweeps away the deficiencies of the old order such as the need for the temple, racial segregation, darkness, impurity, and the like? How irksome do you find these deficiencies?*

Theme for the day 'Light' Try Genesis 1; Isaiah 60; John 9

3. God's new world
Revelation 22:1-5

To gain the full impact of this new creation, we need to be reminded of the first creation.

1 *So read these verses, then turn to Genesis 2:4–3:20. Write down the similarities and differences between the two, e.g. the tree, the curse, the relationship to God.*
2 *Fill your mind with these images. Following on from yesterday, how much do you long for the recreation of the fallen world? Turn your thoughts into prayer.*
3 *Water has often been identified with the Spirit and his activity. From these verses, what part does the river as the Spirit have to play? How does that add to your understandng of this new world?*

4. God's own words
Revelation 21:5; 22:6-10,18-19

1 *Can you think of three occasions (in a variety of ways) when God communicated with the world? The 'theme for the day' will give you some ideas. You could turn to Hebrews 1:1-2 which sums up the truth that God does speak to mankind.*
2 *In these verses the stress is upon God's word. Read them. Then write down the stages given here in which God communicated his true words to us. (Revelation 1:1-3 will add to the picture.) What, if anything, does John tell us about each stage? Why is it important that God's words can be trusted? What would happen if his word was untrustworthy?*
3 *These words expressed the gospel itself. What was the right way to react to them – both for John and for those who heard later?*
4 *In what ways is the gospel distorted today, such as in sects, or even in an unbalanced emphasis in the church itself? How should you react?*

Pray for any known to you who are affected by such distortions.

5. God's work... finished
Revelation 22:11-21

In creation God declared, 'Let there

be light' and his spoken word was fulfilled. So here God makes statements about the eternal status of the righteous and unrighteous – and that word will also be fulfilled.

1 *Read verses 11-15 and then make a note of the statements. How do you react to the finality of these statements as they affect both yourself and those who don't know God?*
2 *It is fitting that the book, indeed the whole Bible, ends by focusing upon Jesus. In verses 16,20,21 what is John saying about Jesus? Write down your observations.*
3 *Look back over chapters 21 and 22 and remind yourself of what else John has said about Jesus. Then accept the invitation of verse 17 (which sounds so similar to Isaiah 55) and turn to the praise of the Lamb. Revelation 1:9-20 may help. Maybe you too will want to fall at the feet of Jesus in silent and amazed adoration. What other response is appropriate?!*

Theme for the day 'Jesus as the sacrificial lamb' Try Isaiah 53; John 1:29; the hints in John 18–19 of Jesus as one who is passively led to be slaughtered.

Weekend

1 *Plan your next programme of Bible reading and study. Many people find that IVP's The Bible Speaks Today series is a useful companion, with its emphasis on practical application and its non-technical readability. Michael Wilcock's The Message of Revelation, quoted this week, will make a good introduction. Alternatively, many people find*

Scripture Union daily Bible reading notes helpful, such as Daily Bread or Daily Notes. *These follow a systematic plan, taking you through the Bible over several years.*

2 *Underlying all parts of the Bible is* an integrated and powerful theology. *To grasp something of the richness of biblical teaching, why not read* Foundations of the Faith *by James Boice (IVP), a preacher's portrait of God's message to us?*

Part Seven

Part Seven/Week One
The Acts of the Apostles 11-15 (A historical study)

How did the Christian faith spread from being a small group of Jewish believers to become a major world religion? What sort of people did God use? How did they set about the job? What was the message they preached? And how much of their Jewish culture was essential for people who became Christians? All relevant questions for us, as we think about passing on God's message to others!

The Acts of the Apostles is Luke's second book, showing how the church spread after the events of Jesus' life and death recorded in his Gospel (see Acts 1:1-2).

1. A small start?
Acts 11

Peter was called to account by the Jerusalem church for his actions in associating with Gentiles and preaching the gospel to them. Verses 1-18 are his explanation (you can read the full story in ch.10).

Note: *Verse 6 refers to 'unclean' animals which Jews did not eat (Leviticus 11).*

1 *What points does Peter particularly emphasize in his account? Why?*
2 *What might have prevented Peter from telling these Gentiles about the gospel? What causes us to miss*

some of our opportunities to share our faith with others?
3 *The church in Antioch was to be Paul's base for each of his three missionary journeys. What sort of church do you think it was (vv.19-30)? Make a list of the things you can find out about it from this passage.*

Guided by your answers to question 3, pray for your own church, and for your own part in it.

(We are omitting ch.12 as it continues the story of the church of Jerusalem, the subject of the first part of Acts.)

2. A mission begun
Acts 13:1 – 14:7

Read the passage, concentrating on finding out how Paul and Barnabas set about their job. We will look at the sermon (vv.16-41) in detail in the next study.

Note: *Verses 16, 26.* 'Godfearers' is a technical term for Gentile adherents of Judaism who had not been circumcised.

This missionary campaign was initiated by the Holy Spirit who guided the church at Antioch to set apart two of their leaders for service. The whole account is frustratingly silent about the way the Spirit's leading came, both initially, and to

Paul and Barnabas in some of their decisions.

1 *From the passage, make a list of the factors which determined which towns they visited, and when. (If you have time, look up the towns mentioned in a Bible Dictionary.)*
2 *They seem to have started by preaching in the synagogues in each place. This may have been partly from a theological conviction (see Romans 1:16, but also Acts 9:15), but can you think of any other possible reasons?*
3 *How would you summarize Paul and Barnabas' strategy?*
4 *Is there anything in Paul and Barnabas' method of working to help you in the situations you meet at work, college, where you live, etc.?*

Pray for the guidance of the Holy Spirit for yourself, and also for other Christians you know who are particularly concerned to spread the gospel.

3. A sample sermon
Acts 13:16-41

This is an example of one of Paul's evangelistic talks, given to a mixed audience of Jews and Gentiles who attended the regular meetings of the synagogue.
1 *Summarize the main points of Paul's sermon.*
2 *What was the major theme Paul wanted these people to learn? What response was he hoping for?*
3 *Paul starts his sermon with a potted history of Israel, and uses the Old Testament to demonstrate some of his points. Why does he do this?*
4 *Would this approach work with your non-Christian friends? What*

sort of approach could you use to interest them in the gospel?

Pray for opportunities to talk to them about the gospel, and to find out what they think about God.
    If you're not sure how to set about sharing your faith with others, buy and read a book which explains the gospel for those who aren't Christians, e.g. *One to One* by William M. York, Jr. (IVP), or *Basic Christianity* by John R.W. Stott (IVP).

---

4. A case of mistaken identity?
Acts 14:8-28

In Lystra Paul and Barnabas encountered a town which apparently had no synagogue. There was a local legend that Zeus and Hermes had once visited the area and were entertained by an aged couple who were unaware of their identity. Perhaps the crowd were trying not to repeat that mistake!

1 *Paul's speech here (vv. 15-17) is very different from the sermon at Antioch. Can you think of any reasons for the different emphases?*
2 *Paul and Barnabas obviously thought that visiting young churches was worth the risk of returning to places where they'd been ill-treated (v.21). Why was it so important?*
3 *Would their warning (v.22) be one that you would give to young Christians today? What help and advice might be appropriate?*

It was obviously right that the church that had sent Paul and

Barnabas on their way should have a report of their doings, and be able to share in the praise and thanksgiving to God for all that had been achieved.

Are there people from your church serving God in other places? If so, spend some time now praying for them. Perhaps you could arrange to receive their prayer letter, or find some other information, so that you could pray for them regularly.

5. A big issue resolved
Acts 15:1-35

About ten years after Cornelius and his family were converted, the problem of the Gentile Christians' relationship to the Jewish Law was brought to a head when men came to Antioch saying that circumcision,

the mark of God's covenant (Genesis 17:9-14), was necessary for salvation. Since these men came from Judea it was obviously important to settle the issue at its source, in Jerusalem.

1 *What did Peter say about how people are saved? What conclusions are we meant to draw from this?*
2 *James was regarded as the leader of the Jewish Christians, so his opinion was crucial. What point is he making by quoting Amos' prophecy (vv.16-18)?*

James' suggestion in v.20 (see also v.29) was probably a compromise, asking the Gentiles to refrain from doing things that would be particularly repulsive to Jewish Christians in order to maintain good fellowship. It seems that the Antioch church was happy to accept this ruling (v.31).

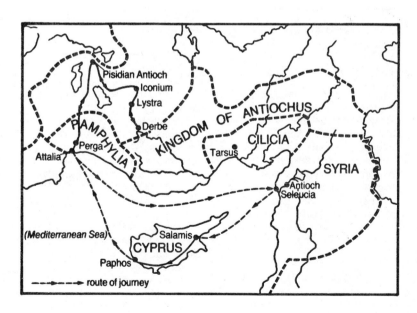

3 *In v.19 James is saying that we should not put any unnecessary barriers in the way of those who want to become Christians. Are there any things we do or say which might make it harder for our friends to become Christians?*

Weekend

You may know quite a lot about Paul (if not, read the account of his conversion in Acts 9), so why not try and find out a bit about Barnabas? As well as references in these chapters you could look at Acts 4:36-37; 9:27; 15:36-41 and Galatians 2:13. What were his special gifts? Try and summarize his contribution to the growth of the church.

Part Seven/Week Two
Ruth (A character study)

This is a moving account of God's overruling in the life of one family. It teaches much about our heavenly Father's care.

1. Yahweh, Ruth's God
Ruth 1:1-18

Verses 1-5 give the background and approximate date. The previous Old Testament book, Judges, records historical events when the judges ruled. It must have been bad enough to leave Judah in search of food, but imagine Naomi coping with bereavement in a strange country. Since Naomi's family had been in Moab only ten years it is likely Ruth and Orpah were still young when their husbands died. Tragedy had struck.

1 *Write down from vv.6-13 the phrases the writer uses involving*

'the Lord'. What do they teach about God and about Naomi's understanding of his ways?

Note: LORD – 'Yahweh', the Hebrew personal name for God.

2 *What do we learn of Ruth's character and her faith (14-18)? Notice she used the same personal name for Israel's God as Naomi had done.*
3 *Despite tragedy Naomi and Ruth acknowledged the Lord as God in their lives. What has been your response when difficulties or tragedies have crossed your path? In what ways have you seen God's purpose in them?*

Write a prayer that expresses your desire to go God's way. As Ruth did, you could think of the different aspects of your life this would involve.

---

2. No flukes with God in control
Ruth 1:19 – 2:13

1 *Naomi was very clear that the Almighty, who was yet her personal God, had been the author of her distress (vv.19-22). Why was it important that she grasped this and did not say 'God has forgotten me; he no longer cares'?*

2 *Ruth gathered up the leftovers of the harvest, not realizing that Boaz, the owner of the field, was a relative (2:1-7). How does the author show that God ordered events for her? (Note v.3).*

3 *Ruth met Boaz and recognized that his kindness was beyond duty (2:8-13). What do we learn of Boaz' knowledge of God and at the same time the way God acts? How did this confirm that Ruth now acknowledged the Lord as her God?*

4 *Read again 1:20-21. Naomi and Ruth both described the same God. How can this be so? How does God both reward and afflict (2:12; 1:21, RSV) — an apparent contradiction? In what ways can this lesson encourage and indeed comfort us? For example, how is God our refuge when we have failed an exam or missed a job we applied for?*

(We will be looking again at the way God can use difficult circumstances to bring good, in the series on Genesis, the 'Suffering with a purpose' study, Week Eight, Day 3.)

Pray today for any you know who need to grasp these different sides to God's character.

For a final example and proof of the truth that following God's guidance brings trouble, look at the life of the Lord Jesus himself. No human life has ever been so completely guided by God, and no human being has ever qualified so comprehensively for the description 'a man of sorrows'.

J. I. Packer, *Knowing God* (IVP)

---

3. Working with God
Ruth 2:14 – 3:13

1 *Boaz' generosity continued. How did Naomi's response in v. 20 show that her understanding of God had held firm despite hardship? She sounded almost excited!*

Think of situations where your faith has been tested. Have you allowed that to strengthen your relationship with the Lord? Be honest!

2 *The situation of two widows is unusual but in v. 9 Boaz would have understood that Ruth was asking for marriage (not necessarily the procedure to adopt today!). Some Christians suggest we should sit back and wait for God to drop blessing from heaven. How do vv. 1-9 and Naomi's previous initiatives show us otherwise? How did Boaz also demonstrate that we need both God's blessing and our God-given mind in action (vv. 10-13)?*

Think of a major decision in your life, like choosing a career. What does the attitude of Naomi and Boaz teach you about finding out God's will?

You can't follow Christ if you stand still.

John White, *The Fight* (IVP)

Pray that you will so know the mind of God that you will increasingly know when to take the initiative and when to wait. Bring to him particular situations where this applies to your life.

---

4. Waiting
Ruth 3:14 – 4:12

1 *How did Boaz show that he was anxious not to discredit Ruth and careful to abide by the customs of his day? In what ways can we cause offence to others by thoughtlessness?*

Note: 4:1 'Gate' means place for public assembly – see Proverbs 31:23.

National customs strike many visitors from overseas as very strange. How much allowance do we make to someone from another culture who seems to misunderstand our way of doing things?

2 *Naomi and Ruth had done their part and had to wait. How can waiting for God to act strengthen our faith in him?*

Naomi and Ruth had to wait a matter of hours, but sometimes God expects us to wait years and years. Examine the situations and people for whom you are praying. How far are you prepared to be patient and wait for God's timing?

You might like to ask an older

Christian how he or she manages to be persistent in prayer.

---

5. A happy ending
Ruth 4:13-22

The Lord had turned Naomi's joy into bitterness and then completed the cycle by giving her joy (not that this is the way he always works).

1 *Looking back over the book, think how many other people had been blessed and would benefit from God's dealings with Naomi. What does this tell us about God's long-term perspective on events in our lives?*

Can you think of ways in which, through hardship in your own life, many people (including yourself!) have ultimately been blessed?

2 *Look back through the whole book and pick out from the phrases which start 'The Lord...' all the activities which are ascribed to him.*

Pray about all these areas of God's activity, and ask him to show you his control and give you faith to trust him.

Weekend

Write a character profile of Ruth, picking out her qualities as a person. (It would be wise to read through the whole book again to make sure you don't miss anything out.)

Which of these qualities would you do well to copy, with God's help? Turn your thoughts into prayer, asking God to help you change where necessary.

Although Ruth lived before Jesus, Romans 8:28 is a good summary of her attitude to God's action and sovereignty. Memorize: Romans 8:28.

Read Psalms 34 and 138.

How does David echo some of Naomi's and Ruth's experiences in these psalms? In what ways does David show us the same God we saw in the book of Ruth? Write down any fresh insights into God's character which you have gained from this series.

An excellent book about Ruth is *The Wings of Refuge*, by David Atkinson (*The Bible Speaks Today* series — IVP).

Part Seven/Week Three
Luke 9 (A meditation)

Like breathing in deeply the summer-evening scent of honeysuckle...like gently stroking a fur coat... like pausing after the main course of a special meal, to enjoy the taste and flavour of good food...so we need slowly to savour and enjoy God's Word to us.

In our activist age, we have tended to look upon meditation as something rather strange and mystical, so a little introduction to meditative Bible study is probably needed.

In meditating on God's Word at least three factors are essential:

1 *We need to allow ourselves TIME, which is why we are taking a week to look at one chapter in Luke's Gospel.*
2 *We need to bring every part of ourselves to the Bible: our emotions, our mind (meditation is not an un-intellectual exercise!) and our spirit. As we ponder a small portion of the Bible we can allow it to go round in our thoughts, focusing on whatever God brings to our attention.*
3 *But before we even start we need to ask God to speak to us.*

PS Sometimes it is hard to concentrate — a half-hour meditation is not an excuse to empty our mind for thirty minutes, nor to devise a Christmas shopping list! Some people find it helpful to think out loud or to write down their thoughts. Memorizing verses also helps concentration.

PPS What we discover about God and the way that he relates to his world should guide us as we pray. Make sure that you turn your thoughts into prayer and action, where appropriate.

You could read *Meditative Prayer* by Richard Foster (IVP), or *Christian Meditation* by Ed Clowney (Presbyterian & Reformed Publishing).

To get started, read through the whole chapter. As you do so, look out for any emphases that Luke made. It may help to write these down.

Remember that Luke was writing the Gospel so that Theophilus would be more certain of what he believed

(Luke 1:1-4). As a result he constantly drew attention to who Jesus was and the persistent way in which Jesus trained his disciples to follow in his footsteps.

identity of Jesus and the **demands of discipleship** which will be explored in this week's studies. But on your own you will no doubt pick up other themes.

1. The disciples' marching orders
Luke 9:1-6

After reading the chapter, read vv.1-6 several times.

Allow your mind to absorb what Jesus was saying to them.

Jesus was not laying down a blueprint for every evangelistic mission. After all, itinerant evangelists today usually take a change of clothes with them!

1 *In what ways would the disciples be sure that they had been sent by Jesus on this particular mission? How far can you share in their confidence?*
2 *How do you know that you have been sent out by Jesus into your own situation? Are you cluttered with personal possessions?*
3 *What have you learned today about the demands of discipleship? Could you explain it to someone else? It might help to write down your summary.*

Pray over what you have thought about today. Pray especially that you will have a power and confidence similar to that of the disciples as you witness to your friends about Jesus Christ.

2. Who is Jesus?
Luke 9:7-9, 18-22, 44-45, 51

The verses are scattered about Luke 9, so start off by reading the chapter and then concentrate on these particular references to Jesus. Read them through several times, slowly.

1 *What can you discover about who Jesus thought he was and how he viewed his task on earth? It might help to write down your thoughts.*
2 *Why does it matter to you that Jesus had to come to earth to die? What would have happened if he had not done so?*
3 *Could you explain to someone else why his task was so important?*

You may want to spend more time looking at Jesus' view of his own mission. To start with, look at Luke 4:18-21; 18:31-34; 20:9-19; 22:7-23.

You may have noticed that Herod's motive in wanting to understand Jesus was very different from the motives of the disciples. Perhaps you can think of some of your friends who are wanting to grasp the truth of Christianity for different reasons. Pray for them and pray that you will be discerning in knowing how to help them.

Herod's desire to meet Jesus was eventually satisfied at his trial (Luke 23:6-12). The disciples were beginning to have some idea about the identity of their teacher but they still had a long way to go.

4 *What have you learnt about the identity of Jesus today?*

Pray over what you have thought about, praising God that Jesus came to earth. You could take the words of a well-known hymn, like 'There is a green hill' and use that to express what you want to say, backed up by what you have been learning.

3. More about Jesus
Luke 9:10-17, 37-43

Read through the whole chapter and then, as previously, focus on the two incidents recorded in these verses. Read them several times, slowly. As you do so, you could imagine that you were one of the disciples with Jesus.

1 *What would you have learned about him from these two occasions? Some suggestions are at the end of this study if you need them. Write down your own observations.*
these different aspects of Jesus' life and ministry. Ask yourself how far you have seen evidence of his activity in your own life or in the life of your church. How much is this the Jesus that you are getting to know?

Jesus has power over evil; he can provide for physical needs; he wants to heal; he lovingly cares for individuals; he is patient with the disciples.

4. The cost of discipleship
Luke 9:23-27, 57-62

The cross symbolizes your willingness to die if needs be, or to give up all else for the surpassing glory of following it. Jesus calls you to pick it up and heave it over your back in the same way that he carried his own cross — not in your lapel or round your neck but over your shoulders. It may look rough and heavy as you stare at it on the ground, but you will be surprised to find how light it feels as you bear it. And it will mark you in the eyes of demons, men and angels as one who despises humiliation and who deliberately chooses the company of the One from whom the world hides its face.*

John White, *The Cost of Commitment (IVP)*

Read the chapter through, reminding yourself of what you discovered about discipleship in the first study.

1 *Examine the verses above in the light of this quotation. Can you pick out the significant features of discipleship pictured here? Write down your observations.*
2 *How far have you 'heaved the cross over your own back', identifying yourself as a follower of Jesus, the one who is more important to you than any other person or thing? Take some time to consider this question. As you do so, you could put under the microscope each of your own ambitions and attitudes to possessions. Write them down as you identify them.*
3 *What is the price to be paid for **not** taking up your cross daily?*

Jesus is not saying that disciples should take their personal responsibilities lightly. But he is saying that any follower needs to weigh up the cost before he embarks on the path of discipleship of Jesus Christ.

4 *Could you explain to a friend what you have learnt about discipleship today? You should be able to. By writing down such lessons it will help you to clarify your own thinking.*

5. Jesus in all his glory
Luke 9:28-36

You will now be quite familiar with the chapter but read it once again to put this passage in context. Then read these verses and try to picture what happened. The glory of this occasion, though, is beyond any human imagination. Make a note of any details that you have not noticed before.

1 *No wonder the disciples couldn't take it all in and Peter didn't know what he was saying. What new dimension would this have given to the disciples as they began to understand Jesus?*
2 *Why else do you think the transfiguration is important?*

Allow yourself to meditate on the truth that this Jesus, seen here in all his splendour as the chosen Son of God, did in fact come to this earth to die.

To help you, you might like to divide a page into two columns. On one side write down all that you have discovered from this incident about Jesus. On the other side make a note of the importance of each of these observations. Then turn what you have noted into praise and prayer.

Weekend

The disciples were still at nursery school — as we all are! What lessons did they learn through the incidents recorded in 9:46-56?

Have you learned them too?

And what about the other lessons learnt this week as you have studied what must now be a very familiar chapter?

It would be good to look back over the notes you have made this week.

What have you discovered about the two themes that were mentioned at the start — the *identity of Jesus* and the *demands of discipleship?*

Thank God for what he has taught you and pray that like the disciples you will be teachable, so that you will be able to answer the question 'Who is this Jesus?'

Try this week to memorize verses that crystallize the two themes:
■ the identity of Jesus — v.35
■ the demands of discipleship — vv.23-24

Part Seven/Week Four
The name of the Lord (A word study)

What's in a name? John Smith or Helena Hebblethwaite. Does it really matter? In the Bible the name given to a person usually has a double significance. It is a means of identification but often also describes the nature or character of the bearer. This series looks at some of the names for God and is a marvellous way of understanding and knowing him better.

1. 'I am who I am'
Exodus 3:1-15

The Lord's revelation to Moses showed that God wants to communicate with and help his people. It came at a critical time in Israel's history when they were being badly treated by the Egyptians.

1 *What did Moses discover about God in vv.1-6? How did he respond initially?*
2 *There was a reason for God's revelation at this moment. What was that? What do vv.7-12 teach about God's character and his involvement with his people?*
3 *Moses' reaction was a very natural one — why me? How should God's promise in v.12 have helped him?*
4 *But Moses was not satisfied and asked 'what is his name?', using a Hebrew word for 'what' that requested the meaning of the name in the answer. How would God's answer be an assurance to Moses? How did God also show in vv.15-16 that he was not altering what Moses already knew of him?*

How is this revelation an assurance to you, especially in any current difficulties?
    Look up John 8:57-59. At the end of a long discussion with a group of Jews, Jesus claimed this title for himself. Why did the Jews respond so angrily?

2. The Holy One
Isaiah 6:1-8

Isaiah prophesied to a nation seeing God's judgment on them for sin and often used the title 'Holy One of Israel' in contrast to Israel's behaviour. Ours is the same holy God and we too can see the Lord through Isaiah's eyes.

> *And it took the breath out of Isaiah. This was no place for him; he was out of his element. The holiness of God is no environment for man to be in.*
>
> R T France, *The Living God* (IVP)

1 *What would Isaiah learn from his vision of the Lord and the seraphim (vv.1-4)?*
2 *How did his response in v.5 show the impact of his vision? Notice what had to be dealt with before he was commissioned (vv.6-7).*
3 *In what terms did Isaiah describe the Israelites at the start of his prophecy (1:1-4)? What was their attitude to God?*
4 *But the Holy One does not act in malice and punitive glee. How does Isaiah 30:8-18 show this? What is God's longing? Note Isaiah's constant use of 'The Holy One'.*

Isaiah 43:1-7 prophesied of God's care for Israel after the exile, which the nation suffered because of her sin. Notice the linking of 'Saviour' with the title 'Holy One of Israel'. The Lord longs to be gracious to you too. Make sure unconfessed sin is not in the way.
    The LORD. Why the capitals? It is a translation of the Hebrew word YAHWEH, a name for God, and is

really *the* name for God. In particular, Yahweh was the God of the patriarchs, as we read in Exodus 3:15. Yahweh is a proper noun, the name of a Person though that Person is divine. It brought God near to man, and he spoke to the patriarchs as one friend to another.

3. The living God
Jeremiah 10:1-16

A relationship with the living God has powerful consequences in our lives and its absence leaves a hole nothing can fill. The Israelites had been influenced by the idol worship of surrounding nations and in these verses of vivid contrast Jeremiah pointed out the futility of idols.

1 *Draw a vertical line down your notebook. On the left, list the reasons Jeremiah gave why idols were useless. By contrast how was God portrayed? Write the answers on the right. Reflect on the two columns for a minute or two.*
2 *What was one of the results of idol worship, described in v.2? Looking at similarities between Jeremiah's time and today, why is astrology increasingly popular now? What part can you play in directing your friends to the living God instead of, for example, newspaper horoscopes? What other idols do we have today, which in effect are substitutes for Israel's wooden ones? Are any of these **your** idols?*
3 *Paul used 'the living God' as a title when describing the conversion of the Thessalonian Christians. Look up 1 Thessalonians 1: 8-10. What is the similarity between Paul's usage and that of Jeremiah?*

Look over your answers today concerning the living God and idols and spend some time praying about the implications.

4. Names commemorating events

There are several places in the Old Testament where compound names for God are used. They are not names in the proper sense but rather they commemorate events. They illustrate God's character and ways with us and for that reason are exciting to study.

Genesis 22:13-18 Judges 6:19-24
Exodus 15:23-27 Jeremiah 23:1-6
Exodus 17:8-15 Ezekiel 48:15,35

Look at each of these passages in turn. For each, write the reference and the name used, as a heading, and then answer the following questions:

1 *What is the context of the incident?*
2 *Why was the name appropriate?*
3 *Is obedience important in the account? In what ways?*
4 *Summarize what the incident teaches of God's character and the way he showed his nature to mankind before we had the example of Jesus.*

You may not have time to do them all. If time is short, do a few completely and the rest at the weekend.

Which incident have you personally found most challenging and helpful?

Meditate on the situations in

which these commemorative names could help you. If you find it helpful, jot such situations down alongside the heading for that name.

Try to memorize the translation of the names.

5. Using Jesus' name

Why is it a privilege to use Jesus' name? This study looks at several examples and will enrich your understanding and worship of him.

John 14 – 16 is Jesus' farewell discourse to his disciples. In it he promises them help for the future, showing the power available in his name.

1 *Pick out the purpose and consequences of the disciples' asking the Father in Jesus' name.*
2 *What does it mean to ask in Jesus' name? (If you are stuck, look up 'Name' in a Bible Dictionary.) What does this teach you about your praying?*

Peter and John were put in jail after healing a lame man in the name of Jesus (Acts 3).

3 *Note the occasions Luke uses 'name' (3:16; 4:7,10, 12,17).*

4 *Why and how did Peter and John use the opportunity to proclaim the name of Jesus? What opportunities have you day by day to tell of Jesus' name?*

Turn the thoughts of this study into prayer, asking in Jesus' name that you may use his name properly, to his glory, day by day.

Weekend

How do the writers of the NT letters think of God the Father? In what contexts do they use this title for God? The easiest way of answering questions like these is to use a concordance. Below are listed some of the entries from the Cruden's Concordance under 'father'. Look up as many as you have time for, writing out what they teach you of God as your heavenly Father.

Romans 6:4; 8:15
1 Corinthians 8:6
2 Corinthians 1:3
Galatians 1:3; 1:4; 4:2
Ephesians 3:14; 4:6; 6:23
Hebrews 1:5; 12:7
James 1:17
1 Peter 1:2; 1:17
2 Peter 1:17
1 John 1:3; 3:1
Jude 1

Part Seven/Week Five
The book of Habakkuk (A detailed study)

A common question as people look at the state of the world today is 'Why doesn't God do something

about it?'

Habakkuk asked a similar question as he looked at the situation around him in Judah — a nation which was supposed to be God's own people. The answers he got were both surprising and shocking, and at first sight seemed to raise more problems than they solved.

Most Christians have to face times when God seems to be acting in unexpected and perplexing ways, both on a large scale and in their own lives. Habakkuk's response may help us to begin to cope with those situations.

Habakkuk lived in a time when Judah was being threatened by the Babylonians. They had defeated some of her neighbours, and were about to attack and conquer Judah. Some twenty years later they took many of her people away into exile. You can read the account of it in 2 Chronicles 36:11-21.

1. Habakkuk's first complaint
Habakkuk 1:1-11

1 *Make a list of the evils Habakkuk complained of in Judah (vv.2-4). How many of these are present in our society?*
2 *Try to summarize Habakkuk's reaction to this situation in a couple of sentences. Do you ever think like this?*
3 *What was God's answer (vv.5-11)? What can Judah expect at the hands of the Babylonians (Chaldeans in the* RSV*)?*

What situations make you question God? God's judgment on Judah was to come through an event which we would interpret as being totally secular. In what ways do *you* expect

God to act in your own life, and the lives of those around you?

2. Habakkuk's second complaint
Habakkuk 1:12 – 2:1

Read the passage, trying to assess Habakkuk's particular reaction to this situation.

Habakkuk's reaction (1:12) seems to be one of faith, both in remembering what he already knew about God, and in accepting what God had just said to him.

1 *Make a list of the titles Habakkuk used for God in this verse. Why is each appropriate to the problem the prophet is facing?*
2 *Despite Habakkuk's faith, he had many questions about God's use of the Babylonians to bring judgment on Judah. Why did he find it so shocking (vv.13-17)?*
3 *How did he set about finding an answer (see 2:1)?*

God sometimes seems to us to be acting unreasonably. Think of specific instances in your own life where this has been the case. How can Habakkuk's response help?

Bring to God any situations that are troubling you or those you know at the moment.

3. God's answer
Habakkuk 2:2-20

As you read the passage, try to pick out the general flow of what God was saying.

1 *Can you summarize God's answer*

to Habakkuk in just one or two sentences?

God's answer was to be written down for all to read (v.2) and it was sure to be fulfilled at the proper time (v.3). It could be summed up by saying that the Babylonians would eventually reap the results of their evil, while the righteous would live because of their trust in God (v.4).

2 *Verses 6-20 are a series of five 'woes' pronounced on the Babylonians (vv.6-8, 9-11, 12-14, 15-17, 18-20). Try to sum up in a few words each of the evils being condemned.*
Notice how the judgment pronounced against each one is appropriate — a serious version of the punishment fitting the crime!
3 *What encouragements are there in this chapter for Habakkuk, and others like him, who want to remain faithful to God in a hostile world?*

Spend some time meditating on verse 20. Consciously bring your own life and the state of the world under God's scrutiny.

---

4. Habakkuk's prayer
Habakkuk 3:1-15

This chapter is a hymn, and the musical directions in vv.1 and 19 suggest that it may have been used in the worship in the temple. It was an expression of Habakkuk's confidence in God, no doubt deeply influenced by the events of the previous chapters.

1 *In verse 2 what was Habakkuk asking God to do?*

2 *Try to write out this verse in words you might use to pray.*

Verses 3-15 form a poetic picture of what happens when God does act. Part of it includes references to God's dealings with his people in the past. For example, the places mentioned in v.3 are the regions around Sinai, and this is a reference to the giving of the Law during the exodus (Exodus 20:18-21 gives you part of the account). Other parts appear to refer to future events.

3 *What impressions do you think this passage is intended to convey?*
4 *What was the purpose of God's actions (see especially v.13)?*

Memorize Habakkuk 3:2, a plea for God's merciful action.
Use verse 2 to help you in your prayers. Try to think of specific parts of God's work that need his reviving power.

---

5. Habakkuk's confidence in God
Habakkuk 3:16-19

Read through the passage two or three times so that you get the feel of it. Remember the situation that Habakkuk was facing as he made this moving statement of confidence in God.
His response seemed to be partly one of physical fear (v.16) as he considered what would happen when the Babylonians invaded Judah. (Remember that the events of v.17 would be catastrophic in an agricultural community.)
Nevertheless, he was able to

express his confidence, and even joy, in God

1 *What was the basis of his confidence?*
2 *How had his attitudes changed since the beginning of the book?*
3 *What, precisely, had made the difference?*
   Can you think of examples of your own attitudes changing in this way?

Part of Habakkuk's confidence came from remembering God's dealings with his people in the past.

What events, both historical and personal, can you use to remind yourself of God's faithfulness when life is difficult? Spend some time thanking God for them now.

Weekend

If you have the time, re-read the whole book, looking to see how it all fits together. You may also notice things you missed on the first reading.

Can you sum up the impression left with you after studying Habakkuk? What is its central message? Are there parts of your life and attitudes which it affects?

Habakkuk 2:4 is a very famous verse quoted in the New Testament (Romans 1:17; Galatians 3:11; Hebrews 10:37- 39). Look at these references (in their contexts!), and see if you can find ways in which its meaning has developed with the coming of Christ.

Part Seven/Week Six
Paul's letter to the Galatians (A whole book study)

A personal relationship with God is much more important than getting your doctrine sorted out — or is it?

Paul is writing here to Christians with an undisputed personal experience of God (he can even use it to further his argument; look at 3:2), and yet he is deeply concerned that they have started to believe something other than the gospel he preached to them — with potentially disastrous consequences; read 5:2-4.

We may not have the same problems as the Galatians, but we still need to be clear on the basic issues of the gospel and how to recognize error, so that we too may avoid those consequences.

Scholars disagree about which churches in Galatia Paul was writing to, and when this letter was written, but it seems probable that these churches were the ones in Pisidian Antioch, Iconium, Lystra and Derbe founded on Paul's first missionary journey. (If you have time, either now or at the weekend, read the accounts in Acts 13-14.) It may have been written just before the Council of Jerusalem (Acts 15) which dealt with a similar problem to the one Paul is tackling here.

If you want to go into the letter in more detail than is possible here, *The Message of Galatians* by John Stott (IVP) will be a great help.

1. A bird's-eye study

The idea of this series is to get a grasp of the overall themes of this letter, so start by quickly reading the whole letter.

Don't worry if you can't understand all of it — you can go back and work on the difficult bits later.

1 *As you read, jot down anything you can find about the problems Paul was tackling in the Galatian churches, and also their consequences.*

Pray for your own church, that it will be kept from false teaching, and that the leaders will have the wisdom to recognize error and teach the truth.

---

2. The argument from history
Galatians 1–2

By preaching a gospel different from Paul's, his opponents were challenging his authority to preach.

1 *What does Paul say in these chapters about where he got his message from?*
2 *It would seem that his opponents were claiming the authority of the apostles in Jerusalem for their teaching (but see Acts 15:24). How does Paul refute this claim?*
3 *In 2:11-21 Paul records an incident which caused a public disagreement with Peter (Cephas in RSV) over the basis of fellowship between Jewish and Gentile Christians. Why do you think Paul reacted so strongly?*
4 *What basic principle was at stake?*

The heart of Paul's gospel is that Christ died for our sins (see 1:4; 2:20) — surely something worth defending! Take time now to thank God for this.

---

3. The argument from Scripture, 1
Galatians 3:1-25

Close this book, and try to write a brief summary of each of the paragraphs in this chapter.

Here is one suggested outline to help you along if you get stuck. Don't read it first!

vv.1-5   The Galatians' personal experience — they received the Spirit by faith, not by keeping the Law.

vv.6-9   Abraham, too, was justified ('put right with God' in GNB) by faith, and promised that through him the Gentiles would receive the same blessing.

vv.10-14   No-one can keep the Law perfectly, so trying to be justified that way only leads to condemnation. Justification comes through faith, because Christ redeemed us from that condemnation by taking it on himself.

vv.15-18   God's promise to Abraham came before the giving of the Law, so the Law cannot change it.

vv.19-25   The Law was given to restrain and discipline us until the promise should be fulfilled in Christ.

vv.26-29 The Galatian Christians have been justified through faith in Christ. Therefore they are all the true descendants of Abraham, without distinction between them.

If you had trouble with your outline, go over the one above and compare it with the passage, until you have got the flow of the argument fixed in your mind.

4. The argument from Scripture, 2
Galatians 3:26 – 5:1

1 *'So you are no longer a slave, but a son' (4:7, NIV). What does Paul say in 3:26 – 4:11 about the results of this new relationship?*
2 *4:8-20 are a 'personal aside' about Paul's relationship with the Galatian Christians. What was Paul's attitude to these churches?*
3 *How did this contrast with the attitudes and motives of the false teachers?*

The argument in the last part of the passage (4:21 – 5:1), though difficult for us, is the kind that would have been familiar in the Jewish rabbinical schools, and thus presumably to Paul's opponents. To follow it fully you will need to know quite a lot about the Old Testament (*The Message of Galatians* would be useful here!).

4 *Leaving aside the details, what point is Paul making by using this argument?*

Re-read 3:26 – 4:11 and thank God for the privileges of being in his family.

5. The moral argument
Galatians 5 and 6

If they were not bound by the Law, it would have been easy for the Galatians to use their freedom in Christ as an excuse for immoral behaviour (5:13). Indeed some of Paul's opponents may have used this as an argument against his doctrine; look at Romans 6:1.

1 *What encouragements did Paul give the Galatians, to help them live holy lives?*
2 *How could the Galatians decide whether or not they were living by the Spirit?*
3 *6:1-6 talks about how the Galatians could help each other in this life in the Spirit. What principles can you find here for helping other Christians?*

Take time to think through the different areas of your own life in the light of what you have learnt about living by the Spirit.

Weekend
Read through the whole letter again.
    Now that you have done some more work on it, you should be able to follow Paul's train of thought in more detail than the first time you read it.
    Can you think of any modern situations where people are tending to make mistakes similar to the ones

the Galatians were making?

Are there modern equivalents to being circumcised and keeping the Law?

In the light of this letter, what should our attitude be to those involved in error, either in teaching false doctrine (1:6-9), or being taught it (4:8-20)?

This is always a difficult area! What principles can you find in Galatians to help you?

Part Seven/Week Seven
Genesis 12-50 (part 1) (A bird's-eye study)

Ancient family trees are fascinating. But frustrating too, for they give only the bare facts about a generation—who married whom and who gave birth to whom. Tragedies and pleasures are lost in the mists of time.

In the next 10 studies we are going to look at the first four generations of the family of Abraham. Fortunately, we are not restricted by a family tree for we have plenty of detail about the personal lives of people in this family. In fact, we have so much, that we can take only a quick bird's-eye view.

But that is a good way of reading the Bible — following the main story-line by reading large chunks and examining a few key themes as we go along.

We will skip through several chapters at one sitting and then go over them in a bit more detail.

But you may be asking, 'What is the value of learning about these ancient men of God?'

Their God is our God even though our understanding of him must be greater since we are living this side of the cross. He deals with us and them in very similar ways. And some of the promises that God made to Abraham are affecting us 4,000 years later!

---

1. Making a start
Genesis 12:1 – 20:18

Ask God to help you grasp the amazing nature of the promises he made to Abraham.

1 *As you read through these chapters make a note of all the promises God made. But notice too that these promises were accompanied by conditions. Write these down alongside the promises.*

God's people today are descendants of Abraham in that the commitment God made to Abraham he has also made to the church.

2 *What are the results of such a commitment on his part?*
3 *What about times when the church sins or forgets his promises?*
4 *And what happens when you try to*

live as though God has no plans for, or interest in, your life?

Thank God that his promises still stand even though you yourself, and the church as a whole, sometimes ignore or distort them.

---

2. A man of God
Genesis 12:1 – 13:18; 18:16 – 19:38

Abraham, the man God had chosen to set in motion his plan of salvation for the world, was an outstanding character. This is particularly clear when he is compared with his nephew, Lot (although, as we shall see in the next study, Abraham was not perfect himself).

1 *As you read these chapters, list the differences in the character and behaviour of Abraham and Lot. You may note some similarities as well.*

Look at what you have written about Abraham's character. Much of it concerns his relationship with God. How do your character and life measure up in each of these areas?

'All nations will be blessed'
Right from the start God's promises were not just for Abraham and his family (12:3). Israel frequently forgot this – as do we!

What are you doing to bring about the fulfilment of this promise made to Abraham 4,000 years ago?

Can you think of overseas students in your college or people of other nationalities in your town who need to know of a God who makes and keeps promises?

In what ways are you building up relationships with them?

And how are you praying for those who have actually left their own country to take the gospel to others?

Note on 'Covenant'
God had entered into a special relationship with his people, a relationship which was an indispensable part of the covenant he made with them. This was no ordinary business agreement between partners, for God always stated the terms and took the initiative. Its dual purpose was to maintain fellowship between God and his people and to ensure that they were holy and separate from other nations. Israel did have a responsibility to be faithful to the covenant.

Four distinct covenants are described in the Old Testament: with Noah in Genesis 9, with Abraham in Genesis 15, with Moses on Mount Sinai in Exodus 19 – 24 and with David in 2 Samuel 7. There is also the promise of a new kind of covenant in Jeremiah 31:31-34.

There is not a great deal of information on how covenants were actually made, although descriptions in, for example, Genesis 15 do give us some inkling.

2 *Why not read the article on 'Covenant' in a Bible Dictionary?*

---

3. It's a matter of faith
Genesis 15:1 – 17:27

It was not enough for Abraham to receive the promises. A response was required.

Look back to your notes from study 1 to refresh your memory on the conditions that accompanied the promises.

1 *As you read chs.15-17 notice how the promises of ch.15 were expanded in ch.17. What was Abraham's response to these promises? Jot down your conclusions.*
2 *Abraham has been heralded throughout the Bible as a man of faith (see Romans 4, for example). What evidence do you see here that he deserved such a title? Write down your observations.*

Notice that it was *God* who declared him righteous — pure and acceptable in the sight of a holy God.

He had done the same for those who have faith in his power and willingness to make anyone righteous.

3 *Try to explain in your own words why this business of being 'accepted as righteous' is such an important part of God's dealing with mankind today. Why are we unable to make ourselves acceptable to God?*

Do you live as someone whom God has made righteous? In what ways will this show itself?

4 *This man of faith and righteousness was still prone to sin, as we read for example in 12:10-20 and ch.16. What were Abraham's failings?*
5 *Despite such imperfections God still kept his promises to Abraham, although he had to suffer the consequences. (Ishmael's descendants were a 'thorn in the side' of Israel from then on. Look up Genesis 25:18.) How could he have kept himself from sinning?*

What about us? How can we guard against falling into sin? You might like to discuss this with others who have been Christians longer than you have.

4. God in control
Genesis 21 – 25

God's plans are not like castles in the air — unrealistic and highly unlikely to materialize. Having laid his plans, God has the power to see them become reality, although man's waywardness may sometimes appear to alter them.

Ask God to reassure you that he is in control of the affairs of this world.

1 *As you read these chapters watch out for evidence that God is in control of every situation — be it the timing of the birth of Isaac or Isaac's marriage with Rebekah. Note down the evidence that you collect.*
2 *Abraham may sometimes have wondered if God's power could really bring about the impossible. Sometimes we too are fearful and forget God is in control.*
3 *Write down your own fears alongside the evidence that God is all-powerful. What happens to your fears as you look at the God who is in command?*

Pray for any you know who are fearful and pray that you will be able to share with them the hope and confidence which comes from knowing that God is in control.

5. Just testing!
Genesis 22:1-19

Being a man of faith did not mean instant gratification for every one of Abraham's whims and wishes. Faith grows through being tested and Abraham's faith faced just such a trial. Did God make and keep his promises?

1 *Read through these verses a couple of times, seeing it first of all from Abraham's point of view and then from God's angle.*

In what ways was Abraham's faith strengthened through this testing?

Can you think of times when your own faith or that of your church or even the wider Christian fellowship has been tested, yet through it all blessing has resulted?

Are you prepared for your own faith to be tested?

Pause to thank God for the way in which he works and pray for any situations you know in which someone is going through a tough patch.

God not only tested Abraham's faith but also demonstrated that to be in a covenant relationship with him required total obedience, whatever the cost.

2 *Make a list of all the things and people which are precious to you. Is God more important to you than each of them?*

Weekend

Over the weekend find time to read chapters 26 – 36.

As you do so watch out for the ways in which Jacob was like his grandfather, Abraham.

Both were part of God's eternal plan, yet both tried to manipulate God. Both received God's blessing, yet both sinned many times.

Write down your observations.

You may have enjoyed your encounter with Abraham, the man of faith. If you want to find out more about him *A Man and His God* by Denis Lane (Presbyterian & Reformed Publishing) is particularly helpful.

Part Seven/Week Eight
Genesis 12-50 (part 2) (A bird's-eye study)

---

1. I did it my way
Genesis 25:19-34; 27:1 – 28:22

In Genesis 25:23 God promised that Jacob, the younger son, would rule his elder brother.

1 *As you look at these chapters, and in the light of your weekend reading, make a note of the ways in which Jacob tried to make things happen his own way and in his own time.*

What were the consequences of his behaviour?

In what ways have you ever been like Jacob (in searching for a marriage partner ... in resorting to dishonest practices, arguing that the end justifies the means)?

Have you suffered from the consequences?

Such behaviour must grieve God, although Jacob did not appear to be particularly aware of this.

Pause to ask God for forgiveness and for strength to face the consequences.

Despite Jacob's deviousness he was not deserted by God; like Abraham, he received God's blessing.

2 *Look at 28:10-22 and in your own words describe Jacob's response to the Lord.*

Jacob has often been accused here of bargaining with God. Yet he was very conscious of the awesomeness associated with being in God's presence (vv.16-17). So it is probably fairer to say that he was taking the promise of v.15 and translating the general into the particular.

Acknowledging that you are now in the presence of a mighty God, thank him that he does have a plan for you and for his world, and in his own time his plans will become reality.

Pray for patience to wait *with* God, and an awareness of his willingness to bless.

2. God's faithfulness
Genesis 32:1 – 33:20

In some respects Jacob was the same man here as the fugitive of 14 years before, in ch.28.

Yet there had been some change.

1 *Reading these chapters, what changes can you detect in Jacob?*
2 *What promises, made at Jacob's encounter with God at Bethel, had been fulfilled?*
What does that say about the kind of God we have?

Pause to praise God that he did keep his promises to Jacob and that over a period of time he had been changing Jacob.

Thank him that he can and is doing the same in you, if you let him.

One of the similarities that you probably noticed when comparing Abraham and Jacob was that these two men were men of prayer. They can provide us with insights into how we can pray.

3 *What can we learn from Jacob's prayer in 32:9-12 about showing our gratitude to God and persistence in prayer?*
4 *Look again at Abraham's prayer in 18:16-33. Write down what you notice and see how you can use it in your own prayer time today.*

Jacob was a different man as a result of his night-long encounter with God.

Are you marked out from others because you have met with the living God?

3. Suffering with a purpose
Genesis 37 – 50

There was no way in which Abraham could have anticipated God's future dealings with his descendants.

As you read these chapters watch out for the way God fulfilled his promises of Genesis 12, even though suffering was involved.

This is an exciting story, so make sure that you really get into it as you would if it was a detective novel. The hero comes out well in the end!

Pray that you will grow to see that, although God's plans may seem to be nonsensical, involving suffering and hardship, they do ultimately result in great blessing, for he is a God who loves to bless his people.

4. God overrules man's sin
Genesis 37, 39 and 40

Almost all the people mentioned in these chapters illustrate the fact that man is basically sinful.

1 *Make a note of all the sins committed.*
In what ways did God use these sinful acts to good purpose?

This is a common theme in the Bible and it is probably an experience with which you yourself are familiar.

What reassurance is it to you that God can overrule man's sin?

Think of times when you have needed to be reminded of this truth.

Joseph himself may frequently have wondered why he was going through so much hardship. Why had God allowed him to be sold as a slave into a foreign country? Why was he even reduced to being a prisoner in Egypt?

You have no doubt asked God similar questions about the things that have gone wrong in your own life.

2 *How was God preparing Joseph for the future?*

How conscious are you that in the future God has a task that only you can do and for which preparation is necessary now?

Read Ephesians 2:8-10 and meditate on those verses.

What does it mean to you personally that you are God's workmanship?

How should that affect your approach to your life now?

What place for grumbling is there in the behaviour of a Christian?

Pray that you will be willing to be used by God in the future, even though the training school may seem unattractive.

5. A lifetime of trusting God
Genesis 41:41-57; 45:1 – 46:4; 49:29 – 50:21

Over Joseph's lifetime he had matured from the seemingly conceited boy into a man of impeccable behaviour. As an old man he could look back over his life and understand far more clearly God's plans and purposes.

1 *Looking particularly at 41:51-52; 45:4-8; 50:19-20, how would you explain his understanding in your own words?*

Age, experience and a daily encounter with God over the years do indeed help God's people to see life from his perspective. You don't build up this sort of relationship with God overnight.

What patterns and habits are you

establishing with God so that in time to come you will be able to see things from God's viewpoint?

Get to know a godly, older person in your church. Find out how they maintain a living relationship with God and how they have come to trust God and understand his plans and purposes.

There are no expressions majestic enough to tell of the glory I have seen or of the wonder of finding that I, a neurotic, unstable, middle-aged man, have my feet firmly planted in eternity and breathe the air of heaven. And all this has come to me through a careful study of Scripture.

John White, *The Fight (IVP)*

God always works through individuals even though they sometimes don't even acknowledge his existence.

2 *The story of Joseph illustrates that God has his man for each moment and can use secular authorities for his good purpose. What encouragement is that to you?*

Pray for any Christians you know who are in positions of influence in the secular world.

Weekend

Over these 10 studies on Genesis several themes have turned up again and again. Look back over your notes and check that you have grasped them all.

1 *God had a plan for Abraham's family which would have far-reaching implications. Through him, all the families of the earth would be blessed.*
2 *The promises that God made formed part of this plan — and they placed certain conditions on Abraham and family.*
3 *Abraham needed to remember that he was not chosen because of anything that he had done but simply because God loved him. He just had to believe.*
4 *Being part of God's plan did not guarantee an easy life. It involved much heartache and sorrow. Yet God was still in control.*
5 *These men did not always behave as though they believed God would work things out his way. Nor were they sinless. But God remained faithful. Having made his promises about the shape of things to come, he would keep his word.*

Read through Hebrews 11:8-22, a brief summary of the early days of God's people.

Do you have a similar faith in such a God?

Part Eight

Psalm 103
Mark's Gospel
Love
Peter
The book of Jeremiah
Human beings, warts and all!
Beginning the Pastoral Letters

Part Eight/Week One
Psalm 103 (A meditation)

Why should we praise God? The psalmist gives us many reasons here. As we look in some detail at what he says, it should encourage our own thanksgiving. Each study looks at just a few verses, but you should try to see where they fit into the whole psalm. Where cross references to other passages on a similar theme are given, don't feel obliged to look up all of them — concentrate on the psalm first, and use the other passages to help further reflection. You could also follow up other passages you know on a similar theme.

1. 'Count your blessings'
Psalm 103:1-5

The psalmist starts by encouraging himself to praise the Lord — with his whole being (verse 1), not merely an outward show. Like him we probably need the command in verse 2 not to forget how much God has done for us — when we do remember, it should encourage us to praise God, just as it did him.

1 *Look through the whole psalm and write a list of all the things the psalmist says the Lord has done for him.*
2 *How many of these are things you can identify with? — mark them on the list.*
3 *Now look back on your own*

experience *as a Christian and write your own list of things (both spiritual and physical — see verse 3) for which you can praise the Lord.*

Now spend some time in praise and thanksgiving for yourself — use these lists to encourage you, as the psalmist did.

Consider: Can you honestly say with the psalmist 'He fills my life with good things' (verse 5)? — or are there things you do not yet have, and wish the Lord would give you? Now would be a good time to talk these over with God. It may be that these are blessings which God wants to give you at some time in the future, or it may be that God knows these things are not best for you (*cf.* Luke 11:9-13).

2. Looking back
Psalm 103:6-8

Not only can the psalmist look to his own experience of God's blessing to encourage his praise, but also that of the whole people of God down the ages and in his own time (notice the word 'our' and 'we' in verses 10,12,14). These verses recall the Lord's rescue of his people when they were oppressed in Egypt, and particularly his covenant with them at Sinai, when he revealed himself and promised to guide them. Verse 7 recalls such verses as Exodus 33:12-17, and verse 8, Exodus 34:5-6.

1 *What does the psalmist say here about God's character?*

Try to express it in different words from the psalm!

2 *Consider: Can you think of examples of God's faithfulness to believers, either in past times, or in other parts of the world? Stop and thank God for his faithfulness, both to you and to others.*

Reading Christian biographies can be a great encouragement to your own faith in God, such as Dr Helen Roseveare's story, Give Me This Mountain *(Bethany), or Corrie ten Boom's* The Hiding Place *(Zondervan).*

As Christians we look back to Jesus' death and resurrection as the supreme revelation of God's love to us, just as the Jews looked back to the Exodus. Read Romans 8:31-39, where Paul uses this theme to encourage his readers to face their current problems. Why is it such a stimulus to confidence in God?

---

3. God's forgiveness
Psalm 103:8-14

The psalmist turns to one particular example of God's compassion — his forgiveness.

1 *How do we deserve to be treated (verse 10)?*
2 *Why doesn't God treat us like that?*

Not an easy question! — the psalmist's only answer lies in his understanding of God's character — he uses poetic imagery to show how

sure forgiveness is (verses 11-12). We have the privilege of seeing this much more clearly demonstrated in Jesus.

Read: 1 Peter 2:21-25. (Peter is making clear allusions to Isaiah 53 — you might like to read that as well.)

3 *What extra grounds do Christians have for being certain of God's forgiveness?*

Stop and thank God for his forgiveness — it may help to remember specific sins from the last day or so, or even from further back, confess them, and thank God that they are so decisively put away (verse 12).

4 *It is easy to take God's forgiveness too lightly! What attitude towards God does the psalmist expect in those who are forgiven? How will this affect our attitude towards sin?*

---

4. 'We are dust'
Psalm 103:13-18

1 *What does the psalmist mean when he says we are dust (verse 14) and our life is like grass (verse 15)? (Do you ever think of yourself like this?)*
2 *What does he say gives meaning to life?*
3 *Think about your non-Christian friends. What is important to them? What do they use to give meaning to life?*

Consider: Do you ever let such things become more important to you than the Lord? Read Jesus' warning about such things in Matthew 6:19-24.

Read the whole psalm again, and look out for all that it says about the way the Lord loves us. Praise him for that love!

5. 'Our God reigns'
Psalm 103:17-22

As he contemplates all that God has done for him and for his people, the psalmist sums it up by saying that God rules over everything (verse 19).

1 *What response does the psalmist expect people to make to God's sovereignty?*
2 *Why do you think he calls not only men, but angels and all other creatures to join him in praise?*
3 *Read through the whole psalm again, and make a list of all that it teaches about God's character.*

Consider: What does the Lord's rule mean for you personally? Do you have any problems which seem to be insoluble? Are there areas of your life where what you want and what God wants don't coincide? As you think and pray about these, it may help to look back at what this psalm says about God's love and faithfulness.

Weekend

Pray: Since God is king *over all* (verse 19), it follows that we can bring the needs of the whole world to him. Think of the major stories which have been in the news in the past week, and take time to pray for the needs which these represent. Try to understand something of the background to this week's crises, by careful reading of news reports and editorial comments. Do you know of Christian missions working in such areas, who could do with prayer now?

Part Eight/Week Two
Mark's Gospel, 1 (A detailed study)

Traditionally the author of this Gospel is Mark, who appears at various times in the early days of the church. The reference of Mark 14:51 possibly applies to him. He may have been heavily influenced by Peter. This Gospel would therefore be a record of Peter's personal account of the life of Jesus.

This is the shortest Gospel and possibly the earliest. Matthew and Luke may have used it in writing their own accounts.

Mark may have been writing to Christians in Rome who were facing persecution under the Emperor Nero around AD 60-70. Encouragements to Christians in such a situation can be found throughout the Gospel.

Inevitably there will not be time to look at the Gospel in great detail, but this series will hopefully whet your appetite! But above all pray that you will get to know Jesus better as a result of these studies. Allow him to rise out of the pages of this Gospel

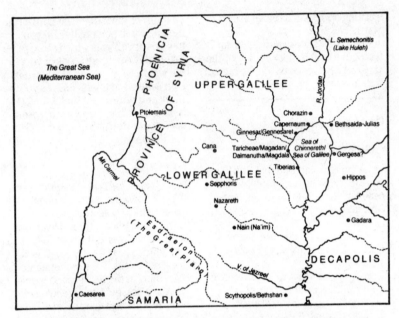

The Great Sea
(Mediterranean Sea)

PHOENICIA

PROVINCE OF SYRIA

UPPER GALILEE

R. Jordan

L. Semechonitis
(Lake Huleh)

Ptolemais

Chorazin
Capernaum
Ginnesar/Gennesaret

Bethsaida-Julias

Cana

Taricheae/Magadan/
Dalmanutha/Magdala

Sea of
Chinnereth/
Sea of Galilee

Gergesa?

Mt. Carmel

LOWER GALILEE

Tiberias

Hippos

Sepphoris

Nazareth

Esdraelon
(The Great Plain)

Nain (Na'im)

Gadara

V. of Jezreel

DECAPOLIS

Caesarea

SAMARIA

Scythopolis/Bethshan

Good commentaries for reference include the Tyndale Commentary on *Mark* by R. A. Cole (Eerdmans), *The Gospel of Mark* by William Lane in the New International Commentary on the New Testament (Eerdmans).

1. The opening section
Mark 1:1-13

Structure
These verses are often described as 'the Prologue to Mark's Gospel'. Here he presents the central figure of his account, Jesus. He did not want anyone to be in doubt about whom he was writing.

Interest point
The common theme running through the opening section is that of the wilderness. It is a theme that recurs throughout the Gospel. For any Jewish reader the wilderness or desert stood for a number of things:

■ a time of testing and failure after they had left Egypt,
■ a time when they were called to repentance,
■ a time when God appeared to them in a new way and when he gave them the law as a sign that they were in a special relationship with him,
■ a time when they knew his care for and guidance of them, and it was anticipated that when the Messiah came, he would gather the redeemed to him in the wilderness.

1 *As you read the Gospel, look out for the wilderness or desert symbolism. Which of the ideas associated with the wilderness do* you find present in the opening section?

2 *Repentance was central not only to John's message but also to that of Jesus. What did John say about it? In your own words write down what else you understand by the word. You could ask other Christian friends what they mean by it as well and look up 'repentance' in a concordance.*

3 *What is Mark saying about the central figure of his Gospel in this opening section?*

What was John's attitude to Jesus? He has been described as the first preacher of the good news of Christ. What is your attitude to Jesus when you are telling others about him? Do you start with what you think about him, so that it ends up with Jesus being almost obscured by you and your experiences? What can you do to prevent this happening?

---

2. The first phase of the Galilean ministry

Mark 1:14-45

Structure
Mark records a similar pattern at the start of the early phase of the ministry to that of the later phase. Both phases start with Jesus' activity (1:14-15; cf. 3:7-12), followed by the call of the apostles (1:16-20; cf. 3:13-19).

Interest point
The ordinary people addressed Jesus as 'Lord' (7:28), 'Teacher' (9:17), 'Son of David' (10:47-48), 'Master' (10:51). But demoniacs called him 'the Holy One of God' (1:24), 'Son of God'

(3:11), 'Son of the Most High God' (5:7). The demons had superior knowledge of Jesus' identity. They were not acknowledging him as God but as a defensive action were trying to call him to order — they failed!

1 *Right from the start the characteristics of the new kingdom or order brought in by Jesus were apparent — both by what he said and by what he did. Note down how you think Jesus' actions here demonstrated its coming.*

2 *It was impossible not to react in some way to Jesus. Contrast the reactions of the following groups. Why did they react as they did?*

- ■ *the disciples*
- ■ *the evil spirits*
- ■ *the sick*

By his words and actions Jesus commanded obedience. Can you think of any time recently when he called you to an act of obedience? What was your reaction?

---

3. The first phase, continued

Mark 2:1 – 3:6

Structure
These Galilean controversies could be said to be balanced by the five Jerusalem ones in 11:27 – 12:37.

Interest point
The term 'the Son of man' appears twice in this chapter. Then it is only after Peter acknowledges Jesus as the Messiah in 8:29 that Mark uses it again, twelve times, as Jesus discloses his identity to his disciples alone. The phrase may simply have

been a substitute that Jesus used for 'I', but at times it possibly had some Messianic connotations (e.g. 14:62). Jesus may have had in mind Daniel's marvellous vision (Daniel 7:9 -14) in using the phrase.

1 *Read the passage and then pin-point what issue was at stake in each of the five controversies (2:1-12; 2:13-17; 2:18-22; 2:23-28; 3:1-6). Then beside each point note down Jesus' response to the controversy. What did you discover about the character of Jesus and how he viewed his mission?*
2 *His claims about himself are stunning in their original context. How challenging do you honestly believe the good news of Jesus is to your own situation? Take each of the five responses and try to apply them to your own circumstances.*
3 *What could the offer of forgiveness mean to those you know whose lives are broken and guilt-ridden?*
4 *What about those who lead good lives, acknowledging their own high moral code, but who do not have any time for God?*

Pray for those of whom you have been reminded as you have considered these five controversies.

4. Later in the Galilean ministry
Mark 3:7-35; 6:1-13

Structure
As with the earlier phase, this starts with a summary of Jesus' activity followed by the commissioning of the disciples.

Interest point
The idea of rejection occurs throughout this section — those who refuse to accept Jesus and his miracles or who fail to understand him do so because of their hardness of heart. Already in 3:6 the opposition is wanting to kill him.

1 *Draw out the similarities in 3:13-18 and 6:6b-13 from the two callings of the disciples. How did Jesus call them and to what? Notice that he first called them to be **with** him. There is a danger that action in serving God can come before spending time with him. How can you safeguard yourself from this? Pray for any you know who are in danger of being so busy serving God that he is actually being squeezed out of their lives.*
2 *Jesus faced rejection from many sources. Why did the following reject him? — members of his family, the teachers of the law, the people of Nazareth, some of those who heard the disciples.*

Jesus came to bring salvation in the face of rejection and hostility — from men and from Satan himself. His disciples too had to face similar rejection. In what ways have you been misunderstood or rejected because of your faith? What reassurance can you find in these verses?

5. The later Galilean ministry
Mark 4:1-34

Structure
This is the largest grouping of Jesus'

parables by Mark. All three parables illustrate the character of the coming of the kingdom of God.

Interest point:
the kingdom of God

The phrase 'the kingdom of God' stands for God's reign of salvation and righteousness at the end of time. This cosmic saving rule of God began in the ministry of Christ, and was strengthened by his death and resurrection, and the pouring out of the Spirit. It will finally be consummated in the end of the world and the re-creation of the universe. Thus the kingdom of God has begun and is with us now, yet not completely.

In the first parable (4:1-20) notice that the sower and the seed are presented as being good and the climax of the story is the good harvest rather than the attempts of the poorer soils to produce a harvest. In your own words, what sort of responses to the seed are characterized here? Can you think of any of your friends who have

responded to the word of God in a similar way to one of the soils? Pray for them now, that they will become more receptive to the truth, or praise God for them if they are already bearing fruit.

Jesus was urging his hearers to listen carefully and act responsibly to his words (21-25). Yet on the other hand it would appear in the parable of the growing seed (26-29) and the mustard seed (30-32) that man's part in the bringing in of the kingdom is non-existent. What was Jesus saying about the kingdom of God in these two parables? How would it come and what would it be like? List some of its features. What does this say about the ways in which God chooses to work?

Weekend

Look up the following references to Jesus' rejection and suffering which are found later in the Gospel: 5:17; 8:31 – 9:1; 9:12-13, 30-32; 10:32-34,45; 11:18; 12:1-12. If you have time, read the account of the crucifixion in chapters 14 and 15 as well.

Part Eight/Week Three
Mark's Gospel, 2 (A detailed study)

1. More of the later Galilean ministry
Mark 4:35 – 5:43

Interest point
A common theme in Mark is that, although Jesus spent much time with the disciples, they often

misunderstood and he had to rebuke them. 4:40 is just one example. See also 7:18; 8:17-18,21,32-33; 9:19.

In these four miracles Mark wrote of the power of Jesus at work over nature, the forces of evil, death and chronic sickness.

1 *If you were reading these verses for the first time, what would strike* you about Jesus? Write down your observations.

2   Pin-point the reactions of the disciples, the demon-possessed man, the people in the Decapolis, Jairus and the woman with the bleeding, to such demonstrations of Jesus' power. How do they give both good and bad examples about faith and the need to respond to Jesus and what he has done?

Write down some things that Jesus has done for you, *e.g.* in saving you from sin, and in removing fear. How have you reacted to what he's done? Then thank him and pray that you may grow in responsive faith and in obedience.

2. Withdrawal beyond Galilee, 1
Mark 6:14-56

Interest point
The New Testament writers relied heavily on their Jewish background in writing, frequently finding parallels between the Old Testament era and the new era brought in by Jesus. One example is here, where Mark could be paralleling John the Baptist with Elijah, and possibly Herod and Herodias with Ahab and Jezebel (1 Kings 19:1-2). The wilderness motif is another example which is brought out in these verses. The feeding of the 5,000 could be paralleled with Israel in the wilderness, experiencing the compassion of God who feeds and teaches them (Exodus 16:4-16; Deuteronomy 29:2-6). Notice also the phrase of Jesus in 6:34, 'sheep without a shepherd', which is also used by Moses in Numbers 27:17.

1   The ministry of Jesus aroused Herod's conscience. What had been his attitude and behaviour towards John while he was alive (verse 20)? Yet he remained untouched by John's message. Can you think of examples of people today whose conscience can be aroused by hearing about Jesus and the truth about him and yet remain untouched? Pray for them and for any Christians who are in regular contact with them.

2   The love and compassion of Jesus are outstanding. In what ways was his love demonstrated in these two miracles — towards both the crowds and his disciples? Note down your comments.

Recently, how have you experienced his love towards you? How far are you willing to allow his compassion to flow through you towards others? (Don't pass quickly over this question!)

3. Withdrawal beyond Galilee, 2
Mark 7:1-37

Structure
7:1-23 forms a single teaching unit which seems to have no clear relation to what has gone before nor what follows after it. Fitted in here, however, it forms a prelude to the three miracle narratives in which Jesus extends his grace to the Gentiles. The unit's position is similar in structure to the place of the teaching unit (4:1-34) in the period of Jesus' later Galilean ministry (3:7 – 6:8).

1 *What was wrong with the Pharisees' view of the law and tradition and what did that mean in practice? How had this affected their views towards the attitude of the heart?*

Note: The law itself was not wrong; it was given by God and written down. Rather, Jesus was calling into question the authority of the oral law of tradition accumulated over the centuries.

2 *How easy is it to be bound by traditions or customs of the church or Christian group to which you belong — so that they become more important than God himself? Is this so in patterns of worship, or the way that you spend Sunday?*
3 *So what, then, is Jesus saying to those who keep the letter of the law without the spirit of it?*

Note on verses 26-30

At first sight, it looks as if Jesus is insensitive to the Gentile woman with her crying need. Is Jesus out of character here?

The faith of the Gentile woman and of the deaf man with his friends provides a sharp contrast to the behaviour of the Pharisees, crowd and the disciples. Write down all the contrasts you can see in their attitudes and behaviour. You might find it useful to make two columns.

4. Withdrawal beyond Galilee, 3
Mark 8:1-30

Structure
In 6:31 – 7:37 Mark has presented a pattern of incidents which includes a feeding of a multitude, encountering the unbelief of religious leaders and acts of healing. 8:1-30 has a similar pattern, climaxing in the confession of 8:27-30. The first pattern ends with the deaf ears of the man being opened. The second pattern ends with the deaf ears and the blind eyes of the disciples being opened.

Interest point
The conversation at Caesarea Philippi (8:27-30) is the climax of the preceding chapters. Up to now, Mark has made no clear statement about Jesus' identity except in 1:1. From this point he shows Jesus talking openly about his death. He has set his face towards Jerusalem. This dominates the rest of the Gospel.

1 *The disciples could hardly have forgotten about the previous feeding of the 5,000, yet they seemed unsure of what Jesus would do (8:4). Their lack of faith, however, was different from the blatant unbelief of the Pharisees. From verses 1-21 what differences can you detect?*

Note: 'Yeast' was a common metaphor for corruption.

2 *The unbelief of the Pharisees meant that they wanted to judge him on their own terms: 'Give us a sign'. What was Jesus' response to them? Ask God to forgive you if at any time you have made demands on him and judged him when to do so is like throwing an insult in his face.*

If someone were to ask you what you thought about Jesus, what would you say (without using any jargon)?

Write down your answer. What about getting a friend to read it and talk about it with you?

5. Journey to Jerusalem, 1
Mark 8:31 — 9:50

Structure
In this section Mark records three times Jesus' explanation of his death to his disciples (8:31; 9:31; 10:33) and each time it is followed by misunderstanding and then teaching by Jesus on the nature of true discipleship.

1 In your own words, summarize what Jesus said and taught in the first two declarations about his death and then about the subsequent call to discipleship — 8:31 – 9:1 and 9:31-50. You will need to write down your summary.
2 Putting the interests of God and others before your own is never easy. In practical terms, what does this mean to you? From these verses what motivates you to live by this standard?

3 In what ways could the transfiguration (9:2-13) have helped the disciples to understand Jesus' identity, forthcoming death and glorification?

As you read verses 14-29 try to enter into the weary exasperation of Jesus towards his disciples and their misunderstanding. And yet he did not give up on them. Do you think that Jesus is often exasperated with you and your slowness of heart? Spend time thinking over this and praise God that he has not deserted you.

Weekend
1 Look back on your notes. Some of the studies may have taken longer than you expected or had time for. But above all, remind yourself of what you have learned about Jesus.
2 Pick out one incident from Jesus' life that has particularly struck you this week. Now tell it in your own words from the point of view of one of the people involved (it could even be Christ's!)

Part Eight/Week Four
Mark's Gospel, 3 (A detailed study)

1. Journey to Jerusalem, 2
Mark 10:1-52

Read verses 1-12.
Jesus' purpose in explaining the Mosaic law on divorce

(Deuteronomy 24:1) in verse 5 was to restate that divorce was not acceptable but may be necessary to limit sinfulness and control its consequences, a direct response to the question of verse 2. God's pattern was, and has always been, that of a lasting partnership between a man and a woman. In the subsequent discussion with the disciples he put man and woman on the same level in marriage — which was truly shocking for his time.

1 What does this indicate about God's intentions for human beings which are so often higher and better than our way of doing things?
2 Can you think of other examples?
3 Pray that you will always strive to let God mould your ideas.
4 God does not always give to people what they ask of him. Blind Bartimaeus got what he asked for, but the rich young ruler went away sad. Read verses 17-23 and 46-52. What do we see here about the way that Jesus granted requests which people made of him? In what attitude of mind do you ask God for things?

To complete the observations you made in the last study about the statement of Jesus' death and the call to discipleship, look at verses 24-45. Jot down what these add to your understanding.

2. Ministry in Jerusalem, 1
Mark 11:1 – 12:44

Structure
This section is divided into two: 11:1-25 consists of the symbolic actions accomplished during the three days in Jerusalem, and 11:27 – 12:44 the five conflicts with priestly and scribal authorities (possibly paralleled with the Galilean ones, 2:1 – 3:6).

Interest point
In fulfilment of Zechariah 9:9 Jesus was coming as Messiah into Jerusalem, coming as Lord to his temple, although the disciples did not understand the significance until afterwards (John 12:16). It was unlikely that Jesus wanted his action to be understood as a claim to political messiahship. The cursing of the fig tree could be seen as another Messianic act, since the fig tree often symbolized Israel's status before God (e.g. Jeremiah 8:13) and its destruction was associated with judgment (e.g. Hosea 2:12). In cleansing the temple forecourt Jesus was symbolically enabling the Gentiles to worship God — a fulfilment of Zechariah 14:16.

1 As you read 11:1-25, make a note of all the indications that Jesus was always in control of events and not vice versa. What grounds for praise does that give you?
2 Briefly summarize the criticisms levelled at Jesus in 11:27 – 12:44. How did he handle such criticism? What hints can you get from him on how you can confront those who criticize you for your faith? When, if ever, are you entitled to attack such critics in the devastating way that Jesus did?

Praise God that even in the face of such opposition Jesus remained firm, refusing to act in any way other than might be expected of God-become-man.

3. Ministry in Jerusalem, 2
Mark 13:1-37

Structure
This is the longest uninterrupted discourse of Jesus in Mark's Gospel.

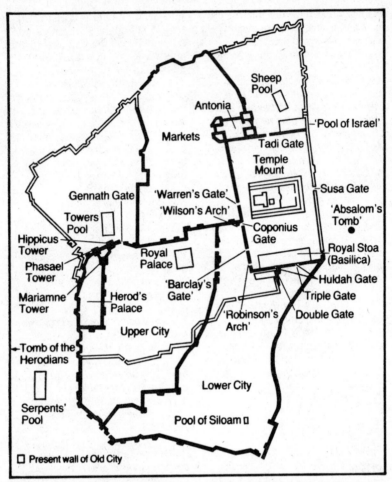

□ **Present wall of Old City**

It provides a bridge between Jesus'
public ministry and the account of
his death, showing a link between
the judgment of Jerusalem and the
death of Jesus (see 14:58; 15:29).

Interest point

The primary function of chapter 13 is
not to predict details of future events
but to promote faith and obedience
in a time of distress and upheaval.
This would be particularly relevant

to the original readers undergoing
persecution. As you can imagine,
much scholarly debate has been
focused upon the chapter. Was Jesus
referring to the fall of Jerusalem in
AD 70, or to his second coming, or
what? In this study we shall not
attempt to answer such questions!

1 *What were the motives of Jesus in
instructing the disciples on how they
were to view the future? Consider*

each of the following statements to see which of them gives a clue as to his motives. Note down which verse(s), if any, applies to which statement.

Jesus taught his disciples about the future because...

■ he wanted them to be prepared for whatever happened.
■ he did not want them to be deceived.
■ he wanted them to be confident in the face of persecution.
■ he wanted to motivate them to preach.
■ he wanted them to take a long holiday every winter.
■ he wanted to increase their trust in the sovereignty of God.
■ he wanted them to spend all their lives analysing the signs of the times.

2 Take each of the above **relevant** *statements and prayerfully consider how you yourself are taking the teaching of Jesus to heart.*

4. The road to death, 1
Mark 14:1-52

Structure
So many of Mark's themes are down together in what is obviously the climax of his Gospel: for example, the conflict with the authorities, the plans to kill Jesus, the awareness that Jesus has had all along of his mission and impending death and the ways in which he prepared his disciples for it. Mark was preparing his readers for this moment, for the passion of Jesus.

'He was despised and rejected
    by men,
a man of sorrows, and
    familiar with suffering.
Like one from whom men
    hide their faces
he was despised, and we
    esteemed him not'

(Isaiah 53:3, NIV).

As you read these verses, bear this prophecy about the Messiah in mind. Make a note of all the different ways in which Jesus was rejected. His loneliness and isolation were finally tragically expressed in his cry from the cross in 15:34. What does such utter desolation mean? Then pause to realize that he went to such depths for you. In humility praise God that Jesus was obedient, even to the point of death on the cross.

Even at this late stage, what was Jesus saying to his disciples about the purpose of his suffering? How would you answer someone who said to you that the death of Jesus was a tragedy because it was a pointless death of the best man who ever lived? Use this passage to help you in your answer.

5. The road to death, 2
Mark 14:53 – 15:47

'He was oppressed and
    afflicted,
    yet he did not open his
        mouth;
he was led like a lamb to the
    slaughter,
    and as a sheep before her
        shearers is silent,

*so he did not open his
mouth'*

> (Isaiah 53:7, NIV).

1 *Familiarity can blunt our senses.
As you read this moving and well-
known narrative, bear this prophecy
of Isaiah in mind. Notice the
indignity of the Son of God, who had
left all the glories of heaven to come
to this earth, yet being treated in this
way. What right had any man to do
that to Jesus? You may feel anger
welling up inside you. Allow yourself
to respond to God in a way that
seems appropriate.*

2 *As in his life, so in his death, the
person of Jesus provoked a reaction.
How would you describe the
reactions of the following?*

■ *anyone in the temple at the time
when the curtain split*
■ *the centurion*
■ *the woman*
■ *Joseph*
■ *Pilate*

*No-one can be indifferent to Jesus
when they meet him.*

Interest point, verse 38
The curtain separated the Holy of
Holies, where God was believed to be
present in a special way, from the
rest of the temple. The high priest
went in there only once every year.
Now, by the death of Jesus, access to
God was available to everyone.

Structure
The statement about Jesus, with
which Mark begins his Gospel, is now
to be found upon the lips of a
non-Jew, at the end of the Gospel.
'Surely this man was the Son of God'
(verse 39, NIV).

Weekend

The resurrection of Jesus
16:1-20

1 *Read 16:1-8 (many authorities
believe verses 9-20 are a later
addition to the Gospel). The tragedy
gave way to triumph, as Jesus had
predicted (e.g. 10:34; 14:28). If he had
not been resurrected he would,
among other things, have been a liar.
From your own knowledge and
looking at these verses and I
Corinthians 15:12-34, why is it
important that the cross was not the
end for Jesus?*
2 *Spend some time over the
weekend reviewing your studies in
this Gospel. But above all, ask
yourself how much have you
discovered about Jesus and in what
ways has he met you and spoken to
you over these last three weeks?*
3 *The resurrection of Jesus provides
a solid historical basis for
Christianity's claim to be true. It is
examined thoroughly in **Jesus
Christ: The Witness of History**, by
J.N.D. Anderson (IVP) and **Who
Moved the Stone?**, by Frank
Morison (Zondervan).*

Part Eight/Week Five
Love (A word study)

It would be very difficult to talk about the Christian gospel without mentioning love. But what is it? The word 'love' conjures up all sorts of ideas. We shall look at how the concept comes across in the Bible itself.

1. Love is...
1 Corinthians 13

The church at Corinth had a lot going for it. But it had problems! Not the least of these involved divisions into various party groups and irregularities in worship.

The church had written to the apostle Paul about these and other issues, and time and again he hints at love as being the solution to their problems.

Chapter 13 focuses the reader's attention directly on love — its meaning and importance.

1 *How would you define what love is? Before reading the passage, write down your definition and then test it against verses 4-7. Can you think of any other ways of briefly summarizing the meaning of love, or of other words you could use in its place?*
2 *In verses 1-3 you will read some startling statements. Why, do you think, should lack of love make these apparently highly spiritual activities worthless?*
3 *Verses 8-13 contrast temporary things with the permanence of faith,* hope *and love. How do Paul's pictures about growing up and mirrors (vv.11-12) help you to see the importance of faith, hope and love over 'temporary' things?*

Notice the supremacy of love over even faith and hope (verse 13). Pray about what you plan to do today and ask God to help you to 'make love your aim' (14:1) in everything you do and say.

2. Loving and being loved
1 John 4:7-12

The characteristic word for love in the New Testament is *agapē*. It was not used widely in Greek-speaking society, but was picked up by Christians to bring out the special quality of love that God has for us — and that we should have for him and for other people.

John addresses his readers as *agapētoi* — those who are especially loved. (The translation 'Dear friends' is a weak substitute for the old-fashioned word 'beloved'. In its singular form — *agapētos* — it is the word used by God the Father to describe his special love for his 'beloved' Son, e.g. in Matthew 3:17.)

As people whom God especially loves we have special responsibilities.

1 *'Without love — nothing!' How*

does this principle from 1 Corinthians 13 work out in 1 John 4:7-8? Why can you not be a Christian without having love?

2 Where did your love relationship with God begin (verse 10)? How can you be sure that God still loves you? (Before you write down your answer, compare verse 9 with John 3:16; Romans 5:8; then read Romans 5:6-11.)

3 If God's love is seen through his actions in your favour, how should you love other people (verses 11-12)? What unseen resources can you draw on to enable you to love like God?

4 How can you be confident that God will not stop loving you? (Think again about what you read in Romans 5.)

As 1 John 4:8 says that 'God is love', you may like to substitute 'God' for 'love' in 1 Corinthians 13, and then use these verses to help you worship God.

---

3. Love that lasts
Deuteronomy 7:6-11

One of the great Old Testament words for love is *hesed* (often translated as 'steadfast/constant love', 'loving-kindness' or even 'mercy'). It focuses on the permanence of the relationship that God has with his people to whom he has committed himself.

In Genesis, God promised Abraham that he would be his God and the God of his descendants, and he sealed this covenant commitment with an oath (Genesis 15:18-20; 17:1-8).

God's love involves commitment: steadfast love.

In Deuteronomy 7, set just before Israel takes possession of the promised land, God restates this covenant relationship.

1 Why did God choose Israel (verses 6-7)? Write your answer in terms of (a) motive and (b) purpose. Make a special note of any reasons that clearly are not grounds for God's choice.

2 How was God's love seen in action on Israel's behalf (verse 8)? Note any parallels between this and how God's love for you was displayed. (See your notes on Study 2.)

3 In the last study you saw that your love relationship with God began with God rather than with you. But love is not all one way. How is this brought out in verses 9-10?

Study 5 will pick up the relationship of 'love' to 'law'. Begin to think about how God's love is seen in his action towards us and note any ways in which you can show your love for him in the light of verse 11.

---

4. God loves you!
John 3:16; Ephesians 5:25-27; Romans 8:28-39

1 What does John 3:16 tell you about the extent of God's love — and the conditions of benefiting from it?

2 Ephesians 5:25-27 pictures Christ's love for the church in terms of a bridegroom's love for his bride. (This parallels the Old Testament picture of God's covenant love for Israel as his bride.) In your own words, write down what Jesus wants to do to express his love to you as a Christian, based on this passage.

Read Romans 8:28-39. List what

this passage teaches you about the results of (a) your love for God, and (b) God's love for you. Why can the apostle write with such certainty (verse 32)?

3 Many people encounter difficulties over the Bible's teaching concerning election: how does God's special love for some square with his love for all the world?

The idea of choosing a bride can be a helpful one in appreciating what God has done: that God has chosen a special people for himself — as you saw he did with Israel in the last Study.

The fact of God's undeserved and electing love must not be allowed to detract from God's loving offer of life to all who will believe in Jesus.

4 Think over Romans 8:29-30. Try to grasp the idea of a love which stretches from eternity to eternity — beginning in God's foreknowledge (which means much the same as his 'forelove') and ending in glorification for Christians.

Rededicate yourself to Christ in readiness for the church's presentation as his bride (Ephesians 5:27-29).

5. 'Do you love me?'
John 21:15-17

This is an encounter between Peter and Jesus after his resurrection. Three times Jesus asks his friend, 'Do you love me?', and he then gives Peter a threefold commission to look after his sheep. This must have brought great reassurance to the disciple who had denied his Lord three times.

Two Greek words for love are used in this dialogue: *agapē* and *phileō*. Much ink has been spilt over why these different words are used. It could be that a contrast is intended between different qualities of love. (*Phileō* may be understood as 'tender affection' or 'friendship'.) But the distinction cannot be clearly determined — and it is reasonable to assume that John is just using different words for variety.

1 *Read John 14:15-24 (part of what Jesus said to his disciples on the night he was betrayed). How do Jesus' words help you to know if your love for him is genuine? (NB verses 15,21,23 and 24.) Write your response after looking at Jesus' own example in verse 31.*
2 *Refer to Matthew 22:35-40. Jesus is teaching that all the commands of the law — i.e. everything that God requires of us — hang on the twin cord of love for God and love for your neighbour. How does this reflect what Jesus says in John 14?*
3 *Does this link between love and obedience help you to answer for yourself the question Jesus put to Peter in John 21?*

If you have time, go back over 1 Corinthians 13:4-7 and read your own name in the place of 'love'. Ask God for grace to make that ring true.

Weekend

1 *The word 'love' covers a number of quite distinct concepts. C.S.Lewis' book **The Four Loves** (Peter Smith) would make interesting weekend reading if you want to follow this up.*
2 *The idea of **erōs** — the love that aims to possess, or sexual love — does not appear explicitly in the New*

Testament. However, the Old Testament provides many examples of love used in this and other senses. You can check this out under 'love' in an analytical concordance. Try to work out for yourself what the Hebrew words *'āhēḇ, dóḏ* and *ra'yâ* mean.

3 Song of Solomon is a beautiful poem about human love. You may like to read it and note in your notebook some of the lessons you learn.

4 Alternatively, you may like to read Hosea's love story (Hosea 1-3), which is not only a tragic tale of human love, but a picture of God's love and the response to it.

Part Eight/Week Six
Peter (A character study)

1. Peter, the fisherman
Luke 5:1-11; John 1:35-42

Just suppose that you have been asked to write a biography of Peter. The only source material that you have to work with is to be found in the New Testament. Throughout the week, make a list of all the biographical details you might want to include — his background, activities, attitudes, relationships and any changes you detect in him over the years.

You could also asterisk any characteristics that you share with him. How did God deal with him? Might he treat you in the same way?

1 *Begin by reading these two passages and listing the biographical details you discover. In what ways do you see yourself in Peter?*
2 *Peter followed Jesus voluntarily. But how had Jesus demonstrated that he was greater than Peter and worth following? In your own words,* how did Peter respond to Jesus' authority?
3 *Can you think of any who have such a limited view of Jesus, that they don't see the point in following him? How can you help them to see Jesus as he really is? (It may be that they are so proud and so blind that they are unable to recognize something of his greatness.) Pause to pray for them now.*

In Peter's experience, he first needed to recognize who Jesus was, limited though that recognition may be. It was then that Jesus gave him the commission to follow him. How far has that been the pattern you can trace in your own life, when you became a Christian and subsequently in your Christian life?

2. Peter, jumped in feet first
Matthew 14: 22-33; 16:13-23; 26:31-35,69-75

Each of these incidents will give you

more information for your biography. Note down additional details of Peter's character. Asterisk those characteristics you share with him.

1 *In your own words summarize how Jesus dealt with Peter on each of these occasions. Was Jesus treating him consistently?*
2 *Peter was always a man for action and speaking his mind. At times this was a good thing, but at other times his forwardness led to sin. Recently, when have you been able to speak out for God or acted boldly and God has used you? Praise God that he has used you.*
3 *On the other hand, when have you spoken or acted impetuously and without thought? You may not be reduced to the bitter tears which Peter shed, but pause to ask for God's forgiveness and an openness for him to reveal himself to you as he did to Peter (Matthew 16:17).*

3. Peter, with a job still to do
John 21

After reading this chapter, note the additional material you find there about Peter's life. In what ways can you identify with him? Also, look back to Week 5, Study 5, on love.

Peter's denial of Jesus must have made a very deep mark on him. His bitter tears of regret and failure were not crocodile tears! But by this time, overjoyed that Jesus was alive again, he with the other disciples were in a period of waiting. But they hardly knew what they were waiting for. It would be quite natural, though, for

them to go off on a fishing expedition.

1 *Why was this conversation between Jesus and Peter so crucially important? What does it suggest about Jesus' attitude to failure and the way in which Peter himself responded to his failure? Is there any sense in which you have failed God and need to assure him of your love for him and willingness to serve him despite your failures? (Don't manufacture a failure for the sake of it!)*
2 *Have you known a time of uncertainty and waiting, possibly following a time of humiliation, emotional turmoil? Have you anguished over the need to make a decision about the future? What reassurance can you find from Jesus' conversation with Peter that God does not abandon those whom he loves, whom he intends to use in the future? If you are in such a period at the moment, pray for yourself in the light of what you have read and for any others that you know in such a situation.*

4. Peter, filled with the Spirit
Acts 4:1-22

By this stage there are definite signs that Peter was being changed, although he continued to make blunders throughout his life.

Read this section and note down any further information about Peter. The background of this passage is found in Acts 3.

1 *Compare Peter here with Peter as*

we read about him in Matthew 26.
How do you account for the
difference? Acts 4:8 should give you
one clue.
2 *The Holy Spirit strengthened Peter
for a particular situation when
clarity of speech and boldness were
essential. He was experiencing in
practice the promise of Jesus in Mark
13:11. Pray for any you know who are
involved in the work of spreading the
gospel and speaking in hostile
environments, that they may learn to
rely on God to give them the right
words to say. You ought to include
yourself in this!*
3 *You may not have identified
yourself with Peter today, apart
perhaps from seeing yourself as
ordinary (verse 13)! But Peter made
the most of the opportunity which
was presented to him. How can you
look out today for similar
opportunities, although they may be
of a less dramatic nature?*

For Peter such an attitude involved
considerable discomfort. How
prepared are you for that? (At the
end of the day, think about how you
have used the last 24 hours to speak
out for Jesus and to show him to
others by the quality of your life.
Have people been able to see that
you have been a companion of
Jesus?)

---

5. Peter, feeding the sheep
1 Peter 1:1-2; 5:1-14

Towards the end of his life, Peter
wrote at least two letters to isolated
groups of Christians, obeying the
command of Jesus to be a shepherd
to the sheep. He had some strong
things to say to them, but his deep
concern for his fellow Christians is
very evident. If you had time you
would enjoy reading the whole letter.
However, start by reading these two
extracts.

1 *What insights do they give into
Peter's character?*
2 *List the encouragements and
instructions that he gives to his
fellow Christians, especially the
leaders.*
3 *His care for them is demonstrated
by the high standards that he sets.
Unlike Peter you are probably not in
a position to give such instructions
to many other Christians, but think
of your Christian friends. What are
your ambitions for them? Do you
long for them to apply Peter's
guidance to their own lives? Putting
Peter's instructions into your own
words, turn them into prayer bearing
your friends in mind.*
4 *Peter has a special concern for his
fellow elders, reminding them of
their responsibilities. Pray for the
leaders of your church, that they will
be able to live up to the standards
God requires of them.*

It is easy for leaders to become
discouraged. Can you think of some
way in which you can encourage one
of the leaders in your church this
week?

Over the weekend...

1 *You could look up all the
references to Peter in a
concordance. But do find time to
look over your notes on what you
have studied this week, noting
especially the way in which God took*

Peter as he was, enthusiastic, outspoken and dominant, and used him, refined him and made him like Jesus.

2 We have not had time to read about Peter's contribution to the growth of the early church. You could do that on your own! Look at, for example, Acts 1:15-26; 2:14 – 3:26; 5:12-42; 10; 12:1-19.

Part Eight/Week Seven
The book of Jeremiah, 1 (A historical study)

Jeremiah was called to be a prophet — someone who spoke God's word at a time when his country, Judah, was relatively prosperous. However, during the forty or so years of his career he saw all that change, and he had the unenviable task of warning the people that God's judgment was going to come in a series of disasters, culminating in the destruction of Jerusalem. The book gives us much of his preaching, and also accounts of what happened to the prophet, and his reactions to the events taking place around him.

The Book of Jeremiah can seem confusing, as some of it is arranged topically and some chronologically. Broadly speaking chapters 1-25 are messages from the Lord for Judah and her rulers; 26-45 are events in Jeremiah's life, probably recorded by his secretary, Baruch; 46-51 are prophecies against other nations; and chapter 52 is a postscript describing the fall of Jerusalem.

1. The prophet's call
Jeremiah 1

Read the chapter (preferably more than once), looking out for details of the job Jeremiah was being given.

1:1-3 is the heading of the book, summarizing the extent of Jeremiah's career. Take a sheet of paper and start a time-chart (to which you can add other dates as we go along), so you will be able to see how the events of Jeremiah's life fit together. The 13th year of Josiah's reign was 627 BC and he died in 608 BC. Jehoiakim was king until 597 BC, and the people were taken into exile (verse 3) in 587 BC. (NB — There were two other kings during this time, but they reigned for only three months each — more on this in Study 5.)

The rest of the chapter tells of the events which made Jeremiah realize the Lord was calling him to be a prophet.

1 What can you find out about Jeremiah's character?

2 In what ways does God equip him for his job? What reassurance does he give Jeremiah that he can accomplish the job he is being called to do?

3 How do you think the visions

(verses 11-16) helped Jeremiah to
understand his job better?

Note: *Verses 11-12.* The Hebrew has
a play on words — the word for
'almond' sounds like the word for
'watching'.

Consider: Jeremiah was reluctant to
accept God's call. Was his reluctance
justified? Have you ever been in the
position of not wanting to do what
God has asked you to? What help can
you find here for such a situation?

2. National renewal?
2 Kings 22:1-20; 23:1-4,21-30

When Josiah became king things in
Judah were in a sorry state — idol
worship and social injustice were
common. No doubt this was partly
an attempt to win favour with their
foreign oppressors, Assyria, by
worshipping their gods as well as the
Lord. However Assyria was no longer
powerful, and Josiah was able to take
steps to put things right.

The book which was found in the
temple was probably Deuteronomy,
or the bulk of it.

1 *What practical steps did Josiah
take to implement its teaching? (The
verses omitted, 23:5-20, contain a
detailed description of the
destruction of idol worship.)*
2 *What does the passage say about
the results of disobeying God?*

Note: 23:26 Manasseh – Josiah's
grandfather, an idolator.

3 *What are the results of obeying
God for Josiah?*
4 *In what sense are these results of
obedience or disobedience true for
Christians? (You might find
Galatians 6:7-10 helpful.)*

Consider: What changes of attitude
or action have you made in response
to things you have read in the Bible?
(You may find it helpful to look back
over previous notes, and think about
what you learned.) Pray that you will
be able to take God's word as
seriously as Josiah did.

3. The temple sermon
Jeremiah 7:1-15

Jeremiah 26 gives an account of how
this sermon was preached, and the
reactions it provoked (read that too
if you have time). It was delivered
early in the reign of Jehoiakim (26:1)
and so not long after the death of
Josiah.

Notes: 7:12. Shiloh was a place
where God was worshipped before
the temple was built in Jerusalem. It
had been destroyed by the
Philistines.

7:15. A reference to the
destruction of the Northern
Kingdom, Israel, in the previous
century.

From this chapter, and what you
read in 2 Kings 22 and 23, think about
the effects of Josiah's reforms:

1 *What had been achieved?*
2 *From Jeremiah's denunciations
here, where had the reforms fallen
short?*

It was popularly thought that God would not allow his temple and those who worshipped in it to be destroyed, because of his reputation — if the temple were destroyed it would be assumed that the god of the conquering nation was more powerful than the Lord. However this reasoning was false — God's reputation could also be damaged by the conduct of his worshippers, as we see here.

4. The potter
Jeremiah 18:1-17

This must be one of the most famous incidents in the book! Like the temple sermon, it comes from the early years of Jehoiakim's reign. A potter at work must have been a familiar sight, and the image here is of a pot which doesn't come out quite as intended, so the potter squashes it back down into a lump of clay, and then makes it into something different.

Read: the passage — more than once — trying to work out how the analogy works. In what sense is the house of Israel like the clay?

1 *What are God's plans for his people at that moment? Which alternative applies to them (verses 7-10)?*
2 *What attitude did the people of Israel take? What specific things mentioned here show their lack of repentance?*
3 *If the people do not repent, what will be the result? There is a sense in which even in this case Jeremiah sees a future for the nation — God can remake the pot. But how far is*

this a message of hope, how much is it a solemn warning?
4 *The temple sermon showed the dilemma between God's plan of blessing his people and their response (or lack of it) to him. How does this passage help us to understand this problem?*

Consider: Israel did not repent, so for them this message was a solemn warning. What would you say to someone in the opposite situation, who feels they have failed God, and there is no hope for them? Pray for any who might be in this state.

5. The international scene
2 Kings 23:29 – 25:12

Read the passage, and fill in the remaining kings on your time-chart.
  The international power-struggles described here are amazingly complex! Assyria had been the dominant power, with Egypt as her nearest rival. Her power had waned, however, and Babylon had come on the scene as a strong contender. 23:29 describes an alliance between the former rivals, Egypt and Assyria, against Babylon. Babylon, however, eventually came out on top, leaving Egypt with still a little influence, and Assyria's power virtually non-existent. Judah, as a tiny state caught in the middle of this, was at Babylon's mercy.
  We might attribute Judah's downfall to the power struggle going on around her, and to unwise political decisions at home (e.g. 24:1).

1 *What explanation is given here?*

2 *Do these two explanations conflict? If not, can you explain why not?*

3 *What do we learn here about how God works out his purposes in history?*

Pray: It is often easier to see what God is doing in the world when you look back, particularly in the history of Israel with her unique position as God's people. The conflicts and power struggles going on in the world today may make little sense. Pray for the trouble-spots which are in the news at the moment in the light of what you have learnt from this passage.

For the weekend

In this series of studies, we are concentrating on the history of the times in which Jeremiah lived. The book, however, also contains fascinating glimpses of him as a person, particularly his prayers, as he struggles with the task God has given him. Already you have learned a bit about Jeremiah from chapter 1 — see what else you can learn about him from 11:14 – 12:6 and 20:7-18. (Some other passages you could look at: 7:16-20,27-34; 8:18 – 9:1; 10:23-25; 14:13-18; 15:10-21; 17:14-18; 18:18-23.)

Part Eight/Week Eight
The book of Jeremiah, 2 (A historical study)

1. The scroll
Jeremiah 36

This chapter gives us a fascinating glimpse of how some of Jeremiah's prophecies came to be written down. The scroll was probably the first stage in the compilation of the Book of Jeremiah as we now have it.

Note the timing of this incident (verses 1 and 9), probably soon after the temple sermon, which may explain why Jeremiah was banned from the temple (verse 5). The fourth year of Jehoiakim (605/604 BC) was shortly after the Egyptians had been decisively beaten by the Babylonians at the Battle of Carchemish, and the fast (verse 9) may have been in response to national danger, as Babylon had just defeated one of Judah's neighbours, Ashkelon.

Note: Baruch, a close associate of Jeremiah. See 32:12-16; 43:3-6; 45.

1 *What can you find out from this chapter about the contents of the scroll? What was its basic message?*

Note: Verse 23. Scrolls were written sideways, in vertical columns.

2 *Look at how the different characters in the chapter reacted to the message. If you were a political commentator, how would you describe the political situation in Judah? (The officials in verses 10-12* were important ones — the contemporary equivalent of cabinet ministers.) You might try writing a newspaper article assessing the situation.

Consider: We see here some more examples of people's reactions to God's word. How do they compare with Josiah's (Week 7, Study 2)? Has what you learned then affected your attitude to subsequent studies?

2. The letter to the exiles
Jeremiah 29:1-32

This letter, and the response to it (verses 24-32), perhaps came from the fourth year of Zedekiah's reign (594/593 BC). Some of the people were in exile in Babylon, and this letter may have followed a period of unrest among them.

Note: *Verse 2.* Jeconiah (RSV) is another name for Jehoiachin. *Verse 17.* The reference to figs comes from Jeremiah's oracle in chapter 24, about God's plan for the exiles, and those who remained in Jerusalem.

1 *What message do you think the false prophets were preaching to the exiles?*
2 *Why were the people likely to believe them, rather than Jeremiah?*
3 *What aspects of Jeremiah's message do you think the exiles would have found unexpected? (Remember that the Jews thought that the Lord hearing their prayers was associated with the functioning of the temple and the sacrificial system in Jerusalem.)*

Consider: The exiles must have felt very confused as they tried to work out God's purposes for them in the middle of what was going on. Have you ever known such a confusing situation? How did things work out? What can you learn to help you cope with such situations in the future? You may find Romans 8:28 a helpful verse to meditate on and memorize as you consider this.

3. Hope for the future
Jeremiah 31:23-40

Chapters 30 and 31 contain a collection of sayings about Israel's hope for the future and probably originally circulated as a separate scroll (perhaps with chapters 32 and 33 as well) — a Book of Comfort.
   As you read the passage, try to put yourself in the position of the exiles in Babylon, and think how they would have reacted to these promises.

Notes: 31:23 The mountain is Mount Zion, where the temple stood in Jerusalem.
   31:29 This popular saying probably reflects a feeling among the exiles that they were being punished unjustly for the sins of their ancestors.

1 *What promises does God make here?*
2 *How can the Israelites be sure the promises will be kept?*
3 *How many differences can you find between the old form of religion (its worst forms were denounced by Jeremiah in chapter 7) and the new covenant promised here (verse 31)?*

The concept of the new covenant is very important in the New Testament. It appears in the words of institution at the Last Supper (Luke 22:20; 1 Corinthians 11:25) and the concept is used elsewhere by Paul (e.g. 2 Corinthians 3:6). This passage from Jeremiah is quoted by the writer to the Hebrews (8:10-12; 10:16-17) in his argument to show that Jesus has brought about a new state of affairs in man's relationship with God.

4. Jerusalem under siege
Jeremiah 37–38

These incidents can be dated to 589/588 BC. It would seem that Zedekiah, although installed as a puppet-king by Nebuchadnezzar, had rebelled against his masters (see 2 Kings 24:20) and that in consequence the Babylonians (Chaldeans, RSV) had laid siege to Jerusalem. Chapter 37 begins with a lull in the siege, caused by an Egyptian army moving towards the city. Imagine the feelings of joy and relief! Jeremiah, however, had the job of telling people that this is not the end of the matter — the Babylonians will return to the attack — and by the time we get to 37:17 it seems that the siege has been resumed.

Note: 37:12 Perhaps a field Jeremiah bought. See 32:1-15.

1 *What can you learn about Zedekiah's character from these chapters? What factors affected his political judgments?*

Note: 38:10 Probably 'three men', not 'thirty' (some translations).

2 *What do you learn about Jeremiah's character from the way he copes with opposition? (NB. The officials who are hostile to him are different from those in chapter 36, who were presumably by now in exile in Babylon.)*
3 *Compare this with what you learned about Jeremiah last week. How has his character developed during his ministry?*

Consider: Jeremiah's strength of character is a tribute to God keeping his promises (1:17-19). That did not mean, however, that he found life easy, as we see in these chapters. What evidence can you find of God's faithfulness in your own life at the moment?

5. The fall of Jerusalem
Jeremiah 39:1–40:6

The event which Jeremiah had first prophesied forty years previously (1:13-16) finally happened. Jerusalem fell to the Babylonians and became subject to their rule (39:3 describes the setting-up of a military government). We have read already a fuller account of this in 2 Kings 25:1-12 (repeated in substantially the same form in Jeremiah 52, as a postscript to the book).

1 *Look back to Week 7, Study 5 and see what you found out about the causes of Judah's downfall. Do you want to add anything in the light of your subsequent reading?*

2 *In the general judgment which was coming on Judah, the exiles had complained that some of them were being punished unjustly (Jeremiah 31:29-30). How does the example of Ebed-Melech (39:15-18) and indeed Jeremiah himself help to understand what was happening? (How had Ebed-Melech shown his trust in God (39:18)?)*
3 *Presumably Jeremiah was treated kindly because he was thought to be a friend to Babylon. From this passage, and from your previous reading, what do you think his attitude was to his own country?*

Consider: The popular definition of a prophet is someone who foretells the future. How far does Jeremiah fit this definition? Look up 'prophet' in a good Bible Dictionary to see all the main features.

For the weekend

There is plenty more of the book for you to read! If you read on, you will find out what happened to Jeremiah in the confused situation in Judah after the fall of Jerusalem. This is followed by a collection of oracles to foreign nations (chapters 46-51) from different points in Jeremiah's career. Alternatively, you can go back and fill in some of the bits we skipped over. As you read, remember that the material is not in chronological order, and look out for any indications of when particular prophecies or incidents are to be dated.

You could read further into Jeremiah's life and message with two IVP publications: *Run with the Horses* by Eugene Peterson, and *The Message of Jeremiah*, by Derek Kidner.

Part Eight/Week Nine
Human beings, warts and all! (A topic study)

1.Human nature as it was meant to be
Genesis 1:26-31; Psalm 8

Read these two sections. Then see what they say about each of the following descriptions of human nature. Write the relevant verse(s) beside each statement.

A person in his nature is:-

■ deliberately created, the climax of God's creativity

■ made in God's image
■ enabled to communicate with God
■ a sexual being
■ made for human companionship
■ God's representative on earth to exercise lordship over the rest of creation
■ a pleasure to God, evoking his care
■ given a purpose in living

Rushing waterfalls, majestic mountains and delicate flowers cause us to marvel at God's creativity. But if a person is the climax of all creation, he or she is more precious to God than all these. After all, he or she alone can communicate with God. As Jesus said, 'Look at the birds of the air... your heavenly Father feeds them. Are you not much more valuable then they?' (Matthew 6:26, NIV). Since humans have such a privileged position, what responsibility does that place upon them? (E.g. treating every person as someone, like you, made in God's image, ensuring that God's world is not spoiled.)

Praise God for his world and for his care of you in that world. Pray that you will take seriously your responsibility towards it.

2. Human nature corrupted

Genesis 3

1 God had made human nature perfect, but the serpent in Genesis had serious limitations. What were these?

2 The serpent's powers of persuasion won the day. Take each of the statements made in the last study and note down how each of these aspects of human nature was affected by the fall. As with Adam and Eve, so with all of us. Think about how these particular elements of corrupted human nature are present in your own life.

3 But all was not lost. How did God respond to this corruption?

4 Read the commentary on Psalm 8 found in Hebrews 2:5-11. What grounds for hope are to be found there?

5 You may be acutely aware of your own fallen nature. In the light of Hebrews 2 how are you to view your imperfection? Think of what it cost Jesus to make you holy and the fact that he has made you so and in the future will do even more.

In your prayer time, concentrate on Jesus, the perfect man, whose body suffered corruption and who tasted death for everyone so that we might have a new nature. Praise God for him.

3. Fallen nature has far-reaching consequences

Ephesians 2:13; Romans 1:18-32

These two passages contain a vivid description of what the fallen world is like. Write down a summary of what the passages say about our fallen world.

1 We have already seen that Adam and Eve's sin affected their own relationships. But it also led to the corruption of the world and society itself. As you look at the world we live in, how true are Paul's descriptions in his letters to the Ephesians and Romans? For example, you could think about family relationships, law and order, public honesty. What can people do about it?

Again we should not despair, for God is still making the truth about himself plain to people.

2 Think of two aspects of society which you are particularly interested in, e.g. education, family life, national politics — all of which reflect the distortion (on some level) of our world from what God intends. Then pray specifically that God's way and righteousness will be revealed here, bringing about change in our world. You could challenge members of your Bible Study group or fellowship to do the same.

How far would these verses help you to answer a non-Christian who came out with a statement similar to the one Lenin made in 1919? Lenin said: 'The workers are building the new society without having turned themselves into new men who would be free from the dirt of the old world. They are still in it up to their knees.'

4. Human nature restored
Romans 8:1-17

1 *Divide a piece of paper in half lengthways. On one side write down what Paul says about the sinful nature. On the other write down how he describes the new nature. The contrast is startling.*
2 *Now go through the passage again, noticing all that God has done. It is his initiative all the time. Only he can make anyone righteous. The privileges of being a co-heir with Christ are enormous. Take each of the privileges that you have found in this part of the letter and turn them into praise. God has given us guidance for living which we must strive to observe. (We shall look at these in the next Study.)*

He also wants us to relax in him, knowing that we have been given his Spirit so that his righteous demands might be fully met in us.

5. My new nature
Colossians 3:1-17

Although every Christian has a new nature and status, we are all aware that the old nature is still fighting for a survival — a survival which, we are assured, it will never achieve. Paul told the Colossians that they must resist every attempt of the old nature to rear its ugly head.

1 *Read this part of his letter to the Colossian church. Then, put in your own words what he says it means in practice to 'set your minds on things above' (v.2, NIV), both in terms of what things are to be deliberately excluded and what things are to be consciously included in our lives. Pause to assess your own life by these standards of behaviour. Notice that Paul is talking mainly about attitudes.*
2 *Glance back at Romans 8:12-14 to see how Paul puts it another way. Pray that God will help you to put to death what is wrong in your life.*
3 *Paul was not just writing to individuals but to a church. They were to help each other to resist the claims of the old nature. In what ways recently have you helped another Christian to exercise the qualities of a restored nature?*

Think of some way in which this week you will be able to help another Christian to live a holy life, the kind of life God expects from someone whose fallen nature has been restored. Remember however that we do not do this in our own strength. God's Spirit within us is working to make us like Jesus, who came to show us what perfect human nature was meant to be.

Weekend review

Over the weekend look back over your notes to trace the progression of human nature. Then read Romans 5-8 in one sitting. This summarizes what God has done in restoring our nature.

For further reading, John White's *Putting the Soul Back into Psychology* (IVP) looks into biblical and modern scientific understandings of human nature.

Part Eight/Week Ten
Beginning the Pastoral Letters (A bird's-eye study)

These Epistles (1 and 2 Timothy and Titus) are so called because they have more to do with the practicalities of church life than the other letters of Paul. They are basically letters to individuals, rather than to a congregation (although they may have been read publicly) and all three deal with similar problems.

The aim of this study is to get an overall grasp of the contents of these letters. (You can go back and work at the difficult bits later, once you see where they fit in to the whole letter.) First of all, we will study 1 Timothy, and then you can look at the other two on your own. We shall be looking particularly at three themes, how we can serve God in his church, the problems caused by false teachers, and then at the practical teaching on the life of the church.

1. 1 Timothy – a bird's-eye study
1 Timothy

Timothy has been told by Paul to stay in Ephesus (1:3) and has been given a specific job to do there (1:18). It seems that Paul is writing to encourage him and give him some practical help with this job.

Read the whole letter (fairly quickly — don't let yourself get bogged down with any difficult bits — you can sort them out later). As you do, make a list of the particular areas of church life Paul wants Timothy to deal with.

1 *What can you find out about the activities of this church?*
2 *What were the particular problems it faced?*

Pray for your own church — for its regular activities, for those who lead it and for any particular problems it faces at the moment.

2. The qualifications for Christian service
1 Timothy 1:12-20; 3

1 *Read 1:12-20, where Paul is*

266

talking about his own ministry, in contrast to that of the false teachers (1:3-11). What qualifications does Paul have for his job?

2 Read chapter 3. What qualities is Timothy to look for in those he appoints to leadership roles in the church? Some of these probably don't apply to your situation. Can you think of equivalent qualifications which would apply?

Consider: All Christians are called to serve God in some way. How many of these qualifications do you have already? Are there any areas in which you ought to take some action? What are you doing with the qualifications you have got? Take time to pray for those areas of Christian service in which you are already involved (and remember that service for God is not necessarily equivalent to an official title in church or other Christian groups) and also perhaps to ask God if there is anything different he wants you to be involved with. Remember — since gifts are given for the upbuilding of the church, other people are usually better than you at spotting your talents and hidden abilities — ought you to ask someone else for some honest advice?

3. 'Handy hints' for Timothy's ministry
1 Timothy 4:6 – 5:2; 6:11-21

1 What advice does Paul give Timothy about his personal spiritual life?
2 What public duties does Paul give Timothy, both here and in the rest of the letter? (Look back to Study 1!)

3 In what ways will the state of Timothy's spiritual life affect his public duties?

Consider: The personal application should be obvious! Look again at Paul's advice on Timothy's spiritual life, and try to translate it into practical terms for your own situation.

As you come to pray, pray not only for yourself, but also for the personal spiritual life of Christian leaders you know.

4. False teaching in the church
1 Timothy 1:3-11; 4:1-5; 6:3-10

One of the problems which was very common in the early church was that of people who came into the church teaching variations of the apostolic teaching, often with a Jewish slant.

Read the passages which deal with this subject (1:3-11; 4:1-5; 6:3-10) and from them make a list of contrasts between true and false teaching (perhaps in two columns in your notebook).

1 How did Timothy know what was true teaching? (There's a lot more on this in 2 Timothy — look out for it there.)
2 Can you think of any forms of false teaching which are commonly found today, either within the church or outside it? Can you find anything here to help in knowing how to deal with it?

If one of the sects — such as the Jehovah's Witnesses, or the Moonies — is common in your area, it would be worth finding out a bit about it. Perhaps read a book on the subject, such as *The Guide to Cults and New Religions* and *The Lure of the Cults* by Ronald Enroth *et al.*; both published by IVP.

---

5. The life of the church

1 Timothy 2:1-10; 5:3-16

These Epistles do not give us a 'blue-print' for church life; they are mainly concerned to correct things that were going wrong. You may be able to think of other areas for concern in the life of your church, but it's worth looking at the things Paul picks up to see if they need some attention as well.

1 *What is the church to pray for, and why?*
2 *How is the church to pray? What is the relevance here of instruction on the way they live?*

Consider: What is the scope of the prayer of your church or other Christian group. Is it as wide as Paul envisages here? If not, what practical steps could you take to encourage a wider interest? (And what about your own praying?)

The financial needs of widows in the first century may seem remote to us, especially with the welfare state to care for those who have no other means of support.

3 *What does Paul say here is the responsibility of individual Christians, rather than the church as a whole?*
4 *Do you think the church has a continuing responsibility in this area? If so, what are the equivalent needs? How might they be met?*

Weekend work project

Now go on to look at the other two Pastoral Epistles (2 Timothy and Titus) on your own. You may find it helpful to continue looking at our three themes — start by reading a whole Epistle and noting sections which apply to these themes, and also any other subjects which occur. Then you can go back and work on bits of particular interest in more detail.

Part Nine

John's good news
Kings and Chronicles
Marriage and the family
Four prophets—Micah, Nahum, Obadiah and Zephaniah
The book of Nehemiah

Part Nine/Week One
John's good news (A bird's-eye study)

How would you have reacted if you had been a member of that proud and long-suffering Jewish race when Jesus came? For years you've attended temple sacrifices and read the Torah waiting for the Messiah.

Then this astonishing man Jesus appears, yet he doesn't quite fit the image. What's more the educated religious authorities tell you he's a fake and the Romans execute him. Just how can a plain man know the facts?

John, the disciple, wrote down what he saw. Everything in his Gospel is designed to bring the inquiring reader, from all periods of history, to faith. It mainly comprises what Jesus said about himself and includes seven selected 'signs' to back up these claims. These are the facts and every person must come to terms with them. The aim in this week's study is to gain a view of the broad sweep of the Gospel, which requires more Bible *reading* than usual.

Learning verses
Each of your studies this week contains a memory verse. This is because God commends memorizing and meditation (Joshua 1:8). Learning verses will help you to be accurate when you speak about Christ. In times of difficulty you will have God's Word in your mind to fight temptation or discouragement.

Look at the context of the verse.

Then break the verse into phrases and learn the first one. When you're sure you know it, add the second and so on. From time to time revise them so they stay fresh in your memory. Perhaps you could enlist a friend's help and learn verses together.

When you have learned the verse, meditate, so that the truth of Scripture will mould and shape your thinking. Otherwise, it can become a mechanical exercise. Consider the verse from every angle and restate it in your own words. Ask yourself questions about the verse and how it applies to you.

1. Could this be the Christ? – Samaritan claim
John 1 – 4

The Gospel begins with some stupendous statements about who Jesus is and his recognition by John the Baptist. He gathers his first followers and then begins his public ministry in the temple at Jerusalem.

1 *List the different signs and testimonies that Jesus is the Son of God.*

Note: 1:48 It was customary to read the Scriptures under a fig tree. 1:51 suggests that he was reading Genesis 28:12.

2 *Write out in six or seven lines the message that Jesus brought. What is its significance for a world of suffering and sin?*

Memory verse: For God so loved the world that he gave his one and only Son, that whoever believes in him shall not perish but have eternal life (John 3:16, NIV).

Pray for those of your friends and family who have not yet understood who Jesus is and the great gift of salvation he offers.

Memory verse: When Jesus spoke again to the people, he said, 'I am the light of the world. Whoever follows me will never walk in darkness, but will have the light of life' (John 8:12, NIV).

There will be people who make their decision about Jesus according to what you do and say. Pray that your deeds always live up to your words, and that your words are accurate and true to the gospel records.

Out of the Saltshaker by Rebecca Manley Pippert (IVP) will give you helpful advice in this area.

2. Testimony not valid – Pharisee challenge
John 5 – 8

Jesus demands a reaction. He is not a person you can be indifferent towards because of the incredible deeds and even more amazing claims he makes. Jesus now returns to Jerusalem and to a people who almost immediately reject him.

1 *Note down the things Jesus says about himself. On what authority does he make these claims?*

Note: 7:2 'Tabernacles'. An eight-day harvest festival commemorating the exile.

2 *Pick out the reasons why some people refuse to believe Jesus is God, (a) from what Jesus says, (b) from their own words. Is it possible to study Scripture and still fail to see the truth? (5:39-40).*

3. Lord, I believe – a blind man sees
John 9 – 12

Meeting Jesus means you must make a choice. Yesterday, we saw that some people prefer to stay in darkness. Today, we meet others who gradually realize the implications of accepting him.

Consider questions 1, 2 or 3.

1 *Chapters 9 and 11. What effect does meeting Jesus have on the blind man, Mary, Martha and Lazarus? How are their lives changed?*
2 *Chapter 10. What makes a good shepherd? List the things Jesus will do for those who follow him.*
3 *Chapter 12. God wants all men to be saved. But what are the consequences of rejecting Jesus?*

Note: 9:6 Jesus follows a medical custom to help onlookers understand.

Memory verse: 'I am the resurrection and the life. He who believes in me will live, even though he dies; and whoever lives and believes in me will never die'
(John 11:25-26, NIV).

Has your life changed? Pray through Psalm 139:23-24, asking God to show you which parts of your life aren't under his Lordship.

---

4. How can we know the way? – disciples question
John 13 – 16

The days of public teaching are over. Jesus is with his disciples and must now prepare himself and them for the dramatic and shattering events that follow.

1 *What does Jesus say about his own future?*
2 *Note down the examples, promises and commands he leaves his followers to act upon. How much do you put into practice?*

Note: 13:1 'Passover'. See Exodus 12:1-14. Now the 'Lamb of God' offers himself as the sacrifice. 13:23 refers to the author himself.

Memory verse: 'Do not let your hearts be troubled. Trust in God; trust also in me. In my Father's house are many rooms; if it were not so, I would have told you. I am going there to prepare a place for you'
(John 14:1-2, NIV).

---

5. 'What is truth?' – Pilate confounded
John 17 – 21

Jesus has accomplished everything he set out to do. God has spoken to man, through the Son. Before him now lies betrayal, a fixed trial and a cruel death. He leaves behind him a band of followers in a world which will be as hostile to them as it was to him.

1 *Chapter 17. How does Jesus glorify God?*
2 *Why does Jesus have to die (a) according to his own view, (b) according to his enemies?*
3 *What evidence is there to prove to a sceptic that Jesus rose again?*

Note: 17:12 refers to Judas. 20:6b-7 Jesus' body passed through the clothes without disturbing them. John realizes this.

4 *You could examine this further by reading* **Who Moved the Stone?** *by Frank Morison (Zondervan) or* **The Evidence for the Resurrection** *by J.N.D. Anderson (IVP).*

Memory verse: 'Now this is eternal life: that they may know you, the only true God, and Jesus Christ, whom you have sent' (John 17:3, NIV).

Look at your diary for this week. Do you only go to Christian events? In 17:15-16, Jesus prays we'll be protected in the world, not separated from it. Pray this for yourself and your Christian friends. If necessary, pray that you'll develop wider interests and avoid a holy huddle mentality. (Hang-gliding is taking off!)

Weekend

1 *Jesus promises his disciples they will not be left alone. The Holy Spirit will be sent to continue teaching them. What further work will the Spirit do? (John 14:15-31, 16:5-16). In order to answer this question fully read part 5 in* **Know the Truth** *by Bruce Milne (IVP).*

2 *We're often apologetic about our belief in the power of the Bible, but why defend a lion! Let it speak for itself. List the key passages and verses you would need to explain the gospel. What are the main points you need to make?*

Review your memory verses, adding your own to the list. How about buying a friend a copy of John's Gospel – and discussing Jesus' claim with him or her?

Part Nine/Week Two
Kings and Chronicles, 1 (A historical study)

The books of Kings and Chronicles cover the often tragic story of four centuries of Israel's history from the Judges to the exile. Under David and then Solomon, the kingdom had some stability. But it is gradually eroded as a consequence of the ungodliness of the kings who followed.

In Chronicles, the author concentrates on two major themes: those of true worship, and true kingship. Kings is more comprehensive, recording the history of both Kingdoms.

These books were originally compiled for those returning from the exile to rebuild Jerusalem, many years later. Their generation needed to know the mistakes of the past, if history were not to repeat itself. Like them we study these books to remind ourselves that peace and stability depend on our relationship with the Lord of history, not on our efforts.

For this type of study, it is necessary to read fairly long sections of the Bible.

---

1. David recaptures the Ark
1 Chronicles 13; 15:1 – 16:36

Israel had begged God to give them a king! (1 Samuel 8). God warned them no earthly leader could be as benevolent as he, but they wanted to be like all other nations. After a promising start Saul, the first King, died because he disobeyed God. Then David, Israel's most famous

King, ascended to the throne. One of his many deeds was recapturing the Ark from the Philistines (the symbol of God's presence with his people) and returning it to Jerusalem – City of God and capital of David's Kingdom.

1 *Note down reasons David gives for their initial failure. What would the people learn about God from his judgment on Uzzah? What does David overlook when he gets angry with God? (13:11).*
2 *If you have time, list the reasons David gives as to why all nations should worship God. What aspects of God's character does he specifically mention?*

As David did, look back on all the wonders God has performed, and prayers answered, and give thanks.

2. A thwarted ambition
1 Chronicles 17 and 28

It has been usual for the Israelites to erect a tent in which to perform their sacrifices. But David laments the lack of a permanent central shrine to act as a focus in their worship of God.

1 *What desires has God given David? In what ways does God modify them? To what extent should one trust feelings for guidance?*
2 *From David's speech, note down those things God has taught him throughout his reign.*
3 *The sum of David's hard earned wisdom goes into the charges given to Solomon. List the duties Solomon is to perform, and the priorities he should have.*

Pray that you will give God an opportunity to guide your actions rather than just following your own ideas or ambitions.
    Look up *Temple* in a Bible Dictionary and find out about its importance to Israel.

3. The temple is dedicated
2 Chronicles 6 and 7

Solomon becomes King and carries out the charges David gave him. The temple is built and its dedication is one of Solomon's greatest days.

1 *What guide-lines can we find in Solomon's prayer which might help in our own prayer life (6:14-42)?*
2 *If you were present when Solomon had finished praying what effect might it have had on you?*
3 *God also answered Solomon privately. Note down the warnings God gives.*

Pray that God will cleanse you of motives of personal gain in the things you do for him. *Daring to Draw Near* by John White (IVP) would be an excellent introduction to other prayers in the Bible.

4. Wisdom and foolishness
1 Kings 10 and 11

Not all was well with Solomon beneath the prosperous exterior. Today's study shows the two sides to his character – his godly wisdom and his weak will.

1 *God fulfilled all his promises to Solomon. Read through 3:5-15 noting down all the ways God was true to his word.*

Note: 11:5-7 Worship of these gods was perverted and cruel. 11:13 Judah and Benjamin comprised the Southern Kingdom after the division.

2 *Imagine the extent of Solomon's fame for a neighbouring queen to have made such a long, arduous trip to visit him. In what way is the queen of Sheba an example to us?*
3 *God sees a man's heart. What did God have against Solomon? Trace the action God takes as a consequence of this.*

The queen suffered great inconvenience to seek out Solomon. Rarely do we find someone so earnest to find Christ today. Pray for your friends and ask God to give them this sort of thirst for truth.

5. A kingdom divided
1 Kings 12 and 13

The twelve tribes of Israel often suffered internal tensions. Their unity and power lay in their worship of God and when he wasn't central the bonds weakened. Rehoboam

officially succeeds Solomon but the 10 Northern tribes make Jeroboam their leader. A split occurs creating Israel in the North and Judah in the South.

1 *Compare the characteristics of Rehoboam and Jeroboam. How do they make a bad situation worse?*
2 *What was the purpose of Jeroboam's actions in chapter 12:25-32? Secularly, they were clever, but why did they ultimately fail?*

Read 1 Corinthians 3:10-15. In the light of this passage, consider the foundations of your own life. Are you building truly on Christ? Pray that your 'work' will prove to be permanent.

Weekend

1 *Thinking of King Solomon, why might a close relationship with God go sour? Are any of these obstacles beginning to creep into your life? Meditate on Proverbs 4:20-27 to help direct your thought. Perhaps memorize these verses.*
2 *A succession of bad kings continued until Ahab came to power. During his 22 years reign an 'all-time low' was reached. Read the story in 1 Kings 16:29 - 22:40. What does it teach us about eternal values and the standards by which God judges?*

Part Nine/Week Three
Kings and Chronicles, 2 (A historical study)

As the decades pass, Israel and Judah drift further from true worship

and kingship. Israel is less stable than Judah, who still has the same dynasty on the throne throughout. The catalogues of the kings show that they are all mediocre, bad ... or worse. But God continues to send his prophets to warn the people. In the next two studies, we begin by following the fortunes of one of these men – Elisha.

1. Elisha's double portion
2 Kings 1 – 4

1 *Contrast the actions of Ahaziah and Elijah as they near their deaths. What's the difference between them?*

Note: 2:9 The eldest son inherited twice that of other sons. Elisha is asking that he may be Elijah's heir; not that he may be twice as powerful. 3:11 'Pour water on' *i.e.* 'used to serve'. 4:39 'Gourds' were usually used as a laxative, poisonous in quantity.

2 *Describe to yourself the part Elisha plays in the encounter with the Moabites.*
3 *Elisha's miracles are also parables. Make a list of them and in each case try to work out the spiritual truth involved. What specific lesson do you learn from the first miracle?*

Faith meant that Elisha believed God whatever the odds might be. Pray God will strengthen your faith through life's tests.

2. Elisha gives hope
2 Kings 5:1 – 8:15

1 *Naaman's knowledge of God is*
slight but sincere. What does he learn through his meeting with Elisha?

Notice that God's blessing is not confined to the Jew in Old Testament times.

2 *Summarize how Elisha helps the servant overcome his fear. How can you be helped to conquer your fears?*
3 *The famine and siege are severe. The people's faith is giving way. Note down ways in which Elisha helps to sustain the people.*

Ask God to help you to be conscious of the spiritual realities behind the troubles of this world. Meditate on Hebrews 12:1-3 and fix your eyes and will on Christ.

3. The Northern Kingdom collapses
2 Kings 9; 10 and 17

The last of Elijah's charges to Elisha is to anoint Jehu as king (1 Kings 19:16). A new but short-lived dynasty begins.

1 *Note down the ways in which God used Jehu as a scourge against the evil in Israel.*
2 *In what ways did Jehu fail God? God demands whole-hearted allegiance. Do you ever go only halfway when working for God?*

God began reducing Israel's territory even in Jehu's time. Eighty years and several bad kings later, the reduction becomes complete. Hoshea is the final king, reigning as a vassal of the Assyrians.

3 *List the reasons given for the downfall of Israel. Is there any sense in which these sins are apparent in the life of God's people today?*

Sin undermined and weakened the kingdom until it collapsed. Our lives are likewise hindered by wilful rebellion. Ask God to point out problem areas in your life and deal with them in his time.

Next time you are browsing in a bookstore why not obtain *Holiness* by J. C. Ryle (*Baker Book House*).

---

4. Hezekiah's reforms
2 Chronicles 29 – 32

The Southern Kingdom, Judah, was to continue for over a century longer. During that time some of the kings were quite good! One of these was Hezekiah.

1 *Try to work out what Hezekiah's priorities were during his reign.*
2 *In what ways did he meet opposition? What can we gain from his example?*
3 *Hezekiah's life was godly though imperfect. Note down the things he did that pleased God.*

Sometimes it is harder to be fruitful when things are going well, and it is easy to pray in a crisis. Pray for consistency and ask God to show you when you become self-centred.

---

5. Judah's final years
2 Chronicles 33 – 36

1 *Make a list of Manasseh's evil deeds. From the account of Manasseh's repentance (33:10-17), and God's words (34:23-28), what can be deduced about God's attitude to the penitent? What are the consequences of sin?*
2 *What effect did finding the book of the law have on Josiah and the nation?*
3 *Note down the reasons that eventually brought the downfall of Judah.*

God of course hates sin and seeks to eradicate it from our lives. Pray that God will give you the willingness to surrender to his rule areas of your life which at present are not glorifying to him. This is so that you may grow more into the likeness of his Son (Romans 8:29).

Weekend

Read Deuteronomy 28, which sets out the blessings and curses of the covenant on the threshold of the Promised Land. Look over your notes of the past two weeks. From the record of blessings and judgments in Kings and Chronicles, trace the ways God was always faithful to the covenant, despite the Israelites' increasing departure from it.

Part Nine/Week Four
Marriage and the family (An issue study)

To walk by faith is seldom easy. Some things in the Bible are hard to understand. Some of Scripture's teaching may appear to cut across accepted thinking in our society. But for most Christians, the crisis of faith does not arise through these problems, but through knowing what Scripture clearly says and not wanting to do it! Where the Bible says something we do not like, we are not at liberty to disregard it or explain it away. It stands as God's own Word.

According to the Bible, marriage and family life are part of God's original purpose for mankind. The subjects come up in the earliest chapters of Genesis, and out of these chapters spring much of the Bible's teaching about marriage and the family. The Lord Jesus as well as the New Testament writers refer to them to give teaching to Christians on marriage and the family. So let's start there at the very beginning ... (By the way, Genesis means 'beginnings'.)

1. In the beginning
Genesis 1:26 – 2:25

Genesis 2 elaborates on the summary account of man's creation given in the opening chapter. Together, these chapters show that God's plan for marriage and family life is integral to the way he made man.

1 *What does Genesis 1:27-28 tell you concerning God's intentions in making man male and female?*
2 *From Genesis 2:18-25 list as many things as you can see that make marriage either unique or good as a relationship.*
3 *Genesis 2:24 talks about **leaving** father and mother, **cleaving** to a married partner, and becoming **one flesh** (symbolized in sexual union but meaning that two formerly distinct people should now be regarded as a single unit).*

How important is each of these elements in forming a successful marriage? Why might failure in any one of them cause marriage difficulties?

4 *Genesis 1:28 gives God's command to 'be fruitful and increase in number' (NIV). Families, as well as marriage, are part of God's idea. How is this brought out in Ephesians 3:14-15 (GNB) and Psalm 68:5-6?*

Thank God for what you know of family life. Pray for your own parents and for any other families where you have shared the joy of God-centred family life. Pray about your own relationships and needs for companionship.

279

2. As Christ loved the church
Ephesians 5:21-23

1 *What does this passage tell you about: (a) the love of Christ for the church; (b) the church's relationship to Christ?*
2 *Look at verses 21-28. In what ways should Christ's relationship with the church help you to understand: (a) a husband's 'love' for his wife; (b) a wife's 'submission' to her husband?*
3 *Christ's relationship with the church is pictured not only as 'husband and wife' but as 'head and body' (verse 23). How is this picture worked out in verses 28-30?*

Verse 31 refers back to Genesis and reminds us that in marriage there is 'one flesh' – the two become one. This is indeed a mystery – but nevertheless a truth that we would not have known unless God had revealed it. A husband may not neglect his wife any more than he may neglect his own body.

4 *Are you subject to Christ in everything? Are you willing for Christ's sake to be subject to other Christians? (See verse 21.)*

Spend time thanking the Lord for his love to you as his *bride* and as his *body*. Ask him to assure you of his love and provision for you today. Pray that his love for you will be reflected in your relationships, which do not come right automatically, and especially with your partner if or when you are married.

3. Parent and child
Ephesians 6:1-4

1 *What reasons does the apostle Paul give for a child to obey his parents?*
2 *Is the command to obey parents an absolute command, or is it qualified in any way? (Look up Colossians 3:10-21 before you write your answer. Acts 4:19 also may give you a valuable sidelight on the thought of obeying 'in the Lord', pleasing him.)*

Consider: Look back to Ephesians 5:31. The right relationship of obedience of child to parent necessarily changes when the child marries. A person then has an allegiance firstly to the new marriage partner. Although obedience may not then be required, the commandment to 'honour your mother and father' (Exodus 20:12 quoted in Ephesians 6:2 and 3) is not rescinded – but it has often been shirked. (See Jesus' reaction in Mark 7:9-13.)

3 *According to Ephesians 5, a wife should be safeguarded from exploitation by her husband when she submits to him because of the husband's duty to love his wife. From what you have read today, how should a child be protected from parental exploitation?*

What might honouring your father and mother mean in practice? (You may like to write down your conclusions in your notebook.) Pray in the light of what this means for you.

4. 'I do – or do I?'

1 Corinthians 7

In New Testament times, Corinth was a byword for sexual immorality – conjuring up similar ideas to London's Soho. Some of this immorality had found its way into the church (see chapter 5). In reaction to sexual abuse, the church was in danger of being affected by teaching that all sexual activity was unspiritual, and that it would certainly defile a Christian to remain related to an unsaved partner. The positive teaching of 1 Corinthians 7 clearly contradicts these errors.

1 *How is the principle that husband and wife are one flesh reflected in verses 1-7?*
2 *Marriage is clearly the God-appointed outlet for sexual passion. Is it ever right to have sexual intercourse without marriage? Is it ever right to have marriage without sexual intercourse? Can you demonstrate your conclusions from this chapter?*

Notes: *Verse 10* shows that it is God's intention for marriage to be permanent. This principle of permanence continues to apply when one of the partners becomes a Christian.

Verse 14. 'Sanctified' does not mean 'saved'. It does mean that rather than being unclean in God's eyes and so defiling to a Christian, he or she is in a special sense consecrated through his or her relationship with one of God's children.

3 *What limit does verse 39 place on a Christian's freedom to marry?*

4 *Although marriage and family life are obviously God's provision, can you see any good reasons from 1 Corinthians 7 why singleness should be considered as a serious option for a Christian? Write down what you find. Alongside your findings, write what the chapter says in favour of marriage.*

Ask God to help you to serve him to your full potential, whether married or single. Commit yourself to allowing no change in your marital status unless that change will result in God's glory through your increased liberty to serve him, in line with what you have read today.

5. Divorce

Matthew 19:1-15

In Jesus' day, as today, there was much debate among religious people about circumstances in which divorce may be right. Jesus' teaching is truly radical. Not only is it revolutionary in contrast to much current thought, it takes us back to the *roots* of the issues.

1 *How does Jesus use the teaching of Genesis 2:24 to answer the question about divorce?*
2 *If the one-flesh relationship which God creates in marriage is essentially permanent, are there any circumstances in which divorce might be an option for a disciple of Jesus?*

Note: *Verse 9* would seem to indicate that Scripture permits a new marriage after a divorce on biblically permitted grounds. But verse 8 equally clearly shows that divorce is never required – only permitted under God's law.

3 Consider what Jesus has to say about divorce (verses 4-9) and singleness (verses 10-12) in the light of what you read in 1 Corinthians 7. Write down a summary of your findings on marriage, singleness and divorce.

4 Divorce is always a tragedy – even though it may seem to offer the best solution in a broken relationship. Think about how Jesus' teaching might help people today to avoid the traumas of divorce. Consider how the gospel of forgiveness and healing, of reconciliation and peace might bring comfort to those who are suffering the effects of marriage break-up.

Think about Jesus' attitude to the children in verses 13-15. He is still the same today. As you pray, specifically ask the Lord's blessing on any children in your family – or children you know.

Weekend

1 Follow up your interest in marriage and the family by looking up the relevant articles in the **New or Illustrated Bible Dictionary** *(IVP).* These will set your thinking in the wider context of Bible times.

2 Alternatively, you may like to begin reading one of the following books. You should find that at least one is relevant to your circumstances!

Single and Whole by Rhena Taylor (IVP)

Growing into Love by Joyce Huggett (IVP)

Two Into One by Joyce Huggett (IVP)

I Married You by Walter Trobisch (Harper & Row)

Life in the Spirit: In Marriage, Home & Work by D. Martyn Lloyd-Jones (Baker Book House)

Parents in Pain by John White (IVP)

Part Nine/Week Five
Four prophets: Micah, Nahum, Obadiah and Zephaniah (Whole book studies)

The prophets in the Old Testament had the often unpopular task of applying God's standards to the political, social and religious scene. This they did with devastating directness.

Micah's message, for example, was a mixture of doom because of impending judgment, together with hope, based on the certainty that God would continue to care for his people.

As you study these four prophets, imagine how you would have felt if you had been on the receiving end of their words.

To find out more about these men and their situations, use a Bible Dictionary.

While it is better to read through the whole books, selected readings have sometimes been suggested in view of length.

1. Message from the country
Micah 1:1-9; 5:10 – 7:1

Outline of book

God's judgment on Jerusalem and Samaria (chapters 1-3)

Future restoration and glory of the kingdom (chapters 4-5)

Contrast of prophetic and popular religion (chapter 6)

Message of warning and hope (chapter 7)

1 *Read through the whole book, if you can, or at least Micah 1:1-9; 5:10 – 7:7 noticing the reasons for God's judgment.*
2 *What were some particular social injustices causing God's wrath? (Micah 2; 6:10-12) Think out some examples of religious hypocrisy in our society today which might similarly cause God's anger. What should be our response to these in the light of God's 'requirements'? (Micah 6:8)*
3 *Can you discover what God had against Israel's leaders, both secular and religious? (Micah 3; 7:3-4)*

Let's pray specifically today for leaders both in our nation and in our

churches 'that we may live peaceful and quiet lives in all godliness and holiness' (1 Timothy 2:2, NIV).

Memory verse: He has showed you, O man, what is good. And what does the LORD require of you? To act justly and to love mercy and to walk humbly with your God (Micah 6:8, NIV).

2. The faithfulness of God
Micah 2:6-13; 5:1-4; 6:1-8; 7:8-20

We left Micah yesterday bemoaning the fate of his countrymen. Read the whole book through again or at least Micah 2:6-13; 5:1-4; 6:1-8; 7:8-20, noticing what Micah says about the character of God.

1 *Throughout the prophecy, Micah reminds the people of Israel what God is like. Jot down aspects of God's character he mentions. What difference does this make to their plight (Micah 2:12-13; 5:4-5; 6:1-8; 7:18-20)?*
2 *Because God is merciful and faithful to his people, judgment gives way to hope. How does Micah see the fulfilment of God's promises to the people of Israel (Micah 4; 5:7-15; 7:7-13, 16-17)? Look at the same verses again and see, in turn, what effect God's vindication of his people would have on the nations around Israel. Can you see ways in which God's dealings with us over-spill on to those around us?*

Let's praise God for those aspects of his character highlighted in today's study. As we face circumstances that sometimes are overwhelming, let's thank God that he does not leave his people without hope.

3. The downfall of Nineveh
Nahum

Nahum's message was about the destruction of Nineveh, the great capital city of Assyria, predicted by Jonah some 150 years before and confirmed by Zephaniah. The fulfilment of the prophecy was in 612 BC and today there is nothing left of Nineveh except a mound known as 'Tell Kuyunik' or the 'mound of many sheep'.

1 *How does Nahum describe God in chapter 1:2-8 in relation to (a) his own people, and (b) his enemies?*

2 *Note the way Nahum describes Nineveh. He takes up various images to illustrate aspects of Nineveh's sin. Try to picture these images in your own mind. Why do you think Nahum uses them (Nahum 2:8, 11-12; 3:1, 4, 12)?*

3 *What clues do we get to the reasons for Nineveh's fall? (Nahum 1:11, 14; 3:1-4, 16-19. See also Zephaniah 2:13-15.)*

4 *Twice God declares the solemn words: 'I am against you' (Nahum 2:13; 3:5, NIV). What, in each case, is the consequence of having God as your enemy?*

In the struggle for peace, it is easy for justice and righteousness to be overlooked. Pray for troubled areas of the world.

4. The doom of Edom
Obadiah

Obadiah has a vision of God's judgment on the Edomites, who lived in a mountainous region to the south-east of the Dead Sea. Their geographical supremacy had given them strength in their conflicts. The final outrage, which resulted in this prophecy, was the treacherous invasion of Judah by the Edomites while Jerusalem was being sacked by the Babylonians (verses 13-14).

1 *Why do you think God had to punish Edom?*
2 *Obadiah uses various pictures to describe Edom's fate. Imagine what it would have felt like to have your future described in these ways (verses 4-5, 16, 18). What do you think is the impact of these descriptions?*

Note: *Verse 18. 'House of Jacob ... and Joseph' = whole of Israel.*

3 *'The day of the Lord is near', says Obadiah. What will this mean for Edom on the one hand (verse 15) and Israel on the other (verses 17-21)?*

We may identify more easily with the Lord's promises to Israel, rather than his judgment on Edom – maybe there is a warning here in case we should be falling under the same condemnation. With verse 3, and verses 10-14 in mind, pray that God will show us such attitudes in our national and individual lives.

5. The day of the Lord
Zephaniah

Zephaniah was probably of royal blood, tracing his ancestry back to Hezekiah 70 years or so before.

1 *In popular thinking the 'day of the Lord' (chapter 1:7, 14-15) would bring great blessing to God's people and destruction to their enemies. What did Zephaniah warn the 'day of the Lord' would mean to (a) Judah, (b) the heathen nations and (c) to the 'humble of the Land'? (cf. also Obadiah verse 15.)*
2 *Trace God's complaint against (a) his people (chapter 1:4-6, 8, 9, 12) and against (b) the leaders of Jerusalem (chapter 3:3-4).*
3 *The final verses of chapter 3 are a hymn of praise for God's deliverance. It applied to the people of Israel then, but can you work out any promises that reached further fulfilment in Jesus?*

Meditate on chapter 3:17, learn it by heart, and take the promises into your activities today.

Weekend

1 *Look up some background to the prophecies we've studied this week to put them in their context.*

Micah
Jeremiah 26:17-19
2 Chronicles 30

Obadiah
Genesis 25:23; 27:39-41
2 Samuel 8:13-14
2 Kings 16:6
2 Chronicles 21:8-10
Ezekiel 35

Nahum and Zephaniah
Compare the prophecies relating to Assyria in Isaiah 10:24-34 and Jonah.

2 *Make a chart showing the historical position of the four prophets you have studied. You will find dates in a Bible dictionary or commentary.*

Part Nine/Week Six
The book of Nehemiah (A detailed study)

With Jerusalem destroyed, and the Jews taken into exile in Babylon (587 BC), few of them believe that God still has a plan for the nation (2 Chronicles 36:15-23 tells the story). But God remains faithful to his promises. Babylon falls to Persia and the Jews are allowed to return. Ezra recounts the home-coming of the first two parties. Nehemiah tells the story of the third. It is under his dynamic leadership that the rebuilding of the city wall begins.

1. Man of prayer, man of action
Nehemiah 1 and 2

Though Nehemiah is far from Jerusalem it is his homeland; so he is thunderstruck when his brother brings bad news from there. He grieves and prays for four months.

1 *Chapter 1:6-11. Note down those aspects of God's character which he mentions. What expectations does he make of God? His prayer shows he is a man who knows God intimately. By what means has he got to know God so well?*

Disagreement with the king could be costly and Artaxerxes had already halted the rebuilding once (Ezra 4:7-23). But when the opportunity for action arises, Nehemiah disregards himself and has a well-thought-out plan to put before the king.

Notes: 1:1 & 2:1 Kislev = November; Nisan = March, approximately. 2:1 King Artaxerxes I of Persia, 464-423 BC.

2 *Chapter 2:1-10. What gives Nehemiah the confidence to be so forthright to the king? What new aspect of his prayer life do we see?*
3 *Chapter 2:11-20. Because Nehemiah is a man of prayer and faith, he has his feet firmly on the ground. What practical measures does he take to begin the work?*

Nehemiah knew the secret of long periods given to prayer, but also of constant communion with God. Consider your own prayer life. Pray that God will teach you both of these important sides to prayer.

2. United, they stand ...
Nehemiah 3 and 4

Remember the desolate scene from yesterday of Nehemiah walking alone through the rubble and charred ruins. Chapter 3 acts as a contrast to this as the walls come alive with activity.

1 *Chapter 3. List the different occupations of the people who took part in the building. What makes them willing to work together despite their social differences?*
2 *Chapter 4. Why should Sanballat, Tobiah and the others oppose the rebuilding? See especially verses 1-3, 7-9.*

Note: 4:1 Sanballat, Tobiah and Gesham – leaders among the Samaritans, and Governors of Persian colonies. 4:4-5 The prayer is motivated by zeal for God's honour, not personal revenge.

3 *Chapter 4. Note down the steps Nehemiah takes when the builders come under threat. What hints from his actions will help us face opposition? Also see Ephesians 4:3, and 6:10-11.*

You may have already experienced ridicule about your trust in God. Jesus tells us to expect problems. (John 15:18ff.) In what other ways might you meet opposition (e.g. at home, at work, union meetings, lectures, students' union)? Pray that God will teach you to give a clear but sensitive witness to those who oppose you.

3. ... But what if they should be divided?

Nehemiah 5:1 – 7:4

While Nehemiah had been giving money to the poor and buying Jews out of slavery, rich Jews had been charging heavy interest to their countrymen. God clearly prohibited this (Exodus 22:25), and the onus was on Nehemiah to prevent division.

1 *Chapter 5:6-13. What action does Nehemiah take to put the situation right?*

2 *Chapter 5:14-19. Nehemiah proves the strength of his leadership through the firm handling of this dispute. Note down the other qualities which make him such a good Governor.*

3 *The opposition now concentrates on Nehemiah. Summarize the two different approaches used, (a) in chapter 6:1-9; (b) in chapter 6:10-14. Why don't they succeed?*

4 *Chapter 6:15 – 7:4. The wall is built in a record time of two months! Even their enemies have to acknowledge God's hand in it. But this is not the end of the story. What further steps does Nehemiah take for the public good?*

Make a list of all the things you have learned about Nehemiah's character. Pray that God will help you develop similar strengths.

---

4. Repentance and renewal

Nehemiah 7:73b – 9:38; 10:28-39

Imagine how Ezra felt facing that massive crowd. How thankful to God he must have been, that such an assembly could take place. God had sent their fore-fathers into exile for persistent disobedience. Now the people were humbled and wanted to renew their covenant with their Almighty God. Significantly, their first action was to gather to hear God's Word.

1 *What feelings do you think the people had on this solemn occasion (8:3, 9,12; 9:1-2)?*

2 *Chapter 9:6-37. What things had been done to grieve God (verses 16-17, 26)? Summarize the evidence that God remained faithful and loving to them, despite their disobedience.*

The renewed covenant is signed by the leaders on behalf of all the people (10:1-29). They pledge themselves to keep the law, specifically mentioning marriage, the sabbath debts and temple dues.

3 *We are now under the new covenant, but God's holiness hasn't altered. What does he require of our lives (Philippians 1:27; 1 Peter 1:13-21)?*

In spite of the way in which we've treated God, he continues to love and forgive us. Meditate on the fact of his love, maybe reading 9:15-21.

Memory verse: But you are a forgiving God, gracious and compassionate, slow to anger and abounding in love (9:17b, NIV).

Find out more about God's holiness by reading *The Knowledge of the Holy*, by A. W. Tozer (*Harper & Row*).

5. The people rejoice
Nehemiah 12:27 – 13:31

Picture the joyful celebrations as the walls are dedicated. Two massive processions, each with a choir and musicians, march in opposite directions round the top of the wall. The two companies meet at the temple where they offer sacrifices.

1 *List those things which Nehemiah did on his return to restore morality (chapter 13:1-3, 17-18, 27). What are the benefits of obedience? (12:43.) Why must sin be dealt with so severely? (13:18.)*

2 *Chapter 13 Nehemiah has been absent from Jerusalem (verse 6) and already standards are slipping. What things might have caused the people to slip into their old ways so quickly? (Jeremiah 10:23-24; Romans 7:14-25.)*

Look over your notes for this week. What are the main lessons God was teaching the Jews? Which of them are relevant to you and to today's world? Pray God will help you not only to hear his Word, but to put it into action (James 1:22-25).

Weekend

The Jews had to learn to work together. They became united behind one leader and in a common task. Likewise Christ is our head and we are his body to carry out his will. Examine some of the passages which explain this and note down your feelings. Does today's church match up to the biblical picture? How can you play your part? (Romans 12; 1 Corinthians 12:4-31; Ephesians 4:1-16; Colossians 3:12-17.)

Part Ten

Genesis 1—11
Paul's letter to the Romans
Jonah
Revelation 2
The book of Ezra
Mission matters
The letter to the Hebrews
What about other religions?

Genesis 1-11 (A detailed study)

This week's study concerns part of Scripture often used today as 'evidence' that the Bible cannot be true. It is handed down to us as primeval *history* and we must treat it as such. We should be willing to let it instruct us about God and his world; if we have preconceptions picked up from whatever source about its being a fairy tale, let's take another look...

1. How it all began
Genesis 1:1 – 2:3

1 *Note down which things were called into being on which day. What are some implications of man's order in creation?*

Some interpreters feel that 'a day' here doesn't seem to refer to the 24-hour span as we understand it, but a period of time or epoch.

2 *Depending on which translation of the Bible you are using, you'll find several repetitions of 'When God commanded...' or 'And God said...'. Read John's account of the creation (John 1:1-2) and see how he links God's word with the Lord Jesus, who is God's Word. Paul does the same in Colossians 1:15-17.*
3 *God made the seventh day to be different; how can we follow his example in the way we spend our 'day of rest'?*

We've been reminded today of God's overall authority, and that human beings are superior to anything else in creation. Thank him for the glory and existence of the world, and worship him as creator.

2. The Garden of Eden
Genesis 2:4-25

These few verses give us a picture of life as God intended it to be. Man was the crown of God's creation, the 'apple of his eye'. Notice that he was placed in a garden, where there was much beauty.

1 *List the things God provided for Adam to enjoy. What task was he set to do? What was prohibiting him?*
2 *Man had been given beauty to behold in the creation, a purpose to fulfil, and the company of the beasts. But this was not enough. God wanted him to have a partner, so woman was created, one of his own kind. Try to imagine his joy at this fulfilment of his being!*
3 *Someone might ask, 'How can there possibly be a God of love when this world is in such a mess?' Is there any way you could use this passage to help them? We shall gain a fuller picture in the next study.*

Despite the wretchedness of the human heart now, we may still look upon a beautiful creation. Think of the craggy wonder of some mountain regions, or the sunsets over islands ... Let's thank God today for the splendour of our country's nature reserves. Thank him also that the beauty of love and companionship is a real part of the same world.

To be reminded that we sin because of a built-in weakness does not excuse us at all. Let's be sorry before God in our prayers for the falsehoods in our life. And let's thank him most of all for planning to forgive us, even from this very earliest rebellion.

3. Man's disobedience and what followed
Genesis 3

In order to understand our human condition now, we have to look back to Genesis 3, and the account of how sin (disobedience to God) entered human experience. Since then, it's as if sin got into the very bloodstream of humanity and has been passed down to every generation since. It's important for us to understand that we don't become sinners when we start to do wrong, but rather that we start to do wrong because we are sinners.

1 *Summarize in your own words the origin of sin and separation from God, as though you were explaining it to an unbeliever. Notice how the consequences of sin quickly work themselves out.*
2 *Look back at the first five verses. Should Eve have parleyed with Satan? What lessons are there here for us to learn about how to deal with temptation?*
3 *Adam and Eve had broken their fellowship with God for ever, but God broke the silence by taking the initiative. How is this typical of the Lord who is the Saviour?*
4 *Because of this sin, how did God punish Adam and Eve?*

4. Noah's ark
Genesis 6:9 – 9:17

Sadly all that very many people 'know' of this part of human history is what they remember of a frieze on the wall in their primary school. Today's reading is long, but it's important that we get the whole picture of what is happening. People had grown so wicked that God became sorry that he had created them. Noah, however, was a godly man and he was to be spared the punishment to befall the rest of the world.

1 *What sort of man was Noah?*
2 *Imagine what people must have thought of the Noah family building a huge ark when there was no sign of any water. We read that Noah did everything God commanded him (verse 22). Would you be willing to follow God's lead, doing right despite the mockery of friends, colleagues, neighbours?*
3 *What do we learn of God and his attitude to the world from this passage – e.g. his judgment, covenant keeping, and provision for those that live in the right way?*
4 *Look again at 8:20-22. How did God view Noah's sacrifice? Can this be seen as a development of God's unfolding plan of salvation?*

You might like to write out, then

learn by heart, verse 22 as a reminder that God is faithful and always keeps his promises. Thank him that we do not live on a dying planet.

We've been reminded again today that sin is a serious matter. God takes it so, and we must too, remembering his complete goodness. Let's ask today that we may become the more willing to serve him whole-heartedly no matter what others think.

5. The tower of Babel
Genesis 11:1-9

This is a well-known story of misplaced human initiative in seeking independence from God, and a disunity which happened as a result. Let's be careful that we don't interpret this as meaning that creativity is wrong – far from it. For God has made us in his image, and he is a creative God. It was the arrogance of the people which was being condemned (verse 4).

1 *What does verse 6 suggest about why God took such action? Remembering that these were descendants of Noah, consider how God must have felt about their scheming.*

Here we see God confusing people by dividing a single language into many. In another part of Scripture we see God enlightening people of many different tongues (cf. Acts 2:1-13). Both are the result of a supernatural intervention, and remind us that all our words, whether thought or spoken, are given us by him, the source of all communication.

2 *How much is language a barrier today, not only between cultures, but also in close relationships? How may such barriers be healed unglibly?*

Let's pray that we will have our thoughts, longings and ambitions cleansed by God, that they will be unified in the purpose of loving and serving God, instead of being a 'babble' of conflicting and selfish interests.

Weekend

1 *You may well have come across attack from others on the 'truth' of these early chapters. If so, then make time to re-read them (preferably all at once) to make sure that you see exactly what the Bible says, and if you want to take the matter further, you may find* **Evolution and the Authority of the Bible** *by Nigel Cameron useful (Attic Press), or* **In the Beginning** *by Henri Blocher (IVP).*

2 *It is easy to get the impression that Genesis 1-11 is merely a collection of vivid stories which strangely move our imaginations. Or it is easy to see them simply as brief historical incidents, unparalleled in secular histories, viewed through breaks in the mists of time. They also, however, provide the framework for the unfolding history of God's plan to save mankind from the all-pervading effects of its rebellion. We saw a hint of this in Study 3. See if you can trace the emerging pattern of this plan in God's treatment of Adam and Eve, and the serpent, his attitude to Cain and Abel, and the saving of the human race through Noah's family.*

Part Ten/Week Two
Paul's letter to the Romans, 1 (A whole book study)

Paul's manifesto – that's how Romans has been described. In it we have the fullest statement of the basic Christian truths. Its theme is that faith in Christ is the only way to be accepted by God. We are all condemned, even the Jews who knew God's law. The only answer is a new start through Jesus. This new power of faith from God will transform us and empower us to live lives pleasing to God.

We also glimpse the warm and caring personality of the author. Paul was a Roman citizen. But he'd still not visited the capital when he wrote this letter, probably in AD 57. Rome was the trading centre for the known world, and the church was as cosmopolitan as the city.

1. What in the world has gone wrong?
Romans 1:1 – 2:16

God created man, and the evidence for that lies all around. Reason and conscience are rejected and mankind seems to sink deeper and deeper into selfishness and hopelessness.

1 *What does Paul say about the origin and power of the gospel (verses 1-18)?*
2 *Summarize what Paul says about man's state without God. Does it give*

man any grounds for optimism?
3 *How does God's wrath manifest itself (a) in the future? (b) in the present?*

Memory verse: I am not ashamed of the gospel, because it is the power of God for the salvation of everyone who believes: first for the Jew, then for the Gentile (Romans 1:16, NIV).

Salvation comes from responding to the gospel. Pray that God will give you the opportunity to study a Bible passage with someone who isn't a Christian.

You could follow up today's study by reading 'The Wrath of God', chapter 15 in *Knowing God* by J. I. Packer (IVP).

2. New leaf or new life?
Romans 2:17 – 3:31

The Jews (and indeed Gentile moralists) would be quick to condemn the decadence of the Roman way of life. Yet are they really any better off than other people, or is the Jew as spiritually bankrupt as the pagan? In the next two studies we'll begin to see that God doesn't just require us to turn over a new leaf. The solution is more radical than that. We need new lives.

294

1 *What advantages do the Jews have over the Gentiles? In what situations does circumcision have value?*
2 *So, why are Jews also condemned?*
3 *What was the purpose of the law?*
4 *On what grounds will God forgive both Jews and Gentiles?*

Memory verse: For all have sinned and fall short of the glory of God, and are justified freely by his grace through the redemption that came by Christ Jesus (Romans 3:23-24, NIV).

'Is God the God of Jews only?' No, of course not. But do you fall into the trap of thinking the gospel is only for certain types? All people need God's salvation. Pray that you don't fail to witness to someone because you think God couldn't save them.

3. Who is righteous?
Romans 4 and 5

Abraham was the prime example for the Jew of a righteous man. So, Paul sets out to explain precisely why God credited Abraham as being righteous.

1 *Explain why God accepted Abraham and David.*
2 *Make a list of the blessings arising from being justified by faith (5:1-11).*

Note: To 'justify' means to 'reckon' or 'declare right' (4:1-3).

3 *How can one man's death be the acquittal for millions?*

Pray that you will learn to take God at his word and act on his promises as Abraham did.

You could read George Muller of Bristol (Revell) to see how God kept his promises in the life of an individual.

4. New life for old
Romans 6 and 7

'If God's forgiveness is so extensive and complete, can't Christians just carry on exactly as before?' asks Paul's reader. The questioner misunderstands the nature of God's plan. We have become one with Christ in an exchange of our old sinful lives for the new life of Christ.

1 *Describe the Christian's new relationship to God.*
2 *What is our position in relation to sin? What conflicts will we experience in life?*
3 *Does the law have any limitations?*

Note: 6:6 refers to 'the sinful self'. 6.11 'Dead to sin' – the penalty of the old life is settled, but we still feel its influence.

4 *If someone asks you why a Christian should strive to avoid sinning, what arguments of Paul's might you use to answer the question?*

We have been set free from sin (verse 22) and empowered to lead holy lives. But Paul makes it clear that he struggled to overcome sin. Pray that God's Spirit will point out those things in your life that displease him.

5. 'The likeness of his Son'

Romans 8

Christ has set us free – not to do as we please, but to follow him. He has given us the potential to do this by providing the Holy Spirit.

1 *What role does the Holy Spirit play in our new lives? What must we do in order to allow God to reshape our lives?*
2 *Note down the assurances we have about the future. Does this knowledge help us in the present?*

Note: 8:10 Christians do not die spiritually.

3 *Paul gives us many reasons for rejoicing. Make a list of some of them.*

Memory verse: For those God foreknew he also predestined to be conformed to the likeness of his Son, that he might be the firstborn among brothers (Romans 8:29, NIV).

Rarely do we spend the time to pray in the way described in verses 26-27. Pray that God will teach you to spend more time in meditation and waiting on him; as well as in asking for things.

Why not do some further study on prayer by reading *Daring to Draw Near* by John White (IVP).

Weekend

1 *What would you say if someone of another faith asked you what you believed? Re-examine this week's notes and work out the important points you would need to explain. Paul shows that it is vital to be able to reason your faith. Study for a firm grasp of the fundamentals by reading* **Know the Truth** *by Bruce Milne (IVP).*
2 *The devil is alive and out to cause havoc in the Christian's life. Look up the word 'devil' or 'Satan' in a Bible dictionary, and study some of the Bible references it gives you.*
3 *Read through the entire book of Romans looking out for the conflict between Jew and Gentile.*

Part Ten/Week Three
Paul's letter to the Romans, 2 (A whole book study)

In the previous chapters, Paul explained the gospel, showing how God used the Jews to prepare the way. Now the gospel is to be preached to all men. Knowing their failure, Gentile nations are turning to God for pardon. But Israel, thinking they are God's favourites, are hardening themselves. What future does Israel have?

1. Israel – Children of the promise
Romans 9 and 10

1 *Write a summary of the two ways of seeking God that Paul contrasts. Why have the Jews failed?*
2 *What is the purpose of God's election? (You could look up the word 'election' in a Bible dictionary.)*
3 *List the responsibilities we have in proclaiming the gospel.*

Memory verse: If you confess that Jesus is Lord and believe that God raised him from death, you will be saved. For it is by our faith that we are put right with God; it is by our confession that we are saved (Romans 10:9-10, GNB).

Read through 10:5-15 again and let the implications sink in. Pray for the boldness and opportunity to proclaim the good news.
Evangelism and the Sovereignty of God by J. I. Packer (IVP) tackles these issues.

2. A faithful God
Romans 11

Is this the end for Israel? No, because God always keeps his promises. We have evidence for this in that some Jews were becoming Christians. God's sovereign ways are sometimes beyond us, but we know he purposes forgiveness for all, even though not all will accept his offer. Today we see his future plan for that nation.

1 *List some of the ways God has dealt with Israel.*
2 *Pick out a lesson from God's dealings with Israel which you can apply to yourself.*
3 *What is God's future plan for Israel?*
4 *List the attributes of God mentioned in verses 33-36.*

Pray that God's faithfulness and forgiveness will be expressed in your behaviour to others.

3. Living the new life
Romans 12 and 13

God gave his Son for us. Now we are to give our lives to him in gratitude. He will shape them into the likeness of his Son (8:29).

1 *Carefully list the characteristics, qualities and attitudes that those who have a new life should demonstrate. Assess yourself in the light of this.*
2 *Note down the reasons Paul gives for submitting to the authorities. Are there any grounds for opposing them on occasions? (See Acts 5:29.)*
3 *What incentives do we have for living the life described here?*

Memory verse: Do not conform any longer to the pattern of this world, but be transformed by the renewing of your mind. Then you will be able to test and approve what God's will is – his good, pleasing and perfect will (Romans 12:2, NIV).

Pray through the list you made for question 1, asking God to show you the areas in which you particularly need his help.

4. Let Christ dwell among us
Romans 14:1 – 15:13

A writer once described church life as 'building with bananas'. He was explaining that we are all far from perfect, yet through the Holy Spirit, God has given us the potential to live in peace, and work together in the Christian community. Today's study will give us some insights about how this can be worked out.

1 *From Paul's illustrations, try to work out the most important principles which govern our relationships with other Christians.*
2 *What sources of help do we have to achieve these?*
3 *What practical things ensue from following Christ's example?*

Pray that you will learn to bear with others' failings, be forgiving and cultivate compassion, kindness, humility, gentleness and patience (see Colossians 3:12-13).

5. 'Friends, Romans and countrymen!'
Romans 15:14 – 16:27

Despite Paul never having visited Rome he includes a long list of personal greetings. His hectic life never came between him and his priority of care for other believers.

1 *Examine what Paul says about himself and his work. Paul doesn't intend to sound superhuman, but to be an encouraging example. Can you see yourself having similar ambitions and priorities?*
2 *Look down the long list of names. Write out those expressions used by Paul to describe these people. What's the significance of your findings?*
3 *What characterizes false teachers (verses 17-18)?*

Pray that, like Paul, you will develop godly aspirations, seeking to put the Lord first in all things.

Weekend

1 *In last week's study on Romans we saw the incredible truth that we can be justified in God's sight by Christ. This week we have seen that he has the power to bring us into the likeness of Christ himself. Go back over your notes and list all the practical hallmarks that demonstrate this new life within.*
2 *Make a study of the demands of Christian living by reading one of the many fine books available, such as* **The Cost of Commitment** *by John White (IVP). You could ask your someone at your local bookstore for further suggestions.*

Part Ten/Week Four
Jonah (A character study)

That Jonah was a real person is shown by a reference to him, in 2 Kings 14:25, indicating that he lived during the 8th century BC. Who actually wrote the book *Jonah* remains unknown. It could be autobiographical, but nowhere is the first person used. Its main message is that God loves Jew and non-Jew and offers salvation to both. Peter was given a similar message, through a vision, resulting in the conversion of a Roman centurion. Peter then realized that 'God does not show favouritism but accepts men from every nation who fear him and do what is right' (Acts 10:34-35, NIV).

1. What me? No way Lord!
Jonah 1:1-6

Jonah was a prophet, one bringing God's special messages to the people, particularly concerning future events (2 Kings 14:25). In this role he would have expected God to speak to him from time to time, giving directions to go to a certain place and deliver God's word to a certain person or people. From Joppa (Jaffa), Tarshish (possibly in Spain) was in the opposite direction to Nineveh.

Nineveh, the last capital of Assyria, an enemy of Israel, had temples, palaces and a famous library. Water was provided by dams and canals. The metropolitan district would have taken three days to cross (3:3). The inhabitants worshipped a national god, Ashur, and a local goddess of war and love, Ishtar.

1 *List all the information given in these verses, concerning Jonah. What does this tell us about his character?*

2 *How did God deal with his rebellious servant?*
3 *Can you see any parallels in your own experience with that of Jonah in both his rebellion and God's response?*

Pray that you may be willing to obey God as he speaks to you through Scripture.

2. It's your fault!
Jonah 1:7-16

The casting of lots was used also by the Jews: for example, the choice of a goat for sacrifice (Leviticus 16:7-10) and the choosing of Matthias as a disciple (Acts 1:21-26) were decided by lot.

1 *What more do we learn here concerning Jonah's character? Add to your list of yesterday.*
2 *As Jonah talks with the terrified sailors, how does his attitude begin to change?*
3 *What has the Lord taught you, following times of disobedience?*

Pray that you may have a willingness to recognize the need for repentance and act upon it.

3. Help, help!
Jonah 1:17 – 2:10

Jonah's vivid prayer from inside the 'great fish' has been likened to a Psalm.

1 *As Jonah considered his position before the Lord, what were his feelings? Why do you think the Lord sometimes seems to withdraw his presence from us?*

2 What does Jonah's prayer teach
   you about a repentant heart and
   the response of a forgiving Lord?

Praise God for his forgiveness in
salvation and in daily experience!

---

4. Repent!
Jonah 3

Jonah now faces the great city of
Nineveh, its king and people having
been given a second chance.
Sackcloth, a coarse black material,
was worn as a sign of mourning or
penitence for sins. The people of
Nineveh seem to have worn it as a
robe over their other clothes.
Repentance (v.9 RSV) on the part of
God has more the meaning of
relenting (NIV).

1 What did Jonah preach and what
   was the depth of the response as
   measured by the king's decree?
2 In what sense is Jesus 'greater'
   than Jonah? Read Matthew 12:38-
   41 and Luke 11:29-32.
3 Contrast the rapid response of
   Nineveh with that of Jonah's
   attitude from the beginning of the
   book.

Consider the thought that it is best to
obey first time! Pray about your own
attitude to obeying God.

---

5. All is revealed!
Jonah 4

Jonah has been described as a
'narrow little nationalist' (Bishop J.
B. Taylor). But was he angry because
his ability as a prophet could be
questioned if they repented? In this
chapter you will see what kind of

man he really was. God has to teach
him a lesson which is hard to learn.

1 What is now revealed as Jonah's
   real motive for sailing towards
   Tarshish? What did he hope would
   happen (v.5)? Why did he now
   want to die?

Jonah was sorry for the plant but not
for Nineveh, angry over the former's
death and the latter's reprieve.

2 Write, in your own words, God's
   answer to Jonah, noting
   particularly how patient he was
   with his servant.
3 From God's dealings with Jonah,
   how can you better understand
   the merciful way in which he has
   dealt and is dealing with you?

Pray that you may not be selfish with
your faith, reserving it for those you
consider 'worthy', but love to 'give it
away' to all.

Weekend

1 Re-read the book and write a
   personality profile of Jonah.
   Where can you identify with him?
   What have you learned about the
   way God deals with disobedience?
2 Jonah was in a missionary
   situation. What situations similar
   to Nineveh exist today? What
   principles does the book teach
   about missionaries and
   missionary work?
3 How does the book of Jonah
   reveal God's love for people of
   other religions?

Revelation 2 (A meditation)

John the apostle was banished to the island of Patmos, which now belongs to Greece, during the reign of the Roman Emperor Domitian. He wrote the book around AD 95 or 96, following a vision of Jesus Christ and the events which will occur when he comes again to judge the world and take Christians to live with him for ever. The glorified Christ is portrayed in 1:12-16, together with the effect of this meeting upon John. Christ gives John a message for each of seven churches, but all are to take notice of the contents.

1. Your first love
Revelation 2:1-7

The church at Ephesus, a major Roman city but now a ruin on the west coast of Turkey, was established by Paul (Acts 19). There was a great temple to the goddess Diana where people were expected to join in the rites of worship which involved immorality and magic. Within the church were problems due to false teachers (Nicolaitans).

1 *Think about the type of church*

described in verses 2-4, correct in its beliefs, hard-working and yet without the vital spark of love for Jesus with which it started. Use your imagination to build up a picture of this church, its people, its worship, its outreach.

2 Note down what Jesus says to this church (verse 5). Following from point 1, imagine the various reactions this could have provoked among the members.

3 What things can cause a church to lose its love for Jesus?

Pray for yourself and your own church, that your love for Jesus will go on growing.

2. Be faithful
Revelation 2:8-11

Smyrna was a beautiful city, north of Ephesus, loyal to Rome. Today it is the modern Turkish city of Izmir. Bishop Polycarp died there for his faith, in his eighties, around AD 156-160. When asked to swear 'Caesar is Lord' to save himself from burning, he replied, 'Eighty and six years have I served him, and he never did me an injury: how then can I blaspheme my King and Saviour?'

1 Think about the riches which this church had, not silver and gold, but much more precious things.

2 Consider the comfort which Jesus' words would have given to these people.

The 'first' death is physical; the 'second' is eternal.

Thank God for his faithfulness to his church and pray that you may be a faithful member of your local church – that you may be loyal to the leadership, pray for its members and activities...

3. Keep the true faith
Revelation 2:12-17

At Pergamum there was a temple to Zeus, Satan's throne (verse 13). Within the church were those who held views inconsistent with the teaching of Christ and who compromised, becoming involved with the sexual evils of the temple and buying meat which had been offered to idols. The church neglected to discipline these people.

1 Jesus both commended and condemned this church, which must have presented a very mixed witness. How may outsiders have viewed this group of Christians?

2 Those who were faithful were promised spiritual refreshment from Christ (hidden manna) and a transformed character (a person's name implies their character to the eastern mind) – verse 17. Consider the generosity of Jesus Christ!

Pray for yourself and your church that you may be faithful witnesses to the truth of the Christian gospel. Pray for wisdom and strength to resist Satan's attacks – he tries to divide and weaken the church.

4. Steadfast love
Revelation 2:18-29

At Thyatira, a trading city, most church members loved the Lord whole-heartedly. Nonetheless an evil woman in a place of leadership (a prophetess) led some into great immorality, mixing pagan activities with Christian worship.

1 *Try to imagine the tensions which must have built up in this church, due to the powerful influence of one person. Consider the reactions of those who held fast to Christ in this situation. Remember – many of the cults started when people followed apparently quite orthodox individuals.*
2 *Jesus promises the 'morning star', that is himself, to those who persevere to the end. He also promises authority over the nations. Let your thoughts dwell upon the power which lies in the hands of Jesus Christ and which he will delegate to his people!*

Pray for yourself and your church that each member may have the grace to bring harmony and forgiveness in times of tension. Pray that the leaders may show a godly wisdom in discerning the cause of problems and in dealing with them in love.

5. 'I fell at his feet as though dead'

Revelation 2

Each letter gives a credential of Jesus Christ. The language is symbolic and follows that of 1:12-20. The stars or angels (verse 1) are the pastors or ministers of the churches (the golden lampstands). The first and last (verse 8) refers to the all-embracing nature of Christ (Isaiah 44:6). The two-edged sword (verse 12) indicates the manner in which Christ will cut out evil.

1 *List the characteristics of Jesus and the evidences of his love, as you re-read the chapter.*
2 *'Gentle Jesus, meek and mild' says the children's hymn – meditate on this contrasting vision of the righteous, conquering Christ.*

Pray that in corporate and private worship there may be always a remembrance of Jesus' position as King of kings.

Weekend

1 *Read Paul's letter to the church at Ephesus, in the Good News Bible, and find out what made them 'fall in love' with Christ in the first place.*
2 *Work through Revelation chapters 2 and 3 with Leon Morris'* **Tyndale New Testament Commentary** *(Eerdmans) or Michael Wilcock's* **The Message of Revelation** *in 'The Bible Speaks Today' series (IVP).*

Part Ten/Week Six
The book of Ezra (A historical study)

Ezra takes up the history of Israel where 2 Chronicles leaves off. (Compare verses 1-3 with the end of 2 Chronicles.) Ezra gives more than a record of the major events around Jerusalem spanning the reigns of five Persian emperors (see chart). He gives an insight into that history from a divine perspective.

1. The God of history
Ezra 1

1 *'In order to fulfil the word of the LORD spoken by Jeremiah'* (verse 1, NIV). *Look up Jeremiah 29:10-14. Note (a) God's timescale; (b) God's conditions so that people will enter into the good of his plans. Who caused the people to want to meet these conditions (Ezra 1:5)?*

Note: *Verse 2.* These Persian Emperors were certainly very powerful men. One of Cyrus' successors actually used the title 'king of kings' (Ezra 7:12).

2 *As in the story of the exodus, God made sure that his people did not return empty-handed to the Promised Land (see verses 4 and 6). God used many means of providing for his work – including the gifts made by his own people. Write down the basis on which they decided how much to give – Ezra 2:68-69.*
3 *Think about the ways in which the Sovereign God has provided for your needs. In many cases probably we have far more! Think about how much you are able to give back to him.*

2. A good start, but ...
Ezra 3:1 – 4:5

1 *What was the first thing the Jews*

did to re-establish worship at Jerusalem? Write down why they did this. What was the 'feast of booths' (RSV) all about? Why was this feast so appropriate for the returned exiles? God had done it again!

Note: 'Feast of booths' see Leviticus 23:33-43

2 *When God's people heed God's word and start to do God's work in God's way, opposition is almost guaranteed. How does 4:4 show that the Samaritans were not really wanting to help? Why did the Jews not want their help if they had been worshipping the Lord as they said? (See 2 Kings 17:24-34 for some ideas.)*

Ezra 4:6-23 need to be put 'in brackets'. They break into the flow of the historical sequence to show that the opposition of verses 1-5 became a recurring feature in the reigns of Ahasuerus and Artaxerxes. (The kings' names provide important historical pointers – see chart.) Verse 24 brings us back to the reign of Darius to give the link with chapter 5.

The people's song at the foundation ceremony was probably Psalm 136. Use it as an aid to your worship today. Celebrate God's goodness and steadfast love in the history of creation and redemption – and also to you (Psalm 136:23). God is still the same!

3. On with the job!
Ezra 5 and 6

You can read the forceful words of Haggai and Zechariah in their books

Persian kings		Events in Ezra			At the same time elsewhere in OT
Dates BC		Dates BC		Ref.	
539-530	Cyrus	537	Return from exile Altar set up	chs. 1-2 ch. 3	End of Daniel's life – Daniel 1:21; 10:1
		536	Foundation of temple laid: opposition begins	chs. 3-4	
530-522	Cambyses		(not mentioned)		
522-486	Darius I (Hystaspes)	520-516	Opposition continues	ch. 4:5,24	Haggai & Zechariah
			Despite protests to the king, temple completed in response to the prophets	chs. 5-6	
486-465	Xerxes I (Ahasuerus)		Further opposition	ch. 4:6	Esther
465-424	Artaxerxes I (Longimanus)	458	Opposition again! Decree to stop building Ezra sent to Jerusalem Ezra's journey and safe arrival Ezra deals with mixed marriages	ch. 4:7-23 ch. 7:1 ch. 8 chs. 9-10	Nehemiah Malachi

in the Old Testament. They certainly got the building work going again – and weren't above lending a hand themselves (5:1-2)!

1 *From chapter 5, how would you assess the reactions of the Jewish leaders to the enquiries of the governor? How do they show respect for both God and king? What lesson had history taught them about giving obedient service to God?*

Notice the touch of the good historian in giving us copies of the original letter sent to king Darius (5:6ff.), of the official minute in 6:2-5 and of the king's reply (6:6ff.).

2 *Note the ways in which chapter 6 illustrates the fact that 'the Most High is sovereign over the kingdoms of men' (Daniel 4:17, NIV). There is no necessary conflict between obeying God and submitting to God-appointed authorities. How is this truth brought out in Ezra 6:14 and applied in Romans 13:1-7? (See your notes for Week 3, Study 3.)*

The temple was completed in time for Passover. Ezra 6:21 is a valuable counter-balance to 4:3 as it proves beyond doubt that the Jewish leaders were not narrow-minded nationalists.

Think over what you have written today. Do you 'obey God rather than men' (Acts 5:29, NIV), yet give due respect to God-appointed rulers and to the laws of the land? Pray for several important leaders by name, and about your attitude to them.

4. Ezra ... at last!
Ezra 7 and 8

Between chapters 6 and 7 there is almost a sixty-year gap. Building progress at Jerusalem had been minimal, and you can read about the continuing opposition to the work during this period in 4:6-23. During this time also, the events of the book of Esther took place. Now Artaxerxes had succeeded to the throne and in the year 458 BC he sent Ezra to Jerusalem. Ezra was a scribe who knew God's law well and who could trace his ancestry back to Aaron. Furthermore, he enjoyed the favour of the king (7:1-6).

Words like the 'good hand' (or 'the blessing') of his God was upon him, or 'God helped', keep cropping up in Ezra and Nehemiah. From these chapters, make a note of (a) the results of God's blessing being upon Ezra; (b) the kind of person upon whom God's hand rests for good.

Do you depend on God for daily protection, provision and wisdom? That question can be answered by looking at the priority you place on prayer, on seriously studying the Bible, and your expectations. Think about how you can follow Ezra's example in 7:10 and 8:22-23 and ask God to keep your heart set in that way. Then praise him for some of the things that have happened to you under his good hand.

5. Not race – religion
Ezra 9 and 10

A superficial reading of these chapters might leave the impression that Ezra was a hardened racist and an advocate of divorce. Neither description would fit him – any more than it would fit God, whose law Ezra had taught with such devastating effect.

1 *Write down the cause of Ezra's violent reaction in 9:1-5. Why was marriage to foreign wives considered 'unfaithfulness', an offence, or sin (verses 2 and 4)? Look up Deuteronomy 7:1-6. Why was marriage to foreigners outlawed for God's holy people?*
2 *Ezra's concern was not only that Israel had broken faith with God by disregarding his law (9:10-12), but that the returned exiles had also sinned against God's mercy (9:13-15). Look over his prayer of confession in 9:6-15. How does he sum up the history of Israel?How does he interpret his own day – especially for the small part of Israel (the 'remnant', 9:8) that had returned to the land?*

Malachi (probably Ezra's contemporary) gives a valuable insight into the situation in Malachi 2:10-16. It would appear that Jews may have been divorcing their Jewish wives in favour of the women of the land.

3 *What is God's attitude to divorce? Why do you think that divorce was the only solution to Israel's problem in Ezra 10?*

Ezra identified himself with the sin of the people as he prayed to God (9:6ff.). Try to enter into his attitude as you confess your sin in the light of both God's law and God's grace. Then pray for the nation and for God's church today.

Weekend

1 *The book of Ezra provides a good way into reading the other Old Testament literature relating to the same period. Try to read as much of it as you can over the weekend. (You will find a list of the relevant biblical books in the chart.)*
2 *Look up the reference to 'divorce' in a good Bible Dictionary, and follow through some of the New Testament references.*

Part Ten/Week Seven
Mission matters (A topic study)

Doubtless you know of the appalling physical and spiritual needs present in our world. But have you considered how it is possible for you to help alleviate them? Every believer has a part to play in Christ's church and its mission. Through these studies we'll see what's involved in being a missionary (Studies 2 and 3) and how you can help (Studies 4 and 5). But first let's see why mission is important.

1. 'As the Father has sent me, I am sending you'
Mark 16:15; Luke 24:47; John 20:21

1 *Put into your own words the task given to the church.*
2 *Why do you think the same commission is repeated in all four Gospels?*
3 *What would you reply to the sceptic who says, 'Christians shouldn't interfere with those who hold other beliefs'?*
4 *How would you answer the person who says he's too busy with the spiritual needs of his own land to care about other places?*

Read Matthew 9:35-38. For what purpose does Christ send his people? Buy a world map and a copy of *Operation World* by P.J. Johnstone or some Operation Mobilisation prayer cards to help you begin to pray for other countries.

'I know that I have opportunities of usefulness at home: nevertheless in heathen lands there is gross darkness and scarcely any gleam of light.'
Thomas Gajetan Ragland.

2. Paul – a missionary in the making
Acts 7:54 – 8:4; 9:1-31; 13:1-3

It's easy to put missionaries on pedestals and assume them to be especially holy types! But this is sometimes a way of evading God's demands on you. Today's study shows how a highly unlikely candidate for a missionary found his calling.

1 **Saul.** *List what you know about his background and previous actions. Is he the 'type' you'd expect to become a Christian? Once converted, what natural gifts does he have that God makes use of?*
2 **Crisis.** *What happened to Paul was exceptionally dramatic, but what elements are common to everyone's conversion?*
3 **Paul.** *What new priorities does Paul have, now he's a Christian?*
4 **Commission.** *Can you work out the respective roles played by Paul, the local church and the Holy Spirit in determining Paul's career? Are there any hints in this study about what may constitute a missionary 'call'?*

Think about what qualities are needed to be a missionary.

3. For the sake of Christ ...
Galatians 1:11-24; Philippians 3:1-24

The two passages today show something of Paul's attitude towards his missionary life, revealing his worries and goals. God did not insulate him from life's difficulties despite his key role in the church.

1 *Where does the gospel come from? Note down the preparations*

Paul undergoes before starting his ministry (Galatians).

2 Make a list of those things which most dominated Paul's life. What might get in the way of commitment to Christ? List some of the priorities which should take the highest place in your life (Philippians).

> 'There is nothing in the world worth living for but doing good and finishing God's work – doing the work that Christ did.'
> David Brainerd.

Are there any aspects of your life that you aren't prepared to surrender for the sake of Christ? Why not read a missionary's life, such as the *Biography of James Hudson Taylor* by Dr and Mrs Howard Taylor (Overseas Missionary Fellowship)?

---

4. How can I help ... now?
2 Corinthians 1:8-11; 9:1-15; Philippians 4:10-20.

It's neither possible nor right for all of us to serve God overseas. But there are ways in which we can all help. Today's study investigates how.

1 *2 Corinthians 1:8-11. Why does Paul want others to know of his sufferings? What part to play have the people to whom he writes? In what ways could you support someone away from home for the sake of the gospel?*
2 *2 Corinthians 9:1-15. Why should you give money away and to whom?*
3 *Philippians 4:10-20. How does God look at this and repay it? What kind of giving does God value most?*

Ask your minister what missionaries your church supports. Find out about them and start supporting one or more with your prayers, money and letter writing.

---

5. Being prepared
Isaiah 6:1-10

> No child of God can claim exemption from the directive to let the whole world know what Jesus has done. The initial call of Christ to his disciples was to 'Follow me' and its immediate result would be 'and I will make you fishers of men' (Matthew 4:19). So often we hear the question, 'How do I know if God is calling me to his service?' ... The question should rather be framed 'Since God has called me to this tremendous task, what particular part does he want me to play?'
> Elizabeth Goldsmith

1 *Note down some of those things which Isaiah's vision teaches him about God's character and his own needs.*
2 *Why is Isaiah prepared to take on God's tasks?*
3 *Look at the message he's to take – will everyone accept God's message? Imagine what discouragements Isaiah will face.*

Lord, help me to be prepared to do whatever you ask of me.

Read *Out of the Saltshaker* by Rebecca Rippert, an excellent book on evangelism.

Weekend

1 *Begin your prayers for the world by adopting one particular country of your choice. Find out all you can about it, such as: the number of local Christians and missionaries; what missions operate there; what the people are like; how the economy runs; how you can find up-to-date prayer information. You could compile a file of information on it.*

Don't forget that the country is an organic whole with real, live inhabitants! Perhaps get to know about the country of an overseas student or immigrant family that you know.

2 *Mission also includes social action in its meaning. To view the relationship between telling the good news and social action read* **Involvement** *by John Stott (Revell).*

Part Ten/Week Eight
The letter to the Hebrews (A bird's-eye study)

The Jewish nation was going through hard times and the religious authorities were urging loyalty to their heritage. They were hostile to Christians, now excluding them from the Temple. Being a Christian was made to seem unpatriotic. Hebrews was written to these Christian Jews who were being tempted to turn back to the old ways.

Hebrews teaches us that Christ is the final, perfect revelation of God to man. It gives a full picture of both his deity and humanity, in a way no other book of the Bible does.

This week's study therefore asks you to read the whole of it!

1. The Son of God
Hebrews 1 – 3

God had spoken to man many times through his servants, but never before by his Son. Hebrews stresses the absolute supremacy of this final revelation, over all others.

1 *List some of the statements made about Christ. In what ways is he greater than angels, prophets and Moses?*

Note: 2:10 Although morally perfect, Jesus became more perfectly equipped for God's work.

2 *What do you learn about the nature of man? Why did Jesus become a man?*

The Israelites are warned they must obey God. Think of any ways in which you are disobeying him. Pray that God will keep you mindful of his glory and majesty; and make you responsive to hearing his word.

2. The promise of God
Hebrews 4 – 6

As the Israelites entered the Promised Land, so we can enter God's rest by accepting his gift of salvation. Christ has made this possible, but it brings certain responsibilities. We don't just settle our sins and live as we please. Our behaviour in the 'wilderness' (*i.e.* this life) shows whether we have truly believed.

1 *Summarize the main evidence that God's promises are irrevocable and unshakeable.*
2 *Note down some reasons why Christ's priesthood is better than the Levitical one.*

Notes: 4:11 'Disobedience' is not believing. 6:4-6 'Enlightened' – hearers, but not necessarily believers.

3 *What responsibilities do you have concerning your spiritual life?*

The Adventure by Jerry Sittser is a superb book about spiritual growth.
One responsibility we do have, is to store up God's word, so remind yourself of this, by learning 4:12.
Have you grown as you should? Pray that God will help you remove the things that hinder your growth and cultivate those helpful activities.

3. The High Priest of God
Hebrews 7 and 8

God regarded the Levitical priesthood as imperfect and obsolete. As made clear in Galatians 3:24-25, the law existed to lead us to Christ. A Jewish Christian may be tempted to keep the law as well as accepting Christ, so it is important to explain the temporary nature of the old covenant.

God always intended the more ancient and perfect Order of Melchizedek to come to fruition in Jesus. The Levitical system could never meet our needs. In today's study we see only Christ can do this.

1 *List some reasons why the new covenant is superior to the old.*
2 *What are some ways that Jesus Christ is unique?*
3 *Why do we need a High Priest?*

Consider all that Jesus endured for our sake, such as the crucifixion. Thank God that he has provided a way of salvation, and pray that you will be a faithful witness to it.

4. Entering the presence of God
Hebrews 9 and 10

The annual Day of Atonement was an awesome occasion. The people stopped work, fasted, and in sacred assembly watched the High Priest enter the Most Holy Place. God was seen to be separate from sin. This elaborate system was only the shadow, pointing forward and preparing men for Christ. He gave himself as a perfect sacrifice and became High Priest for ever. Unlike the Jews, we can now come right into God's presence at any time – if we want to.

1 *Make two lists showing the differences between the sacrifices in the Tabernacle and Christ's sacrifice. What has been achieved by Christ's sacrifice?*
2 *What are some encouragements and warnings we are given to guide us in the Christian life?*

Memory verse: Let us hold unswervingly to the hope we profess, for he who promised is faithful. And let us consider how we may spur one another on towards love and good deeds (Hebrews 10:23-24, NIV).

What effect do you have on other Christians? Are you helpful, sympathetic and positive, or negative and critical? Pray that you will be a blessing to other people.

5. Pleasing God
Hebrews 11 – 13

The Jews had a choice. They could accept Christ and follow God through faith, or continue with a code of religious observance. It is not possible to do both because, as we've seen, the heart of Christianity is that there is one way to God – through the sacrifice of Christ. It is neither an easy choice to make or an easy path to follow. But God is able to save and keep us, using the trials of this life to equip us for the next.

1 *How did some of the individuals in chapter 11 prove their faith in God?*
2 *What are some privileges we have*

that these Old Testament heroes didn't? (See 11:39-40; 12:18-24.)
3 *List those duties we should perform. Have you neglected any of them?*

Memory verse: Let us fix our eyes on Jesus, the author and perfecter of our faith, who for the joy set before him endured the cross, scorning its shame, and sat down at the right hand of the throne of God (Hebrews 12:2, NIV).

Meditate on this verse, training yourself to remember Christ at all times. Many grow weary and lose heart. Pray for those you know who seem in danger of giving up.

Weekend

1 *Hebrews contains much practical advice about how we are to live. Look through your notes and summarize (a) some dangers we're warned of; (b) some things we're encouraged to do; (c) some incentives we're given. Do you neglect any of these?*
2 *One of the major themes in Hebrews is faith. It is neither vague nor wishy-washy, but a lifelong solid confidence in God's promises. Find out more by reading chapter 6 in* The Fight *by John White (IVP) or by looking up the word 'faith' in a Bible dictionary.*
3 *Why not visit a local synagogue, or discuss with a pious Jewish friend the importance to Jews of the law and their various festivals?*

Part Ten/Week Nine
What about other religions? (An issue study)

It is clearly a dreadful thing to reject God's offer of salvation in Jesus Christ. But what about the people who have never had a chance to say 'no' – who have never even heard the gospel? Will a God of love and justice condemn them to an eternity in hell?

Then there are those who are faithful members of other religions. Are they excluded from salvation if they do not acknowledge Jesus Christ as Saviour and Lord?

Many sincere people would shudder at the suggestion that the un-evangelized, and those who adhere to other faiths, are lost. Your task this week must be to discover what the Bible actually says in answer to these questions – and it says much! The notes select passages which represent the main thrust of the Bible's teaching, but you may want to read more widely. (Use cross references in your Bible, or a concordance, to help you find relevant passages.)

To speculate further than what the Bible actually says is dangerous. But you can always trust what you find in its pages, and you can be assured that God, as Judge of all the earth, will always do right (see Genesis 18:25).

1. No other God
Isaiah 45:5-25

1 *As you read through verses 5-19,*
write down the ways in which the Creator God is distinct, and differs from the gods men create.

It is not necessary to worship a physical idol to be guilty of idolatry. Worship of any invention of man's mind, or any created being, is idolatry. Exodus 20:1-6 and Romans 1:18-25 spell out the consequences of idolatry. (Look up these passages and make a note of what they say, if you have time.)

1 *What hope of alternative means of salvation through other religions is given by the Lord in verses 20-25? How does this unique Saviour-God describe himself, and what response does he require from every man?*

It will not do to say that members of other religions who do not worship the God who reveals himself in the Bible are worshipping the same God in their own way. The Bible's condemnation of all other gods is sweeping and universal.

As an act of worship, read (*aloud* if you can) Isaiah 40:9-31, then go on to express in your own words your worship of this God who is uniquely and supremely great.

Idols of Our Time by Bob Goudzwaard (IVP) vividly explores our modern idols of materialism, nationalism, revolution, and guaranteed security.

313

2. No other way
John 10:1-18

Jesus Christ is unique – and made outstanding claims about himself. Either he was an ego maniac, or his claims were true! None of his claims are more egocentric than the 'I AM' sayings in John's Gospel. Today's study looks at some of these exclusive claims of Jesus.

1 *Look over the passage and note down those characteristics which mark out Jesus' sheep. How do your notes compare with verses 25-30? In contrast, what does Jesus say about those who are not his sheep (see verse 26)?*

2 *Jesus speaks slightingly of other would-be rivals for the affections of his flock. How are they described? Why do you think he is so critical of others – who may well have been well-intentioned religious leaders?*

3 *Verse 10 shows Jesus' purpose over against that of the 'thief'. How is the qualification of faith in Jesus as the only way to eternal life with God confirmed in John 14:1-7, John 3:16-21 and Acts 4:12?*

Verse 16 must be carefully understood as it might be misread to mean that 'other sheep' from other religions might find their way into Jesus' fold. Clearly, Jesus is talking to Jews and saying that he has other, non-Jewish sheep. But notice the qualifying characteristic of *all* his sheep: 'they will heed my voice'.

Are you willing to be as extreme in your faith in Jesus as he was in his claims about himself?

3. No racial barriers
Acts 10

1 *As a strict Jew, Peter would have been concerned to obey the Old Testament food laws, and he would not have had any social contact with people of other races on religious grounds. Summarize in your notebook how God prepared him for the visit of the messengers from Cornelius and note his response to them.*

2 *How had God prepared Cornelius to receive the good news about Jesus? Write down especially your observations about the parts played by (a) his awareness of the God of the Bible through his contact with Jewish religion, and (b) the ministry of angels.*

3 *This story has been used by some people to justify the view that God will accept 'men of good faith' no matter what their race or religion. To what extent does that view accurately reflect the text of verses 34-35? From the rest of Peter's talk, what condition must be met to receive forgiveness of sins, and how did Cornelius and the others with him show they had met it?*

Write down the names of any people you know who have a background in a religion other than Christianity. Start to pray for them that God will prepare them to receive the message of Jesus. Go on to pray that you – and perhaps other Christians – will find opportunities to tell them the good news.

4. No justice
Romans 2:1-16

1 *In the last study you saw how God does not show partiality on the basis of race. How do verses 6-11 back up this view of God's fairness?*
2 *What is God's standard of righteousness according to verses 12-13? When judged by this standard, who deserves eternal life? (When you have written down your answer, a glance into chapter 3 and especially verses 9-20 will confirm if you have got it right!)*

Verses 14-15 show that even those who don't know what the Bible says have an innate knowledge of God's basic requirements. Their conscience approves them when they do right and accuses them when they go wrong.

3 *On the basis of your understanding of human nature as well as what the Bible says, how likely is it that anyone will be able to stand before the Lord Jesus with a clear conscience (see verse 16)?*

'Surely God won't condemn a man to hell just because he hasn't heard the gospel.' If you haven't heard – or thought – something like that, you certainly will sooner or later! God's righteous judgment (and his condemnation of all men as sinners) is on the basis of works – not on whether we have had an opportunity to respond to the gospel. His salvation, on the other hand, is totally a matter of grace on the basis of the work of Jesus, and is to be received by faith.
    When you have time, either now or at the weekend, why not read on in the letter to the Romans – at least to the end of chapter 5? Review the notes that you made on the earlier studies of Romans – 'Paul's manifesto', Weeks 2 and 3.

5. No shirking!
Romans 10

Isn't the gospel **GOOD NEWS?** No more need we fear condemnation under the law because we fail to observe it (verse 5). God has his own way of putting us in the right through faith in Christ alone (see verse 4). Romans 10 is set in the context of God's dealings with the people of Israel, but its principles bear wider application.

1 *How does anyone – Jew or Gentile – come into the goodness of God's salvation? (Read through verses 1-13 again, and write as full an answer as you can in your notebook.)*
2 *According to verse 17, what must happen before someone comes to faith and is then able to 'call on the name of the Lord' (verses 13-14)?*
3 *Read Jesus' words in Matthew 28:18-20. What do you think is the weak link in the chain of events in Romans 10:14-15?*
4 *Verse 18 refers to God's self-revelation in his creation. In itself this is insufficient for salvation. According to Romans 1:19-20, though, this general revelation does have an important consequence for everyone. What is it?*

Have you ever read Ezekiel 3:16-21, or Ezekiel 33:1-9, where God speaks to the prophet about the responsibilities of a watchman? Could it be that we Christians have a similar responsibility towards those who have not yet heard about the Lord Jesus, or who are trapped in false religion?

Weekend

1 *You may like to re-read Romans 1-5 to broaden your understanding of the gospel of justification by faith in Christ alone. Alternatively, you may like to study Ephesians 2 to see what God has done in bringing complete outsiders into the full benefit of a new relationship with himself. Don't forget: the God who by sheer grace saved the formerly pagan Ephesians – and you! – can do the same today as the gospel comes to people of other religions and to those who are until then unevangelized.*

2 *Try to get hold of a copy of* **What On Earth Are You Doing?** *by Michael Griffiths (Baker Book House), or read the relevant chapters of Dick Dowsett's book,* **God, That's Not Fair!** *(OMF/STL) for a missionary's eye view of the problem of the unevangelized and other religions – and what to do about it!*

3 *If you are unsure about the Christian claim that Jesus provides the only way to God, you should read* **One Way to God?** by Brian Maiden, or else read right through the Gospel according to St John.

Part Eleven

The Exodus
The second coming
Paul's letters to the Thessalonians
Guidance
The book of Proverbs
Timothy
Matthew 5
The book of Daniel

Part Eleven/Week One
The Exodus (A historical study)

By the time of the Exodus, which most scholars take to be in the first half of the thirteenth century BC, the family of Abraham had multiplied, fulfilling the promise made in Genesis 12:2. Outside the Bible, there is little evidence for the Exodus, since for the Egyptians it was a shameful event not worthy of mention. But this does not alter the fact that it was a historical event which had a deep and lasting impact upon the people of God and demonstrated God's power to rescue. Moses is traditionally the author of the book of Exodus.

Here is no heroic epic of migration but the recollection of shameful servitude from which only the power of God brought deliverance.

John Bright, *A History of Israel* (Westminster Press, 1981).

---

1. Help!
Exodus 1:1 – 2:10

Rameses II was probably the Pharaoh. He was acting from fairly shrewd political motives.

1 *What threat did he see the immigrant minority posing to the native Egyptians? How would you summarize his victimization of the descendants of Israel? With what result?*

Throughout these studies we shall

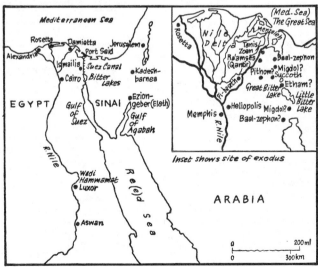

Inset shows site of exodus

see the stark contrast of God's determination and ability to deliver, with Pharaoh's feeble efforts to thwart God's power.

2 *What examples of this contrast do you notice in this passage?*

The Jews have never underestimated their desperate plight in Egypt. From then on God was seen as one who rescued them.

3 *In what ways personally, or as a church, or society in general, do we need to experience God as one who comes to the rescue? For example, think of situations of danger, moral decline, effects of sin. How true is it that the more we realize our need for deliverance, the more we will depend on God's power to deliver? How would you encourage those who felt their situation was so awful that God couldn't deliver them?*

Pray for any you know who need God to rescue them.

2. The means of rescue
Exodus 3:1 – 4:17

Israel's suffering continued for at least eighty years. Yet in all that time, God had not abandoned them, although at times they must have wondered if he had (2:23-25).

1 *Read 3:1 – 4:17 and make a note of all that God said (a) about himself and (b) about his plan to rescue Israel. Take one of these aspects of God's character and spend some time thinking what he means to you. Thank God that he is such a God.*

2 *In the face of all that God had shown him, Moses still hesitated. What excuses did he make (see 3:11, 13; 4:1, 10, 13)? What was the basic reason behind these excuses?*

Has there been a time recently when you knew God wanted to use you but you were reluctant? Ask God's forgiveness and consider if there are ways still open to rectify your action.

3. A brick wall?
Exodus 6:28 – 11:10

The situation for the Israelites went from bad to worse and Moses was blamed for this (chapter 5). But God had not deserted them (chapter 6).

1 *Look at 6:28 – 11:10. As you do so trace the progress of Pharaoh as he gradually relented, compromising all the way (see 7:3,13 etc.).*

Note: The plagues probably lasted over at least a six month period. So Pharaoh's resistance was prolonged as was the judgment upon Egypt.

2 *Had they been open to God, what could the Egyptians and Pharaoh have learnt about the God of the Hebrews?*

Note: Commentators have written at great length on the hardening of Pharaoh's heart. The phrase does not imply that Pharaoh isn't responsible for his stubbornness.

God's power yet awesomeness was very striking. What situations personally, nationally or internationally do you know where you need to be reminded that God is all-powerful? Pray to the great God to act.

---

4. Rescued at last
Exodus 12:1-39

1 *In the instructions for preparation for the Passover, what signs of God's love towards Israel can you see? Read these verses carefully as they are full of fascinating detail.*

In verse 28 the Israelites did just what the Lord had commanded. We do not always anticipate obedience as the response to love. Yet both the Old and New Testaments demonstrate the demand that we show our love for God by obedience.

2 *Are there any commands of God which you are finding hard to obey at present? Pray that God will help you to express your love for him by obedience.*
3 *God gave the Israelites the ceremony of the Passover to enable them to remember forever his goodness to them at the Exodus. Why might they need a reminder? How easy do you find it to remember how good God has been to you? Make a note of all that God has done for you this week.*

Jesus himself took part in a meal which certainly bore a strong resemblance to the Passover meal. He then bequeathed it to his church as a reminder of his death until his return. Read 1 Corinthians 11:17-34, and Luke 22:7-23, especially verses 7, 8, 11, 15.

4 *How important is that meal in your life as a reminder of God's goodness?*

---

5. Backs to the sea?
Exodus 13:17 – 15:18

This is an action-packed story. Read Exodus 13:17 – 14:31, and as you do, try to picture the scene.

1 *How would you have felt if you were an Israelite?*

Note: The crossing probably took place north of the present day Gulf of Suez. These waters are still affected today by the strong east wind, similar to the wind of Exodus 14:21. The miracle lay in the timing of the wind.

2 *What can we see here of Moses as (a) a leader and (b) a servant of God? What had he learned since his first encounter with God by the burning bush? How far do you expect your experiences with God, and your work for him, to leave their mark on you?*
3 *God's ability to rescue Israel stirred Moses to lead the people in a song of praise. As you read Exodus 15:1-18, written using much poetic language, note down some of the things he says about God.*
4 *Is it important to you that there is no-one like the Lord (verse 11)?*

Praise God that he was, and is, a God who rescues his people from all danger.

Weekend

1 *The Exodus always played an important part in the history of Israel, and biblical writers took up the theme again and again. For example, prophets reminded the people of God's greatness and faithfulness. The Psalm writers used* *the Exodus to evoke praise and gratitude. Read through Psalms 77:10-20; 78:1-16; 106:6-13 and 114 to see how they viewed the Exodus.*

Then read Hosea 12:9; 13:4.

2 *List some events in your life that remind you that God is a rescuer.*

Part Eleven/Week Two
The second coming (A topic study)

'The nuclear age' — a time when all the news seems full of gloom, and doom, and uncertainty about who might accidentally push a button and end the world. But knowing that God is in control of history, and that Christ will come again, fills the believer with joy, confidence and hope — not despair!

1. The king is coming
1 Corinthians 15:12-28, 35-49, 50-58

The Greek term most often used in the New Testament for the second coming of Christ is *parousia*. This means 'arrival', 'coming' or 'presence', and was often used in other Greek literature to describe the arrival of a king or visiting dignitary.

Just as a king's coming is announced and eagerly expected beforehand, so we are not surprised that the Bible is full of references to Christ's second coming, as King of kings. In fact there are over 250 references in the New Testament alone! But we shall look at only a few!

1 *Read 1 Corinthians 15:12-28. The word* parousia *appears in verse 23. What changes will Christ bring about at his second coming?*

Note: The NIV translates this as a verb, 'when he comes', in verse 23.

1 *Read 1 Corinthians 15:35-49. Paul is answering questions (verse 35) which some Corinthians may have raised about what their future resurrection bodies would be like. Make a list of the differences Paul shows between our earthly bodies (now) and resurrection bodies (then).*

Read: 1 Corinthians 15:50-57. These are glorious, hopeful verses for the Christian. Read them out loud and take a few minutes to use them as a basis for thanking God that you too, one day, will 'be changed'.

2. Why come a second time?
Matthew 16:26-27; Romans 2:5-11

History has sometimes been

described as 'His (God's) story'. Christ, by his life, death and resurrection, has undoubtedly affected human history more than any other person. And the climax of all history will be when he comes the second time. It is then that the great divide will be fully made between those who belong to Christ and those who do not.

Throughout this study make a note of the various points made in each passage.

1 *Jesus will come as Judge. Read Matthew 16:26-27; Romans 2:5-11. From these passages, on what basis will God judge? How will he decide who to welcome and who to turn away? How will anyone escape such judgment? – Look at Acts 2:17-21.*

2 *Those already dead will be resurrected. Turn to John 5:28-29. But what happens in the meantime to those Christians who die before Jesus comes again? See 2 Corinthians 5:6-10; Philippians 1:23. Notice that the Bible does not teach an 'in-between' time of purgatory or limbo.*

God's judgment is a sobering thought. Turn some of these Scriptures into prayer:

■ Confess anything in your life worthy of God's judgment.
■ Praise God that his justice goes hand in hand with his love.
■ Thank him for sparing you because of what Jesus has done.
■ Pray for a friend who is not yet a Christian, that he or she may believe and experience God's mercy.

3. The Christian hope
Matthew 24:30-31; Revelation 6:9-17

God has promised us that Jesus will return again. Not only will he come as Judge and wind up history as we know it, but there are several other reasons for his coming:

1 *To gather the Church and deliver his people. What can you glean of this from Matthew 24:30-31; Revelation 6:9-17; 1 Thessalonians 4:16-17?*
2 *To complete God's purposes for the Christian. We shall be like Christ and be with him for ever! What insights of this can you gain from John's glimpse into heaven in Revelation 20:1-6, 11; 21:1-8?*
3 *Read Romans 8:18-25. What difference will Christ's second coming make to the whole of creation and to you as a Christian?*

Write out Romans 8:18 on a slip of paper. Take it with you today, read it often and learn it by heart.

4. Signs of the times
Matthew 25:1-30; Mark 13:32-37

The Bible does not tell us exactly when Christ is coming again. In fact, trying to predict a date when the world as we know it will end can lead into serious error.

1 *One of the things marking out cults or sects from Christian truth is their over-emphasis on one point of belief at the expense of others. This is true, for example, of some, where their preoccupation with detailed* predictions of future events (including several wrongly predicted dates for the end of the world!) has distorted what the Bible is really saying. Try to work out how you would use this study to answer such predictions.

2 Read Matthew 25:1-13, 14-30; Mark 13:32-17.

In these three passages Jesus used concrete illustations to show what things will be like when he comes again. Notice that each one is not concerned to give a detailed timetable of events, but a challenge to live in the light of his coming.

3 How far does Jesus emphasize this challenge?

4 For each of these illustrations or parables write down a title which expresses in your own words the main challenge for you to put into practice.

5 What do you learn from each story about the timing of Jesus' coming?

Pray about your response to the challenge in today's readings.

---

5. The last days
2 Peter 3:3-13; 2 Timothy 3:1-5

1 We are certainly nearly 2000 years nearer to the return of Christ than was the early church. But how should that affect the way that we live now?

2 As you read 2 Timothy 3:1-5, assess how far these are true of our times today. Are any of these things true of your life? If so, take some minutes to come to God in repentance and ask his forgiveness.

3 2 Peter 3:3-13. What are the main points which Peter describes here about the last times and Christ's second coming?

Note: The early disciples believed they were living in the 'last days'. In fact, this refers to the whole period between the ascension of Christ and the *parousia* (his literal return, or second coming).

4 Taking up Peter's question in verse 11, what sort of a person ought you to be in response to this teaching? Is there anything you would change in your life if you knew Christ was coming tomorrow?

Weekend

1 The 'Day of the Lord' is an important theme in the Old Testament, referring to a future day of God's judgment. You may like to do your own word study on these verses. What do they tell you about the character of God? Isaiah 10:3; Joel 2:30-31; Malachi 3:2; Matthew 7:22; 1 Corinthians 3:13; Hebrews 10:25; Revelation 6:17.

2 There are two other New Testament terms used of the second coming of Jesus. Apokalypsis — which means 'uncovering', 'laying bare' or 'revealing'. Look at 1 Corinthians 1:7; 2 Thessalonians 1:7; 1 Peter 1:7, 13. What do you learn from these verses concerning what will be 'revealed' about mankind and about Christ at his coming?

Traditionally 'Epiphany' is the time in the church calendar celebrating the showing of the baby Jesus to the Magi or wise men. The Greek word, epiphaneia, means 'manifestation' or 'appearing'. It also has the idea of opening a curtain in order to see what is there hidden behind it. Look at 2 Thessalonians 2:8; 1 Timothy 6:14; 2 Timothy 4:1, 8; Titus 2:13. What can you gather from these verses will be made clear, or manifest, when Jesus appears again?

3 Further reading: Stephen Travis, The Jesus Hope (IVP); Michael Wilcock, The Message of Revelation (IVP).

Part Eleven/Week Three
Paul's letter to the Thessalonians, 1 (A detailed study)

Young Christians usually need a fair amount of teaching and encouragement to grow in their faith. But due to circumstances beyond his control Paul was unable to spend very long with this infant church. (You can read the account of its beginnings in Acts 17:1-10.) Imagine his feelings when trouble forced him to depart, leaving the church to face continuing opposition! These letters, written quite soon after he had left Thessalonica, show us something of the relationship between Paul and the church – they are letters of encouragement to young Christians, and advice on living the Christian life.

1. Thank God!
1 Thessalonians 1:1-10

Paul starts his letter by recounting the reasons he has to be thankful for the church in Thessalonica.

Note: *Verse 7.* Thessalonica was the chief city of Macedonia, the northern part of modern Greece, and Achaia was the southern part.

1 *What does he say about their initial response to the gospel? Try and put it in modern terms – what might it mean for your non-Christian friends to respond to God in a similar way?*

How ought you to be praying for your non-Christian friends? What specific problems would they face in becoming Christians? Stop and pray for them now.

2 *What can you find out from this passage about the quality of the lives of the Thessalonian Christians?*
3 *How does your life match up to theirs? How far is it marked by the sort of commitment to God and his work suggested by Paul's description in verse 3?*

2. Paul at work, 1
1 Thessalonians 2:1-16

Paul's ministry was not always easy. Here he talks about suffering in Philippi, and opposition in Thessalonica. It looks as though people had accused him of preaching for personal gain, as some preachers of other sects had done.

1 *What pieces of evidence does Paul give here for his sincere motives?*
2 *Why did he preach the gospel?*
3 *What is your attitude to telling others about Jesus? Do you hold back out of fear? If so, can you find anything to help you here? Or do you tell your friends, but for the wrong reasons? Perhaps it gives you 'status' in the eyes of your Christian friends, or a feeling of superiority over non-Christian friends – or perhaps your motives are mixed, some good and some bad.*

Pray that God will help you see things from his perspective.

4 *Verses 13-16 talk about the persecution the Thessalonian Christians suffered as a result of their faith. How do you think what Paul says here would encourage them to stand firm?*

3. Paul at work, 2
1 Thessalonians 2:17–3:13

It seems likely that Paul's enemies were also trying to cause trouble by accusing him of neglecting the church in Thessalonica.

1 *How would you have defended Paul? Think both about the practical steps Paul took, and about his attitude to the Thessalonian Christians.*
2 *What picture of the Thessalonian church do you get from these verses? Make a list of their strong and weak points. (If you have time, look back through the previous two*

studies to see what else you've learned about this church.)

Think about Paul's prayer in verses 12-13. What might it mean for your church if this prayer were answered? What would you expect to change? How would it affect you personally? Pray for your church along these lines.

4. Practical Christianity
1 Thessalonians 4:1-12

1 *Make a list of all the reasons you can find in the passage for holy living.*
2 *Now think of particular temptations you find difficult to cope with. Is there anything in your list which will help? If you need encouragement, turn to God's promise in Hebrews 2:18 and ask him to fulfil it in your life.*

The issues Paul raises here were probably the most significant problems for the church in Thessalonica – sexual immorality was an accepted way of life for the Greeks, and they despised manual work.

3 *To what extent are these significant problems for us? How might Paul's comments apply to today's permissiveness?*
4 *Can you think of any other temptations which are major hindrances to Christians wanting to live to please God today? Are these among the temptations you identified as difficult to cope with? If not, to what extent do they apply to you?*

5. The Lord's return

1 Thessalonians 4:13 – 5:11

It seems that the Thessalonian church had taken Paul's teaching on the Lord's return very much to heart, but were confused when some of them died before it happened, and thought they might have missed out on salvation.

1 When a Christian has died what encouragements can you find here for relatives and friends?
2 What reasons does Paul give for that encouragement?
3 What practical affect should the Lord's return have on Christians living in this world?
4 Do you let the expectation of the Lord's return affect your life? What differences does it make to the way you live? Is there anything you would do differently if you thought it would happen today?

An ancient prayer: O Lord our God, make us watchful and keep us faithful as we await the coming of your Son our Lord; that when he shall appear he may find us not sleeping in sin but active in his service and joyful in his praise, for the glory of your holy name. Amen.
Adapted from Gelasian Collect from Frank Colquhoun, *Contemporary Parish Prayers* (Hodder & Stoughton) and David

Silk, *Prayers for use at the Alternative Services* (Mowbray).

Weekend

1 *Spend some time looking back over what you have learnt from the church at Thessalonica so far – it would be useful to read the letter again, and see if anything strikes you that you missed first time through.*

While it is true that many of the important Pauline doctrines are absent, it is also true that the letter reveals to us something of Paul's pastoral zeal and his intense interest in the spiritual well-being of his converts. Here we catch a glimpse of Paul the man in a way we do not always do when he is taken up with questions of more profound theological significance.

Leon Morris, 1 & 2 Thessalonians, Tyndale New Testament Commentary (Eerdmans).

2 *If you have time, read through 2 Thessalonians, in preparation for next week's studies.*
3 *If you haven't already done so, you might find it interesting to read the account of how the church in Thessalonica was started, in Acts 17:1-10.*

Part Eleven/Week Four
Paul's letter to the Thessalonians, 2
(A detailed study)

We should communicate our knowledge and experiences one to another. We should join in prayer and praise one with another. We should set a good example one before another. And it is the duty of those especially who live in the same vicinity and family thus to comfort and edify one another; and this is the best neighbourhood, the best means to answer the end of society. Such as are nearly related together and have affection for one another, as they have the greatest opportunity, so they are under the greatest obligation, to do this kindness one to another. This the Thessalonians did ... and this is what they are exhorted to continue and increase in doing.

Matthew Henry (1662-1714), *Commentary on the Whole Bible* (World Bible Publishers, Inc., 1986).

1. More on practical Christianity
1 Thessalonians 5:12-28

This looks like a collection of odds and ends of instructions – but there's a lot here!

1 *Go through the passage and make a list of any of Paul's instructions which seem particularly relevant – either to you personally, or to your church.*

Pray about each of the things on your list. Ask God to show you where he wants you particularly to take action.

2 *It's easy to feel discouraged when you read a passage like this! Meditate on verses 23-24 – how should they affect your attitude to any changes God wants you to make in your life?*

2. Thank God – always!
2 Thessalonians 1:1-12

This letter was probably written shortly after the first, and picks up many of the same issues.

1 *What can you find out from here about the Thessalonians' reaction to suffering? How was it affecting their Christian lives?*

328

2 *What features of the Lord's return does Paul draw attention to here?*
3 *What effects do you think these features would have on the readers?*
4 *What is Paul praying for the Thessalonians in verses 11-22? Try to write each petition in different words.*

Pray for Christians who are suffering for their faith. Try to find specific things from the passage to use in your prayer for them.

For examples of Christians suffering in other countries, you could read *By Their Blood: Christian Martyrs of the Twentieth Century* (Baker Book House).

---

3. More about the Lord's return
2 Thessalonians 2:1-12

In this passage Paul reminds the Thessalonians of what he had already told them (verse 5) and adds to that. Unfortunately we don't have his original teaching, and in consequence this passage is not always easy to understand.

'The man of lawlessness' or 'Wicked One' (GNB) is a mysterious figure who must appear before the end. He is also known as the antichrist in John's letters. It is not clear whether he is human or a supernatural figure, but he is the agent of Satan (verse 9) and the ultimate embodiment of evil. Lawlessness is already at work in the world (verse 7 – see also 1 John 2:18) but is held back by a restraining power. Again the identity of this restraint is difficult, but the most likely explanation is that it is the

principle of law and government, embodied for Paul in the Roman Empire.

1 *What are the characteristics of evil – in both Satan and his agents – found in this passage?*
2 *What attitudes do you think Paul expects the Thessalonians to have towards evil?*
3 *The effects of lawlessness and evil in the world are only too obvious in every news bulletin. How do you think Christians should react? How should this passage affect your prayer for world events?*

---

4. God at work
2 Thessalonians 2:13 – 3:5

Paul turns from considering the fate of those who reject God to the future of the Thessalonian Christians.

1 *What future does he expect for them?*
2 *What is God's part in their conversion and continuing Christian life?*
3 *What have the Thessalonians done, and what does Paul expect them to do in the future?*
4 *In what areas has God acted? What are the areas in which the Thessalonians are expected to act? How would you respond to a Christian who said that he or she didn't need to bother reading the Bible, or to make a real effort, as God was bringing them to maturity anyway?*

In 3:1 Paul asks his readers to pray for him as he preaches the gospel. Pray for anyone you know of engaged in missionary work elsewhere. How much do you know about God's work in other places? You could find out more by reading a missionary society's literature, perhaps by taking their magazine regularly, or by reading some biographies *e.g.* Jim Elliot, *Shadows of the Almighty* (Harper & Row) or Helen Morgan, *What Price Glory?* (Christian Literature Crusade, Inc.) or Sally Magnusson, *The Flying Scotsman: Biography of Eric Liddell* (Charles River Books).

5. Practical Christianity — again!
2 Thessalonians 3:6-18

1 *What principles does Paul teach here about work?*
2 *How would you apply them to someone currently facing unemployment?*

3 *Consider verse 16. The outward circumstances of the church at Thessalonica were anything but peaceful! What might peace have meant to them? What troubled circumstances do you face at the moment? How might the Lord's peace affect you?*
4 *In this passage we learn more of how Paul preached in Thessalonica. From here, and from what you learnt in the first letter (especially studies 2 and 3) what picture do you get of Paul's ministry?*

Weekend

Go through both letters and look out for all the teaching on the Lord's return – both what Paul taught would happen and also the effects it should have on the lives of believers. How does it add to what you learned from the study on the second coming.

Part Eleven/Week Five
Guidance (A topic study)

Guidance is never a simple matter for a Christian, because it cannot be reduced to a formula applicable to all individuals or circumstances. The heart of guidance is a personal relationship. It lies in knowing God, loving him and speaking with him yourself.

This week's studies concentrate on how we can know God better, his goals for us and the attitude we should have towards him. We are probably all good at asking God for guidance but it is also a question of trusting and listening. A number of

books are referred to during this week. You could check at the outset to see if you have access to any of them.

---

1. God's goals
Romans 8:28-39

God has an overall plan for our lives. God's concern is not simply a matter of telling us to do A or B (as we often wish it was) but of changing and maturing us. Let's look at some of the things God wants to do for us.

1 *List what God has already done for us in Christ. What are God's goals for us now and in the future?*
2 *Can anything prevent God's will taking effect?*
3 *Try to put verse 29 in your own words and then meditate on its truth during the day. You could memorize the previous verse.*

Thank God that Christ's sacrifice is complete and will bring us so many good things. Praise God that *nothing* can separate us from the love of Christ.

Read the chapter entitled 'Fear of the Future' in D. Martyn Lloyd-Jones, *Spiritual Depression* (Eerdmans).

2. The God who guides
Psalm 25

God is intimately concerned with the whole of our lives because Christ lives in us. This is the basis of our confidence that we can hand over control of our lives to him. Supremely, God is a person who wants our fellowship, trust and love. Guidance is almost a by-product of that relationship. Today's Psalm, or song, reads like a prayer for guidance. Read it meditatively several times before you tackle the questions.

1 *What sort of person receives God's guidance? Make a list of those things God requires from us* before *he guides.*

Note: *Verse 12.* 'Fear' in this context suggests awe and reverence.

2 *The word 'guidance' does not occur in the song as such, although it is entirely concerned with being directed by God. (In the* NIV *'guide' comes in verses 5 and 9.) Make a list of those various expressions used to describe guidance.*

Use verses 4 and 5 as the basis of your own prayer.

3. Knowing God
Psalm 19

It may be surprising to know that as you ask God for help in making a decision he is as much interested in the manner in which you make your choice as the choice itself. He wants us to be people who are learning to know him and his mind. We need to know how to share his outlook and values.

1 *Jot down the two ways in which God has revealed himself.*
2 *From verses 1-6 make a list of what you can learn about God's character from the world around you.*
3 *From the rest of the song make a list of what reading the written Word of God will do for you. Notice how much more you can learn about God from his specific revelation, the Bible.*

Note: Theologians speak of God's 'general' and 'special' revelation to show the difference between this revelation of himself in the universe, and in the written form of the Bible.

4 *Note down all the different words used to describe God's written revelation. Then make a second list of the words used to describe their* value. *Is this your experience of Bible study? If not, ask God to speak to you through his Word.*

Pray that God will mould you through Bible study to share his outlook and mind.

4. A loving Father
Psalm 139

As we learn to accept that God is able to direct us, so we must learn to accept that he is also best equipped to give us that direction. He leads us out of love, knowing what we need, even if we don't know ourselves.

1 *From your reading of the song make a brief list of some of the different things God knows about you.*
2 *Which aspects of God's character highlighted in this song do you need to remember when seeking guidance?*
3 *Why did the song writer pray the words of verses 23-24? Do you ever experience this feeling? God can still guide even when you are confused and unclear about your own feelings.*

Pray that you will learn to accept God's direction, even if it conflicts with your own ideas.

Read the chapter entitled 'Thou our guide' from J. I. Packer, *Knowing God* (IVP).
   More generally Paul Little's *Affirming the Will of God* (IVP) has been widely helpful.

5. God's voice
John 10:1-10, 25-30

How can I know that it is God speaking to me? It is easy to confuse the voice of your own emotions with what God is saying. That's where Bible study is so useful. You can test your feelings against the constant, impartial, revealed Word of God. Scripture reassures us that we can learn to distinguish God's voice from others.

1 *Can you find reasons in the passage why Jesus describes himself as the* door *(RSV) or* gate *(NIV)?*
2 *Starting with these verses, and adding to them from other passages you have studied this week, write out some reasons why the* sheep *will recognize the* shepherd's *voice.*
3 *Jot down a list of privileges enjoyed by the sheep. Pray that God will help you to trust and listen to him, as well as ask things of him.*

Weekend

1 *Anyone who sincerely tries to be guided by God will from time to time experience problems. Arm yourself for this by reading the chapter called 'Guidance' in John White's* The Fight *(IVP).*

2 *Look up the words relating to guidance in a Bible concordance, for instance 'lead', 'guide', 'instruct', 'direct'. You could copy some of these verses on to cards. Then in times of doubt or anxiety you could refer to them to remind you of God's care for you.*
3 *'Words of prophecy' are increasingly common in church life today, and are used for guidance by*

many. How do this week's Bible passages suggest that such prophecies are different in authority from the written Word of God? For more on the question of prophecy today you could read chapter 14, 'Prophecy and tongues', in David Prior's The Message of 1 Corinthians (IVP).

Part Eleven/Week Six
The book of Proverbs (A whole book study)

Wisdom literature, a type of writing found in the Bible, was common throughout Old Testament times. Either it consisted of instruction for a successful life (as in Proverbs) or else considered the perplexities of human existence. Ecclesiastes and the book of Job belong to the latter type.

It is generally agreed that Solomon did not write the whole book of Proverbs. Rather, there were a number of writers, whose collections of what are often just common-sense sayings go to make up the book as we have it. They used a number of poetic devices to aid memorization e.g. riddles, parables or comparisons. Much of this however is sadly lost in the process of translation from the Hebrew.

1. Acquiring wisdom
Proverbs 1:1-7; 3:5-6

To start you thinking about proverbs in general make a list of some modern-day ones. How would you describe these proverbs? Upon what are they founded? Does God have any place in them? Then turn to Proverbs 1:1-7.

1 *What reasons for studying Proverbs are stated here? Yet what should be the starting point, undergirding the pursuit of all knowledge and indeed life itself?*

Note: You may sometimes think that Proverbs is nothing more than good worldly wisdom. But time and again you will encounter God's perspective on life slipping in.

2 *As you read Proverbs 3:5-6, which are well-known verses, try to put them in your own words. In what ways have you relied on your own understanding? What caused that self-reliance? How would God's perspective have altered the situation?*

Through the day try to memorize Proverbs 3:5-6, remembering that wisdom is not something gained overnight. Pray that you may always consciously acknowledge God and his will in every decision and situation.

Wisdom as a person

In the Old Testament, wisdom was, for the most part, seen as a characteristic of God, like his justice or mercy. The Hebrew mind however tended to avoid abstract ideas, and to think of wisdom poetically as a person. This personification may be seen beautifully in Proverbs 1:20-33; 8:22-31 (even to the point of having a part in creation). But wisdom probably was not seen as a literal person, *i.e.* the Son of God rather than simply an attribute of God, until after Old Testament times.

2. The fool

Verses from Proverbs chapters 14,15,18,20,21,23.

Sometimes in Proverbs the fool, who makes frequent appearances throughout the book, is described as simple – that is, one who is not stupid but who prefers to reject disciplines and wisdom and to go his own way. At other times the fool is referred to as one who is dull and obstinate (without referring to his intellectual ability).

1 *To build up a picture of what the writers thought of foolishness you could look up in a concordance the references in Proverbs to 'fool' and 'simple'. However, to get you started, look up the following verses: 14:3,8,15; 15:2,5; 18:2,6; 20:3; 21:20; 23:9.*

2 *Note down on one side of the page what is said about the fool and on the other, the contrast of the wise.*

3 *Does your behaviour always match up to that of the wise?*

Take time to consider your own life in the light of what you have written down.

3. Idleness

Proverbs 6:6-11; 19:24; 21:25-26; 24:30-34

The way of the sluggard is another common theme in this book. As in the previous study, note down the point made about him in each of the verses given below. Then consider your own attitudes in the light of these verses!

1 *6:6-11 – How long does it take you to offer to help out in your church, to help your friends or family? With what result?*
2 *19:24 – How often can you just not be bothered to complete a job you have started?*
3 *21:25-26 – What place does wishful thinking have in your life? With what result?*
4 *24:30-34 – Are there things you need to put right now before it is too late? The sluggard will always put off things till another day!*

4. Friendship

Verses from Proverbs chapters 14,16,17,18,19,25

The commonest word used for friend has a wide range of meanings. The context should help to clarify the meaning.

1 *Jot down a summary of 14:20; 19:4-5,7. Then contrast this type of friendship with that spoken of in 17:17 and 18:24. How guilty are you of befriending or paying attention to* the seemingly important or influential people in your church or social group?

2 *Take time to reflect on the friendships you have. What motivates that friendship?*

3 *Relationships are frequently vulnerable and they need to be protected and cultivated. Look at 17:9,17 to see one way in which a friendship can be developed.*

4 *According to 16:28; 17:9 and 25:17 what can so easily destroy friendship?*

Perhaps you have recently been hurt by the damaging of a friendship. Jesus at least understands what it means to be betrayed by a friend (Luke 22:1-6, 47-53). Or perhaps you have been the cause of damaging a friendship. Ask God for his forgiveness (if you are truly sorry) and see if you can bring some reconciliation.

---

5. Wives
Proverbs 31:10-31

There are some amusing but alarmingly apt comments about wives in Proverbs e.g. 27:15-16! But one of the best known parts in the whole book is 31:10-31.

1 *As you read these verses, note down each characteristic of this resourceful woman, trying to use twentieth century language and images.*

2 *Not every woman is involved in trade or buying property, yet this view of womanhood suggests a* wholeness which many in society today are searching after. How could you use the Bible's view of this woman to help those disillusioned by the lot of women?

3 *What do you notice about her relationships with God, her husband and children? What about their approach to her? Could that be the reason for her 'wholeness'?*

4 *If you are a woman, whether or not you are married, how can the example of this woman encourage you in your daily life? If you are a man, how far do your expectations of your wife or women in general tie in with this woman's character? If married, can you help your wife to gain greater fulfilment in her daily life?*

Weekend

1 *There are so many other themes which we could have explored in this study of Proverbs. Over this weekend you could look up the words 'tongue', 'lips' and 'speech' in a concordance to see what wisdom the book has to bear on this sensitive matter!*

2 *Some Christians have made a habit of reading a chapter of this book a day, covering it every month. What about it?*

3 *If you wanted to look into the book in greater detail, Derek Kidner's commentary on* Proverbs, Tyndale Old Testament Commentary *(IVP), would be an invaluable addition to your bookshelf. Linking Proverbs to the other rich wisdom literature of the Bible is his* The Wisdom of Proverbs, Job & Ecclesiastes *(IVP).*

Part Eleven/Week Seven
Timothy (A character study)

Timothy's words go unrecorded in the Bible but he endears himself to those who meet him through the eyes of Luke and Paul in the book of Acts, and the letters. A gentle young man, he is timid in his approach to people, but faithful to his Lord and prepared to suffer the very real dangers of friendship and travel with Paul. He spent time in the jail at Rome because of his faithfulness.

1. A recipe for a 'mixed-up' kid?
Acts 14:8-18; 16:1-5

Timothy lived in Lystra, a Roman colony in a remote mountainous farming region of Galatia (in the south of modern Turkey). Jews also lived there, some having intermarried with the leading families as a way of climbing the social ladder. He probably became a Christian during Paul's stay at the town on the first missionary journey (Acts 14).

1 *Timothy was surrounded by Jews, Romans and Greeks. As you read Acts 14:8-18, note down the differences in belief held by these peoples. How do we as Christians today respond to similar diverse religious views?*
2 *Timothy's Jewish mother had become a Christian but his father, a Greek, apparently retained the old religion as you will read in Acts*

16:1-5. *What kind of problems can such a situation bring about in family life?*
3 *Consider the importance of godly teaching and prayer on the part of parents and relations as illustrated by Timothy's experience – 2 Timothy 1:5 and 3:14-15 – especially bearing in mind your answers to questions 1 and 2. Are there children and parents for whom you could be praying regularly?*

2. The young Christian – too young?
1 Timothy 4:11-13; 2 Timothy 2:20-26

In Old Testament times superior wisdom and authority were considered to be the characteristics of the aged, although Job, a middle-aged man, was revered by old and young alike (Job 29:8). However, Proverbs 16:31 shows that age alone doesn't warrant respect.

1 *From Paul's advice to him in both these passages, what problems do you think Timothy was going to meet as a young man leading a church? Note down ways by which older Christians might have helped him.*
2 *'Youthful passions' (RSV) or 'evil desires of youth' (NIV) in 2 Timothy 2:22 might have included a craving for pleasures, power and*

possessions beyond the reasonable needs of a young man (or woman). How was Timothy told to overcome them? Again how might other believers have helped a Christian such as Timothy?

Pray for those you know who are young in years yet in a position of authority – the Christian Union committee members, youth leaders, young missionaries, house group leaders.

3. Too timid?

1 Corinthians 16:10-11;
1 Timothy 5:23; 2 Timothy 1:3-7

Timothy was not strong physically. He had been brought up in an isolated area, off the trade routes, and possibly had been protected by his mother and grandmother. This was no sophisticated tough guy itching to set out on an adventure.

1 *Corinth was a rough sea-port, international in its population, crude in its ways. What does Paul's First Letter to the Corinthians suggest Timothy's reaction to such a place might be? Note them down.*
2 *What does Paul's advice in 2 Timothy 1:3-7 suggest as the way to overcome the timidity that most Christians feel, if not always, at least in some situations?*
3 *From 2 Corinthians 12:7-10 how might Paul's view of physical hardship and weakness have encouraged one such as Timothy?*
4 *It is easy to dismiss those who always seem anxious or timid. What can you learn from Paul's approach to Timothy which will help to shape our attitude to such people?*

Why not accept 2 Timothy 2:1 as a personal challenge and ask the Lord to make you 'strong in the grace that is in Christ Jesus' (NIV)?

---

4. The faithful fellow worker

1 Corinthians 4:14-17;
Philippians 2:19-24;
2 Timothy 4:9-22

Timothy's name 'pops' up everywhere after he sets off with Paul and Silas. We find him in Asia Minor, Greece and Rome. And the jobs Paul sends him to do might appear most unsuitable! Some people reckoned without God's strength.

1 *As you read these verses in 1 Corinthians and Philippians, make a list of the qualities that Paul finds in Timothy. Are you now better able to understand the truth of 2 Corinthians 12:9a?*
2 *Why was Paul confident in sending Timothy to Corinth and Philippi? From what you have read so far, why might he be able to sort out the problems of doctrine and behaviour occurring in the churches?*
3 *Much is written and talked about the 'generation gap'. Paul and Timothy were years apart in age yet Paul longed for his company (2 Timothy 4:9-22). What do you think made them such great companions?*

Examine your attitude to those older than yourself. In the light of what you have learned, does it need changing? Pray for an open and teachable mind on this matter, a matter which can divide churches, and cause individuals great pain. If you are older than most in your church, do your attitudes to the young need to reflect more of Paul's concern for this young man?

5. The faithful pastor
1 Timothy 1:3-7,18-20; 4; 2 Timothy 1:3-14; 4:1-5

During Paul's third missionary journey, he and Timothy were in Ephesus. This was the great city dedicated to the worship of the goddess Diana. Timothy remained there as pastor after Paul left, despite his possible failure at Corinth.

1 *The passages indicate that God had given Timothy special gifts required for the task. List some of the problems that he was going to have to resolve, despite his youth.*

2 *What practical advice and encouragement did Paul give to his young friend?*

Note: Third missionary journey: AD 53/54-57/58

3 *From the earlier studies this week, what qualities have you seen in Timothy which would help him to become accepted by the church? Would you be willing to listen to and respect such a servant of God? Why?*

Pray for your church leaders. The ones you rate poorly are the very ones who *need your* prayers! And practical help won't come amiss!!

Weekend

1 *Put together a short biography on the life and times of Timothy. Useful references are: Acts 16-28; Romans 16:21; 1 and 2 Corinthians; Philippians; Colossians 1:1; 1 and 2*

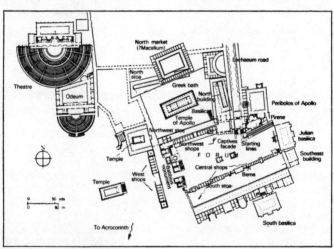

Timothy's Corinth – from The Illustrated Bible Dictionary, *Part 1 (Tyndale, 1980) p. 314.*

338

Thessalonians; Philemon 1:1; Hebrews 13:23. Find a Bible atlas such as the excellent New Bible Atlas (Tyndale) and a dictionary to trace his travels, provide a time-scale and produce a background.

2 Don't be surprised if the Holy Spirit teaches you a thing or two!!

Part Eleven/Week Eight
Matthew 5 (A meditation)

Jesus' words in Matthew 5 must have shocked his Jewish hearers deeply. They expected certain things from the Messiah and Jesus seemed to be completely undermining their precious hopes.

As you read the chapter, try to imagine how those early disciples might have felt. Then as you start to understand and apply this radical teaching to your own life, be prepared for a few shocks yourself!

Note: Two essential ingredients are required for a meditative study. One is an openness to let the Holy Spirit of God be your teacher. The other is a willingness to take time to think and pray over what you are reading.

---

1. Upside-down kingdom
Matthew 5:3-12

1 Start by reading the whole chapter then concentrate on verses 3-12. The kingdom of heaven that Jesus describes here, would be quite different from the one the disciples expected him to rule.

2 Reflect on verses 3-12, known as the Beatitudes. Don't settle for your initial reaction to the words — think on. What does 'blessed' or 'happy' mean here? Is it linked with having God's approval? What does it mean to be poor in spirit, to mourn? What are the areas of your life which you mourn over or see a need for God to work in, areas where you need to hunger and thirst for his work?

Ask the Lord to show you if you've adopted any attitudes or opinions of the sinful world around you.

> The ways of the God of Scripture appear topsy-turvy to men. For God exalts the humble and abases the proud, calls the first last and the last first, ascribes greatness to the servant, sends the rich away empty handed and declares the meek to be his heirs. The culture of the world and the counter-culture of Christ are at loggerheads with each other. In brief, Jesus congratulates those whom the world most pities, and calls the world's rejects 'blessed'.
>
> John Stott, *The Message of the Sermon on the Mount* (IVP).

2. Purity
Matthew 5

All the Beatitudes are radical, but 'Blessed [or 'happy'] are the pure in heart, for they shall see God' is perhaps the most demanding.

1 *Look up Psalm 24:3-4 and Habakkuk 1:13. Think about what 'seeing God' involves. How far are we seeking to be pure in our thought life?*
2 *Look through the rest of the chapter and see how Jesus teaches that purity of mind and heart affects behaviour e.g. where does purity come into Jesus' teaching about salt (verse 13) and about what you say (verses 33-37) and so on?*
3 *How does this help us if we think we may be getting involved in slightly underhand actions or dubious conversations?*

Pray for any of your friends who are finding difficulty with the high standards of behaviour that Jesus expects. Pray for purity of heart for yourself.

> *The glory of the gospel is that when the Church is absolutely different from the world, she invariably attracts it. It is then that the world is made to listen to her message, though it may hate it at first.*
>
> Dr. D. Martyn Lloyd-Jones,
> *Studies in the Sermon on the Mount* (Eerdmans).

3. Relationships
Matthew 5

'Love your neighbour as yourself,' commanded Jesus (Matthew 19:19, NIV). This chapter helps us to see to what limits he took those words.

1 *Jesus said, 'Blessed [happy] are the peacemakers, for they shall be called sons of God' (verse 9). Think through what this may involve in the light of the example of Christ, the Son of God, in Colossians 1:19-20, although his supreme act of peacemaking needs never to be repeated.*

> *The peacemaker has only one concern, and it is the glory of God amongst men. That was the Lord Jesus Christ's only concern. His one interest in life was not himself, but the glory of God. And the peacemaker is the man whose central concern is the glory of God, and who spends his life in trying to minister to that glory. He knows that God made man perfect, and that the world was meant to be Paradise, so when he sees individual and international disputes and quarrelling, he sees something that is detracting from the glory of God. This is the thing that concerns him, nothing else.*
>
> D. Martyn Lloyd-Jones,
> *Studies in the Sermon on the Mount* (Eerdmans).

2 *Look through Matthew 5, concentrating on verses 21-37, and see how Jesus revolutionized already accepted values. In each case, what is he saying about our response to our neighbour?*
3 *With the pressures of society in mind, what practical steps can you*

340

take to ensure that all your relationships are distinctively Christian?

Pray for Christian families you know today, one area where broken relationships are all too frequent.
Peace in our time? by David Atkinson (Eerdmans) explores the biblical framework of peacemaking in our violent modern world, dominated by a nuclear arms race.

4. More on relationships
Matthew 5

For Jesus, loving your neighbour included loving your enemies.

1 *Read through verses 38-48 carefully.*
2 *Think of examples of how Jesus lived out these words, such as at his unjust trial.*
3 *Reflect on what 'loving your enemy' may involve for you.*
4 *'What are you doing more than others?' asks Jesus about our relationships (verse 47). Think about this.*

Persecution seems to be the expected lot of the New Testament Christians, not just to be faced with toleration, but rather to: 'rejoice in that day and leap for joy! (Luke 6:22-23, NIV). Jesus said, 'Happy are you when people ...persecute you...' (Matthew 5:11, GNB).

5 *Look at verses 11 and 12 and meditate on what Jesus meant.*

Write a prayer for those facing persecution. In some countries this may amount to rejection by family and friends, imprisonment, or even death.

5. Like Father – like son
Matthew 5

Jesus says, 'Be perfect, therefore, as your heavenly Father is perfect' (verse 48).

1 *Think about this as you memorize the verse.*

Note: Perfect = complete or whole.

2 *Look carefully at the two illustrations in verses 13-16. Think what it means to be living in the world as salt and light.*
3 *How would you answer someone who said the teaching in this chapter is totally unrealistic? Write a brief answer.*

Allow the Lord to show you where you are missing out on his lifestyle and pray that your light will indeed so shine that God will get the glory.

Weekend

1 *What do you think Jesus' teaching on adultery and divorce (verses 27-30) tell us about his attitude to marriage?*
2 *Look up what else the Bible has to say on divorce.*

Leviticus 21:7
Deuteronomy 24:1-4
Malachi 2:13-16
Matthew 5:31-32
Matthew 19:1-9
Mark 10:2-12
1 Corinthians 7:10-16

3 *Try to get hold of a commentary on the Sermon on the Mount and read the section on Matthew 5. Two classics are John Stott,* The Message *of the Sermon on the Mount (IVP) and Dr D. Martyn Lloyd-Jones,* Studies in the Sermon on the Mount *(Eerdmans).*

Part Eleven/Week Nine
The book of Daniel (A bird's-eye study)

Daniel was a man after God's own heart. He learned how to play a full and active part in a corrupt institution without wavering in his devotion and loyalty to his Lord God. At this crisis point in Jewish history, when the people were exiled from their homeland, God placed Daniel in a powerful position of influence in the heart of the Babylonian empire. Even there he was influenced by Jeremiah and what had gone on in

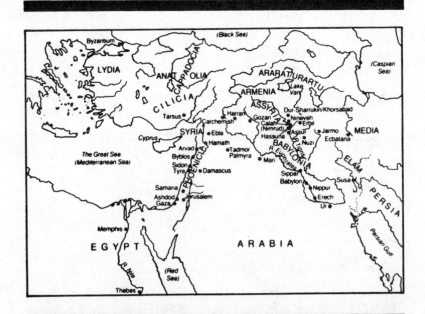

Jerusalem (see Daniel 9:2 and Jeremiah 29).

The book falls into two parts — history and prophecy. The first six chapters describe Daniel's life and the second six, his visions of what was to befall the Jewish people. But the most striking point about this book is the man himself. In the face of amazing pressures and threats he chooses to serve God every time.

To cover the book in the week we shall concentrate on the first six, more familiar chapters. Weekend reading looks at the last chapters. R. S. Wallace, *The Message of Daniel* (IVP) and Joyce Baldwin's *Daniel, Tyndale Old Testament Commentary* (IVP) are a great help in understanding the book as a whole.

1. Daniel the student
Daniel 1

Doubtless there would have been Babylonian youths who would have loved to study in the King's court; but for these Jewish boys it presented potential conflict with their worship of Yahweh. Even as a student Daniel displayed the unashamed resolve and commitment to God which become a hallmark of his adult life.

Note: *Verse 2.* Jehoiakim was probably king from *c.*608, see 2 Chronicles 36:5-8.

1 *Read Daniel 1. Why would Daniel and the others not eat Babylonian food? What could have been their motives for refusing? Leviticus 20:22-26 may help.*

Another reason might have been that to eat from the king's table was

simply an expression of dependence and allegiance.

2 *Describe their manner in dealing with the authorities.*
3 *Compare this story with John 17:11, 16. What qualities did Daniel display which enabled him to be 'in' the world, but not 'of' it?*

Pray that God will help you to copy Daniel's example of involvement with diplomacy but without compromise.

Read 'Being Salt and Light', in *Out of the Saltshaker* by R. Manley Pippert (IVP).

2. Daniel's bravery
Daniel 2

The threat of death hung over the four. Daniel reacted by trusting God entirely to deliver them. He did not attempt to find any short cuts by taking matters into his own hands.

1 *Note down carefully the steps Daniel took when confronted with the King's threats.*
2 *Examine the prayer of the four. Write down exactly what they asked for and how God answered them.*

Note: *Verse 39ff.* The four kingdoms – Babylonian, Medo-Persian, Greek and Roman.

3 *Daniel obeyed God and acted in faith with his life at risk. Note the effect this had on the King.*

When faced with a crisis, is your first reaction to turn to God? Pray that you will be like Daniel in this respect.

3. Whom will you worship?

Daniel 3–4

What appears to be repentance is sometimes only a short-lived remorse. As the years passed Nebuchadnezzar forgot about Daniel's God, and built his own! Other officials, jealous at the success of the Jews, were quick to inform the King that Daniel's colleagues, Shadrach, Meshach and Abednego, would not worship it.

1 *Consider the response to authority of Daniel and his three friends. In chapter 2 Daniel obeyed the King's command to interpret his dream, but in chapter 3 the king's command to worship idols was disobeyed by the three friends. Why was this so? What guidance does this give for when you should or should not obey secular authority?*

Again the King was forced to acknowledge the God of Israel, but in chapter 4 God took him through a far more humiliating experience.

2 *Compare the several 'repentances' the King made. How does this one differ from earlier attempts?*

Pray that God will identify sources of pride in your life and then deal with them in a way that will last. You could take Nebuchadnezzar's statement of praise in 4:34-37, to form a basis for your prayer.

4. Belshazzar

Daniel 5

23 years after Nebuchadnezzar's death, the next King needed Daniel's godly powers just as much.

1 *Try to work out what sort of man Belshazzar was. Write out the accusations Daniel made about him.*
2 *To what did Daniel ascribe Nebuchadnezzar's success?*
3 *In what ways did Belshazzar aggravate his sins against God?*
4 *Read Psalm 47 and make notes on how God is in control of the nations. Even the most ungodly of Kings will face divine rule.*

Use the Psalm that you have just read to praise God that he is the ultimate ruler of the nations. All forms of injustice in the world will be subject to his authority. Pray for any situations in the world where you are now aware that injustice appears to reign.

Note: *Verse 29.* Daniel was the third highest ruler in the kingdom as Belshazzar was son of King Nabonidus, ruling in his absence.

5. The lions' den

Daniel 6

Even Daniel's colleagues could find no fault in him. The only way they could attack him was to persecute him for his relationship with God. Daniel could have compromised by praying in secret but the zeal of a lifetime knew no such weakness.

1 *To have your enemies acknowledge your religion is a marvellous testimony. Make a list of those qualities which made Daniel a man of God.*
2 *The King's hands were tied by his decree, but God's were not. How did*

God demonstrate this fact? With what effect? As you consider this, what clues from Daniel's example can help you?

As in study 3, take the words of King Darius 6:26-27 and let them mould your praise to God today.

Weekend

The story of Daniel's life is an inspiration, and in the following six chapters his statements about the future were also a tonic which helped the Jews endure their years of exile. Despite the fact that they are hard to understand, they are an integral part of Scripture, helping us especially to understand Jesus' teaching about his second coming, the man of lawlessness and the book of Revelation (2 Thessalonians 2). Their themes are picked up again in the book of Revelation. This type of literature is known as apocalyptic.

1 Read Daniel 7 – 12 over the weekend with the help of a good Bible aid or commentary such as R. S. Wallace, The Message of Daniel (IVP). You would find it especially useful to read the article in the Illustrated Bible Dictionary (Tyndale) or the New Bible Dictionary (Tyndale) on the prophecies of Daniel, entry 'Daniel, Book of'.
2 Look up the entry on 'apocalyptic' in the New Bible Dictionary or the Illustrated Bible Dictionary.
3 Daniel's prayer recorded in chapter 9 is one of a number of key prayers recorded in the Bible. Think about it as a possible model for your own prayers. John White writes about it helpfully in Daring to Draw Near (IVP).

Part Twelve

The book of Ecclesiastes
Loneliness
The Gospel of Luke
The cross
John 15
Selections from Leviticus
Hosea and Gomer
Work

Part Twelve/Week One
The book of Ecclesiastes (A bird's-eye study)

'Wisdom literature', of which Ecclesiastes is an example, was a popular style in Old Testament times. The books of Proverbs and Job are other examples. For us it takes a bit of getting used to because it is not a familiar form. The style seems a little disconnected by our standards. Though 'Wisdom Literature' is ancient, the theme of Ecclesiastes is as poignant as it ever was. Mankind searches for meaning, but without God you are better off never having been born.

Many contemporary writers use this theme, such as Samuel Beckett in *Waiting for Godot*. Secular writers are not always sure what their lives lack, but they do know that something is missing. As you read Ecclesiastes, bear in mind that the majority of people we meet every day are in this position. Like the writer of Ecclesiastes they are discovering that everything under the sun is meaningless.

---

1. 'Meaningless! Meaningless!'
Ecclesiastes 1 and 2

'Ecclesiastes' — or Qoheleth — translates as 'the Preacher'. Some feel he may have been Solomon. Whoever he was the Preacher limits his scope to a description of life 'under the sun', that is, in the world

as man sees it without God. If this was the case, then we would have to agree that his findings are the only ones feasible. But the Christian knows that the apparent meaninglessness of the world contrasts sharply with the abundant life found in Christ, and the new interpretation of reality that he gives us.

1 *Write out concisely the author's main theme. To what extent do you agree with the Preacher's promises and conclusions?*
2 *Why is his enjoyment of pleasure hollow?*
3 *Note some of the reasons why the pursuit of wisdom fails to satisfy.*

Read John 10:10b and use it as the basis of your prayer of thanksgiving that we need not face life alone.

---

2. From dust to dust
Ecclesiastes 3:1 – 4:12

Man understands the passing of time, but if he cannot see it from the all-important spiritual point of view then it is bleak. Pleasures do not satisfy. Life is full of cruelty and unhappiness, and anything of promise is rendered meaningless by death. Such are the findings of the Preacher.

1 *Describe the Preacher's attitude*

towards (a) the natural world, (b) human history. Does he see any way to escape the endlessly repeated pattern of life?

2 *Following on from this, what view of life does he put forward?*

3 *List the four examples given of the futility of life. To what reflections do these give rise?*

4 *Loneliness is a terrible plight, but for those who have friends there is much consolation. Write down the ways in which the privilege of friendship helps us as Christians. See Matthew 18:19-20 and Hebrews 10:24-25. You might like to refer back to the study on friendship in the Proverbs series in Part 5.*

Pray that God will help you seek out someone who is lonely and befriend him or her.

3. In awe of God
Ecclesiastes 4:13 – 6:12

The unrelieved pessimism of the early chapters gives way from now on to advice and teaching. The Preacher believes that wisdom, even though it looks foolish in the eyes of the world, is the only way to live.

1 *Make notes on the advice given concerning worship. What is the right spirit in which it should be conducted? Why is it important to fulfil promises?*

2 *Are you known as a trustworthy person who keeps his or her word? (See Numbers 30:2; Proverbs 11:13; Daniel 6:4.)*

3 *'Money isn't everything'. Make a list of the reasons why the Preacher would agree with this saying.*

Consider your own attitude to

material wealth, praying that God will keep you from envy, always being prepared to help those in need. Ian Coffey's *Pennies for heaven* (Kingsway) is helpful on our responsibilities in handling money.

4. Death — the great leveller?
Ecclesiastes 7:1 – 9:12

The Preacher has found that the most satisfactory way to live is to know that your life comes from God. It is foolish to compare what you have with others as this will breed discontentment.

1 *Read chapter 7 and then write down the practical points of wisdom the Preacher gives. What is the guiding principle behind these tips?*

2 *Then turn to chapter 8:1 – 9:12. How should the fact that no one knows his or her future influence the way he or she lives? See also chapter 11:1-6 and James 4:13-17. What about you?*

The Preacher envisages no eternal life beyond death. But we know that death hasn't the same meaning for the righteous and the wicked. The injustices of this life will be dealt with.

3 *Read Luke 23:39-43 and 1 Corinthians 15:54-58 and use them to explain what deficiencies there are in the Preacher's Old Testament understanding.*

Why not commit 1 Corinthians 15:54-

58 to memory? You could write it down on a card or piece of paper and use odd moments today to learn these verses.

5. Fear God
Ecclesiastes 9:13 – 12:14

The Preacher has described life without God realistically. He has shown it for what it is, hollow and purposeless. In this final section he highlights the pivot on which man's life turns — his relationship to God.

1 *The Preacher expected too much from wisdom when he tried to base his reasons for living on the pursuit of it. Now he puts it in its right perspective. Make a list of the values of gaining wisdom.*
2 *Death and old age are gloomy prospects without Christ. Contrast the Preacher's view with that of a Christian's. See 2 Corinthians 4:16-18; 1 Peter 1:3-5.*
3 *Reading Ecclesiastes 12:9-14 consider the Preacher's conclusions. How then should we live in the light of these?*

> 'The end of the matter' (12:13-14) ... does bring into full view what has earlier been glimpsed only fitfully and, for the most part, in deep shadow. Now the fear of God emerges as not merely man's duty (that word has been supplied by the translators) but as his very raison d'être; and the judgment of God has, as it must have, the last word.
>
> Derek Kidner, *The Wisdom of Proverbs, Job & Ecclesiastes*
> (IVP)

Jesus lives! Praise God that he has provided us with so great a salvation.

Weekend

1 *An awareness of the meaningless of life, outside of Christ, is only realistic. Much of modern literature and art portrays a sense of meaninglessness. But for a Christian, pessimism is a state of mind that cannot be defended. Michael Green shows how this topic can be a stumbling block, preventing a response to the gospel, in chapter 3 of* You Must Be Joking *(Hodder).*
2 *How would you answer someone who said he couldn't believe in God because life is meaningless? Prepare your case.*
3 *In the face of all the evils mentioned in Ecclesiastes, the Christian still enjoys a life worth living. Why not investigate the richness of life more closely by undertaking a Bible study on the word 'joy', using a concordance?*

> Now his eyes were afresh opened to see that in his nature and thoughts lay large spaces wherein God ruled not supreme – desert places, where who could tell what might appear? For in such regions wild beasts range, evil herbs flourish, and demons go about. If in very deed he lived and moved and had his being in God, then assuredly there ought not to be one cranny in his nature, one realm of his consciousness, one well-spring of thought, where the will of God was a stranger. If all

was as it should be, then
surely there would be no
moment, looking back on
which he could not at least
say,

Yet like some sweet beguiling
melody,
So sweet, we know not we are

listening to it,
Thou, the meanwhile, wast
blending with my thought,
Yea, with my life and life's
own secret joy.

George MacDonald,
The Marquis of Lossie
(Kegan Paul)

Part Twelve/Week Two
Loneliness (An issue study)

To be lonely is not to be alone! You can be lonely in a football crowd, a packed underground station, a church, a family. An estimated four million people in Britain are lonely – both young and old. This is characteristic of modern society. The causes are many and the need for human contact desperate. The first step is to admit your feelings to someone – to God.

Whether you are lonely or not, remember you have been called to care for others. The lonely are much more able to understand the needs of those with similar feelings. And above all, the Lord Jesus, who experienced the ultimate in loneliness on the cross, understands and offers the solution through a variety of means.

Loneliness is the major problem of our day.

Malcolm Muggeridge

1. Where's all that brotherly love?
1 Peter 4:7-11; Matthew 25:31-40

Lonely Christians? Yes, many of them. Are you the only one in your family, or at work? Do you feel like compromising just to feel one of the group? Have you listened to everyone's problems but no one will listen to yours? Have you ever been surrounded by chattering people in church but you feel isolated? Are there any practical ways by which you can overcome your own loneliness and that of others?

1 *Read 1 Peter 4:7-11. What does Peter tell Christians to do to help others? Why should they? From the passage jot down practical ways in which we can be committed to the needs of others.*
2 *Read Matthew 25:31-40. Look out for the various areas of need that*

352

Jesus talks about meeting. 'Prayers may have feet' – how does the passage confirm this saying?

> You will not find ... the Christian by staring in his eyes as if he were your mistress: better fight beside him... pray with him.
>
> C. S. Lewis, *The Four Loves* (HBJ, 1963).

Ask the Lord that you might be able to 'fight beside' and pray with the lonely.

---

2. Down to earth with a bang!
1 Kings 18 and 19

Elijah experienced God's greatness in a fantastic way (1 Kings 18) and then the rot set in with loneliness and despondency. Have you ever experienced a greatly inspiring time followed by dullness, loneliness, even defeat? Elijah experienced the lot but God had the answer.

1 Read about Elijah's experience of God in 1 Kings 18. Then turn to chapter 19. Note down Elijah's thoughts, especially 19:3-5,10,14. How would you summarize the ways in which God dealt with him?
2 Have you ever felt like Elijah did? How did God provide for him?
3 What comfort might this same God offer us? How often have you ignored the comfort which he offers because you are full of self-pity?

You can be only outward looking as you trust the Lord Jesus for strength.

This has been promised (1 Peter 4:11). Hand your loneliness over to Jesus — you can't use it, but he can!

---

3. I'm the odd one out!
John 5:2-9; Philippians 4:6-7; John 8:1-11; 1 John 1:9

Have you learned to accept yourself? Do you feel unaccepted by others? Some are to be congratulated for being different – Christ-like for Christ! Others feel outcasts because of events in their lives – a relationship, drugs, a scar either physical or within... On what basis does Jesus accept you?

1 What does the passage in John 8 say about Jesus' attitude to outcasts? Divide your sheet, and note down the main points on one side.

2 The attitudes of the scribes and Pharisees were opposed to those of Jesus. Write the corresponding contrasts on the other side.

3 Philippians 4:6-7 and 1 John 1:9 contain promises that assure the believer of Jesus' acceptance and comfort. What are these promises? Have you met the conditions given?

Ask yourself if you really believe Jesus accepts you, not because of, but in spite of, what you are, as he accepted the women. Ask him to make this a reality for you.
    Memorize the Philippian verses you have read today.

---

4. He'll have to speak first!

Ephesians 4:1-7, 25-32; Romans 12:14-21

Most people aren't on speaking terms with God. Because of this the world is full of broken relationships. You may come from a broken home yourself, or have experienced a break-up with a close friend. Bitterness and an unforgiving spirit often go with these, along with a sense of loneliness, and of being let down.

1 *What do these verses have to say about bitterness and revenge? Note down the positive attitudes suggested.*
2 *A pattern for the way of forgiveness is shown. From where does the strength for this come?*
3 *Romans 12:21 'overcome evil with good' (NIV). What practical ways are there for fulfilling this?*

Consider whether you need to put right any relationships in your own life. Tell Jesus and look expectantly for his working in your situation. Remember, however, that he has to prepare at least two hearts for reconciliation!

---

5. All alone

Luke 10:25-37

People cause loneliness! They do it by forgetfulness – have you written home lately? By 'busyness' – does everyone have a life as full as yours? By climbing to the top – who've you stepped on this week? By grabbing their own pleasures – who have you used, or misused, recently?

1 *Read Luke 10:25-37. Jot down the ways in which you love yourself. Taking verse 27, do you have as much love for others?*
2 *There was a centuries-old friction between Samaritans and Jews (the priest, levite and traveller were of this latter race). Contrast the behaviour of the priest and levite with that of the Samaritan. What does Jesus teach us about real caring?*
3 *Consider how observing the first commandment can be instrumental in helping us keep the one of secondary importance.*

Resolve not to be a cause of loneliness, by positive prayer followed by action. Write that letter, make time to talk, encourage those around you, respect others.

Weekend

1 *Read When You're Feeling Lonely by Charles Durham – a very practical book both for the lonely and those who really want to help. Also worth reading are Elizabeth Skoglund, Loneliness (IVP Booklets) and W. E. Hulme, Creative Loneliness (Augsburg).*
2 *Put into practice what you have learned. If you are lonely ask Jesus to give you the courage to seek out the right person to tell – perhaps a minister, a Christian known to you, someone in a local Christian bookshop... Whoever you are – invite someone for coffee or pop out to see someone who you know is often alone. And pray for sensitivity to the needs of others.*

*Loneliness is not a sin and we
have no need to feel guilty
about lonely feelings recurring
even if we belong to God. What
is senseless is the Christian
either refusing to acknowledge
he can be lonely or else giving
in to the helpless lethargy that
self-pity suggests. In Jesus we
have a friend who can
sympathize with our
weaknesses.*

Alan MacDonald, *Tea for One*
(UCCF Booklets).

Part Twelve/Week Three
The Gospel of Luke, 1 (A historical study)

Can a historical study of Luke be
justified? Is Luke's Gospel a work of
history – or of theology?

Until recently, few would have
doubted that this book –
traditionally seen as from the pen of
the 'beloved physician' (Colossians
4:14, AV) – was a work of carefully
researched history. But some
modern scholars have argued that
Luke's interest is theological rather
than historical.

Undoubtedly, theology rather than
strict chronology may have affected
the sequence of events in Luke's
'orderly account' (*cf.* Luke 1:3). As all
historians must be, he has been
selective, theological importance
often being an obvious criterion of
selection.

But as you will see from Luke's
own introduction to his Gospel (as
well as the opening verses of its
sequel – the Acts), his intention was
to write history. And his work shows
all the marks of a careful historian,
even if it does not always meet the
demands of a modern work of
history.

What is this Gospel then? It is a
record of the historical facts of
Christ who has come into the world
to bring salvation to sinners.

Over the next three weeks we shall
consider Luke's orderly account in
three sections. This week we see
how Jesus came **in** to the world; next
week, how he went **on** to Jerusalem;
and finally, the narrative
surrounding his going **out** of this
world.

1. From the beginning
Luke 1 and 2

1 *Write down those reasons you can
draw from Luke 1:1-4 which might
support the claim that the author of
this Gospel is writing a historical
account.*

Note: 1:3 'Excellent' – socially
prominent (?). 'Excellency' – GNB.
'Theophilus' means 'lover of God'.

2 *Since it is probably familiar ground, read chapters 1 and 2 straight through. As you read, make a particular note of Luke's attention to detail: his use of political rulers to pinpoint dates; his precision in recording movements; the intermingling of the stories leading up to the births of John and Jesus. (You may find it easier to highlight significant points in your Bible rather than making full notes in your notebook.)*
3 *As you have read Luke's account – with all its miraculous events involving angels, prophecies, and supernatural births – did it strike you as fantasy or as history? Why?*

Thank God for the Bible and for the attention to detail taken by men like Luke, so that all 'lovers of God' may 'know the certainty of things you have been taught' (Luke 1:4, NIV).

2. Jesus' preparation
Luke 3:1 – 4:13

John the Baptist's ministry was intimately linked with that of Jesus. Not only was he his cousin, who went before him to 'prepare the way' (Luke 3:4), but his message was to be echoed by the Lord Jesus as he began his ministry.

1 *Read Luke 3:1-22. What was John's message according to 3:3? What was of greater importance: the act of baptism, or the repentance i.e. turning from sin, a true change of heart. How can you support your conclusion from Luke's account of John's preaching?*

Repentance resulted in practical action – see 3:10-14. In your life, what

does repentance mean to you?

2 *Jesus' public act of baptism was not left unchallenged. As you read Luke 4:1-13, make a note of the temptations the devil placed before him to do something other than the revealed will of God.*

The devil's temptations are intended to stir selfishness. Jesus' response was a firm 'no'. Just as he was committed to God's will as written in the Bible, now commit yourself to live for God today (and always) – and expect that commitment to be tested!

Note: God's preparation of the way for Jesus didn't begin with John's baptism and the desert encounter with the devil. The genealogy in 3:23-38 (another historical marker) sets Jesus firmly within the context of biblical history. The whole Old Testament prepares the way for him.

3. Teaching for everyone
Luke 4:14-21; 6:17-49

Early on Luke showed that Jesus himself saw his ministry in the context of Old Testament teaching and prophecy, and the Old Testament itself has a historical basis.

1 *Notice how Jesus' ministry is rooted in Scripture. Looking at 4:14-21, how does he see his mission and message in the words of Isaiah? (Compare 3:16-21 with Isaiah 61:1-2.)*

Jesus was a man with a message for *everyone*, as you will see when you look up the following incidents. He couldn't be tied down (see 4:42-44). His pulpit might be in a synagogue (4:44) or a boat on the sea (5:3). He sometimes spoke with individuals (5:12). At other times large crowds followed Jesus and he taught them on a level place (Luke 6:17).

2 *Jesus' God-centred values are very different from those of self-centred society. Try to summarize his teaching in Luke 6:20-46 by drawing out the principles of living approved by Jesus.*
3 *Look over your notes. How do you rate your life? Would Jesus give you a 'blessing' or a 'woe'?*

What strikes you most forcibly from your summary of Jesus' sermon? Read the relevant verses again and ask God to help you to live a more God-centred life today.

4. Not talk ... but power
Luke 4:31 – 5:11

In 1 Corinthians 4:20 Paul writes that 'the kingdom of God is not a matter of words but of power' (NIV). Certainly, Jesus' ministry could not be criticized as being so much 'hot air'! The things which Jesus 'accomplished' (Luke 1:1) included not only teaching but *action*.

1 **His authority over demons.** *How did Jesus silence the demons in 4:33-37 and 4:41? How did this indicate that he had real authority? (Compare 4:31-32 with verse 36.)*
2 **His authority over disease.** *What do verses 38-40 show you about Jesus' approach to disease,*

and his power over it?
3 **His authority over the deep.** *Jesus only had to say the word and it was done (see verses 35-36 and 39). What part did Jesus' word have in Luke 5:1-7?*
4 *Simon was willing to respond in obedience to Jesus' word of authority (verse 5). He had witnessed the authority of Jesus over demons and disease – even in his own home (4:38-39). How do you explain his reaction in Luke 5:8-11?*

How do you react to Jesus' authority? Do you believe that his word still **works** today?

5 *If you want help in studying Luke in greater depth, make use of a good commentary like the one by Leon Morris in the* Tyndale series *(Eerdmans). Other expositions of Luke are David Gooding,* According to Luke *(Eerdmans), and Michael Wilcock,* The Message of Luke *(IVP).*

5. Who is Jesus?
Luke 9:1-50

Luke began his Gospel with the intention of presenting the facts about Jesus so that his reader might know the full truth (see 1:1-4). In this chapter he records incidents where Jesus discovers how much his hearers understood. In the process even more about Jesus is revealed.

Note: Matthew 16:13-17 is a fuller account.

1 *Read through this chapter. On the evidence of verses 1-17, why were the disciples able to give such a clear answer to Jesus' question in verse 18?*

2 *Jesus' disciples had witnessed many incidents which indicated the extraordinary nature of their master (such as the miracle recorded in verses 10-17). How was their appreciation of Jesus confirmed, corrected and strengthened on the mountain (verses 28-36)?*
3 *On their descent (verses 37-50) there were more lessons to be learned. Jot them down briefly in your notebook. How do these lessons, and those learned on the mountain, add weight to what Jesus had already taught them in verses 21-27?*
4 *Who do you say that Jesus is?*

Memory verse: Learn verse 23 – and think about what it means through the day.

Weekend

1 *These studies in Luke are inevitably selective. So to get a grasp of what has been studied this week, read right through Luke 1-9. Pay particular attention to lengthier accounts of Jesus' teaching such as in 8:4-18, and make some notes as to how you should respond to Jesus' words.*

2 *Referring to your notes of the week, can you trace a link between Jesus' words and his actions? The incident in 5:17-26 may be particularly instructive, as is the encounter with John's disciples in 7:18-23 where they are told to report what they have seen (actions) and heard (words).*

Part Twelve/Week Four
The Gospel of Luke, 2 (A historical study)

Today we start a new phase in Luke's account of Jesus' ministry. On the mountain, while transfigured, the Lord had spoken with Moses and Elijah about his departure (literally 'exodus') which he would accomplish at Jerusalem. This week we consider Jesus going *on* to Jerusalem (see Luke 9:51, which clearly marks the start of a new section in Luke's account).

In this section, Luke lays considerable emphasis on Jesus' teaching – perhaps more than on his actions.

1. Priorities
Luke 9:51 – 10:42

1 *Survey today's passage and make a note of the priorities that are commended. For example, what was most important for:*

■ *Jesus in 9:51-53?*
■ *would-be followers in 9:54-62?*
■ *those whom Jesus sent out in 10:1-20?*
■ *the lawyer – and the characters in the story in 10:25-37?*
■ *Mary and Martha in 10:38-42?*

2 *What are the most important goals in your life? In the light of Luke 10:21-24, how can you be sure that you have your priorities right?*
3 *How single-minded are you over doing what you know to be right? Do you want to follow God's way whatever the cost, even overcoming deeply-rooted prejudices? Are you holding on to selfish ambitions?*

Don't put your Bible and notebook away without first confessing your own *specific* sins and failings to God in view of what you have learned today. Then ask for God's help to do what is right above all else.

2. Prayer
Luke 11:1-13; 18:1-14

Throughout Luke's record, he showed Jesus' dependence upon prayer (*see* 6:12; 22:39-46). He wanted his disciples to know how to pray by his example and by what he said. As well as giving this example of prayer though, Jesus tells some stories to illustrate important *principles* for praying.

1 *What lessons about prayer are taught by each of Jesus' stories in: (a) Luke 11:5-13; (b) Luke 18:1-8; (c) Luke 18:9-14?*

Note: Luke explicitly records the point Jesus is making in each of these stories. Make sure you get that before looking for other possible lessons in prayer in these passages.

2 *Which aspects of the Lord's Prayer (Luke 11:2-4) are illustrated by each of these three parables?*

Use the form of words Jesus gave to his followers as a pattern for your praying today.

There is an excellent chapter on prayer in John White's book *The Fight* (IVP). Other useful books to look out for are, David Hubbard, *The Practice of Prayer* (IVP), O. Hallesby, *Prayer* (Augsburg) and John White, *Daring to Draw Near* (IVP).

3. Preaching
Luke 12:1 – 13:5

Included in Luke's history is a record of much of Jesus' preaching. While some of his teaching was addressed to a small group of his followers (*e.g.* 12:1ff.), other parts were preached to large crowds (*e.g.* 12:54ff.).

1 *'Fear God ... and fear no man!' (see 12:1-12). What consolation does Jesus give his disciples in view of the threats of the Pharisees? And what reasons does he add that they should fear God, but fear no man?*
2 *'Money isn't everything!' (see 12:13-34). How does Jesus illustrate this statement?*
3 *'This world won't last forever' (see 12:35-53). How does Jesus' teaching put our lives into an eternal perspective? And how ought we to live now?*
4 *'Be warned!' (see 12:54 – 13:5). How does the Lord warn the crowds in view of coming judgment?*

Pray for your friends who are unaware of God's eternal perspective on life. Ask God to show you both how to warn them, and how to demonstrate the relevance of the unseen world and spiritual reality by the way you live.

4. Parables
Luke 15:1-31

As you have been reading through Luke's Gospel, you will have already seen that one of Jesus' favourite teaching tools was the parable: a story with a clear point to it.

Note: It is worth distinguishing a parable from an allegory – such as John 15:1-16 – where the illustration fits piece by piece to the reality. If you look for too much significance in parables you can get strange results!

In chapter 15, Luke records a parable Jesus told in three parts to Pharisees and teachers of the law (verse 2).

1 *What is the point of the stories of the lost sheep and the lost coin? (You will see that this is stated quite clearly in the text.) How is the same lesson taught in the story of the lost son (verses 11-32)?*
2 *Notice Jesus' method: from 100 sheep, through the 10 coins, the Lord sharpens his focus on 2 men. If the younger son's repentance brought joy to the father, what lesson is to be learned from the older brother's behaviour, bearing in mind Jesus' audience?*

How frequently do you rejoice that you have been lost and now found, or do you sometimes forget that you have needed to repent?

5. People
Luke 18:18 – 19:10

Luke portrays the characters in his account in very clear and realistic detail. These are no fairy-tale types. And to see how Jesus deals with people certainly bears a stamp of authenticity. In today's passage we contrast three people. The first is a synagogue official who would be well skilled in the Old Testament Law; the second, a blind beggar; the third, a collaborator with the Roman occupying forces.

1 *Read the passage, then divide a page of your notebook into three columns. In each of the columns, list the characteristics of the three men you have read about e.g. rich or poor; upright or dishonest; self-sufficient or needy; socially acceptable or acceptable to Jesus. Add other characteristics you can see from the text so that you have as full a picture of each as possible.*
2 *At the foot of each column, note which men benefited from their encounter with Jesus. Why did one go away sad, while the other two received what they needed?*
3 *What lessons can you learn about money from the three men you have been thinking about? How does the example of the disciples help you to view your possessions in the light of eternity — and of Jesus' self-sacrifice for us? (see Luke 18:24-34).*

Weekend

1 *Think over this week's studies (your notes will help you to do this). Note again the response of the people to Jesus' words and actions. What produced a good response?*

What had the opposite effect? Why do you think Jesus chose those moments to say or do what he said and did? What was the response he wanted – and what is your own response to Jesus' teaching, e.g. in Luke 14:25-34?

2 Read through the first twenty chapters of Luke to gain an overall picture. It is important not to get into the habit of reading the Bible for only details. As in viewing a photograph or landscape painting, details make more sense in a larger context.

3 David Gooding has written about this book: 'One of the most beautiful features of the Gospel of Luke is the way it depicts Christ as the Champion and Saviour of the outcast and oppressed, as the One who can restore to true human dignity men and women whom life has somehow warped' Windows on Paradise (Everyday Publications). Pen brief sketches of several unfortunate or outcast people you have met in Luke whom Jesus helped. Some suggestions are: a prostitute (7:36 – 8:3), a swindler (5:27-32; 18:9-14), a widow (7:11-17).

Part Twelve/Week Five
The Gospel of Luke, 3 (A historical study)

Chapter headings in your Bible (e.g. 'Signs of the end', RSV/NIV) are not part of the text. They may unduly colour your interpretation of the passage. We need to look at the Gospel text itself to see what Luke is telling us from Jesus' teaching.

1. The servant of history
Luke 21:5-38

1 Read the chapter. What is the context of Jesus' teaching, and what question is he answering (verses 5-7)?

2 Jesus' concern is to relieve the fear of his followers (verse 9) in view of the dreadful things that were to happen within their generation (verse 32). List the things that Jesus

says will happen. What warnings does he give? What comfort can be drawn from Jesus' promises?

3 Verses 25-27 clearly reflect the language of the Old Testament. Look up Isaiah 13:10 and Daniel 7:13-14. (If your Bible gives other cross-references, you may like to check them out too.) What were these Old Testament writers saying: (a) about the destruction of cities; (b) about the coming of the 'Son of Man' to the 'Ancient of Days' to receive power?

Note: This passage certainly applied to the destruction of Jerusalem by the Romans in AD 70 – after Jesus had ascended to a position of authority in heaven.

4 Think about Jesus' words in verses 28 and 33. As his prophecy regarding the destruction of the

temple was so accurately fulfilled in AD 70, what confidence can you have in the words of the Lord of history concerning yet future events?

2. The servant of history
Luke 22:1-38

1 *Everything is going according to plan! Judas has negotiated Jesus' betrayal — but Jesus is no powerless pawn in the hands of the Jewish authorities. How is his command of the situation seen from verses 7-13 and verses 31-34?*
2 *How does Jesus show, during the Last Supper, that he knows what lies before him? Why was he so certain about this? (Compare verses 22 and 37).*
3 *Luke shows us the Lord Jesus as the ultimate Servant of the Lord. What are the implications for us of his submission to God's will? (See especially verses 24-30.)*
4 *The suffering Servant of the Lord is seen prophetically in Isaiah 52:13 – 53:12. It is to this Scripture that Jesus referred in verse 37. Think about how Jesus fulfilled this prophecy in history as you read Isaiah's words.*

Pray about your service in the light of verse 26-27, and ask God for specific ways in which you can serve others today.

3. The man of history
Luke 22:39-71

Probably the genuine humanity of the Lord Jesus is seen as much in these verses as anywhere else in Scripture.

1 *How does Luke portray the Man Christ Jesus (a) through his prayer on the Mount of Olives, (b) his encounter with his captors, and (c) his response to Peter's denial?*
2 *In verses 63-71, Jesus is mocked and charged with claiming to be the Son of God. What does his response add to your understanding of him?*
3 *Meditate on the picture of Jesus given in this chapter. How does this very human Jesus reveal the authority and compassion of God whom we cannot see? Then respond to God in worship.*

Memory verse: So the word of God became a human being and lived among us. We saw his splendour (the splendour as of a father's only son), full of grace and truth (John 1:14, J. B. Phillips).

4. The crux of history
Luke 23:1-56

At the centre of history stands a cross. All of history up to then had been leading to that moment. And from that point, God has invited people to look back to this central, brief period when mankind's separation from God was finally dealt with, and Jesus could cry out – 'Father, into your hands I commit my spirit'.

Before you begin reading today's chapter, remind yourself that this event – Christ's crucifixion – actually happened in a real place at a real time. It is true. Pray that as you read, the reality of the death of Jesus on your behalf may be impressed on your mind.

1 *Ask yourself how the events of this*

chapter, which Luke brings out,
illustrate each of these Old
Testament chapters:
■ Psalm 2:1-2 (compare Acts 4:24-
28)
■ Psalm 22:6-8,18
■ Psalm 69:21
■ Isaiah 53:9,11,12
■ Amos 8:9
■ Psalm 31:5
2 *What does today's passage reveal
about (a) Jesus' innocence, (b)
Barabbas' guilt, and (c) the effect of
the cross on the lives of the two
thieves respectively?*

Note: Turn to Acts 2:22-24 and see
how the early church had already
begun to look back to the cross.

3 *How central is the event of the
cross in your life?*

Memory verse: For our sake he
made him to be sin who knew no sin,
so that in him we might become the
righteousness of God (2 Corinthians
5:21, RSV).

> *There lies beneath its shadow,*
> *But at the farther side,*
> *The darkness of an awful grave*
> *That gapes both deep and*
> *wide;*
> *And there between us*
> *stands the cross,*
> *Two arms outstretched to*
> *save;*
> *Like a watchman set to guard*
> *the way*
> *From that eternal grave.*
>
> *Beneath the cross of Jesus –* a
> hymn by Elizabeth Cecilia
> Clephane (1830-1869).

5. The turning point of history
Luke 24:1-53

What would it need to convince you
that someone had risen from death?
Read through the chapter and let the
facts hit you.

1 *From verse 11 it is clear that the
disciples were less than convinced
by the women's story! Why were the
women convinced by the angel's
explanation of the empty tomb?*
2 *What parts did the word of Christ
and the evidence of their own eyes
have in convincing Cleopas and his
companion that Jesus was alive?*
3 *How did Jesus convince his
friends that his resurrection was real
– and that what they were seeing was
in fulfilment of the Scriptures?*
4 *In what way are we 'witnesses of
these things' (verse 48, NIV)? Why
does it matter that the resurrection
is an actual event in history?*

The resurrection of Jesus is the
turning point of history – and the
turning point of lives! (Did you
notice how the realization of the fact
of the resurrection caused people to
change radically?)
　　Aim to share the facts of the
resurrection – as you find them in
the Bible – today, and pray that they
will cause people you know to turn
round (see Acts 17:30-31).
　　Several excellent books are
available on the facts of Christ's
resurrection – Frank Morison, *Who
Moved the Stone?* (Zondervan), John
Wenham, *Easter Enigma*
(Zondervan) and Sir Norman
Anderson, *Jesus Christ: the Witness*

of History (IVP). The latter also has written a helpful booklet *Evidence for the Resurrection* (IVP).

Weekend

1 In writing his Gospel, Luke was not intending simply to write history and nothing more; his concern was to record history that relates to salvation. Luke 5:31-32 are key verses. Survey the whole Gospel for examples of Jesus healing the whole person. (See how salvation in Luke is more than a spiritual, religious concept; nor can it be restricted to the physical realm. It involves the whole person.)

2 Pay special attention to this theme of salvation in the passages you have studied this week.

3 The writer, Luke, was apparently a medical doctor (see *Colossians* 4:14). There are features in the Gospel which may show his special interest – for example, the account of the woman with the haemorrhage (Luke 8:43-47). Have you noticed any such medical features in this Gospel? Try to find some more. He was similarly interested in death – think about some examples. There was the elderly Simeon (2:25-35), the widow of Nain's son (7:11-15), the only daughter (8:40-56), and the dying criminal (23:39-43). Use such examples to explore your own attitude to death. How biblical is it? Christ's death dominates Luke's account. How central is Christ's death to your thinking about the subject? What is a Christ-like response to death?

Part Twelve/Week Six
The cross (A word study)

The cross is one of the commonest symbols of Christianity (you may well wear one), and one of the key events at the heart of our faith. What does the Bible have to say about it? We shall look at passages which contain the word 'cross', 'tree' (a poetic word for the cross) and 'crucify' to find out.

It would be a useful introduction to read something about crucifixion, for example, the article on the cross in the *Illustrated Bible Dictionary* (Tyndale), or the Lion *Encyclopaedia of the Bible*.

The cross is an enormous subject, and some of these studies contain too much material for one sitting. The material is included so that you can follow up things that interest you. Don't try to tackle too much at once (better to learn one thing properly than have a vague knowledge of a wide area!) – save the rest for the weekend.

Any really serious attempt to understand the Christian way must begin with the cross. Unless we come to see what the cross means we do not understand Christianity, real Christianity in the sense the New Testament writers gave to it. The cross is absolutely central. We must give time and attention to our understanding of what it means.

Leon Morris, *The Atonement* (IVP).

1. Jesus on the cross
Luke 23:26-49

Many of the occurrences of the word 'cross' in the New Testament come in the account of the crucifixion – the obvious place to start this study.

1 *Read the passage slowly and prayerfully. Before going on to the rest of the study, thank God for sending Jesus to die for you.*

Hallelujah, my Father, for giving us your Son;
Sending Him into the world to be given up for men,
Knowing we would bruise Him and smite Him from the earth.
Hallelujah, my Father, in His death is my birth.
Hallelujah, my Father, in His life is my life.

Tim Cullen, 1975, *Spirit of Praise.*

2 *Now try to put yourself in the place of some of the characters in this account. What would these people have thought was going on: (1) the women (verse 27)? (2) the people and Jewish leaders (verse 35)? (3) the two thieves (verses 39-43)? (4) the centurion (verse 47)?*
3 *How does Luke show that Jesus was innocent in his death?*

2. Following the cross
Luke 9:18-27; 14:25-35

The idea that the Messiah would suffer was unexpected – both to the crowds in yesterday's study, and to the disciples in today's. But Jesus calls his disciples to follow him – and that includes the experience of the cross.

1 *Read both passages. (1) Make a list of all that carrying his cross means for a disciple (see especially 9:23-26 and 14:25-27, 33). (2) What attitude does Jesus want his followers to have?*
2 *Discipleship can seem hard and costly at times – but the New Testament points us to Jesus as our inspiration, example and encouragement – see Hebrews 12:1-3; 1 Peter 2:20-25. What do you find difficult about being a Christian? Does Jesus' example help? Meditate on one of these passages.*
3 *If you have enough time, go on to see what Paul says about discipleship and the cross. Look at Romans 6:1-7, 11-14 (there are similar references in Galatians 5:24; 6:14). What attitude does Paul expect the disciple to have?*

Why not commit Jesus' words in Luke 9:23-25 to memory?

3. The cross: God's plan
Galatians 3:1-29

Paul had problems with the churches in Galatia! After he had been there and preached the gospel, others had come along to tell the new Christians that they should be circumcised and keep the Jewish Law, as well as believing in Christ. The implication was that the cross was an afterthought – a bonus for pious Jews – not God's age-long plan of salvation.

In Part One you've studied this chapter before – it might be helpful to look back at your notes on that. Read through the chapter, and try to trace the stages in God's plan. The following questions are to help you on your way – they need only brief answers!

1 *We start with Abraham, the founder-member of the people of God before the Law was given (see verse 17). How was he put right with God, or justified?*
2 *God made Abraham a promise. What can you find out about that promise (see verses 6-9, 15-18)?*
3 *The Law was obviously an interim measure (see verse 19). What could the Law achieve (see verses 19, 23-24)? What could it not achieve (see verses 10-12)?*
4 *How was God's promise to Abraham fulfilled (see verses 13-14)?*

Note: Verse 13 quotes Deuteronomy 21:22-23. The Old Testament custom was for the criminal to be stoned, and his body would then be hung up as a warning to others.

5 *How can people today inherit God's promise through Abraham (see verses 26-29)?*

4. Explaining the cross

Galatians 3:13; 1 Peter 2:24; Colossians 1:20; 2:15; Ephesians 2:16

The Bible, in many ways, tells us what the cross achieved — both in putting us right with God, and in the other effects which follow from that. Choose one (or more if you have time) of the following verses, and try to get the drift of the passage of which it is part, then answer the questions.

■ Galatians 3:13
■ 1 Peter 2:24
■ Colossians 1:20
■ Colossians 2:15
■ Ephesians 2:16

1 *What does your verse say the cross achieved?*
2 *What difference should that make to your life?*
3 *How would you explain the verse to someone who knows very little about Christianity, and doesn't understand religious jargon?*

Note: 1 Peter 2:24. Though the context of this verse is Christ's example, Peter characteristically draws out the doctrine of the cross – Christ's atoning death as our substitute – as he also does later in 3:18.

The Bible has lots more to teach about the death of Christ (in passages where 'the cross' does not appear explicity) and its place in the whole work of Christ. To follow that up, you could read the appropriate section of a book on Christian belief (*e.g.* 'The atonement: biblical teaching' pp.150-163 of *Know the Truth* by Bruce Milne (IVP), or Leon Morris' helpful and readable book, *The Atonement* (IVP).

5. Preaching the cross

1 Corinthians 1:17-2:5

It seems that the church at Corinth was split by personality cults (*see* 1 Corinthians 1:10-16). Paul tackles this by reminding them that it is the message of the cross, not the preacher, which is the basis of their faith. The problem was mundane – but as a result we have this vivid description of how Paul preached.

1 *Verse 22 shows us what Jews and Greeks expected of religion. Look at Galatians 3:13 to see what the Jews would have thought of the cross. For the Greeks 'wisdom' was insight into the nature of God and the world. How does the cross conflict with what they would have expected of religion (see especially verse 23)?*
2 *What do your non-Christian friends think of the gospel? (Can you remember what you thought when you first heard it? – if you can remember a time when you weren't a*

Christian) Are they more like the Jews or the Greeks?
3 *From this passage how can anyone understand the 'message of the cross'?*
4 *What are the implications of that for the way Paul preaches?*

How do you feel if anyone asks you about your faith? Is it anything like how Paul felt at Corinth? Do your feelings put you off saying anything? From this passage, how should you react?

Weekend

1 *You've probably got lots to follow up or finish off from the studies this week!*
2 *If you want some extra material to look at, many of the sermons in Acts refer to the cross (Acts 2:36; 4:10; 5:30; 10:39; 13:29). Choose one of these verses and read it in its context. What does it say about the cross? How does it fit in with the rest of the sermon? How do the hearers react?*
3 *The cross repays a lifetime's meditation. An excellent way to continue your application of what Christ has done is to read through John Stott's major, lucid and inspiring biblical study,* The Cross of Christ *(IVP).*

Part Twelve/Week Seven
John 15 (A meditation)

This chapter forms part of Jesus' farewell discourse to his disciples. Only John out of the four gospel

writers has recorded these words for us.

---

1. Final words
John 13 – 15

Pray for a quiet mind. You need an unhurried approach to the Bible if you are going to benefit from your meditation. So commit every part of your self, including your mind, imagination and emotions, to God.

1 *Having done that, slowly read through John 13-15 (Jesus' final words do in fact cover chapters 16 and 17 as well). As you do so, notice the quality and depth of Jesus' love for his disciples, which motivated him to speak to them as he did in his farewell message.*
2 *Then reflect on how you can best respond to a love of such depth which has been extended to you too.*

> Love so amazing, so divine,
> Demands my soul, my life,
> my all.
>
> *When I survey the wondrous cross*, a hymn by Isaac Watts
> (1674-1748).

Note: The Old Testament frequently referred to Israel as a vine, as in Isaiah 5:1-7; Jeremiah 2:21; Ezekiel 15. The vine had actually become the symbol of the nation of Israel. It was for this reason that it appeared as the emblem on the coins of the period just before Christ. So when Jesus described himself as the true vine, he was claiming to be what Israel had failed to be.

2. Remaining in the vine
John 15:1-6

Take the thoughts that you had from yesterday's study to prepare you for today's meditation. Conscious of Jesus' love for his friends, we turn to look at the picture of the vine.

1 *Read these verses a couple of times, trying to imagine a garden full of vines, in its various stages of development.*
2 *When you became a Christian you were joined to Christ. What does it mean to you to be part of the true vine, dependent upon Christ? Consider this both in theory and practice.*

Note: Pruning is inevitable and unavoidable. Indeed a newly-planted vine would have to wait three years before bearing any fruit because it would be so drastically cut back.

3 *Why does Jesus say that pruning is inevitable? Think over how you have responded to the divine secateurs of the gardener. It may have been a relationship that was wrong, an attitude which needed correction, a habit which had to be broken if you were to be fruitful in serving God.*

Painful as it may be, we can be secure in the knowledge that God wants the best for us and has all things under control.
Thank God that he wants you to be reliant upon the true vine which in turn gives you life in all its fullness.

3. My joy in you
John 15:7-11

Once again, consciously put aside all the thoughts buzzing round in your mind, as you come to God's Word.

Ask God to let his spirit be your teacher.

1 *Read these verses through several times. Pick out what Jesus is teaching about the effects of remaining or abiding in Christ, the true vine. These will include an effect upon –*

- ■ *our prayer life*
- ■ *how others view us*
- ■ *our response to the Father's love for us*
- ■ *our willingness to be obedient*
- ■ *our joy*

2 *Spend time meditating on these aspects of your relationship with God. How real are they in your own life?*

> Jesu, Thou joy of loving hearts,
> Thou fount of life, Thou
> light of men,
> From the best bliss that earth
> imparts
> We turn unfilled to Thee
> again.

Latin (*c.* 11th century), translated by Ray Palmer (1808-87).

4. Love each other
John 15:12-17

We are told that it is impossible to command a person to love. But Jesus breaks the rule. Today we see how and why Christian love is so different.

Ask God to speak to you. Then read these verses through.

1 *What do you notice about Jesus' friendship with his disciples? Is it*

unconditional friendship? If not, what are the conditions? Who took the initiative? At what cost?*

Spend time thinking over your response to the fact that Jesus has called his disciples to be his friends. Then turn in gratitude to God to thank him for such a friendship.

2 *Our love for others is an extension of Christ's love for us. Realizing how much Jesus has loved you, how can that affect your relationships with those you find hard to love? Specifically name those who fall into that category and pray for them in the light of the truth of Jesus' teaching here.*

Memory verse: Greater love has no-one than this, that one lay down his life for his friends (John 15:13, NIV).

But Jesus died even for his enemies!

'While we were still sinners, Christ died for us' (Romans 5:8, NIV).

5. Rejection!
John 15:18-27

Despised and rejected! We shall never experience what Jesus went through. But being a Christian often means that, like him, we are hated for our faith.

Pray that the Holy Spirit will help you to understand this part of Jesus' final words in this chapter.

1 *After reading these verses try to put the main points into your own words. Jesus does not disguise the fact that identification with him has a cost attached. Why is this?*
2 *In what ways have you*

experienced rejection because you
have been closely identified with
Jesus? Jesus was not talking here
about insensitive fanatics. This may
have meant going against the tide of
popular opinion or being the lonely
object of derision.
3 Draw out the encouragements and
instructions Jesus gives to his
disciples throughout this chapter.
Then see how they relate to your
own life or the situation of any you
know who are undergoing rejection.
Turn this into prayer.

He was despised and rejected
by men,
a man of sorrows, and
familiar with suffering.
Like one from whom men

hide their faces
he was despised, and we
esteemed him not
(Isaiah 53:3, NIV).

Weekend

1 Read John 13-17 to get a full
picture of Jesus' farewell message to
his disciples.
2 Andrew Murray's devotional book
on John 15, Abide in Christ
(Lakeland), may be helpful if you
want to look at this chapter in more
depth.
3 Explore more fully (see study 1)
some of the Old Testament
background of the image of the vine,
as in Isaiah 5:1-7; Jeremiah 2:21;
Ezekiel 19:10-14. Find out a little
about the characteristics of the vine.

Part Twelve/Week Eight
Selections from Leviticus (A detailed study)

Leviticus is a rulebook which was
sometimes termed the 'priest's law'
by the Jews. God gave us the book
because he intended that all the
people should know and keep the
law. To us, it might perhaps seem a
strange book – dealing with
unfamiliar and even repulsive topics
such as leprosy, skin diseases, and
blood-sacrifices. It is a fascinating
book too, because it is the
background to the greatest event of
all time — the death of Jesus Christ.
You will have discovered this when
you studied the Letter to the
Hebrews in Part 4.

Unfortunately, we shall be able to
read only a small part of this lengthy
book in these detailed studies. But as
you read the intervening chapters for
yourself, bear in mind that the rites
and regulations are not an end in
themselves. They are a foretaste of
the fullness of salvation that we
enjoy in Christ. In some of the
studies you will find suggested
passages to read in Hebrews which
will illustrate the relevance of
Leviticus for a fuller understanding
of Christ's sacrifice.
'Be holy...' (Leviticus 19:2) is a
recurring phrase throughout the

book, occurring even in the midst of dietary laws, showing how holiness applies to all of life, no matter how ordinary.

1. The sacrifices
Leviticus 1 and 4

Chapters 1-7 describe the instructions that the people were given concerning five categories of sacrifice. These were the burnt, cereal, peace, purification and guilt sacrifices. (We shall be able to look at only two of them.) Similar rites were common throughout all the ancient nations. Yet there are certain unique features in the sacrifices for Israel. The tone was austere and reverent, contrasting with the orgies, sorcery and human sacrifices of the neighbouring nations. All the sacrifices are descriptive of the relationship between God and his people. They knew him as the one, true and holy God who dealt with them in justice and love.

1 *Read chapter 1 about the burnt offering. This was the commonest sacrifice, carried out every day at least. What do you notice about the sacrificial victim? What role did the offerer have to play, and what about the priest's part? What was achieved by the sacrifice (verses 3-4,9)?*
2 *How aware are you that when your relationship with God is being restored, you are in fact pleasing him?*

> Sacrifice is the appointed means whereby peaceful co-existence between a holy God and sinful man becomes a possibility.

Gordon Wenham, *The Book of Leviticus* (Eerdmans).

3 *Then turn to chapter 4 to read about the less frequently performed purification or sin offering. As you do so, note down the distinctions between the sacrifice of the priest, the Israelite community, and an individual.*

> The purification offering ... was designed to cope with a subsidiary problem created by human sin–pollution and defilement.

Gordon Wenham, *The Book of Leviticus* (Eerdmans).

4 *How seriously do you consider the consequences of sin – both your own, and those of the larger community or nation?*

Ask God not only to forgive you for any known sin, but also to deal with the consequences. As with Israel, he still longs to be fully reconciled with his purified people.

2. Aaron's ordination
Leviticus 9

Chapter 8 describes how Moses carried out God's instructions (Exodus 29) by consecrating Aaron and his sons to the priesthood. They were to carry out the duties described in chapters 1-7 that we have already partly examined. Following their ordination, they offered their first sacrifices, which we shall study in this chapter.

1 *Why do you think the priest*

needed to make an offering for himself? How did this compare with Christ's priesthood (Hebrews 7:23-28)?

Notes: The priests were appointed to lead the religious life of Israel. This privilege was reserved for Aaron (Moses' brother) and his descendants (Numbers 3:10). They were assisted in this task by the Levites who had a particular responsibility in caring for the tabernacle.

Verse 2. The perfect calf contrasts with the idolatrous golden one (Exodus 32).

Verse 22. The blessing may have been Numbers 6:24-26.

2 *Note down everything that is said about the Lord in this chapter. How joyful are the times when you worship with others? When joy appears to be absent, why is this?*
3 *How did God show his pleasure in, and acceptance of, their worship?*

Spend time thanking God that in Christ we have a perfect high priest, succeeding where all others had failed.

3. The Day of Atonement
Leviticus 16

Chapters 11-15 cover the rules for daily living. With advances in medical science we can now see that God was working through natural processes to deal with Israel's health problems (as promised in Exodus 23:25). We also can see now how amazingly revolutionary the hygiene rules were.

The Day of Atonement was an annual event for the nation, when the high priest was allowed into the inner sanctum, or Holy of Holies. This chapter sets out the proper rituals he must carry out to enter safely.

1 *Note down from the reading the conditions necessary for entering into God's presence. Then, from Hebrews 9:11-28 and 10:1-25 contrast the advantages held by the believer, since Christ, in approaching God.*
2 *From what you have read in the books, how is guilt dealt with in both Leviticus and Hebrews?*
3 *How important is it for you, in your worship of God, to be reminded that you have a cleansed conscience? Is repentance, along with a seeking of forgiveness, a regular part of your personal devotions? Do you enter God's presence aware of his holiness and purity, as the priest had to?*

4. Feast days
Leviticus 23

Chapters 18-20 describe the various moral laws. Some of these might seem strange requirements to us, so it is well to bear in mind that a few of them are specifically directed against the evil practices of the neighbouring nations. But most reinforce for us what we already know of God's holiness. 'Be holy because I, the LORD your God, am holy' (19:2, NIV).

Chapters 21 and 22 deal with special rules for priests. They were subject to particular stringency because of their privileged position.

1 *Read chapter 23. Make a list of the*

seven different feast days. Write a brief description of the nature and purpose of each of them where the text makes it clear. What are their similarities and differences?
2 Three of these feasts were of particular importance. Take each of them in turn and consider how the original purpose of them applies to the church today.

(a) **The Passover/Feast of Unleavened Bread** – it served to act as an annual reminder of Israel's deliverance from Egypt. How are you reminded of your deliverance? (Your studies on Exodus in Part 5 may help here.) See 1 Corinthians 5:6-8.

(b) **The Feast of Weeks or Harvests** was an annual reminder of God's provision of material gifts in the harvest. How do you consciously express your gratitude for God's goodness?

(c) **The Feast of Tabernacles/ Booths/Ingathering** – an annual reminder that Israel had once lived in booths as they wandered through the wilderness (see verse 42) but God had been faithful to his people. How do you respond to God's faithfulness in all sorts of areas of your life? (Zechariah 14:16-19 refers this feast to the end of time.)

Turn your reflections into prayer.

---

5. Justice and obedience
Leviticus 25 – 26

Chapter 24 turns from the feast days to the regular duties of the weekly offering of the twelve loaves and the lamp which must be kept alight.

God's concern for justice has always been evident.

1 Read Leviticus 25, noting down what commandments are given in terms of seeing justice for the poor, the slave and the foreigner. What does this say about God?
2 How can his people today share this aspect of his character? Spend time thinking over this.
3 Read chapter 26 and then make a list of the blessings which obedience brings. What privileges can you think of which we can have in Christ for our obedience? How does such obedience apply to groups of people as well as individuals?

Note: The Year of Jubilee ideally occurred every 49 years.

4 Why does God punish disobedience? Again, how might such punishment be communal as well as individual? How can we be restored? You might like to compare the ideas here with Hebrews 12:1-13.

Thank God that he treats us as his children even if that means discipline. Pray that you will be willing to accept all that God gives you.

Weekend

1 Throughout our reading of parts of Leviticus we have seen that God is holy and will not tolerate sin. Do some background work on this subject, perhaps by reading Holiness by J. C. Ryle (Baker), or by looking up the entry on 'holiness' in a good Bible dictionary. What practical lessons can you learn from the book of Leviticus' concern for the whole of life, not merely the narrowly spiritual

and religious?

2 Also on the theme of holiness you could study chapters 11-15. They deal with the ugliness of the results of sin. Leprosy is usually taken as an illustration of sin and how it should be dealt with. In chapter 15 you could examine the parallels which exist between it and secret sin. How does sin prevent acceptance with God in chapter 14? Hebrews 12:14-29 can provide a starting point for an answer. In thinking about sin, keep in mind Leviticus' emphasis on communal as well as personal evil. Are there features of your own society which perhaps merit God's judgment? What form might such judgment take today?

3 The New Testament book of Hebrews can be seen as a commentary on Leviticus. Why not make your own study of this book, or at least read attentively through it? Your notes will help you from your study of the Letter to the Hebrews (Part 4, Week 8).

Part Twelve/Week Nine
Hosea and Gomer (A character study)

Intertwined are two marriages that went wrong — that of Hosea with the prostitute Gomer, and God with the wilful kingdom of Israel. Through the pain of his own situation Hosea learnt the extent of God's deep and tender love for his people. Both brides paid the price of adultery. Gomer became a slave. The northern kingdom of Israel fell in 721 BC to Assyria, its people deported, and the land occupied. The southern kingdom of Judah suffered a similar fate in 597 BC although, like the north, the Jews were allowed to return after their period of exile in Babylon.

Hosea's prophecy was addressed mainly to the northern kingdom, but there was a relevance for Judah too (see 11:12). By looking at the characters of Hosea and Gomer we shall see parallels of God's relationship with Israel, and Christ with his church.

In your notebook draw three columns headed, 'Hosea and Gomer', 'God and Israel' and 'Christ and his church'. During the week, or as an alternative weekend activity, jot down parallels which may be drawn between these themes.

It is the people you love who can hurt you most. One can almost trace the degree of potential pain along a scale – from the rebuff which you hardly notice from a stranger, to the rather upsetting clash you may have with a friend, right on to the stinging hurt of a jilting, the ache of a parent-child estrangement, or, most wounding of all, the betrayal of a marriage.

Nothing short of the last two of these could really have conveyed to Hosea or to us how deeply God cares about us. Even then, words alone might have failed to bring home the sharpness of it. It needed acting out, and in real life at that.

Derek Kidner, *The message of Hosea* (IVP).

1. 'I name this child...'
Hosea 1:1-8

God directed Hosea into a marriage with Gomer who was a prostitute at the time, or would soon become one. The first child was probably Hosea's, but the others may well have been conceived as a result of her profession. Hosea's family life became a living prophecy — a parable of pain — to his fellow northerners in Israel.

1 *What do the names of the children tell us about the relationship that could have existed between the 'brides' and their respective 'husbands', Hosea and God himself?*

Note: 1:4 Jezreel: Jehu caused a blood-bath at that city (2 Kings 9 and 10).

2 *From these verses, what is God's attitude to sin? What do we also see of his love? Is God's attitude to sin different from that of man in general? How? Why?*
3 *Meditate on the importance of faithfulness in your relationship with Jesus. Romans 12:1 tells us that we*

can worship by giving our living bodies in service instead of offering a dead animal's body, as in Hosea's day.

2. A light on the horizon
Hosea 1:10 – 2:1

Despite the apparently impossible situation reached in both relationships there is the possibility of reconciliation, if the parties are willing. God does not forget his promises.

1 *List the evidences of hope in these verses. Upon what was this hope based?*
2 *Remembering yesterday's study what can you learn now of the depth of God's love for us as sinners and hence the hope that is ours?*

Meditate on the glorious promises held in Revelation 21:1-4. Perhaps you would like to learn the latter part as a reminder of his love. These verses would help in adding to your three-column chart.

3. Will he have me back?
Hosea 2:2-13

Frustration marks the life of Gomer and of Israel. Sexual freedom often ends up with disillusionment — times haven't changed, men and women are no different now than then! Here Gomer's plight merges into that of the people of Israel.

1 *Jot down the actions of Gomer that are frustrated and suggest what Hosea's agonized responses might have been.*
2 *What does the passage show you concerning God's attitude to and provision for Israel? Punishment was a reality. How dependent was Israel upon God's goodness and mercy? How is this paralleled in Christ's dealings with his church?*

Take stock of your daily needs and how they are met, and other indications of God's goodness towards you. You could take Psalm 67 and use it as a prayer of gratitude to God for his merciful provision.

4. Can I win her back?
Hosea 2:14-23

God speaks of wooing back Israel and sets a pattern for Hosea to regain Gomer. What a beautiful love-poem and that's how God felt about Israel and now about you.

1 *List the ways in which God intends to attract Israel. Have you ever felt him dealing with you in a similar way?*
2 *What do verses 19 and 20 show you about God's relationship between him and his people?*
3 *Go through the passage noticing the use of the pronouns, 'I', 'you', 'she', etc. What do you learn about God's love for Israel – and us?*

Note: 'That day' (verses 16, 18, 21) in the Old Testament points us on to the great 'Day of the Lord'. That day began with Christ's first coming. It will further unfold with his second coming.

Meditate on the love of Jesus Christ for his bride — the church (Ephesians 5:25-27).

5. On probation!
Hosea 3

Action! Hosea buys back Gomer and the marriage is saved. How deeply she must have been loved. Israel too was loved, but though her 'husband' was faithful, she was not.

1 *From verse 3 and earlier studies, what suggests that Hosea was faithful to the marriage bond? What does that say about the need to keep on working at a relationship?*
2 *Note down the parallels between Hosea's treatment of Gomer and God's response to Israel, adding to the three-column chart.*

Consider the price that Jesus Christ paid for your salvation (1 Peter 3:18). Make that the basis of a time of praise to God. Why not memorize this verse?

Weekend

1 *Using* The Message of Hosea, *by Derek Kidner (IVP), dip into the rest of the book for the evidences of God's forgiveness towards, and relationship with, his people Israel.*
2 *If you have not already done so, carry out the project suggested at the beginning of the week, looking for parallels as indicated.*
3 *Hosea is one of a number of Old Testament examples of biblical teaching being dramatically acted out. (You might look at the book of Jeremiah, which we studied in Part 2.*

This is full of other examples, such as Jeremiah 19:10-13.) Think about how drama may be useful today. Some Christians, for instance, have experimented with street theatre, or by putting on Christian productions in local theatres. If you are interested, A Time to Act, *by Murray Watts and Paul Burbridge (Hodder)* is worth reading.

Part Twelve/Week Ten
Work (A topic study)

'Work is a consequence of our creation in the image of God and not a consequence of our fall'.

John Stott

Work need not be drudgery, a necessary evil so that we can enjoy our leisure time! The Bible encourages a positive attitude to work, contrary to the expectations prevalent in our society. In the first study we shall establish a biblical framework for our attitude to work. We shall then examine some practical implications.

---

1. A necessary evil?
Genesis 1 – 3; Exodus 35:30-35

Skim read Genesis 1-3.

1 *What evidence is there that God himself is a worker, finding satisfaction in his work?*
2 *How far did God make man to be a worker like himself? Does man work on God's behalf?*
3 *What do we read here about frustration in work?*
4 *From these verses, what strikes you as being different about the Bible's view of work and that of the world around? How far have you*

adopted our society's negative view of work?
5 *Since God has intended us to work and has enabled us to do so, we have a responsibility to work to the best of our ability. Read Exodus 35:30-35 and see how Moses viewed the way God equipped men as craftsmen. Do you have the same attitude to the use of your gifts as they had to theirs?*

---

2. Not on the scrap-heap
Romans 12:1-13

'I have become a statistic... I am unemployed!'
We need to draw a distinction between work and employment. Because someone is out of paid employment does not mean that they are unable to work, are not working, or are valueless. Within the church, all members belong and have something to contribute, and this is the true pattern of society. Read Romans 12:1-8, noting down the different ways an individual Christian should think of himself and his contribution to others. As a contrast, think how the 'pattern of this world' differs from this, for

example, encouraging conformity, self-absorption, independence from others.

1 *Where do your gifts lie? (A leader in your church, or a trusted friend, may help you to identify your contribution.)*
2 *Confronted by unemployment, how could this passage help you find value and a contribution in the church? How does it help you in your relationship to your society?*
3 *Depression and fatalism often descend on someone who is unemployed. Material need may certainly exist.*
4 *Read Romans 12:9-13 to see how Paul was urging the church in Rome to help those in need. If you are in paid employment think of someone you know who is unemployed. Then think over each of these phrases with them in mind, e.g. how sincere is your love, your prayer, your hospitality?*

3. Drudgery and idleness

Genesis 3:17-24; Colossians 3:22-24; 2 Thessalonians 3:6-15

It may be that you are in a job with little job satisfaction, and you may feel powerless to do anything about it.

1 *Read again Genesis 3:17-24. Contrast that with the fruitfulness in work promised in Genesis 1:28. We need not be overcome by the sin in the world.*
2 *Turn to Colossians 3:22-24. Summarize Paul's advice to slaves in*

Colossae. *How would your attitude change if you consciously applied verse 23 to your work situation? If this is outside of your experience there is maybe someone you know in such a job who would welcome your prayerful interest and support.*
3 *The Bible also says something about those who simply refuse to work. Read Thessalonians 3:6-15 noting down everything Paul says about those who will not work. What effect were they having on the church? How were such people to be treated? Does this have any relevance to your church?*

Note: The word for 'idleness' Paul used here is not 'laziness' but 'a refusal to work where work is expected'.

Paul set a good example to the Thessalonians. Pray that the leaders of your church might be good examples of a Christlike attitude to work.

4. Daniel – God's man at work

Daniel 5 and 6

Some Christians make a false division between Christian and secular work, even having a double standard of behaviour – one for work, one for home and church. Daniel made no such division. In this study we shall look at various ways in which he approached his work as a high official serving a pagan king in Babylon. You could refer back to your studies in Part 5.

1 *Reading Daniel 5, what reputation had Daniel built up? Upon what was*

this founded? Is there any evidence that the power and wealth lavished on him had gone to his head?

2 In no way had God's name been dishonoured by Daniel's behaviour. Is the quality of your work such that God's name is honoured? Pray for any Christians who are in positions of power, that they will continue to be dependent on God. No man of God is automatically immune from making enemies.

3 Read Daniel 6:1-23. Why did Daniel have enemies? As a final resort how did they attempt to bring about his downfall? What was Daniel's response?

4 Is it obvious to others at work that you are a Christian? Some Christians are ridiculed at work because of their faith, the high quality of their work or their moral standards. (A few Christians seem to invite ridicule by being particularly awkward!) What encouragement from Daniel's life is there for those in such a postion?

In the light of this pray for yourself (if relevant) and other Christians who have unwillingly made enemies at work.

---

5. All work and no play?
Genesis 2:2-3; Exodus 20:8-11; Mark 2:23-27

A ten-day working week has been tried and has failed. From the beginning God laid down a human pattern for work and rest.

1 Read Genesis 2:2-3, then Exodus 20:8-11 to refresh your memory

about this pattern. Why did God intend man to rest?

2 Do you work six days and rest on the seventh? Write down anything you did on your last day of rest that you could have done on another day which would have then made the rest day more refreshing.

3 Christians have tended to keep Sunday as a day for worship and refreshment. Are your Sundays so busy that they cannot be described as days of rest? How much time do you really give to worship on that day?

4 The Jews at the time of Jesus had surrounded the keeping of the Sabbath with many rules and regulations. In Mark 2:23-27 the Pharisees thought that the disciples were reaping, an activity of work forbidden in Exodus 34:21. How did Jesus respond to such a rigid approach?

5 How far is your day of rest so wrapped up in rules that it has ceased to be of benefit to you?

Weekend

1 Jesus worked as a carpenter; Paul as a tentmaker. But both, at times, were supported by others. In 2 Thessalonians 3 we saw how Paul described this right. He elaborated on the principle that a Christian worker should be materially rewarded in 1 Corinthians 9:1-15. How would you summarize this principle?

2 If you are not now in full-time employment, find a Christian more mature than yourself who has a job and discuss with them what you have studied this week.

3 For further reading, John Stott is excellent on this subject in chapter 1 Involvement, Vol. II (Revell).

Time with God

1 *Find a time when you can be alone and undisturbed. Most people find that the morning is best.*
2 *Consciously make an effort to slow down and be quiet. Think about the God you are coming to and be prepared to talk to him – about himself, yourself and the time that you will spend together.*
3 *Read the Bible passage for the day – preferably more than once unless it's very long. Try to get a clear picture of what it is about by careful reading. What does it teach me for or about today?*
4 *Have a notebook handy and write down your thoughts.*
5 *Now is the time to use* The Quiet Time Companion. *Don't cheat by letting it do your thinking for you. It is a good principle to learn and then to act upon what you have learnt.*
6 *Spend some time talking to God – praising him, thanking him, bringing personal and wider concerns to him, asking him to help you really to* learn *and* act upon *what you have understood from the Bible today.*
7 *Finally, be ready for anything that God particularly wants to tell you for, or about, today. Be prepared to commit yourself honestly in response.*